Working Women in English Society, 1300–1620

This study explores the diverse and changing ways in which English women participated in the market economy between 1300 and 1620. Marjorie Keniston McIntosh assesses women's activity by examining their engagement in the production and sale of goods, service work, credit relationships, and leasing of property. Using substantial new evidence from equity court petitions and microhistorical studies of five market centers, she challenges both traditional views of a "golden age" for women's work and more recent critiques. She argues that the level of women's participation in the market economy fluctuated considerably during this period under the pressure of demographic, economic, social, and cultural change. Although women always faced gender-based handicaps, some of them enjoyed wider opportunities during the generations following the plague of 1348–9. By the late sixteenth century, however, these opportunities had largely disappeared and their work was concentrated at the bottom of the economic system.

MARJORIE KENISTON McINTOSH is Distinguished Professor of at the University of Colorado at Boulder. Her previous publications include *A Community Transformed: The Manor and Liberty of Havering, 1500–1620* (1991) and *Controlling Misbehavior in England, 1370–1600* (1998).

Working Women in English Society, 1300–1620

Marjorie Keniston McIntosh

Distinguished Professor of History
University of Colorado at Boulder
USA

CAMBRIDGE
UNIVERSITY PRESS

CAMBRIDGE
UNIVERSITY PRESS

University Printing House, Cambridge CB2 8BS, United Kingdom

Cambridge University Press is part of the University of Cambridge.

It furthers the University's mission by disseminating knowledge in the pursuit of education, learning and research at the highest international levels of excellence.

www.cambridge.org
Information on this title: www.cambridge.org/9780521608589

© Marjorie Keniston McIntosh 2005

First published 2005

A catalogue record for this publication is available from the British Library

ISBN 978-0-521-84616-5 Hardback
ISBN 978-0-521-60858-9 Paperback

To the memory of Robert Keir McIntosh 1966–1999
whose delight in beauty
and engagement with the world around him
encouraged others to develop
the richness of their own lives

Contents

List of illustrations   *page* ix
List of maps, tables, and figures   xi
Acknowledgments   xii
Notes on the text   xiii
List of abbreviations   xiv

Part I. Introduction: women and their work

1. Women's work in its social setting   3

2. Studying working women   14
   1 Sources: what information is available?   14
   2 The historiographic context: how have scholars interpreted
     the sources?   28
   3 Continuity and change   37

Part II. Providing services

3. Domestic and personal services   45
   1 Live-in servants   46
   2 Taking in boarders   61
   3 Non-residential household employment, sex work, and health care 72

4. Financial services and real estate   85
   1 Women and financial credit   85
   2 Lending money   98
   3 Pawning goods   107
   4 Renting out property   114

Part III. Making and selling goods

5. General features of women's work as producers
   and sellers   119
   1 Characteristics of production and sale   120
   2 Apprenticeship   133

6. Drink work   140
   1 Brewing ale   145
   2 Aleselling   156
   3 Beer, wine, and taverns   163
   4 A historical puzzle: were women displaced from the drink trades
      around 1500?   170

7. The food trades and innkeeping   182
   1 Baking   182
   2 Other foods   190
   3 Innkeeping   202

8. Women's participation in the skilled crafts   210
   1 Cloth and clothing   210
   2 Other crafts   234

9. Turning the coin: women as consumers   239

Conclusion   250

Appendices   254
Bibliography   272
Index   288

Illustrations

1. Female servant and two men at a table. BL Add. MS 18852, fol. 1 (Italian, c. 1500). By permission of the British Library. *page* 51
2. Servant assisting mistress with her hair. BL Add. MS 42130, fol. 63 (English, 1345). By permission of the British Library. 52
3. Women doing laundry. BL Harl. MS 3469, fol. 32 (German, 1582). By permission of the British Library. 74
4. Two women nursing a sick man. BL Royal MS 15 D I, fol. 18 (Flemish, 1470). By permission of the British Library. 78
5. Birthing scene in an aristocratic bedroom. BL Harl. MS 2278, fol. 13 (English, 1433). By permission of the British Library. 81
6. Childbirth scene, with midwife and two women attending the mother. Woodcut by Jost Amman from Jacob Rueff, *De conceptu et generatione hominis* (German, 1580). By permission of Philadelphia Museum of Art: Smith, Kline and French (now Smith Kline Beecham) Laboratories Collection, Acc. No. 1949-97-12a. 82
7. Women selling fruits and sausages in London's Grace Church market. From "Hugh Alley's Caveat: The Markets of London in 1598," Folger Shakespeare Library MS V.a.318, fol. 12. By permission of the Folger Shakespeare Library. 128
8. Woman outside her alehouse, serving drink to a man. BL Royal MS 10 E IV, fol. 114 (illuminated in England, c. 1340). By permission of the British Library. 141
9. Woman collecting blood from a slaughtered pig. BL Add. MS 25695, fol. 12 (French, 1470). By permission of the British Library. 193

10. Huckster leaving London's New Fish Street market. From "Hugh Alley's Caveat: The Markets of London in 1598," Folger Shakespeare Library MS V.a.318, fol. 10. By permission of the Folger Shakespeare Library.   195
11. Women selling a duck and weighing butter on a scale in London's Leaden Hall market. From "Hugh Alley's Caveat: The Markets of London in 1598," Folger Shakespeare Library MS V.a.318, fol. 13. By permission of the Folger Shakespeare Library.   197
12. Women smoothing, carding, and spinning wool. BL Royal MS 16 G V, fol. 56 (French, early fifteenth century). By permission of the British Library.   213
13. Woman spinning with a wheel. BL Add. MS 42130, fol. 193 (English, 1345). By permission of the British Library.   214
14. Woman weaving on a treadle loom. BL Egerton 1894, fol. 2 (English, 1350–75). By permission of the British Library.   218
15. Women chatting while buying vegetables and grain at a market. British Museum SAT 61, "Tittle-Tattle" woodcut (published in England, 1603, but probably based on a continental source). By permission of the British Museum.   242

Maps, tables, and figures

Map 1. England, 1300–1620   *page* 17
Table 1. The purchasing power of £10 if held as cash for
    a decade, 1500–1619   100
Fig. 6.1. Havering and Ramsey, percentage of brewers plus
    alesellers reported as women   142
Fig. 6.2. Minehead, Northallerton, and Tamworth, percentage
    of brewers plus alesellers who lived in female-headed
    households or were reported as women   144
Fig. 6.3. Average number of brewers reported per year,
    women plus men   153
Fig. 6.4. Average number of alesellers reported per year,
    women plus men   162
Fig. 7.1. Average number of bakers reported per year,
    women plus men   188

Acknowledgments

I am grateful for the generosity that characterizes the world of research concerning medieval and early modern England. Since my own entry into this field, which began in the fall of 1965 with my first timid visits as a graduate student to the Public Record Office in Chancery Lane and the old Essex Record Office, I have learned from several generations of scholars, archivists, and students. Scattered throughout England and North America, they have contributed to this project as to my previous work by suggesting sources, sharing ideas and information, and commenting on early versions of my thinking. During the research stage, this book was enriched by Judith Bennett; Helen Bishop, Archivist at the Keele University Library, and the History and English faculties there, who welcomed me so hospitably; Edwin and Anne Dewindt; Maryanne Kowaleski; and Christine Newman. I am grateful to the Graduate Committee on the Arts and Humanities and the Committee on Research and Creative Work at the University of Colorado for grants that supported research in England. My thanks go also to the graduate students at the University of Colorado who offered careful research assistance, primarily with the market town data bases: Michael Clisham, Susan Duncan, Stephan Edwards, Alison Flynn, Zana Kamberi, and Jennifer McNabb. Anne and Edwin DeWindt, Susan Kent, Philip Morgan, and Christine Newman sent helpful comments about an earlier draft of this book; Judith Bennett, Maryanne Kowaleski, and readers for the Press offered valuable critiques. The penultimate version of the study was completed in Kampala, Uganda, in the congenial and intellectually stimulating environment of the Department of Women and Gender Studies at Makerere University. Michael Watson of Cambridge University Press has been a wise advisor throughout the project.

Notes on the text

All spellings from manuscript sources have been modernized.

Dates are given in the Old Style in use at the time, but the start of the year has been moved to 1 January.

Money is recorded in the system used then, as pounds, shillings, and pence.

> 1 pound (written as £) contained 20 shillings (written as s.).
>
> 1 shilling contained 12 pence (written as d.).
>
> Thus, £2 3s. 8d. = 2 pounds 3 shillings and 8 pence, or 43 shillings and 8 pence.

Abbreviations

BL	British Library, London
CEMCRL, 1298–1307	*Calendar of Early Mayor's Court Rolls of London, 1298–1307* (ed. A. H. Thomas, Cambridge, 1924)
CPMRL, dates	*Calendar of Plea and Memoranda Rolls of London* 1323–1364 (ed. A. H. Thomas, Cambridge, 1926) 1364–1381 (ed. A. H. Thomas, Cambridge, 1929) 1413–1437 (ed. A. H. Thomas, Cambridge, 1943) 1437–1457 (ed. P. E. Jones, Cambridge, 1954) 1458–1482 (ed. P. E. Jones, Cambridge, 1961)
CRRamHB	*The Court Rolls of Ramsey, Hepmangrove and Bury, 1258–1600* (ed. and trans. Edwin B. DeWindt, Toronto, 1990): a printed volume plus 5 microfiche of English transcriptions
CSPML, 1381–1412	*Calendar of Select Pleas and Memoranda of London, 1381–1412* (ed. A. H. Thomas, Cambridge, 1932)
ERO	Essex Record Office, Chelmsford
KUL T MSS	Keele University Library, Archives Room, Tamworth Manuscripts
NYRO	North Yorkshire Record Office, Northallerton
PRO	The National Archives, Public Record Office, London (Kew)
SRO	Somerset Record Office, Taunton

Part I

Introduction: women and their work

1   Women's work in its social setting

During the centuries between 1300 and 1620, women played multiple roles within England's society and economy. In social terms, they were most obviously the bearers and raisers of children. Women were expected to marry (though not all did so in practice), and because birth control was not widely used in this period, many were either pregnant or breastfeeding the newest baby much of the time. Some families contained not only the mother's own children but also her stepchildren, since widowers – like widows – commonly remarried. Many households also included live-in servants, usually young people between their mid-teens and their mid-twenties. It was women who provided most of the socialization of all these children and young adults, teaching them the practical skills they would need in their own later lives, showing them how to function socially within families and communities, and supervising their religious development. Women were also the primary care givers for other adults within their households.[1] By attending to the physical and emotional needs of their relatives, they contributed to a positive social environment and enabled men to pursue work outside the home.

In addition, women had essential economic duties within the domestic setting. They were responsible for obtaining food and cooking it, they commonly brewed the ale their families drank, and they made or bought the clothing worn by members of the household.[2] They fetched water and fuel for cooking, did the laundry, and kept the living space clean. If the head of the family was a craftsman, his wife, daughters, or servants might help with some aspects of his work. Women living in rural areas generally had vegetable gardens and raised poultry, and they often helped with agricultural labor.

---

[1] For women's roles in attending to "the everyday body," see Riddy, "Looking Closely."

[2] See, e.g., Hanawalt, "Peasant Women's Contribution to the Home Economy," and Whittle, "The Gender Division of Labour." I am grateful to Dr. Whittle for letting me have a copy of this unpublished paper. Unlike Dr. Whittle, however, I do not define as market production the growing or making of food or other goods at home for domestic consumption in place of ones that would otherwise have had to be purchased.

All these activities were praised by the male authors of "prescriptive" works that described good women and their roles.[3] Sermons, plays, and written texts taught that a woman should be part of a household unit supervised by a male head at every stage of her life: as a daughter, perhaps as a servant with another family, and thereafter as a wife. At all ages women were encouraged to remain within the domestic context, busily employed in their household labors, supporting others, and responding with deference to the man who was responsible for ensuring their good behavior. All these patriarchal expectations were present by 1300, may have been somewhat more muted during the generations after the Black Death of 1348–9, and were expressed with great intensity around 1600.

What one does not learn from prescriptive works is that women were heavily involved in the market economy outside their homes. They were not just consumers, buying goods for themselves and their families. To the contrary, many adolescent girls and adult women, especially those from middling and poorer families, worked to generate their own income. They provided services in return for pay, they loaned money or gathered rent from real estate, and/or they made and sold drink, food, cloth, and clothing. Such work came on top of their duties at home: women did not shed their domestic obligations just because they were bringing in cash. Women living in urban communities were especially likely to have their own incomes, but many of their rural sisters did so too. Women of all marital statuses likewise participated, with wives supplementing their husband's earnings and singlewomen and widows working to support themselves and sometimes their children. Women's work was necessary both to the survival of many families and to the successful operation of the broader economy. It was women who brewed ale (England's staple beverage) and prepared the yarn needed to manufacture woolen cloth (England's major industry), and it was women who sold many of the goods required by consumers.

Yet their work outside the domestic economy was not valued by the authors of prescriptive texts or town officials. If women's activities were mentioned at all, it was in negative terms. Men worried about the conduct of women who were out in the public world on their own, free from the control of male relatives. Their sexuality and speech were of particular concern. In periods of limited employment, there was also fear that

---

[3] For a useful summary of this ideological formulation during the medieval period, see Mate, *Daughters, Wives and Widows*, pp. 3–7; for examples of its articulation during the early modern years, see Aughterson, ed., *Renaissance Woman*. Despite this approval, women's work as housewives was never regarded as an occupation comparable to that of men.

working women might take jobs away from men, who were regarded as the natural breadwinners for their families. Even singlewomen and widows who were obliged to earn their own money were not supposed to compete with men. But these patriarchal attitudes did not provide an accurate reflection of many women's actual roles. Working women ignored the messages that told them to restrict their attention to their family and home, and their friends and neighbors were prepared to accept at least many of them as responsible and respected women despite their participation in the wider economy.

This book explores the kinds of work that generated an income for women: the various services they provided for pay, and their role in producing and selling goods. Activities that were less directly related to the money economy have been excluded, not because they were unimportant but simply on pragmatic grounds, to keep the project within manageable bounds. Thus, we do not discuss the tasks that women did on an unpaid basis within their own households, agricultural labor performed on their family's or someone else's land, and selling agricultural items like grain or sheep.[4] While village women appear occasionally, we will talk mainly about women who lived and worked in small or large towns and cities. The issues associated with women's right to own, control, and inherit landed property, though they were critical components of their broader status and wellbeing, are likewise not discussed here.[5] To maintain a focus on women's *work*, their role as *consumers* is considered only briefly, in the final chapter.

The study expands our understanding of women's economic roles in England between 1300 and 1620 in several ways. It looks at types of work not commonly addressed before, including the full range of personal services provided by women (like boarding other people in their homes) and their role in money-lending, pawning, and real estate. In examining craft and trading activity – manufacturing and/or selling goods – we go beyond existing studies of particular types of work or specific cities to present a more encompassing picture.[6] The book also explores how women's personal and economic standing underlay their working lives, how women accessed financial credit, and how gender-based disabilities limited their involvement in the increasingly important upper ranges of England's commercial system. In approaching all these issues, we set women's economic activities within a social context.

---

[4] Mate, *Women in Medieval English Society*, esp. pp. 27–38, and Whittle, "The Gender Division of Labour."

[5] For these issues, see, e.g., Mate, *Daughters, Wives and Widows*, Hanawalt, "The Widow's Mite" and her "Dilemma of the Widow," and Erickson, *Women and Property*.

[6] For discussion of earlier works, see sect. 2, Ch. 2 below.

Further, whereas nearly all existing studies stop or start around 1500, this book bridges the transition between the later medieval and early modern periods. In 1300, England was primarily an agricultural economy, though production and export of woolen cloth were to increase rapidly across the following century. By 1620, the economy was marked by large-scale manufacturing, growing international trade, and more formalized systems of credit. Identifying what part women played in the earlier system and how they fared as it changed is essential to our understanding of economic issues, social patterns, and gender relations. We therefore pay close attention to alterations in women's work over time: when they happened, why, and how.

The book also emphasizes variations between regions of England and between types of communities. Thanks to some excellent but previously untapped sources, we show that women who worked in the north of the country operated within an economic and social environment that differed in some respects from the better studied south.[7] Rather than discussing women's work only in large communities, the study considers smaller towns as well, the setting in which most urban women were active. We present new and unusually rich information about women's participation in the drink and food trades in five market centers, located in different parts of the country and featuring distinctive characteristics. These case studies permit a closer look at such issues as how long women worked, how many trades they pursued, whether they gained any occupational identity, and what status married women and their husbands had within the local community. The answers to these questions suggest that some female traders in the market towns during the later medieval period had a more serious commitment to their work and were held in greater respect than other accounts have suggested.

Finally, this account offers a more personal, engaging picture of working women's lives than has been possible before. Research has commonly been hampered by fairly sterile sources that provide the names of women engaged in income-generating activities but tell us little about their actual experiences. Using a sample of 283 narrative petitions submitted to the royal equity courts between 1470 and 1620, we can go beneath the surface.[8] These statements, prepared by people involved in disputes over women's economic dealings, describe the specific events and individual human relationships that led to conflict. While the petitions cannot be accepted at face value, they nonetheless provide welcome glimpses into what work meant for women during that period.

---

[7] These are petitions to the equity courts, which were located in the north of England as well as the London area.
[8] See sect. 1, Ch. 2 below.

As background for later chapters, we need to lay out certain key features of women's work, many of them related to gender issues. Most types of labor were assigned either to men or to women in later medieval and early modern England, but this gender division was not rigid: no taboos made it impossible for people to engage in each other's work. To a limited extent, labor designations rested on physical strength (e.g., the difficulty some women might face in handling a heavy loom) or biological factors (e.g., disruptions of activity caused by pregnancy and childbirth). But far more important was the assumption that because men were the heads of households, they had first claim on those types of work that brought in enough income to support a family. Such occupations were often full time and carried an identity as a member of that craft or trade. The types of paid activity regarded as "women's work" were in most periods part time and poorly paid. Only when there was a labor shortage, when there were not enough men to fill all the available economic niches, were women welcomed into more lucrative jobs. Further, men were free to work away from their homes, to travel to other communities in connection with their business, to participate in public discussion, and to plead in their own right in the courts. Women were not. Although some individual women led active and independent economic lives, and although both husbands and wives contributed to the income of many households, men as a group were privileged over women.[9]

Because women's economic activities were seen as secondary to those of men, their engagement with the market economy was generally shallow and subject to change. Seldom receiving the training that enabled them to enter specialized craftwork, they commonly shifted between different types of economic involvement over time, in accordance with their domestic responsibilities and their household's financial needs. Women were therefore less likely to have a visible primary occupation and were rarely described in terms of the kind of work they did. (While men were usually labeled by their employment, as a carpenter or merchant, women were normally labeled by their marital status.)

Further, many women pursued diverse kinds of income-generating activities simultaneously, in some cases helping their husbands with their work while also taking on assorted projects of their own. Although multiple economic activities were found among men as well, they were a more pronounced feature of female life. In the chapters that follow we will consider the various types of economic participation separately, but we must remember that in practice they were by no means mutually exclusive. A married woman with young children at home, for example,

[9] Fletcher, *Gender, Sex and Subordination*, pts. I and II.

might help her husband, a glover, with fine sewing while also spinning yarn that she sold to a nearby weaver; she raised chickens she could take to market if the household needed cash; and she might earn some money in the short term by caring for an elderly neighbor who had broken her leg. Clearly such a woman contributed to her household's financial security and to the economy as a whole, though she worked largely within the context of her own home and had no occupational identity of her own.

Demographic factors affected women's need and ability to generate an income. England experienced significant shifts in population patterns across the centuries under consideration, with probable (though poorly documented) repercussions for family composition and fertility levels.[10] In periods when the population was large relative to available resources, as was true around 1300 and again around 1600, an abundant supply of labor meant lowered wages. Under those circumstances, many poor women were forced to earn money to help their households get by. But because their labor provided unwanted competition to that offered by men, what little work they could find was likely to be undesirable. In 1348–9, however, the first outbreak of bubonic plague killed 35–40 percent of England's population. The disease continued thereafter, with additional national epidemics and local flare-ups that occurred roughly once per decade. The population thus remained low and stagnant until the early sixteenth century. Because the economy was buoyant until the mid-fifteenth century in many parts of the country, a labor shortage resulted. Some women during the post-1348–9 generations had more choice about whether and how to enter the market economy.

The particular demographic and economic regime operative within a given period and place could have differing consequences for women depending upon their socio-economic level, type of participation in the market, and family situation. Conditions of low wages and high prices, for example, might be damaging to a landless widow who supported her young children through her labor but had to rent housing and buy food and clothing. Under those same circumstances, an older married woman who raised vegetables for market sale and brewed ale commercially, using capital furnished by her husband and employing poorly paid local labor, might thrive.

Marital patterns, too, had an impact on women's work. In simplest terms, singlewomen and widows could be forced to earn their own income since they had no husband to provide for them. These categories of

---

[10] See, e.g., Hatcher, *Plague, Population* and his "Understanding the Population History of England," and Wrigley and Schofield, *The Population History of England*.

women formed a significant fraction of the population. In 1377, following nearly thirty years of plague, at least a third of all adult women in England had never married or were widows.[11] Many young people were employed as servants before they married, and couples generally did not wed until they could afford to set up their own households. As a result, the average age of first marriage for non-elite women was probably high.[12] We lack concrete information about the later medieval period, but during the second half of the sixteenth century, the average age of marriage for women was twenty-two to twenty-seven years. Since some women never married, a considerable number of women were single at any given time.

Other women were left as widows, responsible at least temporarily for their own households. Though some widows remarried, others stayed on their own for the rest of their lives.[13] Bubonic plague and the other epidemic illnesses of the period were not gender specific, but the death of a spouse had a greater economic impact on women than on men, especially in towns. A man could generally continue his previous economic activity without a wife at home, whereas a widow or daughter who had just become a household head had to come up with a way to support herself and in some cases her children or other dependent relatives. Some widows carried on their husband's former business, but others developed income-generating activities of their own. It is not surprising to see more not-married women participating in the public economy during the disease-ridden generations after 1348–9.

A woman's ability to generate her own income depended heavily upon "credit." That term, in its multiple meanings, will recur throughout this book. In one sense, credit referred to a person's individual reputation or standing. A woman's personal credit, which had social and economic components, was created and assessed through human relationships: in her dealings with relatives, friends, neighbors, the people she saw at church or the alehouse, and those with whom she did business. Credit also had more specifically financial meanings, referring to the various

[11] Kowaleski, "Singlewomen," pp. 325–44.

[12] See sect. 1, Ch. 3 below. It has been suggested that after 1348–9 some English women may have delayed marriage so they could continue their independent working lives, and pastoral and medical treatises imply that at least a few women tried to avoid having children through contraception or abortion (Goldberg, *Women, Work, and Life Cycle*, esp. ch. 8, Biller, *The Measure of Multitude*, esp. ch. 8, and Riddle, *Eve's Herbs*, esp. chs. 4–5).

[13] Younger widows and those who had inherited some property were especially likely to remarry. In London, 1598–1619, 35 percent of all women marrying were widows at the time; two-thirds of the widows of tradesmen and craftsmen had remarried within a year of the death of their former husband (Brodsky, "Widows"). See also, among recent works on widows, Keene, "Tanners' Widows," Hanawalt, "Remarriage as an Option," and her "The Widow's Mite."

mechanisms that regulated the exchange of money, goods, or services and the promise of future payment. Loans of cash or property were common, with interest sometimes charged, and many agreements for goods or services were set up with the expectation that delivery or payment would be made later. Most working women were therefore embedded in complex networks of obligations due by them and to them. Whether they succeeded in their business often depended upon their ability to access loans or postpone their debts to others. But due to the gendered assumptions and practices of their society, women were at a disadvantage in obtaining credit. As the scale of money-lending, production/sales, and importing/exporting increased across the sixteenth century, few women could compete in the upper levels of the new environment.

Because the lives of all working women were affected by their personal standing, we will explore that aspect of credit here, reserving discussion of their involvement with the forms of financial credit for a later chapter.[14] English people of middling or lower rank – those examined in this study – employed a variety of terms when describing how they or others were regarded within the community.[15] The wordings "credit," "reputation," "standing," and "good name" seem to have been used interchangeably and could be applied to both women and men. Although the social and economic aspects of a person's reputation were related, different features might be emphasized depending upon the context. You could be seen as a good friend, based upon sociability and your willingness to help in an emergency, but still be regarded as economically unreliable with respect to repaying a loan.[16] The phrase "honor" appears infrequently at lower social levels, though it remained in use among the gentry and nobility, where it kept some of its older courtly or chivalric connotations. In the northwest of England, a sense of collective family credit, in which an individual's reputation was linked to the good name of her or his relatives, continued through the sixteenth century for non-elite people as well as for the aristocracy.[17] Neighborhoods or communities might likewise have shared reputations.

---

[14] See sects. 1–3, Ch. 4 below.

[15] An extensive literature has grown up over the past few decades concerning credit. Selected studies that focus on its sexual/social components include Haigh, "Slander and the Church Courts," Sharpe, *Defamation and Sexual Slander*, Gowing, *Domestic Dangers*, Walker, "Expanding the Boundaries," Fletcher, *Gender, Sex and Subordination*, Foyster, *Manhood in Early Modern England*, and Capp, "The Double Standard Revisited" and his *When Gossips Meet*. Studies that emphasize economic credit include Shepard, "Manhood, Credit and Patriarchy," Muldrew, "Interpreting the Market," and his *The Economy of Obligation*. For an examination of the interrelated meanings of credit in the later eighteenth and nineteenth centuries, see Finn, *The Character of Credit*.

[16] McNabb, "Constructing Credit."

[17] Ibid. and Carney, "Social Interactions." For below, see Capp, *When Gossips Meet*, ch. 7.

Many factors contributed to the social side of someone's individual credit. Earlier research demonstrated that women were deeply concerned about their good names in sexual terms, while men worried mainly about their economic reputations or the behavior of the women under their supervision.[18] Newer studies make clear, however, that while good sexual conduct may have been especially significant for women, a wide range of issues mattered to both sexes.[19] Reliability and generosity were key ingredients. Was a woman responsible in caring for her family? Was she ready to loan a piece of clothing or some spoons to a friend for an important occasion, or to look after a neighbor's children during an illness? Did a man provide adequately for his household? Was he careful to return the harrow he had borrowed in good condition, and was he willing to join with others in repairing the roof of an elderly neighbor? People gained credit through being hard workers, whether in the fields, the market, or at home, and by being fair. But those who "scolded," arguing or spreading malicious gossip about others, lost credit for threatening local harmony. People who drank too much or who failed to keep their children and servants under control were considered weak, unable to govern their own or their dependents' actions.

Interwoven with the social components of personal credit were economic ones. A good reputation in economic terms meant that others regarded you as honest and trustworthy, a person whose word could be counted on in business dealings. Did other people believe that you would complete economic agreements as promised? Repaying one's debts was also important. People could be poor but creditworthy, borrowing no more than they could afford to pay back and completing their commitments as arranged.[20]

While maintaining a positive reputation was a concern for all women, it was especially important for those who engaged in income-generating activities. Their ability to function within a working environment depended in large part upon their own social and economic credit. A woman who sought employment in someone else's house would probably not be hired if she had a reputation for sexual laxity, gossiping about her employers' private lives, or dishonesty. Agnes Peryham of Devon said around 1540 that because Richard Wyll and his wife Margaret had falsely

---

[18] E.g., Gowing, "Gender and the Language of Insult" and her *Domestic Dangers*, Fletcher, *Gender, Sex and Subordination*, Foyster, *Manhood in Early Modern England*, and Shepard, "Manhood, Credit and Patriarchy."

[19] E.g., Gowing, "The Freedom of the Streets," Capp, "The Double Standard Revisited" and his *When Gossips Meet*, Carney, "Social Interactions," and McNabb, "Constructing Credit."

[20] Expectations varied greatly on the basis of status: an aristocratic male might be admired for being extravagant but scorned for keeping careful track of his finances.

accused her of stealing feather beds from a house where she was employed, she was not only "hurt in her good name and fame" but also "mistrusted at such places as she doth come to work in."[21] Someone who was thought to be irresponsible would have trouble getting loans and might not receive informal assistance from neighbors or fellow market-sellers when she needed it.[22] Agnes Wodeward, a market trader in Ramsey in 1400, was disliked because she was disagreeable to other vendors and charged overly high prices for her food.[23] The ability of a trader or craftsperson to negotiate favorable agreements, loans, conditions, and prices rested in part upon the willingness of other people to accept her word as trustworthy.

Working women who came before the courts, as parties to a case or witnesses, were likewise reliant upon their good name, for it determined whether their testimony would be accepted. In 1590, Blanche Houghe, a sixty-year-old alehouse keeper, was one of four witnesses in a dispute concerning a marriage contract heard in the Consistory Court of Chester.[24] After she had testified, fourteen other people were asked whether her statements should be accepted as reliable. Their responses revealed that Blanche's standing in the community was terrible. She herself was "noted for a woman of evil name and fame": she was described as "of small credit," "of light behavior with other men," and "of loose life," allowing the local minister – among other men – to "abuse his body" with her. In addition, her alehouse was said to be a center of wrongdoing: "there hath a report come amongst honest neighbors that men and women of evil disposition hath resorted to the same and there been received"; one of the witnesses had heard that she "keepeth a house of bawdry [= where prostitution took place]." Blanche's poor reputation meant that anything she said, even on oath, would carry little weight.

Some historians have suggested that economic credit grew in importance and became increasing separated from social credit over the course of the sixteenth century.[25] During the later medieval years and to some extent thereafter, economic transactions were based upon friendship, goodwill, and trust between people who knew each other; they operated within accepted social conventions and could evaluate each other's

---

[21] PRO C 1/1053/32.

[22] See Ben-Amos, "Gifts and Favors," for the importance of informal support in the early modern period.

[23] E.g., BL Add. Roll 39639r, a case discussed in sect. 2, Ch. 7 below.

[24] Cheshire Record Office EDC 5, 1590, no. 32 (Ellen Litler of Nether Peover vs. Philip Downes of the Chapel of Witton). Blanche lived in Nether Peover. I am grateful to Jennifer McNabb for this information.

[25] For thoughtful discussions of this issue, see Muldrew, "Interpreting the Market" and his *The Economy of Obligation*, esp. pp. 4–7 and chs. 5–6.

individual credit. Even when credit was extended beyond one's immediate circle of acquaintances, trust remained essential. When goods were
being valued for sale or as security for a credit transaction, the standing
of their owner was relevant. The worth of the items depended both upon
their objective cost or replacement value and upon the personal status of
their owner. Even cash, which might seem the most objectively defined
element of the economic system, was not evaluated solely in terms of
its buying power.[26] By around 1600, however, a person requesting formal economic credit was likely to be assessed primarily or exclusively
in financial terms. As the degree of personal contact and trust between
creditors and borrowers diminished, the mechanisms used to record the
granting of credit and to ensure its repayment became more formal and
elaborate. At the same time, being in debt was acquiring a cluster of negative connotations.[27] These changes had marked gender implications. The
earlier system provided a more even playing field for women, whereas the
later pattern accentuated the disabilities they faced in financial and legal
terms.[28]

Before addressing the types of economic activities that women pursued, we will look in the next chapter at how historians have gone about
studying women's work. We examine the sources that are available and
review the historiographic context, how scholars have made use of those
materials. We can then survey the areas of continuity and change within
women's economic lives between 1300 and 1620, offering a chronological
framework for the rest of the book.

---

[26] As Muldrew has noted, the shortage of actual coins and the uncertainty of their value
in early modern England contributed to a system in which "monetary value remained
enmeshed with other values" ("'Hard Food for Midas,'" esp. p. 81).

[27] Leinwand, *Theatre, Finance, and Society*. For the meanings of debt and credit in the
eighteenth and nineteenth centuries, see Finn, *The Character of Credit*.

[28] See sect. 3, Ch. 2 below.

2 Studying working women

As background to our discussion of the kinds of women's work, we need to understand where historians obtain their information and how they have interpreted that material. The first question concerns sources. What kinds of documents or texts were produced during the medieval and early modern periods that shed light on how women brought in money? Next, we examine how scholars have made use of those sources. Discussion of the historiographic context is followed by a brief chronological summary of the centuries under consideration, highlighting aspects of both continuity and change.

1   Sources: what information is available?

Our ability to understand women's economic roles during these centuries is affected by the nature of the sources. Prior to the mid-fourteenth century, we know very little, and until the later fifteenth century, records address just a few facets of their working lives. Only with the survival of a significant number of equity court petitions beginning around 1470 do we start to gain a fuller picture of their diverse activities.

For the fourteenth century, tax records provide information about many regions of the country. These normally list only the head of each household, usually a man. Although singlewomen or widows who were in charge of their own households are visible in such documents, we learn nothing about the presence or economic roles of the women living within male-headed households, as family members or servants. The most helpful materials for a study of women are the lists of people assessed for the Poll Taxes of 1377–81, which, at least in theory, included all adults aged fourteen or over and in some cases provided occupations. The Poll Tax returns do not, however, survive for all areas, and they were prepared at a time when many demographic and economic patterns had been distorted by repeated outbursts of plague starting in 1348–9. Nevertheless, Poll Tax material provides most of the quantified information for the medieval period in the chapters below.

Even in sources that list male occupations, women's work was rarely accorded a similar designation. Although many men of middling and lower rank were engaged in multiple economic activities, they would normally be labeled occupationally by their most active trade. But women were described differently. A married woman who supplemented her family's income by brewing ale or combing wool for yarn would not have been identified in the records as a brewster or kembster. Even less likely to be recorded were the activities of women who earned money in unrecognized or morally doubtful ways, such as sex work. If women were labeled at all, it was usually by their marital status.[1] When a woman is given an occupational identification in the Poll Tax listings or other records, she was probably a singlewoman or widow who headed her own household and worked with atypical concentration in a particular trade.

The records of private suits heard by local courts can be a valuable source. If the court's clerk wrote down in some detail what each party in the case claimed, as was common practice during the first and sometimes the second half of the fourteenth century, we learn something about the circumstances that surrounded provision of services and production or sale of goods. From around 1400 onwards, however, court rolls were less likely to record the pleadings. In later records we usually get only the bare bones of a case: we might learn, for example, that a widow brought suit against a man for a debt of a given amount, but we are told nothing about the kind of economic activity from which that debt stemmed. By the sixteenth century, private suits were omitted entirely from the records of most local courts, apart from a few towns.

An equally serious problem with all records from local and other common law courts is that married women's economic roles are normally obscured by the requirement that a married woman be represented by her husband if she sued or was sued concerning her own economic activity. Because a woman lost her independent legal identity in the eyes of the common law when she married, becoming a *femme couverte* (a woman "covered" by her husband), she could not buy and sell property in her own right, sign any contracts, or plead on her own behalf before a court. In all instances she needed at least to be joined by her husband; in legal actions he was the person named as the party, and he spoke on her behalf. Thus, we might encounter the record of a plea of debt brought by a male saddler against a male smith for 4s. Unless the pleadings in that case were noted on the roll, we would not know that the debt actually arose from a series of purchases made by the smith's wife, who ran an eating place, from the saddler's wife, who sold fish. Our ability to use local court

[1] Beattie, "The Problem of Women's Work Identities."

records to trace female economic roles during most of the later medieval and early modern period is therefore generally limited to singlewomen and widows who pleaded in their own names. Only in London and a few of the large towns could a married woman work as a *femme sole*, pursuing a business independently from her husband and pleading on her own behalf in court cases.[2]

A source that can be used to trace changes over time within at least a few trades is the lists of workers in the food and drink trades reported to local courts. Officials known as "aletasters" were responsible for enforcing the Assize of Bread and Ale, a national law requiring that producers and sellers of food and drink meet certain standards for weight/volume, quality, and price. The names of those who violated the Assize, which later became a de facto listing of all those who paid a small fine to work in these trades, were recorded on the rolls of the local court. Starting as early as the thirteenth century and stretching in some cases well into the sixteenth, aletasters' reports can provide a long sequence of fairly consistent information, giving extensive if not always entirely complete coverage.[3] The main problem in using these records is that we cannot always be sure whether the person named was actually doing the brewing/baking or was instead the male head of the household within which that work was being done by someone else, commonly his wife.[4]

Market centers are particularly well suited to an examination of women's roles in the food and drink trades for several reasons. England contained 600–700 communities that held regular markets and hence were more economically active than the thousands of purely rural villages; they were, however, smaller and less wealthy than the thirty-eight cities and larger towns.[5] With populations ranging from a few hundred to around one thousand people, the market communities served as centers of trade for their immediate region and funneled goods to larger places for consumption or export. About half of all women who can be described as urban lived in these communities, and women may have had unusual economic opportunities in places that had some degree of commercial development but did not require the heavy capital investment and ability to control labor characteristic of the major centers. Further,

---

[2] For a fuller discussion, see McIntosh, "The Benefits and Drawbacks of *Femme Sole* Status."

[3] See the appendix to Bennett, *Ale, Beer, and Brewsters*, for these records and how to interpret them.

[4] See Ch. 6 below.

[5] Dyer, "Small Towns," and his "Small Places with Large Consequences," and Everitt, "The Marketing of Agricultural Produce," esp. pt. i. For a listing of the larger communities, see McIntosh, *Controlling Misbehavior*, p. 219.

Map 1. England, 1300–1620

because food/drink work was generally supervised by a single court in these places, we avoid the problem of shifting jurisdictions between multiple courts that makes it difficult to trace these workers in many larger communities.

For this study, five market centers in different parts of England were selected for close examination. They are not only well documented in long runs of local court records, they represent a variety of economic patterns and regional variations (see Map 1).[6] Tamworth was an ordinary little market town in the West Midlands, straddling the border between

---

[6] The methods and manuscripts used to study these centers are described in App. 1.1.

Staffordshire and Warwickshire.[7] Its economy was largely unspecialized and its trade limited by a cluster of other nearby towns. In the mid-fifteenth century it experienced heightened local violence as the Wars of the Roses approached. The market center of Ramsey, Hunts., lay in the shadow of one of England's wealthiest monasteries, on the southwestern edge of the fens.[8] Situated on an island surrounded by marshes, Ramsey served a mixed population of people who earned their living mainly from the water and those who engaged in land-based farming. Northallerton was a poor and disrupted North Yorkshire town located on the main road leading from York up to the Scottish border.[9] Struck by occasional raids by soldiers or armed bands, it was prone to disease carried by the many travelers along the road. Northallerton's economic problems during the later fifteenth and sixteenth centuries were accentuated by a tendency to participate in unsuccessful rebellions against the crown. At the opposite end of the scale was the suburban market town of Romford, Essex, located on the eastern outskirts of London within the manor and Liberty of Havering-atte-Bower.[10] This prosperous and dynamic community, situated on the road to Colchester, was on the cutting edge of economic and social change. The port of Minehead, Som., faced Wales across the Bristol Channel.[11] Minehead's life included not only local people but also visiting sailors, their ships (which needed to be stocked with food and drink), and goods being imported or exported. Some voyages were local – fishing or trading with adjoining coastal regions – but larger ships sailed to and from Ireland, France, Spain, and Portugal.

[7] In the tax listings of 1524–5, Tamworth contained around 400 people, placing it in the 74th percentile in size within a national sample of 255 market centers and villages from across the country. Since, however, it was only in the 67th percentile in wealth, this suggests slightly lower than average individual prosperity. For general accounts, see Tonkinson, "The Borough Community of Tamworth," Palmer, *History of the Town and Castle of Tamworth*, Henry Wood, *Borough by Prescription* and his *Medieval Tamworth*, and Studd, *Tamworth Court Rolls*; for the national sample, see McIntosh, *Controlling Misbehavior*. Only those court rolls for the Staffs. side of Tamworth have been analyzed quantitatively in this study.

[8] In 1524–5, Ramsey had around 850 people, in the 90th percentile for size, but was in the 81st in wealth, indicating a large population but below average per capita wealth (CRRamHB). That work and Anne DeWindt's "The Town of Ramsey" will soon be joined by their book on Ramsey.

[9] Tax records for Northallerton do not provide reliable information about size and wealth, since northern towns paid at a lower but uneven rate due to their obligation to assist militarily in the defence against the Scots. See Newman, *Late Medieval Northallerton*.

[10] In 1524–5, Romford had about 480 inhabitants, in the 78th percentile for size, but was in the 88th percentile for wealth. Per capita wealth was thus above average (McIntosh, *A Community Transformed*).

[11] In 1524–5, Minehead had about 530 people, in the 82nd percentile in size, but was in the 70th in wealth, indicating low per capita prosperity (Binding and Stevens, *Minehead*, and Hancock, *A History of Minehead*).

Material from the five market centers appears in several forms below. Aletasters' reports have been analyzed in quantitative terms, enabling us to examine closely the women who worked in the food and drink trades, how their work varied in accordance with social and marital status, how it compared with male activity, and how it changed over time. We can investigate the transition that occurred during the decades around 1500 with respect to who was reported for brewing and selling drink. Whereas the names had previously been almost entirely female, they now became almost entirely male. Was this a change in recording practices, or did it reflect an actual change in who was doing the work? That historical puzzle is investigated at the end of the chapter on drink. Throughout this book we will also present information about additional types of female economic activity in these communities, drawn from various local records.

Women's work is sometimes documented in other kinds of sources as well. Payments by the crown, religious institutions or hospitals, and private households may reveal women as providers of services, such as tending the sick or cleaning houses, or as sellers of food, drink, or clothing. These accounts are summary, giving no information other than the person's name, how much was paid, and for what. For a few places during the later medieval years and for many more by the end of the sixteenth century, we have wills and sometimes inventories of the possessions of singlewomen or widows that give some indication of their economic activities, the composition of their households, and their material circumstances. (Married women did not normally write wills, since in the eyes of the law they owned no goods of their own.) Many urban centers have left town books or court records that tell us about the operation of the market and producers and sellers of goods, especially people who broke local rules in connection with their work: a peddler of fish who bought her supplies from fishermen at the wharf rather than waiting to purchase them in the public market, or a server of drink in an alehouse who offered sexual services as well. These can shed valuable light on women's work and men's reactions to it, as can literary sources, moral treatises, and sermons. During the second half of the sixteenth century and the early seventeenth, we gain a greatly expanded array of contemporary printed materials: prescriptive works and religious homilies written by men that describe what women's social and economic roles ought to be, as well as plays, ballads, and proto-novels that provide stereotypic images of certain kinds of working women and reflect male anxieties about them.

All the sources mentioned thus far contribute to this book, either through direct use of primary sources or through studies done by other historians based upon them. But they have major limitations in terms of the types of economic activity they document and the kinds of women who are visible in them. The sources reveal something about women's roles as producers and sellers of goods – their involvement in craftwork or trade – but they are almost entirely silent about informal economic activities that did not occur within a public context. They obscure the role of married women. And even the best pleadings in common law court rolls give us little detail about the personal interactions that lay behind the problem at issue.

From around 1470 onward, we gain a broader and deeper understanding of women's economic activities from petitions submitted to the equity courts. Functioning as an outgrowth of the king's medieval right to administer justice when it was not available elsewhere, the equity courts were willing to hear cases that did not fall within one of the jurisdictional categories of the common law courts. The "central equity courts" included in this study consisted of the equity side of the Courts of Chancery, Requests, and Exchequer.[12] These sat in the London area but could hear cases from throughout England. Most of the cases heard by the "northern equity courts," those of the Duchy and Palatinate of Lancaster and the Palatinate of Durham, came from those regions. A person requesting a hearing from one of the equity courts had to submit a petition describing the problem and how it arose and explaining why the case could not be heard by one of the normal common law courts. By the later sixteenth century, we also have for some cases the defendant's response and more rarely the questions asked of witnesses and/or their answers. Equivalently helpful but much less abundant records from the equity side of the Exchequer consist of the depositions taken in connection with cases heard in that court.

Although the equity court petitions cannot be taken at face value, they allow us to go beyond the bare outline reported in common law pleadings to examine the context and details of economic interactions. They are particularly valuable for those areas of female activity about which few other sources exist, such as taking in boarders and pawnbroking. The account presented here relies heavily on information from a sample of 283 equity court cases (229 from the central courts, 54 from the northern ones) that document female economic activity of the kinds examined in this study.[13] The cases are summarized in Apps. 1.2–1.4, which lay out by sub-period the types of economic activity in which the women were engaged, their marital status, and the region of the country in which

---

[12] Surviving petitions from Chancery become numerous around 1470, with petitions to Requests appearing in the early sixteenth century. Northern records survive in good quantity only from around the mid-sixteenth century; Exchequer depositions begin in the 1570s.

[13] See App. 1.1 for how this sample was created.

they lived.[14] Although the distribution of women between petitioners and respondents varies with the specific issue (e.g., women were more likely to be petitioners in cases in which they were pleading against a former master for their unpaid servant's wages), women appear as both aggrieved parties and defendants in many sorts of disputes stemming from their work.

As narrative sources for women's economic lives, the best of the equity petitions are unmatched by any other material from the period. These courts were frequently used by women themselves. Amy Erickson's analysis of samples from the manuscript calendars of Chancery proceedings during Elizabeth's reign shows that women were parties to a quarter of all suits opened in the court; Wilfred Prest's sample indicates that the figure had risen to 40 percent by the reign of James I.[15] In Tim Stretton's work on petitions to the Court of Requests, 12 percent of all named litigants were female in 1562, and women constituted 14 percent of all litigants in 1603.[16] Further, the equity courts did not enforce the common law requirement that married women had to be represented by (and hence hidden by) their husbands. Here married women could plead in their own names, though in practice they were sometimes joined by their husbands as co-parties. Stretton found that 36 percent of female litigants in the Court of Requests in 1562 were married, as were 40 percent in 1603.

The equity courts offer the additional advantage that they were used by women of diverse economic levels. Analysis of the size of loans mentioned in these cases and the value of goods traded, together with the content of the stories told, makes clear that in the equity court narratives we are often hearing about the economic activities of middling-rank women and sometimes about wealthy or poor ones.[17] The northern equity courts in particular attracted people of modest status. (The dockets of the central courts within the common law system, by contrast, were increasingly filled by disputes among substantial landowners.) One might have expected that educated and wealthy people were more likely to use the equity courts. Complainants had to have basic familiarity with the legal system

---

[14] Because the selection process used in creating this sample favored not-married women, the distribution by marital status shown here is not reflective of broader patterns.

[15] Erickson, "Common Law vs. Common Practice," p. 28, and Prest, "Law and Women's Rights," p. 182, both cited by Stretton, *Women Waging Law*, p. 39.

[16] Personal communication. I am grateful to Dr. Stretton for this information and that cited below.

[17] For the size of women's loans in this sample, see Ch. 4; for the value of goods traded, see Ch. 5. For examples of cases where complainants were excused from court costs due to poverty, see PRO DURH 2/2/71 and PRO DL 1/272, Rychardson vs. others, 18 November 1617.

even to know that these courts existed, they had to be willing and able to get their petition prepared and delivered to London, and they had to be able to pay the costs of a court case.[18] But other influences gave people of lower level access to the court. During the later fifteenth century the Court of Chancery was popularly thought to be sympathetic to people who lacked power, and during the earlier sixteenth century the Court of Requests was known as "the poor man's court." While the latter may not have referred in practice to the destitute poor, the fact that the equity courts were thought to be open to people of lesser rank expands the range of cases brought before it.

Despite their benefits, these records can by no means be taken as simple reflections of reality. As is true for all legal sources, the petitions record exceptional or contentious interactions rather than normal or successful ones: something went wrong in dealings between people or the problem would not have come before the court. Further, although the narratives purport to be written in the petitioner's own words, many were probably prepared by lawyers or other people who had some familiarity with the law, rather than by the actual complainant. Nor can we assume that the specific stories told were strictly factual. The accounts were constructed to present the claims of that party in a positive legal light, designed to win the case, with evidence excluded, distorted, or even created as appropriate. The specific matter at issue was most likely to be unreliable, e.g., how much of a long-standing debt between the parties had already been repaid. The secondary information provided by the narrative about the circumstances within which that agreement was made, which offers the best material about women's dealings, was less apt to be deliberately re-worked.

Another problem is that many of these petitions were submitted long after the events that had led up to the conflict, with a gap of five to ten years not uncommon. In some cases the delay was due to the initial continuance of good personal relationships between the people involved, so they did not press to have an obligation fulfilled. Only when trust broke down was legal action started. In other cases, women who had entered into some kind of financial arrangement while single or widowed may have waited to initiate a suit until they were (re)-married. They would

---

[18] The cost of initiating a case in the Court of Requests during the later sixteenth century was 16s. 8d., more than the 1s. 6d. required by the Court of Chancery. But subsequent costs in Requests remained relatively low, usually measured "in tens of shillings," whereas in Chancery later cases could cost £50–400 to pursue. Additional expenses included travel, accommodation, and sustenance for the parties, messengers, witnesses, and commissioners. These could easily come to more than the sums owed to the courts themselves (Stretton, *Women Waging Law*, p. 83).

then be better able to afford going to court, and perhaps they thought that their action would carry more weight if they were joined by a man. In these delayed cases, the memory of both parties may have become blurred.

Because petitioners had to allege that they could not obtain justice through the procedures of the common law court where their case would normally have been heard, some narrators presumably tailored their accounts to fit into one of the categories they believed fell under equity court protection. A recurrent claim, for example, was that the petitioner was unbefriended, poor, or unknown within the area in which the problem arose (and where it should have been heard within the common law system), whereas her/his opponent was well connected and able to exert power over a jury in that place, precluding a fair trial. Stretton has shown that women were particularly likely to emphasize their own weakness and lack of power in an effort to evoke the court's sympathy.[19] These allegations may often have been exaggerated. Another problem frequently cited was that the complainant had no written record documenting the debt due to him/her: since the common law courts required proof of an obligation, the case could not be prosecuted there. In these cases, petitioners had to explain why they had not obtained or preserved written confirmation of the debt. In many instances, petitioners emphasized that at the time the arrangement was made, they had full confidence in the borrower's good word and hence did not ask for documentation.[20] In other cases complainants alleged family relationships to their creditor or other special bonds which had led them not to demand a written record.[21] Some petitioners said that there had once been written evidence of their financial arrangement but it had been lost or destroyed.[22]

A question that emerged in some of these equity petitions was the legal status of married women who were lodging a complaint or defending themselves against a charge that stemmed from their own economic activities. Unlike the common law courts, the equity courts were willing under some circumstances to accept petitions from married women in their own right.[23] Likewise, in the equity courts married women could be named alone as a defendant, without their husbands, at least in certain situations. Conversely, a married woman who was being sued with her husband in a common law court could attempt to free herself from that action by petitioning an equity court on the grounds that the problem at issue was

[19] *Women Waging Law*, esp. ch. 3.
[20] E.g., PRO PL 6/2, 1 October 1613, Eccleston vs. Smalshawe.
[21] E.g., PRO PL 6/2, 13 August 1613, Foster vs. John and Alice Rigmaden. See also McIntosh, "Women, Credit, and Family Relationships."
[22] E.g., PRO DL 1/23/H6.   [23] E.g., PRO DL 1/57/A6.

related solely to her husband's activities, not to her own.[24] The equity courts also heard disputes that arose when a married woman claimed that she was trading as a *femme sole* or when she or her husband alleged that she had entered into some kind of obligation without his knowledge.[25] Married women and/or their husbands were therefore able to use the wife's ill-defined legal position to maneuver between courts, sometimes effectively dodging their creditors. This lack of clear legal responsibility for a married woman's economic activities may have made men hesitate before entering into contracts or extending loans to them.

A controversy brought before the Court of Requests in 1610 illustrates the value of the equity court narratives but at the same time shows why we should not accept at face value the claims of either party. This unusually detailed set of statements from both parties and assorted witnesses clearly sets economic interactions within a social context. Emphasizing the importance of personal credit or reputation, it shows how a person's high status and good name or, conversely, her/his weakness and poor standing could be manipulated both in economic dealings and in explanations submitted to a court. It thus highlights the role of gender and power relations in economic interactions.

The petition that initiated this case was submitted by Garrett Daye, a minor London merchant, and his wife Anne against James Meadows of London, Doctor of Divinity and parson of the church of St. Gabriel in Fenchurch Street, and his wife Eleanor.[26] The Dayes' petition alleged that in September 1602, James and Eleanor Meadows came to Anne, one of the plaintiffs, being then "a maid newly come (by the direction of her friends) out of the country to some friends that she had in the city of London, then and there to be placed in service." The Meadows promised that if Anne agreed to serve them, they would use her kindly and that Mistress Meadows, who was Dutch or German born, would instruct Anne "in all manner of curious and strange needle works," skills that would stand her in good stead throughout her life. They assured Anne that her main duties would be to attend her mistress in her chamber, to learn with her needle, and to take care of their children.

In her petition, Anne presented herself as not only young but also eager to improve herself, in both spiritual and practical terms. Having "an especial care and regard to the credit of the person whom she was minded to serve, perceiving that the said James Meadows was a man of good esteem and reverent place and calling in the church, and in whose service she

[24] E.g., PRO C 1/64/1140.
[25] See McIntosh, "The Benefits and Drawbacks of *Femme Sole* Status"; for the latter issue, see Ch. 4 below.
[26] PRO REQ 2/411/34.

did hope for some preferments, besides a good persuasion to be educated and instructed in the fear of God and perfect use of needle work," she agreed to become their servant. Turning down offers of employment, she claimed, from many wealthy merchants and honest citizens, she agreed with Meadows at a meeting in his study that she would receive 30s. in annual wages plus stipulated clothing during a term of five years. For this he gave her 5d. in earnest money.

When Anne began to work for them, she quickly found – so she said – that because Mistress Meadows kept no other servant, Anne was expected to work "in housewifery," preparing food and drink, keeping the house clean, and fetching water. She remained in the Meadows' service for two years, but they refused to pay her any part of the 30s. due annually for wages, nor did they provide her with badly needed hose, shoes, smocks, and other necessary apparel, her own clothing having by then worn out. Further, she was not treated kindly but instead "indured many blows, ill intreatings, and handlings, to her great hurt and prejudice, both in the parts of her body and in her preferments." When she departed their service in October 1604, she had received no wages nor any decent clothing, "by which means she was not then meet and fit for any other men's service of any worth or as was fitting [her] parentage." To make matters worse, Anne claimed that while working for the Meadows she had written to her father to say she needed money to buy clothing; he sent her 40s. through a cousin, who delivered the money to Meadows. Her master, however, never bestowed any of that sum upon her but kept it to his own use. In their petition to the Court of Requests, Anne and her husband therefore demanded payment of her back wages plus the 40s. sent by her father.

The response submitted by James and Eleanor Meadows tells a very different story. They claimed that Anne's suit was brought only from malice: it had been six years since she left their service, during which time she had not demanded any sum of money from them. Her enmity was triggered, they alleged, by Dr. Meadows' refusal the previous summer to "move an offering" (= take up a collection) in the parish church of St. Gabriel Fenchurch at the time of Anne's marriage to Daye. In Meadows' own account of his and his wife's dealings with Anne, he painted a black picture of her. He said that in September 1601, a year before the beginning of Anne's own story, she had come to them to offer her service. At the time she was dressed very poorly, "having then as he remembers no more apparel than one old petticoat, one old waistcoat, two old torn smocks, and [several pieces] of old linen." Within a few days of her joining their household, he noticed that she seemed ill, whereupon he asked "one Mistress Giles, a surgeon, to search what disease [she] then had." Mistress Giles reported that Anne had "a filthy disease" not fit to be named and advised Meadows not to let her lodge any longer in his house. Anne, after confessing that she had a venereal disease, "did in submissive manner upon her knees entreat and desire them to pity her distressed estate and provide some means for her recovery." Because she claimed that her father was an esquire who would willingly repay all charges, Meadows, "in Christianity and commiseration of her misery," asked Mistress Giles to try to cure Anne. Giles was not eager to undertake the charge but eventually agreed. "With great travail and diligence by purging, laticing, plastering, sweating, and bathing," she healed Anne over a period of five weeks. For this, Meadows paid Giles 30s., in addition to the 12s. laid out for Anne's board and room with a married couple during those weeks. (They later told Meadows that "if they had known the plaintiff's disease to be so noisome and infectious they would not have taken ten pounds to have lodged her in their house so long, for that many of [their family] were so infected from the said plaintiff that they brake out in grievous blisters and boches [= boils].")

When Anne was healed, the Meadows tried – they said – to dismiss her from their service. Once more she went down on her knees, begging them "to accept of her service for diet [= food and drink] and apparel only at least until her father's coming to London." This they agreed to do, also paying 26s. 8d. at her request to redeem a box and petticoat that she had pawned before coming to their service. Several months later, however, when Anne's father came to London, he told Dr. Meadows about "the manifold misdemeanors of the said Anne and absolutely refused to see or speak to her, affirming that he would reject her . . . as a daughter." The father encouraged the minister, however, to keep Anne in his service, promising to give him money towards her apparel, in sums growing from £2 the first year to £10 the fifth year. On that basis, Meadows signed the five-year contract with her in September 1602.

During her two years in their service, Anne proved both lazy and dishonest, according to Meadows' statement. Not only were he and his wife forced to hire another maidservant to do her work, Anne purloined silk and other goods from her mistress. Nor did the Meadows receive more than the initial payment of £2 from her father. Meadows' narrative then went on to describe Anne's wicked life after leaving their service, implying that because she was a thief and immoral her petition should not be believed. He said that Anne first worked for another man for a few months but departed that household "in company with one of his apprentices," carrying with them some of their master's and mistress' clothing. After their arrest for this theft, Anne was then "out of service, as they credibly heard, and lived . . . lewdly." When charged by a local officer with sexual misbehavior, she falsely claimed that she was still a servant with Meadows. Finally, she decided to marry Garrett Daye, her co-petitioner, whom Meadows described as "a poor inmate and no householder." (As a subtenant of accommodations within another person's house, he lacked the status that came from heading one's own household.) At the time of their marriage, the Dayes asked Meadows "to move his parishioners to bestow their devotion as offerings," but when he refused to do so, they threatened to trouble him and put him to expense by bringing a legal action.

Although we cannot establish the accuracy of the details of these parties' divergent narratives, they illustrate the value of the equity court records. In the area of personal credit, Anne's approach was to emphasize that her master's apparent religious and social good name was undeserved, as seen by his enticing her into his service by dishonestly stressing the particular skills that his wife could teach her. She defined herself, by contrast, as lacking experience and vulnerable, a young maiden newly come into the city with unsullied reputation. Meadows highlighted his own Christian charity and generosity but undermined Anne's credit by stressing her sexual misconduct (implicitly before and certainly after leaving his service) and her dishonesty. His repeated statements that she went down upon her knees before him and begged to stay in her service drew attention both to her abjectness in relation to him and to her duplicity, thereby casting both her credit and her credibility into doubt.

The case also provides information about the experiences of female servants. Both narratives agreed that Anne signed a contract to work for the Meadows for five years. Since service contracts were normally for a single year only, the length of this one immediately suggests something odd about the circumstances. Both parties' statements illustrate what was always a potentially complex relationship between master/mistress and female servant, where the latter was part of the household, living in close contact with other members of the family, but also expected to work for those around her. We gain a better understanding of why the issue of payment of wages could become so heated and so complex: employer and servant commonly interacted in a number of different ways economically over the course of a year, with wages just one component of their dealings. These narratives suggest the potential vulnerability both of a young woman who agreed to work for and live with an often unknown master for a year or more but also that of a household head who needed to hire a servant but did so with little information about her prior life.

We gain interesting glimpses into other ways in which women engaged with the market economy. Mistress Meadows, foreign born and acquainted with unfamiliar forms of needlework, offered Anne the possibility of learning a skill that would provide her with income later in her life. The surgeon called in to evaluate and treat Anne was a woman, one who had a range of current medical techniques at her disposal. It was a married woman who provided daily care while boarding Anne during her illness and who worried that Anne's disease might be spreading to her own children. Although narratives like these were deliberately written to accomplish particular legal goals and hence may be distorted in some respects, they nevertheless provide a richer, more human look at the ways in which women interacted with the cash-based economy than we derive from other sources.

2   The historiographic context: how have scholars interpreted the sources?

Because the sources are limited in number and scope, historians have had to be selective in deciding what issues to explore and creative in devising techniques that enable them to extract all possible information from the available records. For the same reason, there is room for disagreement between scholars as they interpret and explain the evidence we have. Active debate continues today concerning some key aspects of women's economic lives during these centuries. We will survey what topics historians have chosen to study over time, influenced by more general intellectual trends, and how they have read their sources.

Women and their work were of considerable interest to historians during the earlier twentieth century and again at its end, with attention generally focused on women's roles in producing and selling goods. The first generation of scholars in this field, women like Alice Clark and Ivy Pinchbeck who were active during and shortly after World War I, was concerned with the negative impact of the Industrial Revolution on women and children.[27] They believed that there had been a better era for women prior to the eighteenth century, a Golden Age when men and women worked side by side manufacturing craft goods at home. What they perceived as the rough economic equality of the sexes and the family-based nature of production, which also made possible close contact with children, were portrayed as the opposite of the deleterious consequences of industrialization. These authors were, however, unspecific as to when that better world ended (Clark implies the sixteenth and seventeenth centuries) and what its precise features were. More recent studies suggest that

---

[27] Clark, *Working Life of Women*; Pinchbeck, *Women Workers*.

industrialization began later and had a less profound impact on women.[28] Another cluster of early women historians, contemporaries of Clark and Pinchbeck, found inspiration in the independent and successful economic activity they discovered among women in medieval London.[29] The success of those craftswomen and female traders suggested that since women had proven themselves capable of filling important economic roles even during the Middle Ages, women of the present could do likewise. Subsequent scholars have provided additional examples of women's participation in a wide range of economic activities in London and other towns during the later medieval and early modern periods.[30]

During the closing decades of the twentieth century what may be described as "the Golden Age question" was re-opened but from a rather different perspective and placed now in the late medieval period. Several authors suggested that during the generations after the 1348–9 plague urban women were better able to find employment or to engage in trade or even craftwork but that these favorable conditions did not continue into the sixteenth century. Caroline Barron, an expert on late medieval London, stresses the unusually favorable legal position of married women and widows in the capital.[31] Although women did not hold office in the guilds or city government, a married woman could join her husband in business, enjoying the privileges of freeman status, or could trade independently as a *femme sole*, running her own operation and signing contracts in her own name. Especially those *femmes soles* married to artisans "were frequently working partners in marriages between economic equals."[32] Widows in London inherited an atypically large share of their husband's estate and were not merely allowed but expected to continue his business, and some singlewomen had the opportunity of becoming skilled apprentices, not just servants. Noting that the economic activities of women covered a wide range of occupations, extending from wealthy

---

[28] E.g., Tilly and Scott, *Women, Work, and Family.* Honeyman and Goodman argue that although "industrialization affected the structure of the gender division of labour, it was not responsible for instigating women's subordinate position in the labour market." European women's work in the early modern period already displayed the characteristics of a "secondary labour market where employment was largely unskilled, of low status, poorly paid, casual, seasonal, and irregular" ("Women's Work," esp. pp. 624 and 610).

[29] Abram, "Women Traders," and Dale, "The London Silkwomen."

[30] See, e.g., Lacey, "Women and Work," Keene, *Survey of Medieval Winchester,* Britnell, *Growth and Decline in Colchester,* Swanson, *Medieval Artisans,* Hutton, "Women in Fourteenth Century Shrewsbury," Foulds, "Women and Work" (an unpublished paper kindly sent to me by the author), Roberts, "Women and Work," and Prior, "Women and the Urban Economy."

[31] "The 'Golden Age'," and see also her "Women in London." I am grateful to Dr. Barron for letting me have a copy of the latter, an important new study.

[32] Barron, "The 'Golden Age'," p. 40. For below, see ibid., p. 47.

widows down to many poor women who sold food and small items on the streets, Barron concludes: "The picture of the lifestyle of women in medieval London is quite a rosy one; their range of options and prospects differed only slightly from those of the men who shared their level of prosperity." She adds, however, that women's position deteriorated during the sixteenth century, as demographic rise ended the labor shortage of the later fourteenth and fifteenth centuries. Women were therefore pushed out of the skilled labor market and were no longer offered apprenticeships.

A parallel argument has been made for York by Jeremy Goldberg, who considers the economic and demographic fortunes of late medieval women within three stages.[33] He argues that during the first generations after the plague, until around 1410, the combination of labor scarcity and a thriving economy brought a growth in employment opportunities for women, including younger women who immigrated from rural areas. They were still, however, hired mainly in types of work that had traditionally been done by women. The period between 1410 and 1450 represented the high point of female economic activity. Although economic growth had ended, continued demographic decline further reduced the supply of labor. Under those conditions, he suggests, women may have been drawn into the labor force in even greater numbers, because they were less expensive than men; they began also to fill some economic niches that had previously been defined as male. During the second half of the fifteenth century, however, economic contraction due in part to declining demand from a shrunken population led to a sense that employment for male household heads needed to be protected. Women were excluded from the full range of occupations they had previously enjoyed, especially in the textile industry, and were increasingly forced into marginal and poorly paid positions. Studies like these gain support from research on urban women's work in a variety of continental European settings showing that employment opportunities for women were considerable during the later medieval years but declined across the sixteenth century as the result of changes in the forms of production and sale and in the nature of patriarchal structures.[34] The present book agrees with the general argument that women had more economic opportunities during the 150 years after the plague than was to be the case by around 1600, but it does not argue that their situation was rosy even in the best of periods.

---

[33] Most fully in *Women, Work, and Life Cycle*, esp. pp. 336–7, a summary of his proposed stages.

[34] E.g., Merry W. Wood, "Paltry Peddlers," Wiesner, *Working Women*, and Howell, *Women, Production, and Patriarchy*. Honeyman and Goodman suggest that "intense gender conflict in the workplace" led the patriarchal system to create "a new set of rules defining the acceptable gender division of labour in the workplace" ("Women's Work").

Scholars who emphasize the importance of women's economic contributions have in some cases proposed that the ability to generate an income enhanced a woman's personal agency more generally. R. H. Hilton, for example, speaks of the increased economic independence of peasant women in the Midlands after the plague, comparing their situation favorably with women of higher social ranks; within urban communities of all sizes, he argues, "in their social context working women were better off than upper-class women."[35] Goldberg suggests that the cash women brought into the domestic economy through sale of items they made at home (spun yarn, food, and drink) "may have afforded women some independence of action, and a very real degree of economic clout within the familial economy."[36] He argues further that economic freedom contributed to greater selectivity about marriage. During the later fourteenth and first half of the fifteenth centuries, when urban women could support themselves as servants or through craft or trade activity, they had a choice about when and even whether to marry; some postponed marriage or decided to remain single.[37] By the end of the fifteenth century, however, as women's economic opportunities shrank, most of them married and did so at an earlier age. The strongest case for female independence has been made for widows, who in legal terms had equivalent status with men and may in some cases have actively enjoyed the freedom to control their own lives.[38] Barron speaks, for example, of "the purposeful self-sufficiency of London widows in the fifteenth century."

The entire approach that identifies a pre-industrial period when women enjoyed rough economic equality with men and greater personal independence has recently been challenged on several fronts. This questioning occurs within the context of attempts to evaluate more carefully how women have actually fared within societies dominated by men. In an essay describing the characteristics of female employment in fourteenth-century Exeter, Maryanne Kowaleski emphasizes that late medieval women were normally excluded from regular work in a single, well-paid occupation.[39] Identifying the common features of female employment, she notes that women rarely benefited from formal training in the workplace; they generally held low-status and marginal positions

---

[35] Hilton, *The English Peasantry*, p. 105, and his "Women Traders."
[36] Goldberg, "The Public and the Private."
[37] Goldberg, *Women, Work, and Life Cycle*, pp. 339–40. This would in turn have lowered fertility levels, contributing to the ongoing decline in the population.
[38] For a useful summary of the debate over the status and remarriage of widows, see Mate, *Women in Medieval English Society*, pp. 34–8. For below, see "The 'Golden Age'," esp. p. 47.
[39] "Women's Work."

within individual trades. A woman's marital status and her role within the household dictated the type and nature of her economic activity. Women's work was intermittent in nature, and women often practiced more than one trade. Further evidence of women's economic disabilities during the later medieval period was presented by Sandy Bardsley in a study of the wages paid to agricultural workers both before and shortly after the plague of 1348–9.[40] Women, she shows, were paid less than men for equivalent work even during years of acute labor shortage.

The most important critiques of a "Golden Age" thesis have been provided by Judith Bennett. In an important initial essay she emphasizes the continuities of women's work across the later medieval and early modern period, stressing that any changes that took place were insignificant when compared with the ongoing pattern of poorly paid, low-skilled, low-status work that conferred little if any occupational identity.[41] She claims also that married women did not have the right to control how their own income was spent: their earnings became part of shared household resources for which the husband was responsible. Bennett later explored how "a patriarchal equilibrium . . . has worked to maintain the status of European women in times of political, social, and economic change."[42] In her subsequent book about women's participation in the brewing trades between 1300 and 1600, Bennett shows that a substantial fraction – in some communities the great majority – of all women brewed and sold ale on a small scale at least occasionally during the decades around 1300.[43] Over the following centuries, poorer women, especially singlewomen and widows, were gradually pushed out of competition as the scale of brewing increased.[44] This process, which was already under way before the plague, led to a concentration of production during the later medieval years in the hands of a smaller number of commercial brewers, most of them married women. In parallel with that development, female ale-sellers, who distributed drink they had not produced, emerged as a separate and poorly paid occupational group, especially in towns. During the second half of the fifteenth and the sixteenth centuries, however, opportunities for female brewers disappeared, due in part to the popularity of beer. Because hops acted as a preservative, beer could be brewed in much bigger batches and then stored and transported in kegs. In this new world of large-scale, professionalized production of beer, women were unable to compete with male brewers, due primarily to their disadvantages in accessing credit and controlling labor. By around 1600, women's

---

[40] "Women's Work Reconsidered."   [41] "Medieval Women, Modern Women."
[42] "Theoretical Issues: Confronting Continuity," esp. p. 73.
[43] *Ale, Beer, and Brewsters.*
[44] See sect. 1, Ch. 6 below for the impact of demographic and economic crises on this pattern.

roles were limited to the bottom of the industry: working for male brewers in production or sales, or handling small volumes of ale. This book demonstrates a similar progression in other kinds of production and sales too.

On the basis of that history, Bennett attacks the idea that women enjoyed even approximate economic equality with men during the medieval period and that they descended from a more favorable position to a less desirable one thereafter. "The history of brewsters shows, first, that even the best women's work in the middle ages was humble work (belying any notion of a golden age), and, second, that the enduring characteristics of low status, low skilled, and low profit describe women's work in 1300, as well as in 1600 (belying the notion of a transformation in women's work status)."[45] Stressing that ale-brewing offered little prestige and little profit, she comments, "Compared to the other sorts of work available to women, brewing was a good option, but compared to the sorts of work available to men, it was a poor option indeed." Bennett believes that scholars who have emphasized a dramatic change in women's work "have mingled two things best kept separate: the *experiences* of women and women's *status*." While acknowledging the shifts that took place in women's involvement with the drink trades, the *forms* of their work, she emphasizes that the *substance* remained the same. The history of brewsters, she concludes, is "a story of remarkable stability in women's status – of women 'standing still' in a time of opportunity and expansion."

There is some tension in Bennett's argument between her insistence upon the continuity of women's under-valued and poorly rewarded work across these centuries and certain aspects of the material she describes. She notes, for example, that a commercial brewster during the late medieval period probably gained not just tangible rewards but also personal credit from her trade:

She negotiated with grain suppliers, maltsters, waterbearers, servants, and of course her customers; she talked with local or civic officers about the quality, prices, and measures of her ale; she managed a complex business that involved both production and sales; and she brought income into her household. She might not have been recognized as a worker as skilled as a rural plowman or an urban gildsman, but she was probably recognized as a skilled housewife and a good provider for her family.[46]

That level of participation in the local economy and that degree of female agency are difficult to reconcile with Bennett's claim that the work done by women was humble. Further, if we set the account above against her conclusion that almost no women had independent control over the

---

[45] Ibid., pp. 147–8, for this and the rest of the paragraph.
[46] Ibid., p. 35, for this and below.

production and sale of drink by 1600, it appears that a diminution of economic opportunities and status had indeed occurred for women.

It is also hard to integrate in practice Bennett's assessment of the inherently low status of the *work* done by women with the reality of the socio-economic position of the women who *did* that work.[47] As will be discussed below, considerable evidence shows that households that brewed during the later fourteenth and fifteenth centuries covered a wide range but included families of considerable local standing. In the market centers, some late medieval women worked as brewers and alehouse keepers for several decades, contributing to their families' wellbeing and almost certainly acquiring a measure of occupational identification. Because they were often married to respected men who held office in their community's government, there is thus no reason to believe that their peers regarded the work done by these women as low status.

The particular kinds of women whose work has been analyzed have also changed over time. Initially, scholars concentrated on important urban women, whose contributions are relatively well documented. Recently, however, in a pattern common to many kinds of social history, attention has shifted to peasants and women of lower status in the towns.[48] It is difficult to gather information about these groups, leading some historians to concentrate upon their roles in the food and drink trades, where records are somewhat better. More attention has also been paid in recent decades to the question of a woman's marital status. Because married women's roles are inherently difficult to study, due to their "coverage" by their husbands in the eyes of the common law and hence in most records, many earlier studies focused on widows.[49] Current work attempts some examination of married women, and a new concern with singlewomen, those who had not married, is emerging.[50] The social and

---

[47] For the status of women who brewed, see Ch. 6 below.

[48] E.g., Bennett, *Women in the Medieval English Countryside*, Wright, "Churmaids," and Gowing, "'The Freedom of the Streets."

[49] E.g., Holderness' studies of widows in credit relationships: "Credit in a Rural Community," "Credit in English Rural Society," and "Widows in Pre-Industrial Society." This attention was not misplaced: Peter Laslett has estimated that 12.9 percent of all households in early modern England were headed by widows ("Mean Household Size," p. 147).

[50] Bennett, *Ale, Beer, and Brewsters* and her "Ventriloquisms," Froide, "Single Women, Work, and Community," her "Surplus Women and Surplus Money" (I am grateful to Dr. Froide for sending me a copy of this paper), and her "Marital Status as a Category of Difference," Spicksley, "The Early Modern Demographic Dynamic" (Dr. Spicksley generously sent me a copy of parts of this fine study), and Bennett and Froide, eds., *Singlewomen in the European Past, 1250–1800*, especially Kowaleski's attempt to estimate the number and types of singlewomen in medieval and early modern Europe ("Singlewomen"). For poor women in Paris around 1300 who appear never to have married, see Farmer, *Surviving Poverty*.

economic situations of older women and adolescent servants are likewise being studied.[51]

Recent studies have attempted to break down the notion of "women's work" into more complex categories, a process continued in the present book. Careful distinctions are presented in Mavis Mate's analysis of women in East Sussex between 1350 and 1535.[52] Attentive to differences between regions and to changes over time, she compares the experiences of married women, widows, and singlewomen; of rural and urban women; and of peasants, laborers, those living in craft and trading families, and aristocratic women. In a book about Exeter, a regional center with exceptionally rich records from the later fourteenth century, Maryanne Kowaleski suggests an interesting contrast in the extent to which the households of men in various occupations engaged in commercial brewing.[53] Households headed by a man who worked in a craft/trade that made heavy use of family labor, those involving textiles, clothing, leather, and victualing (= preparation and sale of food), were less likely to brew, presumably because women were more directly involved with the primary activity of the household. If, however, a man worked in an occupation that did not call for female participation (merchants, professionals, or people in the metal and sometimes the building trades), their households – i.e., their wives – were far more likely to brew for sale. Another new study takes a closer look at *femme sole* status, arguing that it conveyed fewer economic and legal benefits and was less commonly used than has been assumed.

Historians are now trying to situate women's work within a broader social, legal, and cultural context. Scholars of the continent like Natalie Zemon Davis and Martha Howell link women's roles to the modes of production and types of familial patterns within which they occurred.[54] Bennett's analysis of female brewers looks not only at changes in the nature of production but also at the changing ideological climate that helped to inhibit commercial brewing by women. Barbara Hanawalt's examinations of women in medieval London emphasize the significance of marriage strategies, widow remarriage, provisions for dowry

---

[51] E.g., Pelling, "Older Women," and for servants, see sect. 1, Ch. 3 below.

[52] *Daughters, Wives and Widows.*

[53] *Local Markets and Regional Trade,* esp. pp. 133–6. She establishes that brewing for sale was practiced by 71 percent of all households at least once between 1365 and 1393, carried out normally by wives or female servants; 29 percent of Exeter families brewed ten times or more, which she defines as a commercial level of activity. For below, see McIntosh, "The Benefits and Drawbacks of *Femme Sole* Status."

[54] Davis, "Women in the Crafts in Sixteenth-Century Lyon," and Howell, *Women, Production, and Patriarchy.* For below, see Bennett, *Ale, Beer, and Brewsters,* p. 123, and cf. her "Misogyny, Popular Culture," and Hanna, "Brewing Trouble."

and dower, and inheritance patterns in determining the social as well as the economic structures of women's lives.[55] Henrietta Leyser touches on women's work into her social survey, while Mate's useful overview balances discussion of women's economic position with consideration of political, educational, religious, and legal factors.[56]

The biggest hole in our knowledge concerns the extended sixteenth century (c. 1480–1620). Historians have previously identified only scattered and indirect evidence, making the equity court petitions especially valuable. Sara Mendelson and Patricia Crawford's compendious survey of early modern women says little about their economic roles prior to the seventeenth century, a statement true also for Anne Laurence's and Jacqueline Eales' shorter accounts.[57] Students of poverty have noted the prominence of women among the needy, especially in the decades around 1600, and Michael Zell's evidence suggests that those crafts or trades in which women were most likely to work with their husbands were located at the lower end of the economic hierarchy.[58] By the later seventeenth century, however, what appears to have been a decline in the economic opportunities open to women was at least partially reversed for some urban women.[59]

Disagreements between historians about various aspects of women's work stem to some extent from scant evidence, gaps that leave open legitimate but differing interpretations. We may never be able to provide a clear answer to the question of what fraction of urban women around 1400 enjoyed unusual economic opportunities (as Barron and Goldberg suggest) and what fraction were suffering from the loss of income from brewing that resulted from the concentration of the industry into a smaller number of hands (as Bennett proposes). It will probably be impossible to determine quantitatively whether a higher fraction of young people went

---

[55] "The Widow's Mite," "Remarriage as an Option," and "Dilemma of the Widow." A dowry was the land or other wealth that a woman brought into her marriage; dower was the provision of land or other wealth she received if widowed. See also Keene, "Tanners' Widows."

[56] Leyser, *Medieval Women*; Mate, *Women in Medieval English Society*.

[57] Mendelson and Crawford, *Women in Early Modern England, 1550–1720*, chs. 5–6, Laurence, *Women in England, 1500–1760*, chs. 8–9, and Eales, *Women in Early Modern England, 1500–1700*, ch. 8.

[58] E.g., Slack, *Poverty and Policy*, and Pelling, "Old Age, Poverty, and Disability"; Zell, *Industry in the Countryside*, pp. 135–9.

[59] Paul Seaver and Joseph Ward have found evidence of improved opportunities for female apprentices in London after the plague and great fire of 1665–6 (see Ch. 5 below); Mendelson and Crawford describe some new opportunities for women of middling status in the decades around 1700 (*Women in Early Modern England*, ch. 6). See also Earle, "The Female Labour Market" and his *Making of the English Middle Class*, esp. ch. 6, and Lemire, "Women, the Informal Economy and the Development of Capitalism" (I am grateful to Dr. Lemire for letting me have a copy of this paper).

into service after 1348–9 than had been true before the plague.[60] We are also dealing with contrasts in emphasis. Bennett presents a history of both continuity and change in her study of brewers but feels that the features that remained the same are more significant than the variations over time; Barron, by contrast, while recognizing that many London women always worked at the bottom of the system, highlights the involvement of some women at higher levels of the economy during the later medieval years. Arguments like these contribute to the intellectual vitality of the field.

3   Continuity and change

Because the rest of this study is arranged by type of economic activity, it will be helpful to present here a broad chronological framework that highlights the main areas of continuity and change within the period 1300–1620. This account, which is derived both from other studies and from the new material that will be presented in subsequent chapters, offers what this author believes is the best way of making sense of the information we now have about women's work as it functioned within its social context.[61]

Certain features of women's economic roles remained fairly constant. For women who produced or sold goods, their work generally required little training, was poorly paid, and carried scant occupational identity. Patriarchal values and domestic constraints meant that when women had their own economic pursuits, those activities were usually seen as secondary to what the male head of the household did. Because women could rarely devote their full attention to income-producing pursuits, almost never gained training in a skilled craft, and had to be able to respond quickly to changing demands at home, they generally worked part time in low-skilled jobs and often pursued multiple activities, either at the same time or sequentially. It was primarily in towns – both large and small – that a limited number of women were involved in a given occupation on a more intensive and profitable basis and for a long period of time.

A cluster of economic handicaps and legal disabilities limited women's participation in the public economy throughout these centuries. The most important was the difficulty of getting credit. Except for those few settings which permitted *femme sole* trading, if a married woman wanted credit, the lender/seller would demand assurance that her husband supported

---

[60] Goldberg, *Women, Work, and Life Cycle*, Smith, "Geographical Diversity," and Poos, *A Rural Society*, who argue that they did, as opposed to Bailey, "Demographic Decline."

[61] References will be provided here only to topics and sources that are not considered in later chapters.

her business transactions and would accept responsibility for whatever debts she incurred. Further, her own creditworthiness rested at least in part upon her husband's social and economic position. For singlewomen and widows, potential sellers or lenders may have been hesitant to extend credit on two grounds: because the woman lacked a husband's economic backing for her enterprises, and because she might later marry someone who refused to assume responsibility for her debts. Women were therefore generally limited to activities that required little capital and involved credit interactions with people in their own community who could assess their individual situation in personal terms.

Gender expectations placed women at a disadvantage in other respects too. Their authority in hiring and controlling workers was weaker than that of men, so the scale of production by women was limited. They were less able to travel freely in connection with their economic activities: it was difficult to abandon their domestic duties, and a woman traveling alone was at physical risk and might be suspected of immoral intent. Because of the common law's definition of married women as having no legal identity apart from their husbands, their ability to enter into contracts on their own or to pursue their interests in the courts was curtailed. Nearly all local and national courts operated under the common law system (the equity courts utilized in this study were rare exceptions), so most women were constrained by those rules.[62] In urban communities with craft or merchant guilds, women might be allowed to join – as a relative of their father or husband or occasionally through their own activity – but they were never chosen for the offices that made economic decisions and did not gain comparable social benefits. At no time during these centuries were women included in the government of any city or town, in the legal profession or Parliament (not even as voters), or in the universities. Women as a group thus remained in a subordinate position across these centuries, not enjoying full economic or legal/political equality with men.

But this book also documents change. It is likely that around 1300 England's population was very large – perhaps higher than at any time again until the mid-eighteenth century – and that many poor families were barely getting by.[63] The purchasing power of wages was low, and when crops failed and food prices shot up, as occurred during the 1310s, mortality rose. Population pressure and economic hardship led some young

---

[62] It is possible, however, that local courts allowed women a somewhat more active voice in practice than the letter of the law dictated. For that phenomenon in Scotland, see Ewan, "Scottish Portias."

[63] For a discussion of the demographic and economic issues, see Dyer, *Making a Living*, ch. 7.

women to seek positions as residential servants, as was to be the case around 1600, but we cannot determine how common this pattern was. Women's involvement in credit relationships during these years was concentrated within the informal system of loaning money, goods, labor, and land. Many women of all marital statuses were brewing and selling ale, but in most cases they worked on a very small scale and on an occasional basis. Some women produced woolen thread for weaving, and many probably assisted their husbands in craftwork or trade in ways that we cannot see. In London and other urban centers, an occasional widow maintained her husband's business, but independent female participation at middling levels of manufacture or sales seems to have been relatively limited.

The atypical period between 1348–9 and around 1500 was marked by a very low population and variable economic conditions.[64] Some women had to support their family after the death of a father or husband. If they had no readily marketable skills, they might try to generate income by transferring what they had previously done within the domestic setting into a for-pay context. One option was by providing services, including boarding and health care. In this period, sex work was tolerated as a necessary evil in some towns. But because labor was often in short supply and wages for other kinds of work were generally high, such activities probably appeared relatively unattractive. A further step outward into the public economy involved preparing and selling items one had previously made for consumption at home: food, drink, or cloth. In many regions and periods, this activity was encouraged by a higher per capita demand for goods, as families of middling and lower rank enjoyed a rise in the standard of living.[65] In brewing, most of the smaller producers dropped out, but the later fourteenth and fifteenth centuries offered a desirable niche for some married women who brewed commercially. So long as production remained at an intermediate level and their husbands backed their activity, women's disabilities in the areas of obtaining credit and controlling labor were less pronounced. Making cloth or clothing provided income for other women, though the more skilled and better paid stages were still usually done by men. Some urban women ran shops or worked in other crafts. Widows were particularly active in this period,

---

[64] Bolton, "'The World Upside Down'."

[65] Dyer, *Standards of Living*. Alehouses became more important as social institutions, due in part to a preference for leisure among wage-earners during a period when better pay meant that fewer hours of work were required to support a household (ibid. and Peter Clark, *The English Alehouse*). In some settings, however, a combination of agricultural crisis, a contraction in England's export trade, and a shortage of coins resulted in lower market demand as well as lower prices and lower wages during the mid-fifteenth century (Mate, *Daughters, Wives and Widows*, pp. 16–17).

either pursuing their own occupations or continuing their husband's business. Even in this period of frequent labor shortages, however, women generally went into the types of work that had previously been considered appropriate for women; rarely did they take up activities that were considered specifically male, such as working with heavy leather items or metals.

Having one's own income and – for widows and some singlewomen – heading one's own household must have increased women's exposure to the public world. Especially in communities with a market, women who pursued an independent economic life were certainly aware of public events and listened to discussion of broader economic, political, and religious issues, though we do not know to what extent they participated in them.[66] Women were members of the fraternities or guilds that flourished in many parish churches during the later fourteenth and fifteenth centuries, participating in their religious and social activities and occasionally even holding leadership positions. Nor were spatial boundaries tightly drawn along gender lines in later medieval communities, restricting women's freedom of movement.[67] It is probably misleading to label these generations a "Golden Age" for women. Expanded opportunities pertained only to some women, they did not overcome the ongoing legal and cultural disabilities that pertained to all women, and they did not result in a long-term improvement in the status of women and their work. Yet this author believes that the period between 1348 and around 1500 offered women more desirable economic options than were to be available in the decades around 1600.

Beginning in the late fifteenth century in urban settings and spreading throughout the country during the sixteenth, a conjunction of factors brought about changes in women's roles. Substantial population growth exceeded the expansion of the economy, causing a drop in real wages and contributing to serious poverty by the 1590s. This intensified concern about the economic competition posed by working women to male household heads. An expanding scale of production, the blossoming of overseas trade, and new techniques for securing large loans all accentuated the

---

[66] Masschaele, "The Public Space of the Marketplace," and Roberts, "Words They Are Women." For below, see French, "'To Free Them from Binding'," her "Maidens' Lights and Wives' Stores," her "Women in the Late Medieval English Parish," and Rosser, "Going to the Fraternity Feast."

[67] Hanawalt suggests in her study based upon the coroners' rolls that "women's chief sphere of work [w]as the home and men's [w]as the fields and the forests" (in her *The Ties that Bound*, p. 145). That conclusion has been questioned on the grounds that her evidence, which is mainly pre-plague, deals with people engaged in especially hazardous activities, not routine work (e.g., Goldberg, "The Public and the Private"). Hanawalt's later "At the Margins of Women's Space" does not emphasize gender distinctions in towns.

disadvantages faced by women in terms of controlling labor, accessing credit, and traveling. These material developments were heightened by intensified social, political, and cultural discomfort about women. Worry about disorder and sexual wrongdoing led to closer supervision of female behavior by local courts.[68] The larger towns became concerned about the economic independence and sexual availability of women who lived on their own, instead of in a male-headed household, or who worked in public settings, especially drinking houses. By the late sixteenth century, women who hawked goods around the streets of urban areas were regarded by local officials as uncontrolled in both economic and social/sexual terms. Anxiety mounted about uncontrolled female orifices, including the vagina and mouth (the source of gossip and criticism of men), culminating in the Jacobean authors of the "woman hater" school: women, ungoverned themselves, corrupt the morality of men and undermine their authority.[69] The homilies read in every parish church in England each Sunday stressed how important it was for women to be submissive and to devote themselves to their roles within the now spiritualized Christian family. Medical writers reinforced these discourses, offering ostensibly objective reasons for women's physical and emotional weakness, which rendered them unsuited to participation in the extra-domestic world. Although earlier historical studies exaggerate both the novelty and the depth of gender tension during the decades around 1600, it is clear that women, their work, their sexuality, and their speech were charged issues.[70]

All these influences together had a negative impact upon the types of work available to women in the market economy. As poverty mounted, more poor women probably resorted to service work as their only way of earning some money, despite its limited financial rewards. Due to economic need and the glut of labor, many needy young women sought positions as live-in servants, but they had to accept increasingly unfavorable terms. Though the term "apprenticeship" was still used in some contracts for girls, it rarely offered training in a skilled craft, becoming instead simply a form of long-term, unremunerated residential labor. Sex work was now castigated as a social and moral evil, though it continued to offer necessary income to some women. In the world of credit, women were active as small- or middling-scale moneylenders and sometimes as pawnbrokers. Especially in London, women with extra resources were beginning to acquire residential or commercial property

---

[68] McIntosh, *Controlling Misbehavior*, and Goldberg, "Coventry's 'Lollard' Programme."
[69] For examples of this literature and that below, see Aughterson, ed., *Renaissance Woman*.
[70] See, e.g., Underdown, "The Taming of the Scold," and Boose, "Scolding Brides"; a more balanced account is given in Ingram's "'Scolding Women Cucked or Washed'."

as a source of rental income. But few women could succeed in the upper realms of the commercial system that developed during the Elizabethan and Jacobean periods, marked by larger transactions and more formal mechanisms.

By the end of the sixteenth century, though many women probably worked with their husbands, few operated as producers or sellers of goods in their own right except at the bottom of the system. Women functioning independently were almost entirely gone from the drink-related trades apart from a few widows licensed to run little alehouses and women hired to retail ale, many of whom peddled their drink on the streets in towns. There they were joined by rising numbers of needy women selling food and used clothing to the poor.[71] All of them were subject to sexual attention and official criticism from men. Many poor women engaged in unskilled or semi-skilled piecework at home (like spinning, knitting, or making pins), but these activities brought very little income. By 1600 the economic role that was being promoted for women, especially those of middling rank, was as consumers of the new and non-essential types of clothing and household furnishings being produced in England or imported from abroad and attractively displayed in urban shops.

The chapters that follow begin with the types of work that required the least departure from domestic activities and move to those that forced women to gain or use new skills. Part II deals first with domestic and personal services, provided generally within a household setting. We then consider women's involvement in financial credit mechanisms, their roles as lenders or borrowers of money, including pawnbroking, and their actions as owners of commercial or residential property that they rented to others. Part III examines women's participation in the production and sale of goods, beginning with trades associated with drink and food and continuing on to more skilled crafts. At the end we look briefly at women's activities as consumers.

[71] Roberts, "Women and Work."

Part II

Providing services

3   Domestic and personal services

In exploring women's roles within the market economy, we move from those types of work that were most closely linked to what women commonly did at home into those that required new skills and/or participation in a public setting. Providing domestic or personal services allowed women to extend the activities they carried out within their own families, without reimbursement, into a for-pay environment, by doing similar work for non-relatives. Many young women and some older ones were employed as residential servants, living with and working for a master and/or mistress in another household. Others earned money by taking boarders into their homes, children or adults who slept and ate there. Little has previously been known about boarding, but we have some fine information from the equity court petitions. Other women brought in cash by laundering, cooking, or cleaning on a non-residential basis, by doing sex work, or by caring for the sick.[1] These activities are examined in the present chapter, followed in the next by the services women provided in the areas of money-lending and renting out real estate.

Such work facilitated the smooth functioning of households, provided necessary personal care or sexual services, and made cash and property available to those who needed it. But, as is true in many societies, the labor of service workers was commonly hidden from sight and undervalued by the rest of society. In England, most service employments offered neither a good income nor enhanced social credit. Domestic tasks were seen as naturally female, and the location of service work employments within a household setting meant that the women who pursued them could be properly supervised by the male head of that unit. Hence there was little objection to women's involvement in service work until the latter part of our period, when discomfort mounted about women who went out to clean men's houses and about sex workers. Moreover, service

---

[1] A few women taught young children basic reading, writing, and arithmetic, but because so little is known about them, they will not be discussed here (see, e.g., Barron, "The Education and Training of Girls," and Anglin, *The Third University*, pp. 75–90).

activities seldom produced enough money to support a family, offering only supplemental income. Even in periods of population pressure and limited employment opportunities, such work was rarely sought by men. Female involvement was therefore not perceived as a threat to the ability of male household heads to provide for their families.

For these reasons, the history of women's service work appears to have followed a rather different trajectory from what we will see with respect to the production and sale of goods. Although we have no quantitative information about service arrangements, largely because they were set up informally, involvement in such work does not appear to have decreased across the sixteenth century, as did women's participation in the trades and crafts. To the contrary, it is likely that after around 1560 poor girls were increasingly seeking positions in residential service, while more poor women may have taken in lodgers. Opportunities to wash clothes, cook, clean, or provide health care through private arrangements were augmented during the later sixteenth and early seventeenth centuries by charitable institutions or poor-relief officials in the parishes who hired women to do similar kinds of work. It may well be that due to poverty a higher fraction of women were providing domestic or personal services in 1620 than had been true in 1400.

1   Live-in servants

Living and working as a servant within a household headed by someone other than one's parents was an experience shared by many young women and probably most young men before the time of their marriage in later medieval and early modern England.[2] It has been suggested that the institution of adolescent service formed a key component within the "northwest European marriage pattern," which featured a late age of marriage for both women and men, a small age gap between spouses, and the expectation that a newly married couple would be financially self-sufficient and set up its own household, rather than moving in with either set of parents.[3] Most of these "life-cycle servants" left home sometime during their teens, in many cases remaining in service until they were financially able to marry, which usually occurred in their early to

---

[2] Goldberg, "Marriage, Migration, Servanthood," Hettinger, "Defining the Servant," McIntosh, "Servants and the Household Unit," Ben-Amos, *Adolescence and Youth*, Whittle, "Servants in Rural England," and her "Women, Servants, and By-Employment" (I am grateful to Dr. Whittle for letting me have a copy of these papers before their publication), Kussmaul, *Servants in Husbandry*, and Capp, *When Gossips Meet*, ch. 4.

[3] Hajnal, "Two Kinds of Preindustrial Household Formation System," and Smith, "Geographical Diversity."

mid-twenties.[4] In return for their labor, female domestic servants normally received room and board, some clothing, cash wages, and training in the sorts of skills they would need when they set up their own households. They generally agreed to serve a given master and/or mistress for a year, at the end of which they were free to change to a different employer if they wished. Especially during periods when labor was in short supply, female servants in craft households might learn in addition some artisanal skills they could later carry into paid employment.[5] Apprentices, who agreed to work for a longer period of years, were supposed to gain more specialized training, but by the later sixteenth century, most arrangements that were called apprenticeships had become simply an extended period of service.[6]

While previous studies have focused on young servants, the equity court petitions shed light on those women who stayed in service beyond the normal age or returned to service later in life. Though most adult women probably preferred to live in their own households, there were few other opportunities that provided comparable security for those who were not married and had no special skills to offer. Service might also provide welcome sociability, and by the later sixteenth century it freed women from the criticism directed at those who lived independently. A detailed household listing from the London suburb of Ealing in 1599 shows that 15 percent of the women described as servants were aged thirty to forty-nine, while 2 percent were fifty years or older.[7]

Some of these older servants were single, women who had not been asked to marry or did not wish to do so. They were likely to remain with a given master for an extended period. During the mid-1530s, Juliana Craunshaw said she had served Robert and Alice Cutlyng of Great Grimsby, Lincs., for fourteen years, while Margaret Cornys, who later married a shoemaker, served John Hall, a Bristol merchant, for eighteen years.[8] In 1605, singlewoman Margaret Jones was asked by Francis Dyer,

---

[4] For the suggestion that some servants in the later fourteenth and fifteenth centuries returned home again before reaching their mid-twenties or married at a younger age, see Bailey, "Demographic Decline."

[5] During the later fourteenth century in towns, for example, women servants were found most commonly in the households of food and drink traders, including tavern- and inn-keepers, and of craftsmen or merchants who dealt with cloth; relatively few served masters in the metal and leather trades (Mate, *Women in Medieval English Society*, p. 47). Male servants were usually trained in agriculture, craftwork, or trade.

[6] For female apprentices, see sect. 2, Ch. 5 below.

[7] Allison, "An Elizabethan Village 'Census'." The proportion of widows and older single-women in service was apparently higher still during the later seventeenth and eighteenth centuries (Froide, "Single Women, Work, and Community"). By the mid-eighteenth century in London, 40 percent of female servants were older than thirty years and 20 percent were older than forty (Kent, "Ubiquitous but Invisible").

[8] PRO C 1/760/19 and C 1/761/18. For below, see PRO REQ 2/420/90.

a gentleman of Tickenham, Som., and his wife Elizabeth, to become Elizabeth's servant. After agreeing to pay her annually 20s. plus cloth for a gown, they "so well liked of her service" that she continued with them for ten years. By 1615, however, Elizabeth Dyer had died and Margaret left her position, going to live in Weston-super-Mare, Som. In this case, most unusually, we are told Margaret's age: she was fifty when she entered the Dyers' service.

A well-documented history of a singlewoman who spent much of her life in service concerns Annis Cowper, the daughter of an embroiderer of London, who was born around 1560.[9] After her father's death when she was a small child, she lived with her mother and stepfather, who made caps. At the unusually young age of eleven or twelve years, she was apprenticed to another London capper, whom she served for nine years; after that she worked as a servant for a third capmaker for eleven more years. At that point, when Annis was in her early thirties, she found that the trade of capmaking was declining, so she went to live with and work for a female apple-seller for twelve years. Next she served a Dutchman for six or seven years until he left the country. Then, as a singlewoman aged around fifty years, Annis had trouble finding residential employment, so she was obliged to take up work as a daily charwoman, cleaning houses for pay, which she did for two or three years. Finally she tried several other ways to make ends meet, probably including begging, before eventually requesting assistance from poor-relief officials.

Widows, too, sometimes had to take work as live-in servants or housekeepers.[10] Pernell Cooke of Greenwich, Kent, was widowed around 1480 when her husband "by misfortune was slain."[11] Because he died in debt and she had no income, Pernell decided to become "a servant for meat [= food] and drink" and was grateful to find even that kind of work. At about the same time, Margaret Shorte, a London, widow, was sued and arrested for violation of the Statute of Laborers by William Lee, an innkeeper of London, who claimed that she had agreed to be his servant by the year but had not filled the terms of her service.[12] Widow Mercy Boxford of Ivylane, London, was approached in the late 1520s by John Corney, vicar of Leamington Priors, War., who asked her to accept service as housekeeper in his vicarage. (Whether this job carried with it

---

[9] Mendelson and Crawford, *Women in Early Modern England*, p. 278.

[10] In the equity court sample, two of five female servants were widows at the time of their employment during the later fifteenth century, as was one of the eight servants during the period 1500–59. Between 1560 and 1619 one widow and one married woman joined eleven singlewomen in the combined central and northern samples. For migration of poor widows into French towns around 1300, some of whom went into service, see Farmer, *Surviving Poverty in Medieval Paris*, pp. 28–31.

[11] PRO C 1/63/138.   [12] PRO C 1/60/208. For below, see C 1/608/41.

the assumption that she would also provide sexual services is not clear.) John promised that if she agreed to work for him, he would give her not only annual wages of 18s. plus a kirtle and a petticoat but also enough extra reward to ensure her financial security for the rest of her life. On the basis of this agreement, Mercy moved to Leamington, taking some of her own household goods with her. During the three years she served him, she later claimed, she laid out £11 6s. 4d. of her own money on their household expenses. At the time of her departure, John promised to reimburse her for those costs and said she could leave her goods at his house until she was ready to remove them. Later, however, he charged her with theft and had her arrested on suspicion of felony, claiming that she had taken some of his possessions away with her. Widow Margaret Lucas worked as a servant to an alebrewer of London for thirty years to support herself and her son during the later decades of the sixteenth century.[13]

Due to the expectation that servants would live in their master's household, married women usually worked as servants only if their husbands had abandoned them. Susan Wright described herself in a petition to the Court of Requests in 1603 as "the forsaken wife" of yeoman John Wright of Willey, War.[14] She claimed that when she was fourteen years old she had been left land and goods worth £250 at her mother's death, whereupon her sister's husband began to plot "how he might take advantage of her nonage and imbecility." He persuaded her to marry John Wright, "who had been her father's man and of small wealth"; over the course of the next two years, John wasted most of her estate. He then left her, disappearing to places unknown, whereupon she was driven to great want. In her extremity she was forced to enter service as a kitchen maid.

Regardless of their age, female servants were brought into contact with the market economy and with credit. Because they received cash wages as part of the reimbursement for their service, they had to extract payment from their employers and to decide how to utilize that money: either in immediate consumption or in some form of investment that would protect and ideally increase their nest egg until they were ready to use it. A thrifty servant might be able to accumulate a nice array of cash and/or goods for her own later use. Service relationships also commonly involved both personal and economic credit. Masters and mistresses looking for servants had to assess the honesty and reliability of the young women who were available, relying often on their reputations, while prospective servants wanted to determine whether employers would treat them well. Economic credit was part of most master/servant arrangements, for wages

[13] PRO REQ 2/398/69.   [14] PRO REQ 2/402/88.

were normally paid only at the end of the year. For the employer, the annual nature of the cash payment was more convenient than frequent deliveries along the way; for the servant it provided a lump sum at the end of the year, to be spent, saved, or invested as she wished. When a servant remained with a given master for a longer span, the credit component was accentuated, for her wages would usually be paid only at the time of her departure. The 1586 will of Joan Worthington, "maiden," who had traveled from Lancashire to work as a servant with a yeoman in Hornchurch, a village in Havering, says that she was owed £3 17s. in back wages, due probably from four or five years of service.[15] Court cases show women servants prosecuting their current or former employers for wages that sometimes stretched back for a number of years of continuous – but allegedly unpaid – employment.

In describing what domestic service for women actually entailed and how servants were hired and paid, we are again fortunate to have personal accounts from petitions to the equity courts. Women who brought suit concerning problems that occurred while they were servants or masters who charged a former female servant with a misdeed accounted for 8–17 percent of all cases within each of the sub-periods in the central court group but a smaller fraction of the northern sample. (See App. 1.2.) The disputes described in the equity court petitions do not, however, reflect how most women experienced service. Many arrangements were presumably completed to the mutual satisfaction of master and servant. Further, those that led to conflict were usually resolved in common law courts. The equity courts were likely to hear two special kinds of cases: those in which the petitioner had no documentation of the initial service agreement; and those in which the (ex-)servant claimed that she was poor and defenseless, whereas her (ex-)master was a person of influence, so she could not get justice in a common law court. While we should there-fore not conclude from these petitions that master/servant relationships were inherently troubled, or troubled in these particular ways, we may use the material provided in the narratives to expand our understanding of what service involved.

The kinds of work done by female servants covered a wide spectrum, depending upon the type of household into which they had been hired. A domestic servant's duties commonly included cleaning, cooking, serving at meals, sewing, washing clothes, and looking after young children.[16] (See Illus. 1.) Women who worked as agricultural servants similarly

---

[15] ERO D/AER 15, 130.

[16] These examples come from early modern Southampton: Froide, "Single Women, Work, and Community," pp. 249–50.

1. A female servant preparing food for two men seated at a table

carried out multiple tasks.[17] In wealthier families, a favored female servant might spend some or all of her time assisting her mistress (see Illus. 2).

Servants in towns or market centers could be sent out to do shopping or other errands as well as performing duties at home. Anne Webb was hired in 1615 as a domestic servant by William Comberford of Tamworth, Staffs., an esquire.[18] In her response to William's petition of 1621 claiming that she and a young man had embezzled grain, wool, linen, and other goods while in his service, Anne said that she was "employed for the most part in brewing, and dressing of meat, and making of white meat [= cheese], and had charge of the brass and pewter in the kitchen." She also bought fresh meat, butter, eggs, and other small items for the

---

[17] Their duties might include running the dairy, milking the cows, caring for small animals, especially poultry, and weeding; these jobs were augmented as needed by helping with domestic work, especially cooking and alemaking (Whittle, "Women, Servants, and By-Employment," and her "The Gender Division of Labour"). By the early modern period, the wages of female agricultural servants were markedly lower than those of their male counterparts: a sample of Quarter Session announcements concerning the level of wages to be paid between the sixteenth and the eighteenth centuries shows that the median ratio of maximum male to maximum female wages was 1:0.6 (Kussmaul, *Servants in Husbandry*, pp. 34–9).

[18] PRO REQ 2/399/10.

2. A servant assisting her mistress with her hair

household, sometimes laying out her own money for them but then having periodic accounting sessions with her mistress. Beatrice Davis, an unusually young servant living in Chigwell, Essex, in 1560, was sent to Romford on an errand by her master.[19] After riding for four miles, the eleven-year-old girl went into the yard of an inn to water her horse. She sat on the edge of the trough to rest while it drank but was "overtaken by sleep," fell into the water, and drowned.

Female servants living in the households of craftsmen or traders commonly spent some of their time in retailing. It could be very convenient to

[19] PRO KB 9/600, pt. 2, no. 104.

have a young woman available to help with sales and deliveries while the
master continued his own work. In fifteenth-century York, Joan Scharp
assisted her master Robert Lascels by weighing the goods being bought,
while another servant, Anne Bawmburgh, carried an unusually large purchase to the customer's home.[20] Thomas Foxe of London, who described
himself as a clothworker in 1618, said that while living in Bishopsgate
Street a few years before he had worked in "the trade of distilling aqua-
vita [= a distilled alcoholic liquor] and strong waters." To assist in his
business, he hired Agnes Miller as a servant, in whom he "placed great
trust" for selling the commodities in his shop and helping him to vent his
brews.

How did a prospective servant make connection with an employer?
Between 1300 and 1620 there were few official hiring fairs of the sort that
would become common during the seventeenth and eighteenth centuries,
although the predecessors of such gatherings are visible.[21] In Coventry
by the early 1450s young people were "let to service" at a fair held on
Good Friday, and in York prospective servants may have gathered at the
Pavement on Martinmas Day to seek employment. Goldberg suggests
that contact between masters and potential servants could be established
through kin relationships, trading ties between the servant's parents or
friends and the employer, or interactions within given geographic areas.[22]
During periods of labor shortage within a given community, sharp competition might exist between potential employers over a good servant. Luring
a servant away from another master was one of the topics addressed in
the Parliamentary statute concerning laborers of 1351, which remained
in effect throughout the following centuries.[23]

Although servants' contracts normally ran for a full year, some young
women set up shorter contracts or decided to leave their employment
in the midst of their term. Elizabeth Bougard claimed that sometime
around 1470, while a singlewoman, she agreed to serve grocer John Pecok
of London for six weeks "upon liking," at the end of which she would
decide whether to agree to work for him for a full year.[24] During the
trial period, however, she became engaged to marry John Barantyne,
whereupon she left Pecok's service, which, she said, "was lawful for her
to do." Throughout her four years of marriage to Barantyne, Elizabeth

---

[20] Goldberg, "Female Labour," p. 25. For below, see PRO REQ 2/410/62.
[21] Roberts, "'Waiting Upon Chance'." For below, see Goldberg, *Women, Work, and Life
Cycle*, pp. 173–4.
[22] Goldberg, "Female Labour," p. 22.
[23] Elaine Clark, "Medieval Labor Law," Poos, "The Social Context of Statute of Labourers Enforcement," Putnam, *The Enforcement of the Statutes of Labourers*, and Kenyon,
"Labour Conditions."
[24] PRO C 1/60/178.

remained friends with Pecock, who was "conversant with her in eating and drinking, as well beyond the seas as this side." (This suggests a very close friendship.) After Barantyne's death, she remained a widow for three years but then married again. At that point, Pecok brought an action of trespass against her, claiming that while she was his servant eight years before she had stolen some of his goods. In the mid-1530s Joan Turner complained against John Lewes of London, haberdasher, her former master.[25] She said that she had worked for him as a servant for three months but then departed, with his goodwill. She left with him a chest containing her clothes and other possessions, to a value of £10, which he agreed to keep safely until she was ready to reclaim it. John, however, opened the chest and gave her clothing to his wife and others.

The payment of wages or clothing due to servants could be problematic. Disputes over such issues account for the majority of cases involving servants that came before the equity courts. In the early 1480s, for example, Joan Chamberleyn, a singlewoman of London, claimed that she had been a covenant servant (= with a written contract) to Richard Swan, a London official.[26] She completed the term agreed between them, but he still owed her 10s. for back wages. Although she repeatedly asked him to pay her, he said he would do so only if she agreed to continue serving him. When she refused, he "vexed and troubled her with divers actions of debt and trespass" in the London courts, acting out of malice, she alleged. If a woman decided to remain in a given master's service for more than a single year, with payment delayed until the end of the full term, the employer might be unable or unwilling to produce the larger sum. Isabel Teychenor of Sussex claimed that she agreed to work for William Heberden starting 1 August 1493, having been promised wages of 2s. in money plus a gown (= a long dress) and a kirtle (= a skirt or apron worn over a dress) each year.[27] She worked for William on those terms for nine years until he died, but his widow then refused to pay her the 18s. plus nine gowns worth £4 and nine kirtles worth £3 due to her.

Working as a servant opened up the possibility of some secondary forms of profit. In addition to the obvious potential of theft from the master's household or shop, a servant might be in a position to use her influence with her master or mistress to her own financial advantage. Before her marriage in 1612, Sara Coxe worked as a servant for six years with William Larkyn, an innkeeper at "the sign of the Rose" near Holborn Bridge.[28] During that time she was approached by William Payne, a London trader in salt and other goods, who wanted to get a lease from Larkyn of a room

---

[25] PRO C 1/912/58.   [26] PRO C 1/61/377. His exact position was not stated.
[27] PRO REQ 2/2/88. These were unusually low wages, even for the later fifteenth century.
[28] PRO REQ 2/398/22.

in his inn called "The Wainman's Hall." Payne thought it would make
a good shop because it was well placed to "obtain great custom of such
persons as came to the said inn." Payne asked Sara to persuade her master
and mistress to lease him the room, promising – so she claimed – that if
she succeeded, he would give her £10 when she married. She managed
to get the Larkyns' approval of the lease, and later, when that room was
no longer adequate for Payne's expanding trade, he again asked her to
use her influence with the Larkyns to lease to him "The Stone Parlor"
as well. When she did so, Payne thanked her warmly for having "done
him so great a pleasure in procuring for him so commodious rooms to
make him so fair and large a shop and so fit for his trading and profit."
Once more, she alleged, he promised her £10 on the day of her marriage.
She also arranged a good price for the food that he and his apprentices
consumed at the inn, and when she went out every day to buy provisions
for her employers, she frequently bought items for Payne as well. At the
time of her marriage, a few months before she submitted her petition
to the Court of Requests, she asked Payne for her £10. He pretended,
however, that the offer was "but a voluntary and idle speech delivered
without any consideration sufficient by the course of the common laws
of this realm to compel him to perform his said promise."

Many relationships between servants and their master/mistress were
positive. When, for example, Alice Jermyn, servant of Richard Grey of
London, was sued by another woman for a debt of 40s. in the mid-1530s
and then arrested and imprisoned in one of the city's Counters (= small
gaols used primarily for people charged with debt), her master hired an
attorney to represent her, paying the man 12d.[29] Female servants might
also collude with their employers in doubtful or illegal activities. Barnaby
Centurian, a young Genoese merchant living in London around 1480,
claimed that Christian Stone alias Griffyth of Southwark, a widow, had
persuaded her servant Grace Austyn to flirt with him and say she loved
him. He asserted in his Chancery petition that he did not respond to
her overtures, other than to buy her wine. But Christian then accused
Barnaby of having removed Grace from her service, demanding some
kind of payment from him in return. When he refused, Christian, Grace,
and a Southwark man brought a plea of trespass against him, for which he
was arrested. They told Barnaby, however, that if he paid £20 to Christian
and took Grace with him, they would drop the charges.

When problems arose between a servant and her employer, they might
in extreme cases result in maltreatment. In Romford, Alice, the wife of
innkeeper William Wood, was reported in 1496 for beating and badly

29 PRO C 1/809/34. For below, see C 1/60/135.

wounding a male servant.[30] Juliana Bulwerke was a young servant (just thirteen years old) who worked for widow Juliana Markes of London during the mid-1530s. According to her mistress, in the early summer of 1536, the girl "did . . . diverse great displeasures, for the which [Markes] gave unto her lawful correction." The following autumn, Markes' petition continued, "it chanced the said Julian Bullok [sic] to have the pestilence [= plague], whereby proceeded from her diverse ulcers, carbuncles, and sores." Widow Markes sent the girl away to be kept and at her own cost hired surgeons to cure her; the surgeons said publicly that Juliana's sores resulted from the plague. Nevertheless, the girl's father complained against widow Markes to one of London's aldermen, alleging that she had beaten his daughter and caused her sores; later he sued Markes for abusing the girl. Elizabeth Smith, a widow of Aylsham, Norfolk, claimed in the 1590s that she had for four years been servant to the wife of John Some.[31] Early on within her period of service Mistress Some had become deranged and wanted to take her own life but was talked out of it by a member of the church. Because of her mistress' "disordered life," which led her to mistreat Elizabeth and call her a whore, Elizabeth wished to leave her position but was persuaded by her master to remain: he was afraid he would not be able to find another person who "could govern and rule her mistress as well." Later, however, Elizabeth and her master fell out over financial matters, whereupon he had her arrested and confined in the gaol at Aylsham. This, she alleged, was "not only unto the great discredit of [her] good name and fame" but also to her great loss in more immediate terms, since she was unable to prosecute suits against those who owed her money.

Though we do not have the kinds of records that would allow us to trace changes in service in numerical terms, the employment situation of young people was probably influenced by demographic, economic, and cultural developments. Such factors presumably affected the number of women who went into service, their socio-economic background, and their ability to seek out a desirable employer and bargain for good terms. For the first half of the fourteenth century, we have almost no information apart from scattered references in local court records. But the decades on either side of 1300 featured the kinds of demographic and economic pressures that around 1600 were to lead many young people into residential service. The population was high, greater than was to be seen again until the eighteenth century, and many peasants had very small holdings. Poor parents may well have encouraged their adolescents to seek residential

---

[30] PRO SC 2/172/38, mm. 6r–7r. For below, see PRO C 1/851/8.
[31] PRO DL 1/213/S25.

employment elsewhere. Opportunities for service were probably more limited than they were to become by the later sixteenth century, however, because urbanization was less marked and the number of middling-level craftspeople and farmers able to employ servants was smaller.

The situation may have reversed after the plague. Because the population between 1348–9 and around 1500 was very low, in settings where the economy was fairly robust, a labor shortage produced high daily or weekly wages. Such conditions may well have made employers eager to hire residential servants: it could be less expensive to hire a young person on an annual contract for relatively modest cash wages than to pay high short-term wages. From the servants' perspective, because they were potentially able to earn more money through non-residential employment, some may have been in a position of strength, able to negotiate with prospective masters for favorable living conditions, good pay, and training in valuable skills, sometimes including craftwork. Further, during the post-plague generations one encounters relatively little criticism of women who lived in female-headed households, so unmarried women who could support themselves probably experienced less social pressure to enter service.

In the later fourteenth century, we gain our first quantifiable information. The Poll Tax listings of 1377–81 commonly included servants, though women may have been undercounted. These records suggest that in northern English towns, 20–30 percent of the total population over age fourteen was in service; in other towns, the figure was around 20 percent.[32] In rural areas the level was only 8–10 percent. Other kinds of scattered evidence from northern England support the idea that service was less important in agricultural and pastoral communities than in towns: in urban settings many/most young men and women went into service, whereas in rural areas a higher fraction of women and some men stayed at home until the time of their marriage.[33] The Poll Tax listings also allow us to estimate what fraction of all households contained servants. In most urban communities, servants were found in 20–33 percent of households, but in only 15 percent in rural areas.[34] How all these values compared with levels prior to the plague we cannot determine. Equally important is the fraction of the servant population that was female. Poll

[32] Goldberg, "Female Labour"; Ben-Amos, *Adolescence and Youth*, p. 2. Hilton's suggestion that in 1381 one-third to one-half of the taxpayers in market towns were servants is probably too high ("Medieval Market Towns"). For below, see Goldberg, "Female Labour," and Smith, "Geographical Diversity."

[33] Goldberg, "For Better, for Worse."

[34] Smith, "Geographical Diversity." For Exeter, the figure was an unusually high 40 percent (Kowaleski, *Local Markets and Regional Trade*, p. 168).

Tax evidence shows that most rural communities contained about twice as many male as female servants; in urban settings, sex ratios varied widely between places.[35] While some of the rural disparity may have stemmed from undercounting of young women, it is possible that fewer adolescent girls than boys left home to become servants in other farming households.

During the later medieval period, the occupations of the people who employed female servants covered a considerable range, especially in towns. When a young woman was hired by a craft or trading household, we cannot tell from the Poll Taxes how much of her time was devoted to assisting her master/mistress in producing or selling goods as opposed to helping with domestic work. Other records indicate, however, that during the later medieval period some female servants received training in specialized skills even though they were not officially bound as apprentices.[36] The Poll Taxes show that women servants were most commonly employed in the households of large merchants, especially those dealing in cloth, retailers of food and drink, and makers of cloth or clothing.[37] Other young women served in artisans' families, who may have needed small or quick hands: skinners or glovemakers among the leather-workers, and goldsmiths/jewelry makers among the metalworkers. An occasional female servant was employed by men engaged in woodworking, transport, candlemaking, and armament-making.[38] Although some women who ran craft or retailing establishments hired their own servants, in general, female-headed households were poorer than male-headed ones and hence less likely to employ servants.[39]

---

[35] Smith, "Geographical Diversity," for general figures; Kettle, "Ruined Maids," and Carlin, *Medieval Southwark*, pp. 173–5.

[36] Swanson, *Medieval Artisans*, p. 116, Laughton, "The Alewives," and Goldberg, *Women, Work, and Life Cycle*, p. 129.

[37] In the woolen cloth exporting centers of York and (King's) Lynn, Norf., 45–6 percent of women servants were employed by large-scale merchants, with another 19–23 percent hired by retailers of food and drink; 7–12 percent worked for masters who produced textiles (weavers and dyers) or made clothing (tailors). In the smaller towns of Pontefract, Yorks., and Oxford, the distributions were quite different: 11–21 percent of female servants were in mercantile households, 38–40 percent in victualing, and 19–20 percent in textiles/clothing. The much poorer community of suburban Southwark, with its emphasis on accommodating visitors to London, had yet another pattern: no female servants at all in mercantile work, 52 percent in victualing, and 5 percent in textiles/clothing (Goldberg, *Women, Work, and Life Cycle*, pp. 187–9).

[38] Ibid., pp. 186–94.

[39] E.g., Goldberg, "Women in Fifteenth-Century Town Life," and his "Female Labour." In the Poll Tax listing for Southwark in 1381, only 7 percent of female house heads had servants, as compared to 23 percent of male householders, most of whom were married (Carlin, *Medieval Southwark*, p. 177).

Across the sixteenth century, the conditions of service for young people, especially women, almost certainly worsened. This is at first glance surprising, for demand for servants by the Elizabethan and Jacobean periods was high. Many households were becoming larger and more complex. This was true not only for great urban merchants and the leading gentry and noble families but also for people of intermediate status, including those tradespeople and craftsmen able to profit from the growing scale of local production and commerce. In Romford, for example, the households of innkeepers and urban yeomen (who worked as middlemen in market transactions and offered credit for interest) were larger in 1562 than any others apart from the knights and gentlemen who lived in the surrounding countryside.[40] Bigger households enjoying a higher standard of living needed more servants.

But demand was exceeded by supply. Population rise that outstripped economic growth led to an increase in poverty, resulting in families who could not provide for all their children. Because of the labor glut and mounting objection to women who lived on their own, poor girls who had to leave home and fend for themselves might have few options other than becoming servants. It therefore seems probable that many young women were at a disadvantage when arranging the terms of service, and they were less likely to receive specialized training. Some servants were hired primarily to sell in shops or do such work as making stockings, lace, or small metal pins, but most were confined to domestic or agricultural labor.

We have only a few household listings from scattered communities in the early modern period, but they suggest that the proportion of households in towns and market centers that contained servants was rising.[41] In 1562, 40 percent of households in Romford contained servants (or, in a few cases, apprentices); in the 1590s, 42 percent of Salisbury households had servants.[42] During the period 1619–32, 38–54 percent of households in the wealthier central parishes in Cambridge contained servants. Increased employment of servants probably stemmed from the growing prosperity of those households: in poorer neighborhoods on the outer edges of several early modern towns, a smaller fraction of households

---

[40] McIntosh, *A Community Transformed*, table 1.11, p. 41.

[41] The figures for Coventry in the early 1520s show a low proportion of households containing servants and an exceptionally high proportion of female servants, due probably to the town's atypical economic and demographical situation (Phythian-Adams, *Desolation of a City*, ch. 20).

[42] McIntosh, *A Community Transformed*, pp. 56–9 (the listing does not distinguish between servants and apprentices); Wright, "Churmaids," p. 117. For below, see Goose, "Household Size."

hired servants, at levels within the range seen in the earlier Poll Taxes.[43] Singlewomen and widows remained less likely to have servants than were male-headed households. In Salisbury during the 1590s, for example, 22 percent of the households headed by not-married women contained servants, as compared with 45 percent of those headed by men.[44]

The ratio of female to male servants varied by setting. Women servants accounted for fewer than half of all the residential employees in urban communities. Thus, in Romford and Canterbury in 1562–3, 42–43 percent of the servants/apprentices were women, as were 39 percent in suburban Ealing in 1599.[45] By the end of the century, young men were willing to take positions as domestic servants in towns if they could not find better employment. In 1617, for example, William Gethin, by then a yeoman of Chancery Lane, London, alleged that when he was younger he had been hired as a "covenant servant in house" by widowed Dame Susan Cesar of Maidstone, Kent.[46] During the three years he worked for her, his duties included shopping for household provisions, including meat, fish, and fuel. The use of female labor in rural households, by contrast, was probably increasing, with young women hired as servants (or nominally as apprentices) to do not only domestic work but also those aspects of secondary agricultural activity that were gendered female.[47] By around 1600, the use of female servants in craftwork had declined,

---

[43] In the outer parishes of Canterbury in 1563, only 27 percent of households contained servants, close to the 23 percent found in the poorer suburbs of Cambridge, 1619–32 (Goose, "Household Size," and Peter and Jennifer Clark, "The Social Economy of the Canterbury Suburbs").

[44] Wright, "Churmaids."

[45] McIntosh, *A Community Transformed*, pp. 56–8, Peter and Jennifer Clark, "The Social Economy of the Canterbury Suburbs," and figures calculated from Allison, "An Elizabethan Village 'Census'," p. 11. The Ealing listing enables us to determine what fraction of young people were engaged in service at different ages: 77–9 percent of all males aged fifteen to twenty-four years were working as servants or other live-in employees, as were 56 percent of those aged twenty-five to twenty-nine years. Of young women, only 50–6 percent were servants when aged fifteen to twenty-four, as were 42 percent of those aged twenty-five to twenty-nine.

[46] PRO REQ 2/300/52.

[47] Whittle, *The Development of Agrarian Capitalism*, pp. 260–1, her "Servants in Rural England," and her "Women, Servants, and By-Employment." Scholars of the later seventeenth and eighteenth centuries in England have found a high fraction of servants, with young people employed mainly for domestic and agricultural work (Meldrum, *Domestic Service*, and Kent, "Ubiquitous but Invisible"). In 1695–1725, a cross-section sample of London's working women showed 25 percent in domestic service, most of whom lived in the household of their employers (Earle, "Female Labour Market," p. 339). In sixty-three parish listings from 1574 to 1821, servants constituted about 60 percent of the population aged fifteen to twenty-four, and the overall ratio of male to female servants was 107:100. Since the ratio in farmers' households was 121:100 and in craftsmen's households was 171:100, the proportion of women hired in domestic service was clearly very high (Kussmaul, *Servants in Husbandry*, pp. 3–4).

lessening their chances of acquiring useful skills for subsequent employment. Although working as a servant was thus an aspect of the lives of many English women throughout the period between 1300 and 1620, service was by no means an unchanging component of the society and economy.

2   Taking in boarders

For women living in their own homes, service work offered different kinds of options. Boarding other people – either adults or children – was a convenient way of generating income. Such work required that the person being lodged have the use of a room (generally furnished) or at least a bed, and either receive food and drink or be given the use of cooking and eating equipment. In some cases, women might serve as wet nurses, breastfeeding the infants whom they took in. The work of looking after boarders was done almost exclusively by women, though in some cases a man functioned as the legal representative of his wife. The responsibilities were well suited to a woman who needed to be at home anyway because she had small children, was caring for an invalid or elderly relative, or was trading or doing craftwork in her house. Boarding seems to have been provided mainly by relatively poor women; those in the middling ranks probably did not find the limited remuneration worth the inconvenience and loss of privacy that boarding entailed.

Boarding has received little historical attention because it is seldom mentioned in most sources. Only occasionally do we find a reference to someone like Christina de Fissheacre of Nottingham. In debt and charged with theft in 1359, she attempted to recoup her fortunes by "boarding scholars at her table" for 6d. per week.[48] We know that by the later sixteenth and seventeenth centuries, some of the cities and towns were paying "foster mothers" to take orphaned or abandoned children into their homes in return for payment provided by poor-relief funds; London charitable institutions were sending out children to be nursed in suburban communities.[49] Private arrangements, however, are largely invisible. Because few agreements for boarding or residential nursing were recorded in a formal written contract or in the presence of witnesses, legal problems that arose from them might be brought to the equity courts. From these petitions we gain a much better view of what boarding actually entailed and the problems that could arise. In the central court sample, 1470–1619, disputes over sums owed for boarding, some of

---

[48] Foulds, "Women and Work."
[49] Willen, "Women in the Public Sphere," Finlay, "Population and Fertility," and Cunningham, "Christ's Hospital."

which included health care, constituted 8–13 percent of the petitions in each sub-period (see App. 1.2). Most of the women in that group who took in boarders (68 percent) were married.[50] Because this material is rare, we will look both at the women who offered boarding and at those who used it.

Credit was once again essential to boarding relationships. In personal terms, both parties had to assess the individual reputation or standing of the other person. Many agreements were made informally and modified over time, so the details of what was to be paid and when might not be clearly specified. Boarding arrangements were also likely to include delayed payment for the services rendered. A case from the 1560s or 1570s reveals the intricate web of mutual obligations that could accompany such a relationship. Elizabeth Watson of London, a widow, complained against Thomas Freman of Leominster, Heref., alleging that she had loaned him £10 13s. 4d. in money about two years ago, which was to have been repaid within a quarter of a year; Thomas had not settled his debt, but she was unable to plead in the common law courts because she had no written obligation.[51] Thomas' answer opens up a far more complex situation. He claimed that around Christmas time two years before, Elizabeth came to Leominster from London and arranged to be "lodged and boarded with him in his house for a time." As the length of her stay was extended, Thomas borrowed money from Elizabeth at various dates to buy food for her. After sixteen weeks she returned to London but came back again early the following summer, this time bringing with her a small child, aged about two years. Both mother and child "continued at bed and board" with him for fifteen weeks before leaving again. During that stay Thomas loaned Elizabeth some small amounts of cash, sold her a gammon of bacon for 2s., and at her request paid Thomas Badicotte 12d. for a dozen loaves of bread she had purchased from him. Elizabeth also arranged that Thomas would board a second child, giving him 2s. in advance payment. When Elizabeth finally departed permanently, she demanded that he pay her the total she claimed she had loaned to him; Thomas in return demanded a reckoning of all the sums she owed to him.

Women who provided board and room found clients of various kinds. Some boarders had just moved into a community or would be there only temporarily. Petronill Rothirford, a widow, boarded for a short time around 1480 in the house of Thomasin Berkeley in London, paying her

---

[50] Of the four women in the northern sample who took in boarders, 1540–1619, three were widows. Ben-Amos believes that the number of lodgers rose from the late sixteenth century onwards ("Gifts and Favors").

[51] PRO C 3/200/28.

for "meat, drink, and other necessaries" as well as lodging.[52] In 1605, Dorothy Wilkinson, a singlewoman who was about to marry, took her lodging and meals in the household of Richard Francis, a merchant tailor of London, for thirteen weeks. Dorothy then wed John Wright of London, dyer, but since he was "unprovided of a competent house or lodging" for her, he asked Richard to let her stay for another five weeks. During those two stays, Richard later alleged, she borrowed a total of £7 6s. from him, which she refused to repay. Men employed away from home also boarded for short periods. The churchwardens of the parish of Hornchurch paid local widows during the decades around 1600 to lodge and feed visiting craftsmen working on the church, including those who cast and hung two new bells.[53] Some boarders needed nursing as well as board and room.

Other boarders had come into urban settings in hopes of improving their social position or finding work. Late in Elizabeth's reign, John Harrys of Ockendon, Essex, approached Philip Baker of London, asking him to board his daughter Elizabeth "for a certain time, to th'end his said daughter might learn some breeding" by being in London.[54] Baker agreed to take the girl for an annual payment of £3 for all her expenses. Elizabeth was apparently slow in acquiring good breeding, for she remained with the Bakers for ten years, until her marriage. Young women who lived in boarding houses rather than working as servants faced public disapprobation: in 1606 and 1613, London's Common Council cracked down on "women brokers" who lodged women who were out of service.[55]

Unmarried but pregnant women might board with another person during the last months before the arrival of the baby. A temporary home was normally sought at some distance from the usual residence of the woman and/or the man who had impregnated her, in hopes of lessening the discredit and possible ecclesiastical punishment that might otherwise befall them both. In Havering, for example, the church courts dealt with two such cases in 1576. Edward Helham, the farmer of one of the large local estates, grudgingly admitted that after impregnating his servant Margaret he had "conveyed her away to the end it might not be espied"; Alice Bishoppe, the pregnant ex-servant of George Malle of Hornchurch, had been carried secretly out of Havering to the Isle of Ely, but the churchwardens were not sure whether the father of her child was her former master or one of his kinsmen.[56] Some men relied upon the anonymity of

[52] PRO C 1/64/1130. For below, see PRO REQ 2/396/29.
[53] McIntosh, *A Community Transformed*, p. 226. For health care, see sect. 3 below.
[54] PRO REQ 2/409/13.
[55] Corporation of London Record Office Journals of Common Council 29, fol. 20v, and 37, fols. 124v–125, and Rep. 27, fol. 7, all as cited in Griffiths, "'Waxey Words'." I am grateful to Dr. Griffiths for letting me have a copy of this paper.
[56] ERO D/AEA 9, fol. 74v, and D/AED 1, fol. 3r–v.

London. Around 1480 Christopher Goswell, a vintner of London, arranged for Elizabeth Blount, a singlewoman, to board in the house of John Hopkyns, a London waxchandler, for eighteen weeks for a payment of 16d. per week.[57] Thomas Chamber of Walberswick, Suffolk, sent a pregnant Juliana Norrey to board with Lucy Browne of St. Bartholomew's, Smithfield, London until the birth of her child sometime around 1540.

Babies were sometimes boarded with and fed by wet nurses, if – for instance – their own mother had died or was unable to provide milk for them. A little is known about this aspect of boarding from other records. In the West Riding of Yorkshire during the later fourteenth century, for example, some women in the rural aristocracy employed wet nurses.[58] A woman in Chester was charged in 1460 with negligence in the death of a young child placed into her care, probably for wet nursing. Likewise in Elizabethan Havering, poor women were hired to wet nurse infants. A few of these children were from the immediate area, usually orphaned or illegitimate babies, and some apparently came to Havering through private arrangements with their London parents, but the majority were from Christ's Hospital in London, which sent out infants for wet nursing throughout the London area. In Romford, the fifty-seven London nurse children buried between 1562 and 1620 accounted for 2.2 percent of all deaths.[59]

As the mortality figures suggest, it could not be assumed that those who accepted infants for nursing would take good care of them. Around 1480, John Edward, a girdler of London, delivered his daughter, then aged twenty-three weeks, into the care of Agnes, wife of William Salmon of Kingston on Thames, Surrey, in return for a weekly payment.[60] The baby remained with Agnes for thirty weeks, for which John paid her the stipulated sum regularly. He later claimed, however, that Agnes had "so negligently kept and nourished" the little girl that she became "lame in both her legs and utterly undone forever." William, Agnes' husband, denied the allegation and tried to force John to sign a general acquittance stating that William "should never be troubled nor sued for hurting and maiming of the said child." When John refused to do this, William sued him for debt and trespass.

Illegitimate children, too, might be sent out to board, whether they needed a wet nurse as an infant or general care later. This was a sufficiently

[57] PRO C 1/64/764. For below, see C 1/955/56.
[58] Goldberg, "Women's Work." For below, see Laughton, "Women in Court."
[59] McIntosh, *A Community Transformed*, p. 47; for broader discussions, see Finlay, "Population and Fertility," and Cunningham, "Christ's Hospital."
[60] PRO C 1/60/173.

common practice in the village of Cranfield, Beds., by the 1510s that an order was passed at the local court that no one should take in the child of a whore to be "mothered" or nursed, under penalty of a fine of 6s. 8d.[61] (Boarding the child of a woman from outside the community who was of good credit was apparently permitted.) In the early 1590s, Anne Abrandon alias Brandon of London, "spinster" (= singlewoman in this instance), was owed £10 in a bond signed by Thomas Smyth of St. Savior's in Southwark, Surrey, a baker of white bread; his debt was to be paid to her at set times during the years 1595 and 1596.[62] Anne then asked Thomas whether he could find a nurse for her baby, promising to allow him that £10 to cover the child's costs. After "long entreaty," Thomas persuaded Goodwife Boxe, wife of Robert Boxe, a husbandman from Southampton, to nurse the child in return for a payment of 20s. quarterly. Over the course of the next 2½ years, Thomas paid Goodwife Boxe a total of £10, which should have cleared his obligation to Anne. She, however, died without canceling his bond and her administrators prosecuted him for the full sum. In the early 1590s, Francis Crispe of Buckton alias Boughton, Northants., made financial arrangements for the care of his illegitimate daughter, Margaret.[63] He began by loaning £100 to the parson of "Scraudwell," stipulating that the interest of £10 annually should be used for the child's care. When Margaret was two days old, he assigned her to the care of Thomas Pertysoyle, with whom she remained for about eighteen months; next she was placed into the keeping of John Stanbancke of Emberton, Bucks., a yeoman in his mid-fifties, who kept her for another nine or ten years. At that point she was probably placed into service, as there is no mention of further charges for her maintenance although she was still alive.

In some cases the person paid to board an illegitimate child was related to it. In 1608, Thomas Alread of Atherton, Lancs., a nailer, and his unmarried sister Ellen Alread agreed with John Astley, a husbandman of Atherton, that John would keep and bring up Ellen's child, then "an infant very young and of tender years."[64] The Alreads agreed to pay John for the child's care for a period of eight years, at the rate of 5s. annually from Thomas and 20d. annually from Ellen. In Astley's petition five years later, alleging their failure to pay him, the child is described as Robert

[61] PRO SC 2/179/82, View for Cranfield held after Michaelmas 4 Henry VIII.
[62] PRO REQ 2/34/116.
[63] PRO REQ 2/392/12. Margaret is not described explicitly as illegitimate, but several of the witnesses said they had always heard her called just Margaret or Margaret Stanley, but not Margaret Crispe, the name under which she brought suit. One of them said caustically that he only once heard her called Margaret Crispe, "by one that said she was her mother, whom . . . he never saw before."
[64] PRO PL 6/2, 27 March 1613, Astley vs. Alread.

Astley alias Alread. This suggests that John was the father or another relative of the child, as does the small amount he demanded as a yearly payment. In 1613, widow Ann Porter of Woodplumpton, Lancs., sued John Watson of the same place, a carpenter, for his failure to pay her costs in providing "meat, drink, lodging, and apparel" for his reputed child.[65] At John's request she took charge of the baby, but after she had cared for it for a year and a quarter without any recompense, she complained to the Justices of the Peace at a Quarter Sessions held in Preston. The JPs questioned both parties and then ordered John to keep the child himself henceforth and to pay Ann 25s. for her previous charges. The child, whose first name is not given, was known by the surname of Watson alias Porter, so Ann was probably its mother or other relative. These cases fit with Adair's and McNabb's suggestion that the northwest of England in the decades around 1600 had a different courtship regime and more relaxed approach to illegitimacy than the southern counties.[66] This is one of the ways that the context of women's work varied by region.

A woman who felt encumbered by a child as she approached marriage, whether it was illegitimate or the offspring of a previous marriage, might likewise seek out someone willing to board it. Around 1580, Thomas Rabley of London, skinner, learned that a woman named Agnes was looking for someone to nurse her child.[67] Thomas contacted John Rede, a London vintner, who arranged with his sister Elizabeth and her husband William Harford to take the child, in return for a payment of 5s. 4d. per month. (Obviously this was intended as a long-term arrangement, since the charge was calculated in months, not the more common weekly value.) John required that Agnes sign a bond that committed her to paying that amount. Because, she claimed in her petition, she was illiterate, she trustingly accepted his statement that the bond was for £5, whereas in fact the amount written on it was £40. Agnes then married John Sanders, who paid the Redes a total of £12 over several years for continuing to care for the child. (Agnes had told him about the child but did not mention the bond.) When Sanders later asked to have the child returned, the Redes refused and instead sued Agnes for the full £40 stipulated in the bond.

Orphaned children were commonly boarded, of necessity if there were no relatives willing to take them in. When Sir Robert Hesketh of Lancashire died around 1550, he named a yeoman and a clerk executors of his will.[68] They in turn asked Laurence Towneley, gent., to "take into his house Anne Hesketh [Sir Robert's daughter] and to find her meat,

---

[65] PRO PL 6/2, 15 January 1613, Porter vs. Watson.
[66] Adair, *Courtship, Illegitimacy and Marriage*, and McNabb, "Constructing Credit."
[67] PRO REQ 2/32/50.
[68] PRO DL 1/32/T6. The community where he lived is not named.

drink, lodging, and apparel," promising that they would reimburse him for his expenses. Laurence kept Anne for four years, spending – as he claimed – 40 marks (= £26 13s. 4d.) for her food, drink, and clothing; he then paid another 42s. 8d. for her funeral expenses. When Hugh Towers of Barcroft in Gainsborough, Lincs., died in 1603/4, he said in his will that his cousin Susan Sheweswell should bring up his daughter Isabel until she reached the age of twenty-one years.[69] In return for caring for Isabel, Susan was to have the profits from an enclosed pasture that Hugh left to his son Thomas. Eleven years later, Susan, twice remarried, sued Thomas for refusing to allow her access to the pasture. She claimed that she had disbursed about £100 on Isabel's food, drink, lodging, and apparel, "in very decent manner fit for her estate and calling." Thomas acknowledged that Susan had looked after his sister for about five years after their father's death. When, however, he learned that she was raising the girl "in base and mean fashion," he demanded to have Isabel given over into his own care. Susan refused to do this, whereupon he excluded her from the pasture. At the time of his petition Susan had taken Isabel to Ireland and left her there: Thomas did not even know whether she was still alive.

The distinction between boarding a child and taking that child as a servant was not always clear. This was a particular problem when an orphaned child was placed with another household. Whereas providing care for a young child required outlays for food and clothing, with no labor received in return, an older child could be expected to contribute to the domestic economy, thereby resembling a servant who would under other circumstances have been paid a wage. The point at which that transition occurred, and what the repercussions were for the child and whoever was caring for her/him, sometimes became matters of law. Alice Quant petitioned against Nicholas Commyn of Church Stanton, Devon, around 1540, claiming that about fourteen years before she had agreed to work as "a laborer and a serving woman" in his house.[70] For this he had promised to give her food, drink, and apparel "according to her degree" as well as £3 in money at the end of her term. She served as arranged, but he did not pay her the £3. Nicholas' answer told a different story. He alleged that when Alice was only two years old, fourteen years before, her friends had asked him to take her in, giving her board, room, and clothing, in return for which he would be paid 4 marks (= £2 13s. 4d.). She stayed with him on that basis for twelve years, during which time she was too young to do any service. Once she was old enough to be useful, she departed from his household and refused to come back, to his great economic loss.

The amount of clothing and education that a boarded child received could also become an issue. Anne Evorey of Somerset was put to board

[69] PRO REQ 2/399/51.   [70] PRO C 1/1054/1–2.

with Anne and Richard Rodes sometime around 1550, with the understanding – as she later claimed – that she would be dressed in decent
and comely apparel, be educated ("brought up at school"), and taught to
use her needle.[71] Instead, she was "put to drudgery" and made to work
as a servant before being removed "discourteously out of their house."
Magdalen, daughter of John Gravenor of Compton in Kinver, Staffs.,
was a child when her father died in 1591. His will placed Magdalen into
the care of his executors, two local men, together with all his goods, which
she later said were worth 100 marks (= £66 13s. 8d.). Fifteen years later,
after her marriage, Magdalen sued his executors, claiming that they had
wasted her property and that Humfrey Bate, into whose hands they had
conveyed her, had insisted that she work for him "in very servile and mean
sort." The executors' response says that John Gravenor left many fewer
goods than Magdalen claimed and that he owed each of them money
at the time of his death. They decided that Magdalen, "being then of
so young and tender years, should be nourished and brought up by and
with [Bate,] being at that time and ever since of better power, wealth,
and ability than ever the said John Gravener was at any time in his life."
Bate provided for Magdalen "in his own house with meat, drink, lodging,
apparel, and other necessaries, as he did his own children, [she] being
unable for a long time to do any work or deserve anything at all." Later,
when she was "grown to some age, she was busied in ordinary labor in
[his] house, for the avoiding of idleness." Magdalen retorted that "her
labor and service [were] much more beneficial and profitable unto him
than the charges disbursed or allowed unto her or for her maintenance."

Boarding and service could also become confused when they concerned people in their later teens and twenties. Katherine, a singlewoman,
boarded at the house of Thomas Warberton of Exeter, chief sergeant
to the mayor, for eight weeks sometime around 1480, paying him 16d.
weekly.[72] She then became engaged to Vincent Ryth, but because Vincent
"was at that time a poor young man and went over the sea with our
sovereign lord," he asked her to go into service until his return to England.
She therefore arranged with Thomas, so she later alleged, to take her on
as a servant. He promised to give her 4d. per week in addition to her
room and board, on which basis she remained in his service for twelve
and a half months. During that time, however, he paid her no more than
2s. for her salary. Vincent then returned from his travels and married
Katherine, but Thomas refused to pay the rest of her wages. Even worse,
he brought an action of debt against Katherine and Vincent in an Exeter
court, claiming that they owed him 6 marks (= £4) for Katherine's food,

---

[71] PRO REQ 2/25/247. For below, see REQ 2/308/37.   [72] PRO C 1/60/168.

drink, and lodging during those twelve and a half months, using the same rate at which she paid when she first boarded with him.

Elderly people, too, sometimes sought boarding. If they had been living on their own but now needed more care, they might arrange with a younger relative to look after them. Because it was often not clear to what extent this was done simply as a matter of family obligation as opposed to being set up on a financial basis, such cases could lead to court action. Sometime around 1560, Robert Cowley married one of the daughters of Agnes Younge of Kilmington, Devon.[73] Near the end of her life, Agnes, "being very old . . . and desirous to dwell near the church," asked Robert "to build for her and to prepare for her dwelling" a set of rooms, added on to his house. He did so, and Agnes moved in, bringing all her personal and household goods. She was subsequently cared for by her daughter and Robert, who also provided part of her food and drink. She often promised, they claimed, to recompense them, but although she left them some legacies in her will and forgave the debt of £8 that Robert owed to her, she did not leave them anything to cover their costs in looking after her. Robert therefore refused to deliver to Agnes' executor the household goods and £23 in money that were left in her rooms when she died. When Agnes Ley of Great Torrington, Devon, could no longer look after herself in the 1590s, being then "an aged woman & decrepit in part of her limbs," she took into her house her niece Joan and Joan's husband William.[74] They looked after her for the rest of her life, spending – so they said – their own money to provide her with necessities.

If they had no relatives to look after them, old people tried to set up other kinds of boarding arrangements.[75] At the end of her life in the 1490s, when she was "greatly vexed with sickness," Elizabeth Lumnor boarded with Ralph Leche and his wife in London.[76] After her death, Elizabeth's executors brought suit against the Leches for detention of a little black chest and some plate of Elizabeth's worth £20. People without family nearby may have assumed that they would be boarded in their final illness. In his 1578 will, Thomas Hoseman, an unmarried Romford yeoman who was well advanced in years, assigned £3 to "the goodwife of the house in which it shall fortune me to die."

The distinction between boarding, charitable assistance to an elderly woman, and domestic service might not be clearly defined. Widow Margaret Lucas of Knightsbridge, Middx., was a servant for thirty years during the later sixteenth century with an alebrewer of London.[77]

---

[73] PRO REQ 2/245/24.   [74] PRO C 3/250/84.
[75] For maintenance agreements based on the use of land, see sect. 1 Ch. 4 below.
[76] PRO C 1/209/24. For below, see ERO D/AER 14, 125.   [77] PRO REQ 2/398/69.

During that time she saved a small stock of money, amounting to £32, which she intended for her son, who was then living overseas. In 1603, having become "very old, weak, and sickly," she began to board with Elizabeth Sharpe of Knightsbridge. Fearing death at the time of a plague epidemic, Margaret decided to put her money into Elizabeth's hands, as her landlady and friend. Elizabeth promised faithfully, Margaret asserted, "that she would safely keep the same for [Margaret], and that if [she] should happen to die before the return of her son into England . . . it should be wholly and solely by [Elizabeth] kept unto the use of him." Elizabeth's response contradicted that narrative. She said that for some years she had provided help and financial assistance to Margaret, a poor woman who "lived partly by the alms of the parish" plus gaining a little income from spinning. During the three years before this court action, Margaret had lived with her, receiving "her keeping as well in sickness as in health, maintenance, lodging, meat, drink, and apparel." Elizabeth claimed that Margaret had given the £32 to her in recompense for this assistance, believing "she should never see [her son] again." Margaret's replication alleged that she had lived for only about a year in Elizabeth's house, "where she did such drudgery work for Elizabeth and her husband as was to be done in her house, and had nothing else for her pains but only her meat and drink and a room to lie in the said house upon her own bed."

In some cases, unscrupulous relatives or acquaintances may have offered to board an ailing older person in hopes of acquiring his or her goods or influencing the terms of the person's will. That is suggested in an action that came before the Court of Requests in 1543–4. An elderly woman named Emma became engaged to John Overye of Gravesend, Kent, a husbandman.[78] Before the marriage took place, however, Emma – described by John as being "aged and in manner somewhat childish" – was persuaded by Beatrice Herbert, a widow whose husband had been a cousin of Emma's, to come to London and live with her, bringing all her goods. Later Emma returned to Gravesend and married John, but Beatrice kept her goods. In defending her possession of the goods, Beatrice claimed that Emma did not want to become engaged to John but was forced to do so (by whom or why is not stated). Out of kindness, therefore, Beatrice had invited Emma to come to live with her, offering to provide "house room, meat, drink, washing, bed, fire, candle, raiment, and all other necessaries" for her and the female servant she brought with her. In return, Emma delivered all her goods to Beatrice and said she could have £7 annually out of a rent of £11 due to her. Because Emma did

[78] PRO REQ 2/12/91.

not pay the promised rent in full, Beatrice claimed it was right for her to have kept Emma's goods when she decided to return to Gravesend. In this case we have the award of the men assigned to deal with the problem on behalf of the Court of Requests, a decision which displays the even-handed approach common to the equity courts, which generally tried to give something to each of the parties.[79] They ruled that Emma's goods should be returned to her and John, but she and John were required to pay Beatrice £7 for her care of Emma.

By the later sixteenth century, boarding was also used by local communities as part of their system of publicly supported care of the poor. In Hadleigh, Suffolk, for example, detailed accounts of the Collectors of the Poor between 1579 and 1596 allow us to examine the nature of assistance provided.[80] In addition to payments made to those poor people who continued to live in their own homes and those with places in the town's two almshouses for the elderly, Hadleigh paid for boarding. Adults constituted a third of the sixty-three people placed into residential care during those years, most of whom remained in another person's home for no more than four months. This group included old people who needed help temporarily due to an injury or sickness and younger ones who were ill or about to give birth. The remainder of those boarded were children. Some were aged just two to four years at the time they entered foster care; many of these were orphans, who commonly remained with their foster family until they were old enough to go into service. The other children were slightly older, aged five to nine years. They came from large and often disorderly families already receiving substantial poor relief. The Collectors were probably trying to lessen the economic burden on the home family while at the same time hoping the child would get off to a better start in a different household. These children were generally boarded with a family engaged in cloth-making or other craftwork, where they could start learning useful skills (and/or be exploited as cheap labor). Nearly all the other people paid by the town to take in boarders were receiving poor relief themselves. Payments for boarding thus filled two social needs at once. Married couples as well as widows boarded people, and a third to a half were over sixty years of age. These elderly households were used especially for care of young children, which featured longer terms of boarding and larger amounts paid by the town. The town fathers probably thought that both the old people and the children would

---

[79] In this respect, their practice resembled arbitration, which was going out of practice in local courts in favor of jury verdicts, which were more likely to give judgments favorable to only one of the parties. See, e.g., McIntosh, *Autonomy and Community*, pp. 198–200, and her *A Community Transformed*, pp. 303–4, plus the references cited there.
[80] McIntosh, "Networks of Care."

benefit from the economic, physical, and emotional stability of such arrangements.

3   Non-residential household employment, sex work, and health care

Several other kinds of service work provided income for a limited number of women. Only a few households hired women to do domestic tasks, for these were normally performed by female members of the family or residential servants. If domestic work was done by an outside employee, it was usually part time and occasional. Sex work offered a means of bringing in money that was chosen by few women on a regular basis but offered a fall-back for poor women desperate to make ends meet. Care of sick people was another option. Most women did only simple bedside nursing, but a few acquired more specialized skills. All these types of service employment were more readily available in towns than in rural areas.

Domestic skills used by most women at home, including laundering, cooking, and cleaning, were sometimes extended into the for-pay economy. A complex conversion into a monetary relationship of what probably started out as services rendered through friendship comes from the early 1590s, when widow Alice Alder was living outside Smithfield Bar, London.[81] Thomas Mason, a grocer, was a regular visitor to her house over a period of two years, an arrangement that one or both of them may have hoped would lead to marriage. Thomas ate a meal with Alice nearly every day, and she made clothing for him and did his laundry. During two periods when Thomas was ill, Alice concocted for him a special but costly drink, to be taken for fifteen days each time, which led to the recovery of his health. When their friendship fell apart, Alice and her new husband sued Thomas for all the charges she had incurred on his behalf. As that example suggests, unmarried men were more likely to need domestic help, but institutions might also be employers.[82] Domestic work is hard to study, for it has left only scattered references.

Laundering was generally done by women who took clothing or bedding home to wash or used public water supplies nearby. In late medieval Westminster, washerwomen were concentrated in the Long Ditch area,

---

[81] PRO REQ 2/80/59. Alder was Alice's surname after her remarriage.

[82] E.g., a woman was hired by St. Leonard's hospital in York as a laundress during the later medieval period, and a woman was named as housecleaner, laundress, and nurse for the workhouse in Salisbury during the early seventeenth century (Goldberg, *Women, Work, and Life Cycle*, pp. 135 and 148, and Wright, "Churmaids").

where running water was readily available.[83] Occasional references to laundering are found in other medieval sources, although it was rarely recognized as a formal occupation.[84] Washing continued as a source of income for some poor women through the sixteenth century, especially in urban areas.[85] (See Illus. 3.) Of 726 adult women included in the Census of the Poor taken in Norwich in 1570, eight (= 1 percent) said they worked as washerwomen, though probably not full time; the wife of a tailor in Salisbury sometime around 1600 brought laundry home for pay.[86] By the early seventeenth century, laundresses were commonly portrayed as physically strong but verbally and sexually uncontrolled.

Cooking for a household other than one's own provided few employment opportunities for women.[87] If cooks were hired on a regular salaried basis for a large establishment, they were almost always male; women found occasional employment only as specialized sub-cooks or kitchen helpers. An official at Barking Abbey in the fourteenth or fifteenth century was told to allow a gown to the "pudding wife" who assisted the other cooks; a woman was employed by Selby Abbey in 1416–17 to prepare offal (probably making sausages or black pudding); and a woman was paid 14d. for washing tripe from twenty-eight oxen in the household of the dowager duchess of Buckingham in 1466.[88] Across the sixteenth century, cooking was increasingly needed at victualing houses and inns,

---

[83] Rosser, *Medieval Westminster*, p. 198.

[84] Few northern English women had a surname that indicated a laundress in the Poll Taxes of 1377–81 or were described as having that occupation (Goldberg, *Women, Work, and Life Cycle*, pp. 135 and 148). A more intensive involvement with the occupation is suggested by the designation of laundress given to six of 137 female household heads described in the 1381 Poll Tax for Southwark, a suburb of London; similarly, five of eighty-eight women were called laundresses in the Oxford Poll Tax of that year. Both those communities had large populations of single men who presumably hired women to do their laundry (Carlin, *Medieval Southwark*, pp. 174–5; Bennett, "Medieval Women, Modern Women").

[85] A woman in fifteenth-century Chester was called Emmota Launder; a few London women were identified as laundresses or were hired to wash clothes; early church-wardens' or monastic accounts include women paid for washing vestments; and a woman received 2s. in 1461 for washing woolen cloths used by the household of the Bishop of Coventry and Lichfield (Laughton, "Women in Court"; Abram, "Women Traders," Lacey, "Women and Work," Goldberg, *Women, Work, and Life Cycle*, p. 135, and Goldberg, ed., *Women in England*, p. 199).

[86] *The Norwich Census of the Poor*, p. 99, and Wright, "Churmaids." For below, see Pelling, "Nurses and Nursekeepers."

[87] This discussion is limited to women who cooked for wages. For cooks as tradespeople, see sect. 2, Ch. 7 below.

[88] BL Cotton MS Julius D. VIII, fol. 42v, Goldberg, *Women, Work, and Life Cycle*, p. 109, and BL Add. MS 34213, fol. 111v. I am grateful to Martha Carlin for the first and last of these references.

3. Women washing, drying, and sun-bleaching laundry beside a stream

but this labor was generally provided by female relatives or servants of the proprietor.[89]

Cleaning for pay became an option only in early modern towns. During the later medieval period one rarely finds an entry like the woman who received 4d. in 1461 for cleaning the buttery and washing vessels at the household of the bishop of Lichfield.[90] By the Elizabethan period, however, some women (called charmaids or charwomen) were cleaning houses on a daily basis in the larger cities. If charwomen lived on their own, especially if they were not married, their activities were viewed with considerable suspicion by urban authorities.[91] Although town fathers were unlikely to have been concerned about the threat they posed to male workers (no men are known to have cleaned houses), officials were troubled by their potentially uncontrolled sexuality. A woman who lived in a household that was not headed by a man, earning her own income through her labor, was bad enough, but it was worse when she went out every day into unmarried men's houses, a setting ripe for wrongdoing. Yet efforts to constrain such work were to prove futile.[92]

Another category of service employment consisted of providing sex in return for money. The various types of sex work covered a wide spectrum. In some cases it was undertaken on a full-time, semi-regulated basis, with young women hired (or, it was sometimes claimed, forced into such activity) by the male or female keepers of established brothels. Other women worked on their own, soliciting partners on the streets or in an alehouse. Beyond that level it becomes increasingly difficult to decide whether a given relationship should be labeled as sex work. Some women had sex with and sometimes lived with men who were not their husbands for weeks, months, or years at a time, in return for financial support. In such cases it is hard to separate the sexual/economic component of the relationship from love or at least a desire for companionship. While sex work was thus potentially an option for many women, especially in urban communities, it was problematic. It exposed women to disease as well as violence, was frowned upon by all Christian moralists, and might be seen

---

[89] See sect. 3, Ch. 7 below. A victualing house served food and usually drink, like a modern restaurant.

[90] Goldberg, ed., *Women in England*, p. 199.

[91] E.g., *Liverpool Town Books*, vol. II, p. 717, and *Court Leet Records [of Southampton]*, vol. I, pt. 2, pp. 186 and 236. See also Froide, "Marital Status as a Category of Difference," and McIntosh, *Controlling Misbehavior*, pp. 110–11.

[92] By the decades around 1700, 11 percent of a sample of employed women in London were engaged in laundry work or went out to clean houses on a daily basis (Earle, "Female Labour Market"). The seventeenth and early eighteenth centuries also saw an increase in the urban demand for women to work on a more regular basis in parish and civic institutions like churches, workhouses, and prisons, where they laundered, cooked, cleaned, and sewed (Froide, "Single Women, Work, and Community," p. 273).

by other people in the community as a threat to solid marriages and good order. Yet for a poor woman who lacked other skills, selling sex may have been her best option if other forms of income were unavailable. Because prostitution has been extensively considered in other studies, we will only point out the changes that occurred across these centuries.[93]

During the later medieval period, prostitution was regarded as a necessary evil in many cities and towns in England and elsewhere in Europe. Brothels were accepted on pragmatic grounds, because they were less harmful to men and society than were individual prostitutes working on their own. In such cases, public officials tried to ensure that prostitutes were readily distinguishable from other women through distinctive clothing (such as a striped hood) and/or that brothels were well run and maintained relatively good health. The most notorious houses of prostitution in England were the "stews" in Southwark, just across the river from London, on property owned by the Bishop of Winchester.[94] In 1381, seven married couples were listed in the Poll Tax return for Southwark as stewmongers or operators of brothels; twelve women probably served as prostitutes, in addition to the female servants living in the households of the brothel keepers. Women of all marital statuses ran houses for sex, serving many kinds of men.[95] In Westminster in 1409, Elizabeth Warren, married to a skinner, and Stephen Essex's wife together operated "a bordelhouse for monks, priests, and others." Even women identified as brothel keepers or prostitutes, however, rarely pursued such work as a full-time occupation. Late fourteenth-century Exeter had seventeen female brothel keepers and fifty-five prostitutes, constituting 17 percent of the town's working women.[96] But all the brothel keepers and nearly half of the prostitutes had a second form of employment as well.

By the later fifteenth century, venereal disease was spreading in Europe, and by the later sixteenth it was present in many English communities. This made paid sex more dangerous for both parties. People at the time were clearly aware that some illnesses were transmitted through sexual

---

[93] For general discussions, see, e.g., Karras, *Common Women,* Goldberg, "Pigs and Prostitutes," his "Women in Fifteenth-Century Town Life," and his *Women, Work, and Life Cycle,* pp. 149–57. Local studies that document late medieval prostitution are Barron, "Women in London," Lacey, "Women and Work," Goldberg, "Female Labour," Keene, *Survey of Medieval Winchester,* pp. 390–2, Kettle, "Ruined Maids," Fleming, *Women in Late Medieval Bristol,* p. 7, and Moore, "Aspects of Poverty."

[94] Karras, "Regulation of Brothels." For below, see Carlin, *Medieval Southwark,* pp. 175–6 and ch. 9.

[95] Rosser, *Medieval Westminster,* pp. 143–4, for this and below. Among the brothel keepers of Westminster were "female entrepreneurs" like Katherine Rasen, a singlewoman who lived herself in St. Olave Jewry in London but was accused with others in 1504 of running a chain of brothels in houses in Westminster and other London-area communities.

[96] Kowaleski, "Women's Work."

contact. In Romford, venereal disease was first mentioned in 1578. Joan Callowaie, called before the church court for having sex outside marriage, claimed that five men had recently had intercourse with her, one of whom "often times had the carnal knowledge of her body and did burn her [= give her a sexually transmitted disease] very pitifully."[97] Five more instances of venereal disease among prostitutes were mentioned in Romford over the following decade. In some cases we can watch the spread of disease. Christopher, the stableman at the Crown inn, was charged in 1580 with having been burnt by a whore; shortly thereafter another woman confessed to having been burnt by Christopher.[98] This situation offered new commercial possibilities to an enterprising woman who ran a brothel in Romford. Agnes Newman, widow, was summoned to the church court in 1580 on a charge of keeping harlots and acting as a "surgeon to common strumpets and such as be burnt." Venereal disease introduced another component to a person's credit. Men and women who were thinking about engaging in sex now had to consider the reputation of their proposed partner in physical terms, her or his trustworthiness as related to health.

Beginning in the later fifteenth century, social concern with sex outside marriage increased. This was part of a broader effort by the leaders of many communities to maintain good order and limit wrongdoing.[99] By the Elizabethan and Jacobean periods, tolerance of sex work was largely gone. The new moral emphasis within certain strains of Protestantism, worry about disruptive behavior among the poor, and fear of venereal disease all contributed to a growing sense that neither open nor private prostitution should be allowed. Many urban governments and the church courts therefore attempted to control women's sexuality outside marriage and to limit or even abolish prostitution. At the same time, however, by the later sixteenth century increasing poverty, disproportionate female migration into towns, and the difficulty of finding a position as a servant must have rendered some urban women so economically vulnerable that they had few choices other than sex work. The little evidence we have about women who operated as freelance prostitutes suggests that most lived on the margins of respectable society, struggling to maintain themselves and their illegitimate children, moving frequently, and resorting to theft or other kinds of petty crime on occasion.[100]

[97] ERO D/AEA 10, fol. 125r.
[98] ERO D/AEA 11, fols. 124r and 135r, for this and below.
[99] Goldberg, "Coventry's 'Lollard' Programme," Mate, *Women in Medieval English Society*, pp. 49–50, Carlin, *Medieval Southwark*, ch. 9, and McIntosh, *Controlling Misbehavior*, esp. pp. 70–2 and 110–11, for this and below. See also sect. 4 Ch. 6 below.
[100] Kettle, "Ruined Maids."

4. Two women nursing a sick (and wealthy) man in bed. Note that the woman stirring the pot is reading a book

Caring for or attempting to cure sick people offered a final form of female service work. In some cases, assistance was given simply as a matter of friendship. When Mistress Boston, the wife of a brewer in early modern Salisbury, lay sick for six weeks, her next-door neighbor, the wife of a bottlemaker, came over every day to take care of her.[101] Mistress Boston gave her an old cloth gown in thanks. But women might also be hired to tend others, paid for their time, and reimbursed for their expenses (see Illus. 4). By around 1600 the label "nursekeeper" was beginning to be applied to those who looked after sick people.[102]

Few of these women had any formal training, though they might have considerable practical experience. In the early 1550s, for example, Thomas Bedforde of Coventry was "sore pained with a very great swelling in his body which of long time he had endured."[103] After lying "at great peril and danger of death" in his own house for some time, he sent for Elizabeth Fysher, a married woman, asking her to "do to him some remedy and ease of sickness." He agreed to pay her for the cost of medicine and her labor. On that basis, Elizabeth bought supplies, including spices from apothecaries, at a total charge of £6 13s. 4d., from which she made medicines that she administered to Thomas. These succeeded in reducing his swelling and "amended his sickness, to his great ease and comfort." More specialized curing skills were claimed by Alice Shevyngton, who was working as a household servant for William Gregory of London around 1480.[104] After she had been with Gregory for about three years, Alice started to leave his house for days and even weeks at a time to earn additional money. Gregory grumbled that she "pretend[ed] her self to have had conning [= knowledge] in healing of sore eyes."

Wealthy people might hire a nurse/care giver to come and live in their own house. Elizabeth Eston alias Gryffyn of Denham, Bucks., agreed sometime during Elizabeth's reign to work as a servant to Thomas Gawen of the Inner Temple, London, esquire, "a sickly man [whom she tended] by the space of many years until he died."[105] She accepted this position because she expected that the wages she earned from Thomas would increase her current savings of 100 marks (= £66 13s. 4d.) in money. As his condition worsened, Elizabeth went with Thomas to his house in Fyfield, Dorset, where she helped him recover from various illnesses and attended him at the time of his death. During the course of her twelve years of service to him, Thomas said initially that he would increase her 100 marks, which she had delivered to him for safekeeping, to £100 when he died; later he promised to grant her a tenement bringing an annual

---

[101] Wright, "Churmaids."   [102] Pelling, "Nurses and Nursekeepers."
[103] PRO C 1/1351/67–68.   [104] PRO C 1/66/264.   [105] PRO C 2/Eliz/E4/64.

rent of 46s. 8d. But neither of those arrangements had been completed by the time of his death.

In other cases, sick people boarded with the care giver.[106] When Remond Siggyn, a foreigner living in Southampton during the 1470s, fell ill, he asked to stay with Barnard de Galis and his wife Marion and be nursed by her.[107] Barnard and Marion later claimed that she purchased medicine for Remond that cost £7 6s. 8d.; their total expenses, including his bed, food, and attendance, came to £29 7s. 8d. When Margaret Porter became unwell sometime before 1558, she went to board with Margaret and John Brandon of London, where she lay for a long period of time.[108] Owing to their efforts, they later claimed, she recovered, but they sustained heavy charges. Sir Anthony Wingfield, the Controller of Edward VI's household, had "in his custody and tuition" one Thomas Philpot, son and heir of Sir Peter Philpot. Thomas, a young man "of small wit and discretion and not able to guide such lands and substance as by inheritance came then unto him," had been committed to Anthony's care by Henry VIII.[109] When Thomas "fell sick and was like to die," Wingfield asked Catherine Studley, dwelling in Aldersgate Street, London, to keep the lad during his illness, promising that she should be well recompensed. Margaret boarded Thomas in her own house for thirty-three weeks, "til that he was perfectly whole again," for a total cost of £30 4s. 8d. Her bill, which averaged more than 18s. per week, was well above values of 12–20d. per week commonly found among poorer people. This may have stemmed from a higher standard of living for a royal ward and/or from the inclusion of medical costs too.

Among the providers of more skilled medical attention, most were probably male throughout our period, as they certainly were in cities by the later sixteenth century.[110] These included the few highly trained fellows of the College of Physicians, barber-surgeons (who let blood and performed simple operations), apothecaries (who prescribed and prepared medications), and those who offered other kinds of medical advice or treatment.

Most of the relatively small number of women with specialized skills were probably midwives. Although we know little about midwifery during the medieval years, women held a virtual monopoly over this field

---

[106] For simple boarding, see sect. 2 above.   [107] PRO C 1/60/230.

[108] PRO C 1/1501/3. John was a shearman, cutting the nap off woolen cloth. In payment, Margaret gave them twelve spoons of silver, various other pieces of plate, two tablecloths made of diaper, and other goods.

[109] PRO REQ 2/14/76.

[110] Pelling, "Trade or Profession?" and Pelling and Webster, "Medical Practioners." More generally, see Webster, ed., *Health, Medicine and Mortality*.

5. A birthing scene in an aristocratic bedroom, with the new baby being warmed by the fire

during the sixteenth and early seventeenth centuries.[111] Midwives were active throughout the social spectrum (see Illus. 5 and 6). They usually trained by serving as an assistant to a more experienced woman, sometimes for periods as long as three or four years.[112] Perhaps a few midwives were ignorant or careless, as was occasionally alleged, but many women took pride in their work and were highly regarded in the community.

[111] One finds occasional references to midwives in medieval London (e.g., the hospitals of St. Mary without Bishopsgate and St. Bartholomew's hired women to care for those in childbirth and for any children born there who were left as orphans), and one was active in Southwark in 1381 (Lacey, "Women and Work," and Carlin, *Medieval Southwark*, p. 175). No midwives were identified in the main records of late fourteenth-century Exeter, but seven were brought in to determine whether a female defendant in a trial was pregnant or not (Kowaleski, *Local Markets and Regional Trade*, p. 168).

[112] See Mendelson and Crawford, *Women in Early Modern England*, pp. 314–18, for this and below.

6. A childbirth scene, with a midwife and two other women attending the mother. Two physicians are casting the baby's horoscope in the background. Note the tools hung on the midwife's belt

In Southampton, for example, a man was admitted to the freedom of the city in 1601 largely because his wife had been for many years "the chief midwife of the town and hath taken great pains and honest care in her function."[113]

By the Elizabethan period midwives were supposed to be licensed by the local bishop, though some women practiced without license. Such

[113] Wright, "Churmaids."

control was not designed to exclude women from the field (men were not yet interested in working in this occupation) but was tied to several other concerns about their activities. Midwives were the most powerful figures within the physical and social setting of childbirth, an occasion attended commonly by the delivering mother's friends and neighbors and an exclusively female setting about which men felt both curiosity and anxiety.[114] Alone among women, midwives were granted the power to carry out emergency baptisms if necessary, and they were associated with issues of female cleanliness and purity that assumed greater importance in the later sixteenth century as venereal disease became a mounting problem.

Women worked occasionally as (barber-)surgeons. In late medieval London, a few women were listed as barber-surgeons; a female barber worked in Southwark, Surrey, in 1381 and another in Coventry in 1499.[115] In York, Isabel Warwike was permitted to practice as a surgeon in 1572 because she had "skill in the science of surgery and hath done good therein."[116] Alice Gordon was paid 40s. in 1598 for her work as a surgeon at St. Bartholomew's Hospital, London. In rural areas, a few women who were called surgeons set bones and dealt with ailments like ringworm and sores that did not heal.[117] Surgeons too were supposed to be licensed, but enforcement was irregular. Between 1550 and 1600, twenty-nine unlicensed women who claimed to be physicians and surgeons were prosecuted by the College of Physicians of London.[118]

Hospitals or institutions for orphaned children offered a little additional employment for women, though generally these positions did not require specialized nursing skills. Instead, they consisted of simple bedside care and housekeeping, thereby resembling the kind of help that women provided in their own or other people's homes. In late medieval York women were hired by hospitals and some of the maisondieus or almshouses, as they were by infirmaries in London.[119] Such opportunities probably declined with the closing of many of the church-run hospitals during the 1530s but increased again during the second half of the sixteenth century and the early seventeenth. Christ's Hospital in London, which opened

---

[114] Cressy, *Travesties and Transgressions*, ch. 7.

[115] Abram, "Women Traders," and Lacey, "Women and Work"; Carlin, *Medieval Southwark*, p. 175, and Fox, "Coventry Guilds."

[116] Mendelson and Crawford, *Women in Early Modern England*, p. 318, for this and below.

[117] Fletcher, *Gender, Sex and Subordination*, pp. 236–7.

[118] Pelling and Webster, "Medical Practitioners," esp. pp. 186–7.

[119] Goldberg, "Female Labour," his *Women, Work, and Life Cycle*, pp. 134–5, and Lacey, "Women and Work." A few women were described as nurses in the Poll Tax returns of 1379 for the West Riding of Yorkshire, but some or all of these may have been wet nurses: Goldberg, "Women's Work."

in 1553, provided residential care for around 400 orphaned children, a quarter of whom were under the age of four. The institution employed a large staff, including a matron and twenty-five nurses, to look after the children. When the nurses were not actively engaged in child care, they were told to keep the wards clean and sew or spin.[120] Women provided more than half of the staff in Norwich's hospitals, which numbered seven to nine after the Reformation, and York's hospitals hired women.[121]

The development of town- or parish-based systems of poor relief during the second half of the sixteenth century created some new kinds of employment. In Elizabethan Romford, women, most of them widows, were hired by the parish to go to the houses of sick people to tend them, especially when plague was present. Bequests to them in wills suggest that the quality of their care bred real affection on the part of their patients if not always a successful recovery from illness.[122] Some elderly poor women in Norwich in 1570 were likewise paid to take care of sick persons or those living in almshouses.[123] By the later Elizabethan years, women experienced in the symptoms of plague and other contagious illnesses were employed in some of the larger communities for the nasty job of examining the bodies of the deceased, to determine the cause of death. Over the following century opportunities for women in health care would remain concentrated within unskilled roles.[124]

Providing domestic and personal services thus allowed women to earn money by transferring their home-based skills into a for-pay setting. It was an essential component of the economies of many households and provided necessary care. Such work remained almost exclusively female throughout the later medieval and early modern periods, in part because those jobs were culturally defined as appropriate to women, in part because they offered so little occupational identification and such poor remuneration that they were not desired by men. Although service work rarely provided enough income to support a household, it generated supplementary income for many women, perhaps a growing fraction of poor women, into the early seventeenth century. We turn now to the services offered by women in the areas of money-lending and real estate.

---

[120] Willen, "Women in the Public Sphere."
[121] Pelling, "Old Age, Poverty, and Disability," and Willen, "Women in the Public Sphere."
[122] McIntosh, *A Community Transformed*, p. 81. When more professional medical care was needed for the poor, Romford's officials hired a male surgeon (ibid., p. 284).
[123] Pelling, "Old Age, Poverty, and Disability," her "Nurses and Nursekeepers," and Willen, "Women in the Public Sphere."
[124] By the period around 1700, 9 percent of a sample of working women in London were engaged in nursing or medicine, nearly all of whom were either wives or widows. The group was comprised mainly of "nursekeepers"; another eight of these fifty-six women were midwives, and just three (none of whom was described as a physician or surgeon) offered more specialized medical care (Earle, "Female Labour Market").

4 Financial services and real estate

This chapter explores women's involvement in several other types of service relationships, those dealing with finance and real estate. These activities are treated here – as in modern economic categorization – as service functions because they helped clients to maintain fiscal solvency and find housing, and because they facilitated the operation of the broader economy. Yet most women who loaned money or bought rental property did so in order to make a profit: the interest they received from loans or rents constituted income for themselves. We first set the context by discussing women's involvement with credit mechanisms more generally, looking then at their roles in money-lending, including pawnbroking. A final section looks at the limited number of urban women who were starting to provide residential or commercial property for rent. Our focus here is upon women who were themselves lenders or landladies, though they appear as users of such services too.

1 Women and financial credit

If financial credit is defined as a postponed or delayed economic obligation, an agreement that leaves one person owing something to another, we find that most women who earned an income in late medieval and early modern England were caught up in multiple networks of credit.[1] At any given time, they owed money, goods, or land to a variety of people; conversely, they had a pool of outstanding debts owed to them, which they might be able to call in as needed. Women who loaned or borrowed money were at the center of the credit system. We therefore need to

---

[1] Muldrew's evidence from King's Lynn in the seventeenth century indicates that virtually everyone living in the town eventually came before the local court as plaintiffs and/or defendants in private suits, most of them involving credit; unfortunately he does not provide a breakdown by sex ("Credit and the Courts"). In 1552–3 and 1612–13, 5–8 percent of all suits in Great Yarmouth had female plaintiffs, while 3–5 percent had male defendants, but Muldrew does not indicate how many of these cases were for debt ("'A Mutual Assent of Her Mind?'"). For the role of a woman's individual credit or reputation, see Ch. 1 above.

understand the types of credit relationships and the mechanisms through which credit was extended.

Women became involved in financial credit through a wide range of activities.[2] Lending or borrowing money – with or without interest – was the most obvious way. It was joined by pawnbroking, where cash was handed out in return for the deposit of goods of greater value; if the money and interest were repaid, the goods could be reclaimed, but if not, they became the property of the lender. Women commonly loaned or borrowed money and sometimes operated as pawnbrokers. Mortgages enabled a landholder to gain cash in return for giving temporary control over the property to the lender. Because women seldom had full control over land, they were less likely than men to take out mortgages. But these were by no means the only kinds of credit relationships. Unfulfilled commitments might also arise from deferred payment for services rendered or unpaid rent. Producing and selling goods often required extending or receiving credit. Rarely during these centuries did a buyer pay the full price for a given purchase and take the goods home immediately. Instead, an agreement for a sale was made, but either payment or delivery of the goods was postponed.[3] Many purchases – at lower as well as upper economic levels – thus linked the seller and buyer in a credit relationship.

Within this system of loans and delayed obligations, working women encountered gender-based handicaps that became more severe over time. They lacked the occupational identity that might have encouraged lenders to advance credit to them, they generally had fewer resources of their own, and they faced questions on the basis of their marital situation that would not have been asked of their male counterparts. If a woman gave credit to another person but was not repaid, she might be unable to travel to recover the sum owed to her or to prosecute the debtor in the courts. These problems were not acute so long as financial transactions occurred on a relatively small scale between people who knew each other and could assess their actual economic and personal situation. A commercial brewer in one of England's little market centers in the mid-fifteenth century who worked with her husband's backing and had good personal and economic

---

[2] Credit obligations could also result from family interactions: see McIntosh, "Women, Credit, and Family Relationships."

[3] If, for example, a brewster sold ale several times each week to a local man but allowed him to pay a lump sum at the end of the month, she was extending credit. If she bought firewood for her brewing operation and took it home with her, paying half the price at the time of the purchase and the rest six weeks later, she was receiving credit. If she purchased twelve bags of malted grain, paying the full price right away but taking only six bags with her at the time, with an agreement that she would collect the rest a month later, she was extending credit.

credit probably had little difficulty in postponing payment for supplies she needed or getting a loan to buy new equipment. But as the scale of production and sale rose, and as money-lending and credit mechanisms became more formal across the sixteenth century, women were increasingly disadvantaged. While they continued to be active participants in the credit system at lower and in some cases even middling levels, they were rarely able to take part in the far more profitable levels of lending, production, and sales that were developing above them during the decades around 1600. In examining the various types of credit mechanisms, we will move from the least formal, those with the heaviest component of social credit and the least reliance upon written contracts and guarantees, to the most structured.

In informal credit relationships, cash, goods, labor, or the use of land were advanced or given temporarily by one person to another. Such loans were extended between people who had personal ties with each other, or who had heard about each other from mutual acquaintances. The social component of these relationships was important, for the loan was based on an assumption that the other person's word was trustworthy and that he/she would perform the promised actions. The agreement was usually made privately between the two people, not documented in writing or in the presence of witnesses. Although transactions other than cash loans were normally assigned a monetary value (e.g., the use of a plough for three weeks might be described as worth 2d.), cash did not change hands at the time. The monetary equivalent facilitated a later reckoning between the parties of their mutual credit dealings, and if goodwill between the parties broke down and legal action became necessary, the amount demanded would be the cash equivalent. There was also considerable flexibility in how the loan might be repaid: through the direct return of the cash or item (with or without some kind of payment for its use) or through reciprocal loans. This system may have been particularly important during periods of acute shortage of precious metals and hence of coins, such as 1395–1415 and the 1440s–50s.[4] Throughout the centuries from 1300 to 1620, many women participated in fairly casual credit relationships like these.

A good illustration of informal, reciprocal credit dealings comes from the Essex manor of Writtle in 1412. During the course of that year Margaret atte Tye, a widow, borrowed various small sums of cash from John Herry, jun., amounting in total to 18d.[5] She also hired him to transport the malt she had prepared to the nearby community of Margaretting,

---

[4] Kermode, "Money and Credit." All money in this period consisted of coins, not paper.
[5] Elaine Clark, "Debt Litigation."

enlisted his wife to help her reap during the harvest, and had the temporary use of one of John's cows. These obligations were assigned a total monetary value of 5s. 2d. On his side, John borrowed from Margaret a spade and a plow-beam, used one of her cows during the winter, and rented some land from her. There is no indication that these transactions were recorded in a written document or arranged in the presence of witnesses: Margaret and John set them up in good faith, based on their knowledge of each other. If, however, amity between Margaret and John were lost, for whatever reason, one of them might demand an immediate accounting of all their mutual obligations or take the other to court. During the medieval years many local courts were prepared to hear cases stemming from the failure of such credit relationships without written proof. The pleadings in debt cases sometimes reveal strings of transactions – including purchases, loans, wages, and/or rents – stretching back for many years but not cleared prior to the time ill-will developed between the parties.[6]

Various types of informal credit were used for the sale and purchase of goods. During the fourteenth and fifteenth centuries, and for smaller transactions throughout our period, if a buyer made frequent purchases of low value from a given seller, the latter might be willing to defer payment.[7] Keeping a running account of the individual charges, the vendor would add up the total periodically and ask the purchaser to pay. For wealthy and reliable customers who made repeated purchases from a shop, the seller might be willing to let even substantial debts accumulate over a considerable period of time before demanding repayment. During the later medieval period many accounts were apparently kept in people's heads, but by the sixteenth century they were more likely to be written down.

At least in London during the decades around 1500, and perhaps especially among foreigners, tallies were sometimes used to keep track of running debts. A tally was a thin wooden rod onto which the amounts owed were notched at right angles to the length of the tally; the stick was then split in two lengthwise, with each party keeping one half. Subsequent debts were notched onto both tallies, which were produced when a reckoning was done. Grace Bartyn, wife of Harry Bartyn, a gentleman living in London during the mid-1480s, bought bread, ale, and other food on a number of occasions from Joan Harold, the wife of John Harold, a tailor

---

[6] Ibid., and McIntosh, "Money Lending."

[7] In larger cities, however, if sellers did not know buyers personally, they normally expected cash on the spot, especially for small, take-away purchases by strangers (Carlin, "'What Will You Buy?'"). Dr. Carlin kindly sent me a copy of this paper.

of London.[8] Joan, who operated her own business independently of her husband, was willing to deliver food and drink to purchasers' houses, as she did for Grace. Joan kept a running record of Grace's debts on their tallies, which eventually came to a total of thirty-six notches. Dispute then arose over what each notch represented: Joan as seller said each was worth one shilling (= 12d.), while Grace as buyer said the notches were worth only 1d. each. Widow Jacomyn Hans of London, who had immigrated with her husband from the Low Countries or Germany, brewed beer for a group of regular buyers around 1500.[9] The man she hired to make weekly deliveries kept a tally with each of her customers, "as it is accustomed within the City of London." After he had scored the latest purchase onto both halves of the tally, he gave one half to the buyer and delivered the other to Jacomyn for her records. Similarly, Peter Wyldank sold beer wholesale to Alice Blunham, who ran an alehouse in London sometime around 1520, using a tally to keep track of the deliveries he made to her.

In another kind of credit arrangement used commonly by both women and men, only part of the payment was made at the time that the agreement was set up and the goods delivered, with the remainder to be paid at some specified later date. These contracts, used often for larger purchases, allowed the buyer to accumulate the necessary money gradually. In some cases the seller preferred to leave the date of payment open (the cash was to be handed over "when requested"), thereby gaining a stock of credit that she or he could draw upon as needed in the future. If a seller doubted the ability of the purchaser to pay, whether on the spot or in the future, she could demand that the buyer deliver into her keeping goods of greater value than the amount owed, to be held as sureties until the original debt was paid. This practice resembled closely the practice of pawning goods in return for a cash loan.[10] Or the arrangement might require full or partial payment immediately, but delivery of goods would happen in the future, in one or more units. This was useful if the seller did not have all the items immediately at hand.

Informal credit left lenders of money and sellers of goods vulnerable in two respects. If the loan or purchase were not documented in writing, it might be difficult to pursue the debt in a common law court should the other party fail to pay as required. Further, in the case of a default, the lender/seller had no legal claim to any of the debtor's other property, no surety or guarantee that the money owed could be regained in another

---

[8] PRO C 1/76/59. Tallies were used routinely by the royal Exchequer to record payments during these centuries.
[9] PRO C 1/252/57. For below, see C 1/564/39.
[10] For pawning, see sect. 3 below.

way. Written contracts, preferably signed by witnesses, took care of the first problem, but a search for greater security led to the use of some new mechanisms of credit. Because these arrangements were generally prepared in writing by a lawyer or at least someone familiar with the law, who had to be paid, they were initially used only for larger debts. Women working at middling or lower economic levels might not have been able to afford a written contract for debts owed to them, though they would perhaps have been asked to sign one for obligations they owed to others.

The most common form of security was a bond for an amount larger than the actual sum owed. In this mechanism, the borrower or purchaser acknowledged the original debt and how and when it was to be repaid. In the written bond, sometimes termed "an obligatory writing," he or she agreed to pay a larger sum at some date in the future if the original agreement had not been fulfilled as specified. If, for instance, Alice loaned £30 to Robert, due on Christmas Day 1520, for which he agreed to pay £3 as interest, Alice might require that he sign a bond stating that he owed her £50 or £60 on 1 February 1521. The condition of the bond, often written on the back of the document, was that if he paid her £33 on or before Christmas Day 1520, the bond was annulled and void.

Bonds had been used for large transactions from the central medieval years, but they were increasingly employed in other contexts too from the fifteenth century onward. By the Elizabethan period, use of bonds to back up loans had become standard practice for middling as well as larger transactions. During the fifteenth and early sixteenth centuries, bonds ranged widely between 1.25 and 2.0 times the value of the original debt, but by around 1600 obligations were more likely to be bonded at twice the value. In a further development, in regular use by the second half of the sixteenth century, a lender or other creditor might demand that a potential borrower find one or two other people to sign the security bond with her or him. These guarantors were then legally responsible with the debtor for repayment of the full bonded sum; should the primary borrower default, the sureties had to cover the debt. A woman who was asked to serve as a surety for another person's bond but did not entirely trust the debtor's ability to repay might in turn require that the debtor sign a second bond to her, for an amount larger than the amount of the first bond.[11]

By the later sixteenth century, security bonds were in use not only for cash loans but in other circumstances as well. Especially in the cities,

---

[11] For example, Richard Daye, a merchant of Southampton, bought merchandise worth £200 from shopkeeper Edith Goddard during the 1550s or 1560s. He and John Jackson co-signed a bond to Edith for £300, but Jackson in turn required that Daye sign a bond to him to cover the £300 (PRO C 3/54/85).

where there was less personal knowledge of people, property owners might require a bond before a lease was signed. In the 1570s, widow Agnes Merydeth of Westminster agreed to lease a house to Richard Foxe for £3. But, apparently not trusting Richard's willingness or ability to pay that rent, Agnes required that he find two sureties who would sign a bond with him for £6.[12] In another variation of the pattern, when John Carpenter of Huwyke, a tinner of Cornwall, and his wife Joan contracted to sell 400 weight of tin to a London pewterer around 1490, Alice Blakealler, a widow of Kingsbridge, Devon, and Rose Rawlyn, a London widow, served as their bonded sureties for the delivery of the metal.[13]

Security bonds, which have survived in abundance, are difficult to use as evidence for the exact nature of someone's participation in the credit system. Unless we have the condition of the bond, we cannot tell what the original obligation was for. Thus, if we encounter a legal action in which Beatrice is pleading against William concerning a £20 bond, we may not be able to tell whether the bond was written to cover a loan of cash, whether William had purchased goods or land from her, or whether he was refusing to deliver her share of an inheritance. Nor can we be sure of the size of the initial debt. This has been a weakness in studies that accepted bonds as evidence of money-lending (not of credit activity more generally) and as the size of the actual debt. It is more accurate to recognize that when we see a woman revealed as a creditor or debtor through a bond, we know she was involved in a credit relationship of some kind but cannot determine the nature or size of the initial transaction unless we have further information.

The equity court petitions illustrate some of the bond-related problems encountered by female creditors. While men certainly faced similar problems, we cannot compare the actual experiences of women and men in quantitative terms from these petitions. Female petitioners generally accentuated their weakness and vulnerability as a rhetorical strategy when appealing for redress of a grievance.[14] Men, who made heavier use of the common law courts, were more likely to define themselves in their equity petitions as powerful and effective. Hence they might hesitate to admit, for example, that they had lost a written document or could not find the person to whom they owed money.

Although a bond was intended to provide greater security for the lender, it was not always easy for women to force payment of the bonded amount after the debtor had defaulted on the initial payment. Margaret Pulton,

[12] PRO REQ 2/33/12. [13] PRO C 1/107/83.
[14] For a fuller discussion of female vs. male strategies in one equity court, see Stretton, *Women Waging Law*.

widow, was owed £4 by William Mylles of Staines, Middx., in 1540.[15] He and Robert Stokys of Eton, Bucks., were bound for £8 to cover the obligation. William did not pay the original debt as required, so Elizabeth sued Robert as his surety, claiming that his failure to pay had left her "in extreme poverty, having 2 young Children in her keeping." Keeping valuable documents safely at home could be difficult. When Elizabeth Pearson, a widow of Durham, petitioned the Court of Requests in 1588–9, she claimed that she had previously had two written bonds at her house, one recording the obligation of Robert Walter and Thomas Willson to pay her £12 to cover an unspecified smaller debt, another documenting that Nicholas Dearwin and John Michellson were bound to her for £24.[16] Her son Robert was apprenticed to Roland Richardson, a glover of Durham. According to her petition, Roland, "a man of bad behavior and lewd disposition," lured young Robert into "dissolute company," enticing him to "bestow great part of his time in dicing and carding and other unlawful & forbidden games." Because Roland loaned the lad money with which to pursue these recreations, Robert became heavily indebted to his master. Having established his power over the boy, Roland persuaded him to steal the two bonds from his mother. Roland then went to the people named in the bonds and renegotiated the arrangements so that they were now bound for a smaller amount, but to him, not to Margaret Pulton. Because Margaret no longer had the original bonds in her possession, she could not prosecute either Roland or the signers of the bonds in the common law courts.

A particularly sustained and determined action by a female creditor began in August 1512 when Henry Palmer, a draper of Coventry, signed a "bill obligatory" to Agnes Delfe of Coventry, widow, as bond for a debt of £9 13s. 4d.[17] When Henry did not repay the amount owed, Agnes lodged a plea of debt against him in the common law court of King's Bench at Westminster, asking for damages of £5 plus the original sum. The jury found against Henry and awarded her the original debt plus £3. Henry still did not pay her, so she obtained a writ of *capias* that ordered the sheriffs of the city of Coventry to seize Henry and keep him in prison until he had satisfied the order from King's Bench. He was duly arrested and placed in the keeping of Henry Wall and another man, then Coventry's sheriffs. But instead of performing his duty, Wall allowed Palmer to go free and even helped to convey him out of Coventry with his personal goods and three cartloads of merchandise. That had happened fourteen years before, but Palmer still had not repaid his debt and damages from the earlier suit. So, in spring 1527, Agnes sued Wall before the king's council,

[15] PRO REQ 2/4/231.   [16] PRO REQ 2/34/13.   [17] PRO REQ 2/7/157.

arguing that by his error in freeing Palmer, he had become responsible for Palmer's debts. Wall later appeared and promised to bring the money to satisfy her. When he failed to do so, she petitioned the Court of Chancery to hear and settle this problem.

Conversely, women could themselves be sued if they had signed a bond as a guarantor on behalf of someone else who failed to repay the loan or complete the contract as agreed. London women may have entered into this role earlier and more fully than did those in smaller communities. In the later 1370s, for example, Isabella, wife of Ralph Whithors, agreed to become the surety for a debt of 80 marks (= £53 6s. 8d.) owed by Ralph Barry, knight, to Robert Culham, armorer, a transaction recorded in a formal bond.[18] When Ralph failed to pay, Isabella was obliged to cover his debt, which she did except for 5 marks. (Since she was allowed to sign a bond in her own name as a married woman, she was probably trading *femme sole*.) Widow Agnes Knesworth acted as surety to Catherine Butteler, a silkwoman of London, for payment for "stuff and wares" that Catherine purchased from John Porter during the 1470s.[19] Five or six years later, after Catherine's death, John alleged that he had not been paid and sued Agnes as the surety. Agnes Weste, another London widow, agreed around 1510 to serve as a bonded guarantor for Nicholas Weste, a grocer, when he bought madder (used in dyeing cloth) from Thomas Gerton of London, skinner; both Agnes and Nicholas were later sued by Thomas.

Bondholders might be also charged with trying to force a debtor to default on the original amount so as to collect the larger surety. George Walpole, a yeoman from the market center of Hickling, Norfolk, claimed that in April 1575 he had become bound to Christian Amys, a widow of the same place, for £30, under condition that he pay her £21 in money on 3 May 1577.[20] Shortly after signing that obligation, Christian married Francis Shillinge. On the day that his £21 payment was due, George had to be in London, so he gave the money to his wife Margaret, telling her to deliver it to Christian and Francis at their house. When Margaret arrived there, however, and explained to the servants that she had come to repay the money, the Shillings "hid themselves in an inner chamber of the house where she could not find them." Because they deliberately absented themselves from her, George alleged, she was unable to make the payment. Later the Shillinges sued George for the full bonded amount.

Several kinds of credit mechanisms drew upon land as surety. Especially during the fourteenth and fifteenth centuries, land was sometimes

---

[18] CPMRL, 1364–1381, p. 271.   [19] PRO C 1/64/808. For below, see C 1/456/31.
[20] PRO REQ 2/33/10.

assigned to a creditor's use for a period of years or rented on favorable terms to settle another debt. In the interactions described above between Margaret atte Tye and John Herry of Writtle in 1412, when they eventually rendered account for all their mutual obligations, Margaret found that what she owed John came to more than she was able to repay as cash.[21] She therefore cleared the slate by renting to John and his father some land and a house that she promised to keep fully repaired at her own cost. Wealthier people used landed property as security when they needed to raise capital during the later fourteenth and fifteenth centuries.[22] In another arrangement, Anne Mallyson of Blyth, Notts., allowed a neighboring farmer to use some land and barns of hers for his cattle in 1613 in exchange for delivering coal for her inn.

Land could produce a different kind of credit through a "maintenance agreement." In such a contract, an elderly or ill person who was no longer able to farm granted her or his land to another for term of the donor's life.[23] In return, the recipient agreed to provide food, housing, and/or physical care to the grantor. Maintenance agreements are well documented in local records during the later medieval years, but the equity court petitions show that they continued into the early modern period, especially in the north of England. In 1605, Alison Silvertop, the elderly widow of John Silvertop of Coundon, Durham, claimed that at the halmote court of the Bishop of Durham in 1598, her husband had conveyed their dwelling and lands to the use of Thomas Heighinton, a yeoman.[24] This holding, worth at least £35, was granted to Heighinton under condition that he provide for Alison "meat [= food], drink, house room [= lodging], and all other necessaries whatsoever during her life natural." Heighinton took possession of the property on that basis, but after John Silvertop's death, he refused "utterly to help or relieve your poor aged [petitioner] but suffereth her to go a begging, not having anything to maintain her withall, to her utter undoing, contrary to all right, equity, and good conscience."

The difficulty in enforcing maintenance agreements is illustrated further by a petition from Edward Rychardson of Clare, Suffolk, a butcher, in 1617.[25] He said that he had received title to a cottage and five acres of land in Stoke, Suffolk, on behalf of his wife Anne, for the rest of her life. (This was probably land she held as dower from a former marriage.) He

---

[21] Elaine Clark, "Debt Litigation."

[22] Kermode, "Money and Credit." For below, see PRO REQ 2/416/75.

[23] For medieval maintenance contracts, see Elaine Clark, "Some Aspects of Social Security," and Smith, "The Manorial Court and the Elderly Tenant."

[24] PRO DURH 2/2/71.

[25] PRO DL 1/272, Rychardson vs. others, 18 November 1617.

and Anne then granted the property to six local men, under condition that they pay Edward and Anne £7 annually throughout her lifetime. The new tenants took over the property but refused to make the required payments. This, Edward claimed, had forced him into destitution, since he had to maintain Anne – who was "lame and bedrid" – at his own costs. In both these last two cases the courts accepted the petitioners' claim of poverty as genuine: they were allowed to plea *in forma pauperis*, that is, without paying the usual court fees.

Gradually, however, mortgages replaced informal use of land within credit relationships, at least for larger loans. In a mortgage, the creditor provided a cash sum to the landholder in return for gaining legal right to the property that was being used as surety; the condition was that the land would be returned to the debtor when the loan was repaid. Mortgages were risky for the borrower. Losing possession of land, even temporarily, was dangerous in a legal system in which the occupant had a marked advantage in the event of a dispute. Further, it was sometimes difficult for the debtor to regain possession from the creditor even if the loan were repaid as stipulated. Nevertheless, by the Elizabethan years, mortgages were widely used by landholders who were short of cash. Women, however, were rarely able to take advantage of mortgages due to the laws concerning landholding in England. Relatively few women had title to land in their own right, with freedom to dispose of it as they wished. (Women formed around one-sixth of all landholders in the early modern period, but in many cases the property was theirs only for life.[26]) The land that a woman brought into marriage as her dowry was regarded by the common law as subject to her husband's – not her own – control. Married women could therefore not raise money for their own purposes by mortgaging land unless they persuaded their husband of the validity of their need, getting him to take out the mortgage. Widows, including those who had remarried, were sometimes holding land temporarily that would pass to their children when they reached adulthood. In such cases, they might have been hesitant to take out a mortgage even if they found a lender willing to grant it.

Although one would like to know how female participation in credit dealings compared to that of men, the nature of the surviving sources limits our ability to assess this in quantitative terms. The main problem is the common law requirement that a married woman's debts and credits were her husband's responsibility. His consent was required when a loan was made, and if legal action ensued, he was named as the party (usually with no mention of his wife). Consequently, whereas widows and

[26] For a fuller discussion, see Erickson, *Women and Property*.

singlewomen are visible in legal records, we can spot the presence of married women behind their husband's name only if the clerk took detailed notes on what the parties said about the issues that had led to the dispute. Full pleadings of that kind are rare, and historians have identified few other sources that reveal the actual degree of participation by married women.

During the fourteenth and earlier fifteenth centuries, local court records commonly name the parties, describe the type of case (e.g., debt, trespass, broken covenant), give the value of any obligations, and sometimes say in brief what led to the suit (e.g., John Williams enters a plea of debt against Henry Smith for 28d. owed for the purchase of woolen cloth). Some fine studies of debt have been prepared on the basis of such entries, but they only allow us to explore the involvement of those women listed in their own name as compared to men, some of whom were acting on their own behalf but others as a legal representative for their wives. Not-married women constituted a much smaller fraction of the total number of participants in debt cases than did men, suggesting that the *extent* of their participation in the credit system was low. A detailed analysis of debt litigation in the manor of Writtle, for example, indicates that 14 percent of all recorded creditors between 1382 and 1490 were women.[27] Of the debt cases heard in the market town of Loughborough, Leics., 1397–1406, women appeared as plaintiffs (and hence presumably as creditors) in only 5 percent of the suits and as defendants (or debtors) in a mere 2 percent.[28] Unmarried women were also more likely than men to be borrowers, not lenders. Of parties in suits for debt in Exeter, 1378–88, 68 percent of the women were defendants, being sued for debts they had not repaid, as opposed to just 49 percent of the men.[29]

In parallel terms, the value of the loans or debts of not-married women was generally lower than that for men. This reflects the *depth* of such

[27] Elaine Clark, "Debt Litigation." In the manors of Oakington, Cottenham, and Dry Drayton, Cambs., between 1290 and 1380, the proportion of (mainly unmarried) female creditors in actions of debt reached a high point of 18 percent in the early fourteenth century but in most decades was 5–12 percent; female debtors formed 26 percent of the total at the start of the fourteenth century but otherwise were usually 5–12 percent. The proportion of female creditors in Great Horwood, Bucks., 1302–60, peaked at 27 percent at the start of the fourteenth century but thereafter was 4–14 percent; women debtors formed 36 percent of the total at the start of the century but thereafter were 11–21 percent (Briggs, "Empowered or Marginalized?" which discusses the problem of whether married women are visible but does not provide persuasive evidence that the records reveal their true level of credit participation).

[28] Postles, "An English Small Town."

[29] Kowaleski, "Women's Work." A low level of unmarried female participation was seen at upper economic levels too. Of 171 accounts for debt from Wiltshire, 1300–1600, most involving wealthier people, only five involved women in their own names (*Wiltshire Extents for Debts*, p. 8).

women's immersion in the credit system. In Loughborough, for example, the average amount owed to women in debt cases was 3s. 6d. and the average owed by them was 2s. 9d., values well below the average for male–male debts of 12s. 1d.[30] In Exeter, the amount owed to female creditors averaged 7s. 6d., while that owed to men averaged 13s. 10d.; for debtors, the gap was even larger, with 6s. 4d. owed by women as compared to 14s. owed by men.[31]

We should remember, however, that widows and singlewomen may well have had different credit patterns from their married sisters.[32] A wife whose husband supported her activity would potentially have had more capital to invest in business or money-lending activity than a not-married woman. Moreover, unmarried female creditors were probably less likely to pursue debts through formal legal action because they did not have a man to represent them; conversely, unmarried female debtors may have been sued more aggressively. For Exeter, we can study the participation of a few married women: in atypical fashion, the late fourteenth-century records named some of the women who participated in debt cases together with their husbands.[33] These married women creditors were owed considerably larger sums than not-married women (14s. 11d. as compared to 5s. 9d.) and – rather surprisingly – slightly more than men. Their debts to others were likewise larger than those of singlewomen or widows (10s. 1d. as compared to 4s. 6d.) but less than those of men.

By the later fifteenth century, most local court records had stopped giving details about cases, but the kinds of evidence that make possible more quantitative research for the period after 1600, especially after 1660, had not yet emerged. Hence we are particularly low on information about female participation in credit relationships for the intervening period, a gap partially filled by material from the equity courts.[34] In the early seventeenth century, the quality of documentation about women's credit begins to improve again, and from the 1660s onwards a wealth of material is available.[35] This shows that many women were still actively engaged in credit relationships but mainly at lower economic levels. With this

---

[30] Postles, "An English Small Town."   [31] Kowaleski, "Women's Work."

[32] Briggs, "Empowered or Marginalized?"

[33] Ibid. Since, however, married women constituted only 1–2% of all creditors and debtors named in these cases, it is likely that many other married women were not listed as co-parties in suits that actually involved their economic dealings.

[34] See Ch. 4 below.

[35] See, e.g., Spicksley's analysis of wills and inventories from Lincolnshire and Cheshire, 1601–1700, which shows that 56 percent of singlewomen in the former county and 63 percent in the latter were engaged in credit relationships at the time of their death. But the majority of the female creditors had loaned fairly small total amounts: 40 percent of Linconshire women and 21 percent of Cheshire women were owed less than £10, while only 14 percent of the former and 30 percent of the latter were owed £50 or more

discussion of the forms of economic credit as a foundation, we can turn to the ways in which women participated in financial services and real estate.

2   Lending money

Many women loaned out money at some time in their lives. Money-lending played a different role within an economy that included no banks for the safe storage of money, no regulated lenders or government backed bonds, no insurance companies, and few means whereby most people (apart from the wealthy) could take part in overseas trading activities or other large-scale enterprises that might bring a high return on their investment. Further, during an inflationary period, such as pertained during the sixteenth and early seventeenth centuries, money that was simply stored lost value in terms of its purchasing power. Sometimes women with extra cash chose to spend it right away. They might decide to buy clothing or household items, expand their own trade, or, if married, help their husband to buy additional land or enlarge his business. But if a woman had money she did not need or want to spend immediately, she had relatively few ways of investing it conveniently and safely. If she bought animals, they might die; if she acquired a piece of land, it had to be worked in order to yield an income. Lending out cash for interest must have seemed a sensible way of getting some benefit from her money, provided that she thought it would be repaid in full and with the stipulated interest.

Interesting changes took place across the centuries under study in how money was loaned, related to the social as well as the economic meanings of credit.[36] Throughout this span, one's individual reputation for reliability and honesty was important. Lenders had to decide whether a prospective borrower was likely to repay the loan as agreed and what kind of security should be required. Borrowers needed to ascertain whether the person from whom they were going to take money, who commonly

("The Early Modern Demographic Dynamic," ch. 3, esp. table 3.1). By around 1700, a smaller number of women with extra resources were loaning money commercially to private borrowers or making safer investments through loans to the government or insurance policies (ibid., ch. 3, Froide, "Single Women, Work, and Community" and her "Surplus Women," Holderness, "Widows in Pre-Industrial Society," his "Credit in a Rural Community," and his "Credit in English Rural Society," Lemire, "Women, the Informal Economy and the Development of Capitalism" and her "Petty Pawns and Informal Lending," Barbara Todd, "The Crown and the Female Money Market" and her "Small Sums to Risk" (I am grateful to Drs. Lemire and Todd for letting me have copies of these papers), and Earle, *Making of the English Middle Class*, pp. 168–71).
[36] See Ch. 1 above.

demanded payment of interest and/or delivery of personal possessions as pawns, was likely to stand by the terms of their agreement. The medieval pattern through which money was loaned has been characterized as local (carried out between people who already knew each other), occasional, and informal.[37] Because lenders acknowledged the importance of cooperation and community values rather than adopting a "rational" approach designed to maximize their profits, most lending was done on a nonprofessional basis through an irregular series of individual transactions between friends, neighbors, and acquaintances.

By the sixteenth century, however, money-lending was becoming less casual. Muldrew suggests that this shift stemmed from the loss of personal trust within an expanding market, which led social relations to be partially redefined in terms of "contractual equality."[38] The mechanisms of credit were also becoming more complex, tied in part to an increase in the size of loans during the later sixteenth and early seventeenth centuries. The assumption had now become that one could not count on a borrower's word, even if given nominally in good faith. Instead the lender required careful written documentation of the loan, as evidence that it had indeed taken place, and some kind of guarantee or surety that it would be repaid. These measures provided additional pressure on the debtor to repay and facilitated legal action if needed.[39] A parallel shift evidently occurred in real estate transactions. By the late sixteenth century, it was becoming more common for property holders to require that a person taking out a lease furnish a bond, backed by other people, guaranteeing payment of the rent.

This credit transition had a profound gendered impact. Throughout the later medieval and early modern periods, many women loaned relatively small amounts of money to relatives, friends, neighbors, and acquaintances. But by around 1600, although women were still active at lower and sometimes middling levels of the credit system, they rarely appear as large commercial lenders, even in London. Only a few wives of prosperous men or widows with inherited resources were able to compete in the more profitable field of activity that was emerging above them.

---

[37] Tittler, "Money-Lending."   [38] *The Economy of Obligation*, p. 7.

[39] Recent work shows, however, that in rural communities and regions farther away from the capital, some features of the older set of attitudes and practices continued at least through the seventeenth century (e.g., Holderness, "Credit in a Rural Community" and his "Widows," and Muldrew, *The Economy of Obligation*, esp. pt. II). Other scholars have suggested that this attitude had already appeared in London and the larger communities by the later sixteenth century (e.g., Tawney, in his introduction to Wilson, *A Discourse upon Usury*). By the later seventeenth and eighteenth centuries, according to the argument of Adam Smith and some subsequent historians, the goals of money-lending had shifted further still, aimed now at the principle of personal profit and individual self-interest.

Table 1. *The purchasing power of £10 if held as cash for a decade, 1500–1619*[a]

£10 acquired and stored in this decade	had this purchasing power in the following decade (in £s)
1500s	9.1
1510s	8.6
1520s	9.6
1530s	8.3
1540s	6.2
1550s	10.1
1560s	9.0
1570s	8.4
1580s	8.0
1590s	10.1
1600s	8.5
1610s	10.1

[a] These figures are based upon the "cost of living" values, which are indexed against a base of 1450–99, provided in table XVI of Thirsk (ed.), *The Agrarian History of England and Wales*, vol. IV, p. 865. The value for a given decade was divided by that of the following one and multiplied by £10.

For women who wanted to make a profit from lending, charging interest was essential. Some loans of goods, money, or land were made simply out of family loyalty or friendship, but in an inflationary economy, a woman needed to collect interest just to maintain the purchasing power of her money at a constant level. To make a gain on her investment, she had to charge more than the rate of inflation. Table 1 lays out the fall in the purchasing power of £10 if it were held as cash for a decade during the period 1500–1619. In only three of these twelve decades would a person have had as much or more spending power at the end of ten years as at the start, and the gains in value during those decades were only 1 percent. During three other decades, the decline in value was 4–10 percent, but in five decades the loss was 14–20 percent. Across the disastrously inflationary 1540s, the original £10 would have dropped by 38 percent. Further, these losses compounded over time: a person who stored away £10 in 1570 would have had the equivalent of only £6.7 by 1590.

During the fourteenth and fifteenth centuries, the amount of interest charged on a loan was usually not recorded, due to the Catholic Church's prohibition of usury. The interest was instead disguised within the amount to be repaid (e.g., if 40s. had been loaned, the agreement would simply state that the borrower owed the lender 42s. at the end of the term). As the sixteenth century progressed, interest was more openly acknowledged, especially after the passage of legislation in 1571 that in practice exempted interest from the potential charge of usury if it was under 10 percent.[40] Interest was now becoming standard even on very small loans, though the exact length of the loan seems to have mattered little to the rate so long as the term was no more than around six months.

Although interest rates during the fifteenth and sixteenth centuries were commonly 5–7 percent, court cases involving women reveal some much higher rates, even in disputes where the amount of interest was not at issue.[41] At the lower end of the interest spectrum were the loans of Anne Martin, wife of Brian Broughton of the Middle Temple, London.[42] During the 1580s she loaned money several times to John Marratt of London, a messenger for the queen, acting sometimes with her husband, at other times in her own right. John was about to repay the £120 he owed her in one of his obligations when she suggested that he keep it for several years more, paying interest of "fifteen pounds in the hundred." Around 1583, Margery Guest, a widow of an unstated place, borrowed £300 to pay her late husband's debts and invest in her own business.[43] She was obliged to pay interest at the rate of £25/£100. An even higher rate was charged by Florence Wymarke, a Suffolk widow who in the 1560s or 1570s loaned Thomas Kempe 100 marks (= £66 13s. 4d.) for interest of £21 (= 31 percent). A few women lenders were formally accused of usury for demanding too much interest. Grace Scott of Retford, Notts., loaned a noble (= 6s. 8d.) to Richard Barley's wife for a week in 1592, but when she demanded 11d. (= 14 percent) "for the use thereof," she was summoned before a church court, "suspected and defamed as a usurer."[44]

Whereas charging interest at a moderate level was thus functionally legal as well as widespread by the later sixteenth century, some discomfort apparently lingered among local people concerning its use. Around Michaelmas 1586, widow Joan Henman of Kent agreed to loan £20 to Edward Norton, a gentleman of Devington, Kent.[45] In return he signed a security bond for £40, which would be due if he failed to pay Joan the £20 at Michaelmas 1587, together with 40s. in interest (which Joan described as the charge for "forbearing" the loan). Before the due date of the original loan, Edward asked to extend it for another year, at the same rate of interest. At Joan's request, however, he delivered to her 3 quarters (= 24 bushels) of barley in place of the 40s. due for the extra year, "for,

[40] Jones, *God and the Moneylenders.*   [41] Dyer, *Making a Living*, p. 327.
[42] PRO REQ 2/40/64.   [43] PRO REQ 2/65/56. For below, see PRO C 3/105/86.
[44] Marcombe, *English Small Town Life*, p. 108.   [45] PRO C 2/Eliz/N5/6.

as she said, she would not have it known that she lent any money upon interest."

When money was loaned out, it and whatever interest had been arranged were not necessarily repaid as cash. In a medieval pattern that continued into the early seventeenth century in the north of England, the loan might be settled through goods and/or labor of equivalent value. In the 1580s, Beatrice Byers, the unmarried daughter of John Byers of County Durham, loaned £11 5s. to Thomas Comyn, a yeoman of "Hebenden Rawe," Durham.[46] He agreed to repay the sum at the end of three years, giving her 33s. 3d. (= 15 percent) in interest annually during that term. When Beatrice married Roger Pattyson of Hampsterly, Durham, yeoman, before the debt was due, Thomas agreed with Roger that he would repay his debt to Beatrice in the form of cattle: two oxen, one mare, and twenty ewes. Margaret Kylner, a widow of Ulverston, Lancs., loaned 5s. to Agnes Corkes, a neighboring widow, in the early 1610s. Part of the condition of repayment was that Agnes would harvest and bring into Margaret's barn some of the grain growing on Margaret's land. When Agnes failed to do so, Margaret sued, claiming she was left unprovided with food. In 1596–7 Robert Smyth, a husbandman of Clent, Staffs., borrowed £6 from Elizabeth Coxe, wife of Thomas Coxe, who lived in the same parish.[47] Elizabeth required that he sign a bill made out to Dorothy Coxe, her daughter, for repayment of the loan plus 12s. interest (= 10 percent) at the end of one year. After Elizabeth's death, Smyth repaid his £6 12s. debt in the form of £3 in cash given to Dorothy's father Thomas, plus 15 strikes of rye worth 35s., $11\frac{1}{2}$ strikes of barley malt worth 28s. 9d., and 12d. in cash given to Dorothy.[48]

During the later 1540s and 1550s, money-lending and other credit relationships became more complicated due to the rapidly changing value of the English currency. Debasement of the coinage offered fine opportunities to knowledgeable and unscrupulous people. John Bengemyn, citizen of Norwich, pleaded against Agnes Sotherton, a Norwich widow, in the later 1550s, claiming that he had previously borrowed £100 from her, with the agreement that he would repay the sum in a year, plus £10 interest; she required him to sign a bond for a larger amount to secure the loan.[49] When, however, he came to Agnes to repay the £110, she asked him to wait another year, for she had learned that the value of

---

[46] PRO DURH 2/1, no. 26 (in pencil), Comyn vs. Pattyson. For below, see PRO PL 6/2, 26 September 1612.

[47] PRO REQ 2/307/48.

[48] The strike, a local unit of measure for grain, ranged from 0.5 to 4 bushels but was commonly equal to 1 bushel.

[49] PRO C 1/1406/34, and cf. PRO REQ 2/25/245.

money was about to change. If he deferred payment of the original £100, she would excuse the £10 interest. He agreed, but later she sued him in a court in Norwich for the full bonded amount. Even in rural communities, lenders attempted to take advantage of the changing value of money. In the early 1550s, John Ingram claimed that Joan and William Kerbye, a butcher of Wedmore, Som., illegally used the debasement of the currency to their own advantage.[50]

Women's participation in money-lending was affected by their marital status. This was probably an especially important economic activity for singlewomen because they had few other ways to utilize productively any cash they owned. In an analysis of a somewhat later period, nominally covering 1550 to 1750 but with nearly all her evidence post-1600, Amy Froide found that nearly half of forty-five singlewomen in a sample of Hampshire wills and inventories had debts owing to them.[51] Some of these were probably for outstanding cash loans. A slightly higher proportion of those singlewomen who were servants at the time of their deaths were owed money, but some of their debts may have stemmed from unpaid wages rather than loans.

Servants who were attempting to accumulate a stock to help set up their own household after marriage sometimes loaned out their wages or any reservoirs of cash or goods. Margaret Prater, a servant in Romford, died in 1598 before her planned marriage.[52] Evidently using the wages she had gained as a servant, she had extended six cash loans, four of them to other women, ranging in size from 2s. to £2 4s. Ellyn Fynche, a singlewoman of Stoke by Clare, Suffolk, pleaded against Peter Lynsell of Saxsford, Herts., in 1581 for £20 which she claimed to have loaned him while she was working as a servant with William Bigge. Lynsell not only denied the debt but noted scornfully that she could not have loaned him that much money since she was only a servant, "having little but her wages." Alice Bankes, the unmarried daughter of a brasier (= brass worker) in Wigan, Lancs., claimed in a petition from 1609 that her father was "but a poor man . . . and hath been for divers years past sore charged with a great number of small children."[53] She, "being one of the eldest sort and being minded to ease her said father of part of his great charge," left home, "being young and of tender years," to work as a servant. After some years she had "by her own industry and the help and assistance of her said father gathered and gotten together" money, cloth, and other

[50] PRO C 1/1304/6.
[51] "Surplus Women." Of the seven female inventories in her sample prior to 1600 (all from the 1580s–90s and five belonging to servants), four had debts owing to them.
[52] ERO D/AER 17, 254. For below, see PRO REQ 2/204/46.
[53] PRO PL 6/1, no. 139.

items worth £6. John Alread of Atherton, Lancs., a smith, knew that Alice had these possessions and persuaded her that she "could make little or no benefit thereof by letting the same lie and remain still in her own hands." If she let him use her money and goods, he promised to return to her later the £6 plus interest at the rate of 2s. per £1 (= 10 percent). At first she refused, telling John that those possessions constituted all, or at least the greatest part, of the estate which she had accumulated for her maintenance and future life. Should she be defrauded of them, "she were utterly undone." Eventually, however, she gave in to his urgings, letting him have those possessions and later delivering to him additional money and goods amounting to another £4. Contrary to his promise, however, John kept her wealth in his own hands for two years, not increasing it at all, and then refused either to return her money and goods or to pay any interest for them.

Inheritances of money or goods were commonly loaned by young women to their masters/mistresses, relatives, or friends. Under these circumstances, where written contracts were seldom drawn up, it might be particularly difficult for the lender to retrieve the items. Sometime around 1600, Maryann Finckle of Maldon, Essex, received a legacy of £5 from her father.[54] She was at that time a servant with Elizabeth Webb, a widow in Maldon, to whom she delivered the money to hold for her. Elizabeth died six years later, not having returned Maryann's money. In the meantime, Maryann had been persuaded by Elizabeth's son, John Hosier, to loan him first £5 and later another £10. That money plus her £5 inheritance constituted her entire wealth. John then died, but his widow denied that Maryann had loaned any money to her husband and challenged her claim that she had possessed such sums: "by her service [Maryann] did not or could not enrich herself in money, but only keep herself in necessary apparel." Widow Hosier claimed that she had repaid the £5 that Maryann had originally deposited with Elizabeth Webb and, moved by pity, had assisted her in various ways. She gave her small sums of money over time, paid some of her debts, bought her a gown and petticoat, and gave her 30s. and a bushel of rye at the time of her marriage to William Pake of Latchingdon, Essex, a weaver of fustian (= a cheap, sturdy cloth). Even one's own family might not be reliable. Jenett Mawdesley of Hoole, Lancs., was left goods worth £15 by her father in 1606.[55] Being unmarried, she asked her brother Thomas "to use and employ her goods and portion together with his own part to both their best commodities, advantage, and profits that might be." When Jenett married Ralph Lach of Hutton, Lancs., a husbandman, Thomas refused to return either her portion or the increase he had received from it, "by color of some fraudulent acquittance or release deceitfully gotten into his hands."

Married women too loaned money, especially if they or their husbands were not involved in economic activities conducive to investment of extra cash in a family enterprise. To do so, however, the law required that they have the agreement of their husbands. This must have been a stumbling block for many married women who wished to loan money or work as a pawnbroker on their own: husbands might not be willing to accept the additional responsibility of their wife's transactions. It is also an obstacle for historians who use common law records as evidence. The petitions submitted to equity courts are more useful, for these courts were willing to accept the claim that a woman had loaned or borrowed money or goods without her husband's knowledge and therefore should be treated as a separate actor. Married women or their husbands were thus free to manipulate what appears to have been in some cases a legal fiction – that the husband was ignorant of his wife's transactions – in whatever ways best suited their needs. In this respect, the stance of the equity courts concerning married women's credit dealings resembled the way that London city courts and the central equity courts treated claims of *femme sole* status among married producers and traders of goods.[56]

In some cases it was claimed that married women had loaned money without their husband's knowledge. Joan Wythers, wife of Thomas Wythers, the parson of the rectory and parish church of St. Martin Orgar in London, was a regular, large-scale, and atypical lender during Elizabeth's reign.[57] Her husband was said to have been unaware of the loans she made, in units of several hundreds pounds. Richard Champyon alone owed her £600 after a reckoning of all his individual debts and payments to her. One wonders whether it was thought inappropriate for a clergyman to be involved with money-lending: if his wife invested their collective resources in this way, he could say he knew nothing about it.

Married men could plead their own prior ignorance when trying to recover money or goods loaned by their wives. Hugh Parker of Whitechapel, alias of St. Mary Matfellow, Middx., yeoman, claimed that his wife Alice, a simple woman, had been persuaded to loan a total of £20 out of his ready money as well as "a certain precious stone called a diamond" to Marcus Bellamy of the parish of St. George, Surrey, a brasier, and his wife Katherine.[58] These loans were made over a period of years beginning in 1591, without his knowledge. When he learned of

---

[56] McIntosh, "The Benefits and Drawbacks of *Femme Sole* Status."
[57] PRO REQ 2/64/33.   [58] PRO C 2/Eliz/P10/40.

them, after Marcus Bellamy's death, he brought suit against Katherine. The claim of a wife's action without the husband's approval could be used in more complicated situations as well. George Manyfolde of St. Botolph without Billingsgate, a London cook, pleaded against Francis West, a trumpeter, in 1604.[59] George said that on 1 August of the previous year, his wife Phyllis "privily and without [his] knowledge" loaned £40 of his money to West, without any written documentation or witness present. When she later told George what she had done, he demanded that Francis repay the debt. Francis refused, whereupon George took action against him in a London city court; there Francis confessed to having received £20 from Phyllis but denied the rest. Another version of the story is provided by Francis' answer. He claimed that Phyllis had previously been married to Richard Gimminges, a neighbor and friend of his. After Richard's death from plague the previous summer, Francis and Phyllis continued their familiarity, and he hoped she had "some affection touching marriage between them." But when the plague continued, killing two of Phyllis' children and a manservant, he decided to "go into his country [= county] to his friends." Out of friendship and kindness, he alleged, Phyllis gave him £20 in early July, "willing him to employ it if he had need" and without any mention that it was a loan. When he returned from the country in August, he found Phyllis married to George, whereupon he voluntarily repaid her that £20.

Widows with extra money were frequent lenders and seem to have been recognized as such by their contemporaries. Around 1480 the prior of Taunton, John Ashe, came to Alice Chester of Bristol, widow, asking to borrow £20 in money.[60] He explained that he was in great poverty "for lack of goods to repair his house and pay such debts as he ought." Alice agreed to make the loan, but only if he found two other people willing to sign a bond with him. Widow Hester Powkes, apparently of London, loaned money during Elizabeth's reign to one of a group of men trying to obtain a royal patent granting the exclusive right to deal in starch for seven years; she also loaned £50 to a gentleman from Kingston upon Thames, Surrey, and a foreign merchant living in London, bonded for a larger amount.[61] These transactions suggest that Hester was a commercial money-lender. Froide's analysis of female credit in Southampton, 1550–1750, shows that of the widows for whom wills and inventories survive, 47 percent had debts owing to them.[62] Widows did not,

[59] PRO REQ 2/395/44.
[60] PRO C 1/60/62. Maud Knight, a widow of an unspecified place, likewise had trouble reclaiming the money she loaned to Sir William Skulser, priest, in the 1490s (C 1/254/50).
[61] PRO C 2/Eliz/A4/60 and C 2/Eliz/E5/34.   [62] Froide, "Surplus Women."

however, loan out as large a fraction of their total estate as did single-women, implying a more cautious policy. Widows were also more likely than singlewomen to have borrowed money themselves.

Women must often have been at a disadvantage when it came to recovering unpaid loans. Quite apart from the inability of married women to bring debt cases before the common law courts in their own name, their domestic responsibilities and the problems that confronted women traveling alone impeded their efforts to force their debtors to pay. A female lender might therefore make arrangements with a man to collect her debts, perhaps someone to whom she herself owed money. Around 1480, a singlewoman of London whose first name was Julian was owed debts amounting to at least £8 by various people.[63] Because she in turn owed a small sum to Robert Berfote of London, woolpacker, Julian agreed to give him 40s. as a reward for collecting and delivering to her the other amounts owed to her. She later claimed, after her marriage to Robert Lynne, that Berfote had collected £7 15s. from her debtors but given not a penny of it to her. During the 1560s or 1570s, Dorothy Shordiche, a widow of Wiggenton, Herts., owed £40 to Thomas Astrie of Stoke Goldington, Bucks., gentleman. Telling him that she had outstanding debts of great value due to her, she named Thomas as her attorney to collect her loans, which he was to use to repay himself. Later, however, Thomas claimed that she had forgiven the debts of many of the people who owed her money, so he was unable to recover the full £40.

3   Pawning goods

Another form of money-lending consisted of granting cash to a borrower who had delivered goods (= pawns) of greater value, to be held as surety. If the loan was repaid as stipulated, plus the interest, the pawned goods were returned. (The pawnbroker sometimes gained additional income by renting out the items to other people in the meantime.) Should the debtor default on the loan, however, the holder of the goods could sell them to recover the value of the debt, keeping any profit. Pawning might be the only means whereby people could get cash if they had a poor reputation for creditworthiness, no relatives or friends willing or financially able to sign a bond with them, and/or no landed property to use as collateral for a loan.

This form of security was used in debt relationships of many kinds throughout the later medieval and early modern periods, in England as

[63] PRO C 1/64/252. For below, see PRO C 3/2/118.

on the continent.[64] In 1465, for example, the Dominican Friars in York used jewels, books, and other precious items as pawns at a time when they were desperate for cash.[65] Pawning was, however, especially common among poor people or those new to a community who had not yet established a credit record. While London women occasionally appear in the equity court petitions as pawnbrokers during the later medieval and early modern period, women were more commonly cited as borrowers. Pawnbroking probably increased in the late sixteenth century as poverty worsened. In early seventeenth-century Salisbury, goods held as pawns are listed in a few widows' inventories, and poor female pawnbrokers were sometimes presented by the court for selling stolen goods.[66]

Pawning was generally done on a fairly informal basis during the later medieval years, with people agreeing to provide cash or a desired item if given some of the borrower's possessions as surety. Local court cases from the fourteenth and fifteenth centuries often speak of goods left with another person "for safekeeping" but not returned.[67] While some of those items may have been stored merely as a favor to another person, many were probably goods that had been delivered as pawns to secure a cash loan. As late as the closing years of the fifteenth century, some pawning arrangements were still described quite loosely, with no value assigned to the goods given as pledge. Elizabeth Langshot, a London widow, borrowed money from William Fosbroke, gentleman, "upon certain gear of hers" sometime around 1480.[68] In the early 1480s, widow Margery Bedon of London – moved, as she claimed, by great pity – agreed to loan 30s. to Richard Luddelowe, for which she received from him "as pledge" three pairs of sheets and two shirts as well as his promise in good faith to repay the loan.

If a lender doubted the borrower's ability to clear the debt, the value of goods required as a pawn might be considerably larger than the loan. In the early fourteenth century, for example, Juliana Coty of Chester received 4d. in cash but only after pledging a cloth worth 16d.; in the later fourteenth century, Margaret, servant of William de Strelley of Nottingham, had to pledge two linen sheets worth nearly 7s. to get a cash loan of

[64] For a general discussion of pawnbroking in pre-industrial Europe, one that emphasizes women's roles as borrowers and men (including Jews) as lenders, see Jordan, *Women and Credit*, pp. 32–8.

[65] Kermode, "Money and Credit," p. 495, note 78.

[66] Wright, "Churmaids," p. 111. For women's pawning during the later seventeenth and early eighteenth centuries, see Lemire, "Women, the Informal Economy and the Development of Capitalism," her "Petty Pawns and Informal Lending," and Earle, *Making of the English Middle Class*, pp. 168–71.

[67] McIntosh, "Money Lending," and Foulds, "Women and Work."

[68] PRO C 1/64/683. For below, see C 1/61/372.

2s.[69] When the wife of a tanner in Writtle, Essex, needed to borrow 8s. around 1390 but did not want her husband to know about it, the lender, a local butcher, demanded that she put up collateral worth more than three times the loan: she delivered to him a bed cover and canopy worth 13s. 4d., gold-buckled shoes worth 3s., silver-plated earrings worth 40d., and cloth worth 6s.

The line between pawning and other forms of credit was sometimes fuzzy. Before it became standard practice for bonds to be co-signed by people other than the borrower, collateral in the form of goods might be required in addition to the debtor's own bond. Around 1480, Alice Deyster, a widow of Coventry, borrowed money from William Broun, a London mercer, for which he required that she become bonded to him (without co-signers) for £21. Evidently doubting her creditworthiness, however, he also insisted that she deliver plate to him worth £21 to keep until the original debt had been paid.[70] On a smaller scale at that same time, Margery Reve, a widow of Winchester, was required to deliver into the keeping of Stephen Braundon, a brewer of Winchester, "divers goods and chattels" of her own which she claimed were worth £4 before he was willing to give her ale worth 16s. on credit.

By the later sixteenth century, some lenders seem to have specialized in pawning, especially in London. These professional or semi-professional pawnbrokers sometimes engaged in long strings of transactions with borrowers, with escalating amounts of credit and collateral. Beginning around 1564, Katherine Fitz James of London pawned a series of her physically transportable, valuable possessions to David Gough of London, fruiterer, and his wife Alice in return for cash.[71] She first "pledged and laid to pawn" for £5 a little chain of gold, three hoop rings of gold, and a gold thimble. Later, needing more money, she returned to the Goughs' house, delivering to Alice a more valuable gold chain worth £20 and receiving back the little chain she had left there before. Sometime after that she conveyed to David Gough a small, locked chest that she said contained diverse goods and chattels worth £40 as well as some written documents, including the bill of sale for the £20 gold chain. Her petition to the Court of Requests against the Goughs was submitted only in 1589–90, indicating a credit relationship extending over twenty-five years.

Another type of pawning is described in a long complaint lodged in 1612 by Robert Radcliffe of Manchester, Lancs., a gentleman, against

---

[69] Goldberg, "Female Labour"; Foulds, "Women and Work." For below, see Elaine Clark, "Debt Litigation."
[70] PRO C 1/60/50. For below, see C 1/64/837.   [71] PRO REQ 2/28/47.

John Glover and his wife Ellen, said to be "wandering tinkers."[72] Robert claimed that the Glovers, whom he described as "of very base condition and disordered life, and getting their living by many unlawful shifts and usurious bargains," had come to the door of his house at various times. There they persuaded his wife Judith, who was known for her "simplicity" and was easily tricked, to borrow a total of £5 from them. She agreed to paying interest at the rate of 6d. per £1 each week, amounting to a startling annual rate of 130 percent. Moreover, as security for those loans Judith had delivered to the Glovers a long list of clothing and household items together worth £23. More recently, she had handed over some pewter platters and a featherbed as further pawns. All these transactions, Robert emphasized, had occurred without his knowledge. He had already brought suit against the Glovers in the manor court at Manchester for detention of goods, but the tinkers shut the door of the house where they were staying and would not allow the bailiff to seize any of their goods in connection with Robert's action. Hence Robert turned to the equity court of the Duchy of Lancaster.

A question that complicated some pawning arrangements was whether the loan had to be repaid by/on a stated day, as was the case with most bond-based debts, or whether the pawned goods could be redeemed at any time upon repayment of the loan. Normally the latter condition pertained, but that could lead to problems if the pawnbroker had temporarily rented out the items to someone else. In 1610, widow Anne Lee borrowed £3 10s. from Thomas Warwicke, for which she pawned to him a long list of women's clothing, bedding, linens, and cooking and eating utensils.[73] When Anne brought suit against Thomas four years later, she said that the condition of this arrangement was that if she repaid her loan on a stated day, she would receive her pawned goods back again. On that day she went to Thomas's house, bringing the money with her, and asked to have her pawned items back. He refused, however, to accept her money and would not even let her see her goods. Because "very few were present at the delivery of the said goods that can justly testify the mortgage of them," she brought suit against him in an equity court rather than in the common law. (Note the verbal equation here between the use of goods and land to secure a loan.) Thomas indignantly denied that a date had been fixed for the repayment of her loan: he "doth much wonder at the impudent and shameless boldness of [Anne], in that she dareth so falsely to affirm in the said bill that there was a day or time prefixed and agreed

---

[72] PRO DL 1/250, Radcliffe vs. Glover, May 1612. "Tinker" was a pejorative term for an itinerant trader or mender of pots.
[73] PRO REQ 2/302/20. She valued the goods at £17 4s. Both parties were from unspecified places.

upon betwixt [Anne] and him . . . for the redeeming and having again of the same goods." If there was no fixed date, he was within his rights to have rented out her goods until she repaid his cash.

Legal action could also result from disputes over how long the pawn holder had to keep the goods in his possession before being allowed to sell them. This issue was at the heart of a suit brought in the Mayor's Court of London by William de Mount Seins, the borrower, against Katherine de Lincoln in 1300.[74] William demanded that Katherine return to him an iron horse-cuirass (= a kind of armor) plus a pair of armor plates covered with cloth of gold and expensive silk fabric; he had pledged those items to her as security for the 35s. he owed to a member of Katherine's household. Katherine said that the pawns had been delivered to her servant, Peter de Armenters, and asked that he be summoned to answer with her. Peter then brought into court an earlier document signed by William stating that if he had not paid the 35s. he owed to Katherine by Easter, she might sell the pledged goods, paying him any surplus over the 35s. When William did not pay, the pledges were sold but yielded only 22s. 1d. On that basis, Katherine and Peter were acquitted. In what was probably a parallel case, Mary Convers of London was imprisoned in 1365 for "parting with" a jewel worth 50 marks (= £33 6s. 8d.) that the Count of Harecourt had pledged with her; she in turn pawned the jewel to a Florentine trader in London, who later sold it to yet another man.[75]

The ambiguity between goods delivered as pawns and those which were intended for immediate sale led to some complicated disputes, stemming from either genuine misunderstanding or fraudulent intent. Alice Whyte of London, a married woman operating independently as a moneylender and pawnbroker, alleged that in November 1531, John Walton, a London tailor, brought to her some silver and other plate worth around £5.[76] He asked her to sell the plate for as much ready money as she could get for it, whereupon she negotiated with John Ducke, a London upholster (= refurbisher of used clothing), who offered £5 for the plate. Since that was the best price she could get, she accepted the arrangement and delivered the money to Walton. He, however, brought legal action against her, claiming that he had given her the plate (which he said was worth £8, not merely £5) not to be sold but rather as a pledge for repayment of £4 that he had borrowed from her. He planned to reclaim his goods as soon as he had the money to pay back his loan. But when he later offered Alice the £4, she refused either to accept the cash or to return his goods.

[74] CEMCRL, 1298–1307, pp. 66–7.
[75] CPMRL, 1364–1381, p. 30.   [76] PRO C 1/712/32 (and compare C 1/712/33).

As with money-lending, married women sometimes claimed in their equity petitions that they had engaged in pawning without the knowledge of their husbands. Margaret Bevington, wife of William, of New Sarum (= Salisbury), Hants., was a pawnbroker in 1613.[77] She claimed that when Alice Jefferies, wife of John, a hellier (= slater), needed money for necessary provisions for her family, she came to Margaret, asking to borrow £5 "for some small time." To guarantee the payment of her debt, Alice gave Margaret a dozen silver spoons. Margaret, acting as she claimed without the consent of her husband, delivered the £5 to Alice, who used it "in providing of diet, clothing, and other necessary things for herself and for the household and family of her husband." Margaret emphasized that Alice's husband was well aware of this transaction and fully approved it. About six months later, Alice asked Margaret to return the spoons to her temporarily, because strangers had come to visit her husband. Margaret accepted Alice's promise that she would return the spoons as soon as their visitors left. Alice and her husband, however, having fraudulently recovered these pawns, refused to give them back to Margaret or to repay the original £5 loan. At that point Margaret told her husband, who confronted Alice's husband, but to no avail. Margaret and William then together petitioned the Court of Requests against both Alice and John.

The petitions used in this study provide a little quantitative information about women's roles in money-lending and pawning. In using this material, we must remember that the size of the sample is small and the material skewed by the courts' willingness to hear only certain kinds of debt-related cases.[78] Larger/better documented credit disputes and problems involving married women in which the husband pleaded on behalf of his wife were generally taken before the common law courts. Petitions about borrowing/lending money or pawning goods in return for cash formed one-fifth to two-fifths of all cases during the four sub-periods within the full span of 1470–1619 in the central court sample and just over half of the northern sample (see App. 1.2). Of the women involved in credit relationships in the central court sample, 66 percent loaned money or gave cash in return for pawned goods; another 11 percent provided surety for someone else's obligations; and 23 percent borrowed money

---

[77] PRO REQ 2/422/17. For another example of a husband's supposed ignorance, see REQ 2/173/18.

[78] The petitions exaggerate the frequency of people who described themselves as poor or weak while trying to get justice against a wealthier, more powerful person; they include a disproportionate number of disputes in which petitioners claimed they had no written documentation of their credit dealings; and they emphasize cases in which married women said they had acted without the involvement or even knowledge of their husbands. For a fuller discussion, see Stretton, *Women Waging Law*.

or pawned their goods. The northern court sample and a small sample of debt cases brought before the Exchequer of the Palatinate of Chester, 1567–95, show variations of the same pattern.[79] Of the women in the equity court samples, 15 percent were married, 67 percent were widows, 13 percent were single, and 5 percent were listed in their own names and hence were probably either widows or single.

The depth of women's credit dealings as shown in the equity court petitions was of low or intermediate level and was no higher in real value after 1600 than it had been before 1500. We know the amounts of cash borrowed or granted in return for pawned goods in eighty-four cases plus five values estimated from the size of the bond that backed up a loan.[80] Between 1470 and 1499, the average amount borrowed was £7.1, with a median of just £4.0. When moving to the later sub-periods, we run into the problem of inflation, forcing us to correct the values after 1500 to make them comparable to those in the earlier period.[81] After correction, the average but not the median amount borrowed increased during the period 1500–59 and reached a peak of £20.5 (average) and £5.9 (median) in 1560–99. Both values then declined, to just £7.4 and £3.1 respectively, in the early seventeenth century. The latter sums are very close to those seen prior to 1500. Within the northern sample, averages were lower, suggesting that women were operating at a lower level of credit, but showed the same drop after 1600.[82] All these sums are well above the average

---

[79] Of the northern sample, 54 percent of the women involved in credit relationships provided loans or gave cash for pawned goods, while 3 percent acted as sureties; 44 percent were borrowers. In the Chester cases, 71 percent of the women were owed money (PRO CHES 16, Box 1, CHES 16/2, Box 1, and CHES 16/9, Box 1, all passim, which together yielded thirty-eight debt cases involving women).

[80] In cases where only the bond size is stated, the size of the actual debt was estimated on the basis of bonded values of 1.5 times the amount of the loan for 1470–1509 and 2.0 times the amount of the loan for later periods. These proportions are derived from the size of other bonds where the value of the loan is specified.

[81] Correction for inflation was done as follows. Table XVI in Thirsk, ed., *The Agrarian History of England and Wales*, vol. IV, p. 865, provides a composite "cost of living" value by decade, using an indexed figure of 100 for the period 1450–99. The "cost of living" figure consists of average decadal prices for arable crops (weighted × 5), animal products (weighted × 2), livestock (single weighting), timber (single weighting), and industrial products (single weighting). The prices for the first period used in this analysis, 1470–99, could be left at face value, since they fell within the base period, but those for later periods were adjusted to match the average corrected value for those decades. For 1500–59, nominal prices were divided by 1.545; for 1560–99, by 3.41; and for 1600–19, by 4.765.

[82] For 1540–99, a corrected average of £4.3 and median of £2.1; for 1600–19, an average of £1.1 and median of £0.8. Debts involving women were even smaller in the Cheshire sample, 1567–95: the average was just 23s. 11d. and the median 8s. 4d. after correction for inflation. Since the court of the Exchequer of the Palatinate of Chester was operating in effect as a local court, these values were probably similar to those reported in private suits before many local bodies in the north.

debts recorded in local court records from the fourteenth and fifteenth centuries but far below the large-scale loans made by professional lenders that were becoming more common after around 1560.[83]

The central court sample contained few substantial loans. During the later fifteenth century, six of the ten loans were for less than £5, three were for £6–19, and only one was for £20–49. By the Elizabethan period, after correction for inflation, the distribution was shifting slightly upwards, with two above £50, but by the early seventeenth century the pattern was again similar to that seen prior to 1500, with none above £50. Loans in the northern sample were concentrated even more heavily at the lower end of the range. While wealthier women engaged in larger transactions may have taken their cases to other courts, it is clear that the credit relationships of many women involved relatively small amounts of money.

4   Renting out property

Another way for women to invest extra resources was to buy urban property which would then be leased out. Owning and renting residential or commercial buildings provided a relatively secure means of bringing in a regular income. Although there was always the danger of fire or the willful destruction of property, holding urban property might be a safer investment than lending money or going into trade. The limited information we have, primarily from equity court petitions, suggests that it became more common during the later sixteenth century for women to hold and rent out urban property for income. While many female owners were widows, married women too could be involved if they acted with their husbands. We may be witnessing here the early stages of the pattern clearly visible during the later seventeenth and early eighteenth centuries, when London contained a substantial group of female *rentiers*, living off the income from their properties.[84]

Landladies necessarily became involved in credit relationships. The personal standing of a prospective tenant was an important factor in deciding whether to grant a lease, and if a renter fell behind in his or her payments, both parties had to make difficult decisions. The property holder could either extend credit (perhaps by lengthening the term of the lease) in hopes that payment would eventually be made, or try to recover

---

[83] See sect. 1 above. Kowaleski found an average debt of £10 16s. in 103 pleas of debt and account brought by Exeter residents, many of them merchants, in the Court of Common Pleas, 1377–88 (*Local Markets and Regional Trade*, pp. 214–15). For a cluster of eight loans ranging from £50 to £300 made by a Romford urban yeoman in 1572–3, see McIntosh, *A Community Transformed*, pp. 139–44 and 158.

[84] Earle, *Making of the English Middle Class*, pp. 168–74.

the property into her own hands, which might require legal action against the tenant. The tenant had to decide which of the financial obligations he or she faced was most urgent, perhaps trying to negotiate an extension on the due date for the rent or a lowering of its value.

In some cases, female owners lived in part of the building, while in others the whole property was leased out. In the 1570s, Katherine Knott, a widow in Chelmsford, Essex, leased a messuage called "Olivers" to John Sympson for a term of years, reserving a chamber for herself over the entryway and shop of the house.[85] She later charged that John did not pay his rent and denied her access to her chamber. His response claimed that after her second marriage, Katherine and her new husband moved to Stratford on Bowe, Middx., to run an inn or victualing house. Because she had left Chelmsford, John made use of her chamber himself, as was legal for him to do. In 1618, Mary West, widow of a London stationer, held a building whose rooms she leased to others.[86] Among her tenants was Robert Jones of London, gentleman, who took the "low parlor or room with a study therein, and a little entry or place to lay wood and coals in adjoining to the said parlor." With his room, Robert gained access also to the yard and privy, to be used in common with Mary's other tenants. His lease ran for thirteen years, during which she was to receive 13s. 4d. in annual rent. Sometime during Elizabeth's reign, Katherine Allen and her husband William rented to Richard Holland, gentleman, "certain chambers and rooms" within a house held by the Allens, paying 5s. weekly.[87] Richard later claimed to have paid his rent each week, into Katherine's or William's hands, but he had no receipts for these payments, which he said came to £6 15s. 4d. in sum. He was therefore vulnerable when the Allens sued him for debt.

Rental property might also be seen by women as a comparatively safe nest egg for their children. In the 1590s, Elizabeth Romsey was left a widow after the death of her first husband, Arthur Parkins, a haberdasher of London.[88] When she later decided to re-marry, to Walter Romsey of Staple Inn, she was concerned about the financial security of her seven sons by her first husband, "unadvanced in marriage and otherwise unprovided for." She therefore bought the lease of a tenement near Newgate market in 1597. Giving control over the property to apothecary William Compton, her son-in-law, she asked him to rent it out on leases of no longer than four years each to the profit of her sons.

Many types of property could yield an income. Joan Ruggewyn, widow, held eighteen booths or stalls at Sturbridge Fair on the outskirts of

Cambridge during the early 1480s, booths that she presumably rented out at fair time.[89] She was cautious in assigning away her right to these booths: when she decided to grant them temporarily to John Wyghton, she recorded the transfer and term in the presence of the mayor of Cambridge. Ursula Bannester, who was described in her own name, not as a married woman, held the farm of the queen's two grain mills in Grantham, Lincs., in 1586.[90] In return for paying an annual rent to the Exchequer, she was allowed to keep whatever profit she could make above that amount. A suit brought against her alleged that she had taken excess toll, failed to maintain the mills adequately, and demanded that all local people bring their grain to her mill instead of to one of the others in the town. Even water could be leased. During the Elizabethan period, Anne and Peter Morrys of London acquired a "conduit or Pipe of Lead" that carried water from the Thames to a house they held but rented out.[91] After Peter's death, Anne was approached by Hugh George of the parish of St. Mary Magdalen in London, who wanted to lease for twenty-one years a side pipe leading from her building to his nearby dwelling. That proved complicated, however, for Anne had already leased the main pipe together with her house to William Harward, gentleman.

Our survey of women's service roles has indicated that although these functions were essential to the functioning of households and the broader economy, most types of participation open to women offered only limited earnings and little occupational status or social credit. The many young women and some older ones who worked as residential servants had to be obedient and deferential to their masters and mistresses and received scant pay. Women who took in boarders, worked in other people's houses, or offered simple nursing care were generally poor. Those who did sex work or loaned money for interest might be condemned on moral grounds. Apart from a few skilled providers of health care, service work did not bring social respect. Only a few money-lenders and landladies – either widows with considerable capital or married women whose husbands at least tacitly backed their activity – gained a good income. We turn now to women's involvement in the world of production and sales, settings in which their labor was again vital and their economic and social standing could in some periods rise a little higher.

[89] PRO C 1/65/166.   [90] PRO E 134/28 Eliz/East 19.
[91] PRO REQ 2/101/17. For the development of a piped water supply for London, see Jenner, "From Conduit Community."

Part III

Making and selling goods

5   General features of women's work as producers and sellers

The remainder of this study examines women's work in production and sales. The manufacturing and retailing sectors of the English economy were reliant upon female labor, but it was concentrated at the bottom of those systems. We begin by surveying some general features of women's roles in making and retailing goods, patterns that will recur in our subsequent discussion of specific types of trade and craftwork. We look here also at female apprentices and at women's roles in training apprentices. The next two chapters deal with types of work in which women could use the skills they had acquired as daughters or adolescent servants to produce something that would bring in cash. Brewing and selling ale were the income-generating activities most commonly pursued by English women, at least until the fifteenth century.[1] In most food trades and innkeeping, women generally played only secondary roles. We turn then to female participation in craftwork, types of activity that required more specialized training and skills. There we consider the extensive involvement of women in making cloth and clothing, where they were concentrated in the least skilled and most poorly paid stages of production, and their limited activity within other crafts.[2] At the end, we glance briefly at women's activities as consumers. Throughout this discussion we must remember that although we consider the various types of market engagement separately, in practice they were not mutually exclusive categories: some

---

[1] While most historians classify brewing and selling ale as a trade, Kowaleski, in her analysis of the economy of late fourteenth-century Exeter, does not count brewing as a separate occupation because it was rarely pursued by men or sustained a family (*Local Markets and Regional Trade*).

[2] We will not discuss the very limited involvement of some women, almost all widows, in mining or other industrial activities. For a few examples of tin mining in Cornwall, see PRO C 1/107/83 and C 1/253/45; for lead and coal mining in the north, PRO DL 1/74/W1, DL 1/250, Bowes vs. Nicholas Marples et al., 14 May 1612, DL 1/179/A36, and DL 1/204/O1; for stone quarrying in Devon, PRO E 134/3 Jas I/Hil 15; for a wich house for making salt in Cheshire, PRO CHES 16/2, Box 1, Katheryne Bromfeld vs. Ellen Bromfeld; and for an industrial patent to make "train oil," PRO REQ 2/43/63, E 134/39 Eliz/East 1, and E 134/39 Eliz/East 27.

women did several kinds of manufacturing or trading at the same time or pursued service work as well.

1   Characteristics of production and sale

Credit, in its various meanings, was an essential component of the practices whereby goods were produced and sold. Vendors needed to assess the ability of prospective purchasers to pay and their reliability in completing transactions before deciding what price to charge and what terms to offer for payment and delivery of the items. If the economic trustworthiness of a buyer was in doubt, she might be asked to leave other items to ensure that she would eventually pay for what she had taken. Around 1520, Dorothy Ferman, a London widow who was retailing textiles on a small scale, took merchandise worth 26s. 8d. from Edward Hollyns, a haberdasher of London.[3] To secure her debt, she delivered other items worth 40s. to him: 15 dozen pincases worth 30s., $1\frac{1}{2}$ yards of white kersey cloth worth 4s., and black cloth for a coat worth 6s. This resembled pawning, but with goods received instead of a cash payment. On the other side, buyers had to evaluate the reputation of producers and sellers with respect to the quality of the items, the price, and the terms proposed.[4] Because many women made or sold some kind of goods and virtually all women made at least occasional purchases, credit assessments like these were pervasive.

More formal credit relationships arose from the widespread practice of delaying payment for goods and/or postponing delivery of them. Women engaged in the food/drink trades, craftwork, and shopkeeping routinely bought supplies or merchandise on credit, to be paid for later, after they had gained some income from sales. Elizabeth Lobbe and her husband James traveled overseas around 1480 to buy linen cloth and other wares from Lewis Gerbray, merchant, for a price of £35 13s. 4d.[5] Although they received delivery of the goods then, they were to pay for their purchases at two times in the future: the following Michaelmas (= 29 September), and Christmas of the year after that. On 3 March 1557, Dorothy Rostyll, wife of Robert Rostyll of Birmingham, yeoman, bought $1\frac{1}{2}$ tuns of herrings from Thomas Byldon of Chester at the fair held in Lichfield, Staffs.[6] Of the purchase price of £16, Dorothy paid 40s. on the spot and agreed to pay the remaining £14 on the following Palm Sunday. Unwisely trusting

---

[3] PRO C 1/504/31. When she did not repay her debt, Hollyns brought suit against her and had her put in gaol, despite the fact that he still had the goods she gave him as sureties.
[4] For consumers, see Ch. 9 below.   [5] PRO C 1/64/525.
[6] PRO C 1/1406/99–103. A tun was a large cask used for storing and transporting both liquid and dry goods.

in her word, Thomas allowed her to take all the herring with her to Birmingham to sell. In a case with an unusually insecure date of payment, Joan Perce, a widow of Yarmouth, claimed around 1540 that she had bought from Christopher Carr of Newcastle upon Tyne 100 chaldrons (= 3200–3600 bushels) of sea coal.[7] The arrangement specified that 60 chaldrons would be delivered to her during the coming year and the remaining 40 during the following year. The value of the coal was assessed at £20, but she paid only 6s. 8d. of that amount to Carr at the time of the agreement. The rest was due to him, she said in her equity court petition, either on the day of her marriage or on the day of her death. To cover this arrangement, she signed a bond to Carr for £30.

For contemporaries, a key question was whether women's work in production and sales threatened the livelihood or social position of male household heads. The lower levels of the drink and food trades and cloth-making generated relatively little profit, enough to supplement a family's resources but rarely enough to live on. Hence there was usually no competition from men. Further, such work was seen as a natural outgrowth of women's duties within the home, so there was no obstacle to their participation in cultural terms. Running a craft shop, however, required longer training (acquired usually through a formal apprenticeship), more expensive equipment, and the ability to hire and control labor. As well as yielding a higher income, it took the head of the establishment into the public world, linked often to membership in craft guilds or urban government. According to patriarchal thinking, such positions belonged naturally to men. Under normal circumstances, the few women who headed craft establishments were widows temporarily continuing their husband's business. Only in periods that coupled low population with a fairly healthy economy do we see women filling such roles on their own.

Even within the types of activity that were seen as characteristically female, if a given form of production or sale required greater capital investment or became increasingly profitable, it tended to fall into male hands.[8] We see this in cloth manufacture, for example, where all the preliminary stages involved in preparing the yarn used for weaving were carried out by women. Yet the looms used for production of traditional woolen cloth were typically operated by male weavers (though sometimes assisted by female relatives or servants), and men gained the profits from sale of the cloth.[9] Because women brewed ale for their own families, it was seen as appropriate for them to do so commercially as well. But

[7] PRO C 1/1053/23.
[8] As Joan Thirsk has observed, "If a venture prospers, women fade from the scene" (as cited by Bennett, *Ale, Beer, and Brewsters*, p. 145).
[9] See Ch. 8 below. For below, see Chs. 6–7.

baking – which might have appeared equally well suited to women – was done primarily by men, due probably to their advantages in obtaining the capital and labor needed to acquire and operate an oven. The pattern applies also to the transition from the brewing of ale (done on a small scale by women using simple equipment) to the brewing of beer (which, because it could be stored in kegs and shipped, supported a much larger scale of production and therefore was done almost entirely by men).[10]

Beginning around 1540, deliberate efforts were being made to introduce or expand some types of manufacturing activity within England. These "projects," as Joan Thirsk has labeled them, were designed to increase national wealth, create more employment opportunities, and lessen the country's reliance upon imported goods.[11] The new consumer goods also helped to fuel the growing demand within England for more comfortable or elegant clothing and household furnishings. Because the semi-skilled work created by such projects was almost always "by-employment," labor that could be done in addition to other responsibilities but was not intended to provide full support for a household, it was commonly taken up by poor women. Throughout the following chapters we will encounter references to Elizabethan and Jacobean women carrying out piecework such as knitting woolen caps, stockings, or "bone lace," making starch for stiffening collars or tableware, or making pins that would be used with clothing or hair. While poor women may have welcomed these additional ways of generating some income without having to undertake extensive training, the work carried inherent disadvantages. Payment was generally by the item produced, so women were under pressure to fit in as many hours of work as possible in order to earn the income they needed to get by. Sometimes they were given a fixed deadline by which a certain number of pieces was expected. Poor lighting and cold temperatures must have contributed to the difficulty of their intensely repetitive labor. Further, there was no guarantee of ongoing employment. If the employer or middleman did not need more of the items a woman manufactured, she was out of work, at least for the time being.

The kinds of production and sales work normally done by women thus shared certain features, all of which had negative consequences. Much of their activity was on a part-time basis, and the degree of their involvement commonly varied over time in accordance with their reproductive and economic situation. Because their work generally required few specialized skills and no formal training, women could step into these activities

---

[10] As discussed more fully by Bennett, *Ale, Beer, and Brewsters*.
[11] Thirsk, *Economic Policy and Projects*.

easily, but they conferred little if any occupational identity. The secondary nature of their work meant that it remained subservient to the needs of the male household head. Their activity often occurred within a household setting, which was convenient for women with other domestic responsibilities, but it limited their interactions with other workers in the same field: they did not gain the economic information and enhanced business/ social contacts that might have arisen from such dealings. Further, women who sold in the marketplace or ran alehouses or inns violated the tenet found in prescriptive sources that they should remain at home, under male supervision. During the post-plague period, social discomfort about women who worked in public settings was relatively muted, but by the later sixteenth century, they faced strong disapproval.

Women marketed their merchandise at many levels and in a variety of ways.[12] In the simplest case, the producer (for instance, a small-scale brewer of ale) sold from her own house directly to the consumer (perhaps a neighbor). As the scale of production or importing increased, however, middlemen were needed to convey goods to retailers. This could result eventually in a pyramid of distribution, involving several ranks of intermediaries. The more elaborate the system, the less likely women were to serve as middlemen. One finds some female wholesalers during the fifteenth century, but by the Elizabethan and Jacobean periods such work commonly required an ability to travel, to arrange for transport on a large scale, to establish significant amounts of transportable credit that was valid in a variety of different places, and to use the courts to force repayment from recalcitrant debtors. Because women were handicapped in all those respects, they were effectively excluded from the expanding middle and upper levels of the distribution system. They therefore served primarily as primary-level retailers, selling directly to consumers.

The equity court petitions provide a little numeric information about female sellers, though the numbers are small and the picture affected by the nature of cases the courts would hear. Of ninety-eight women mentioned in the sample during the full span from 1470 to 1619, 34 percent sold cloth or clothing, 28 percent dealt with drink, and 7 percent with food. The remaining 26 percent sold mixed or other goods. Just under half (46 percent) were widows at the time of the economic interaction described in the petition, 34 percent were married, 7 percent were single-women, and 13 percent were described in their own name. A value was given for the goods sold in single transactions in fifty-five cases from the central court group and eight from the northern sample. Since all

---

[12] The examples in this chapter concern women dealing in general or mixed wares, leaving consideration of the particular features of individual trades or crafts for later.

numbers were taken from the petitions, they are probably high-end figures: the person bringing suit in a case involving non-payment for goods had reason to inflate the value of the items sold. Within the central court sample, the average value of the goods traded in 1470–99 was £47.1 and the median was £19. During the sixteenth century, after correction for inflation, the average and median values of goods traded dropped markedly; by the early seventeenth century the average and median values had declined further still, to corrected levels of just £3.5 (average) and £2.9 (median).[13] Consistent with the information about loans of money, values for items sold in the northern sample were even lower: a corrected average of £1.5 and a median of £1.9 in 1540–99 and just £0.3 and £0.2 respectively in 1600–19. Clearly the equity courts were functioning by the mid-sixteenth century as the venue for business-related cases involving people of middling or lower means. What we cannot tell is how much of the declining value of goods reflects an actual contraction in women's roles in trade and how much stems from the use of other courts for larger cases.

In looking more closely at female involvement in the various forms of selling, we will move from the top downwards. Beyond the reach of most women working on their own were the great import and export businesses and the types of merchant activity pursued by the members of London's leading companies.[14] These men traded in a wide range of goods and sold generally to wholesalers, not directly to consumers. During the fifteenth century, however, there were some significant female exceptions, and they were not limited to London. In the early 1420s, for example, while either a singlewoman or a widow, Agnes Pafford of Southampton was trading on a large scale with Brittany. Although we do not know what kinds of goods she was exporting, she certainly knew how to wield political influence. When she was unable to collect the sums owed to her by various Bretons, she obtained letters of marque in 1424–5 from Henry IV of England and the Duke of Britanny authorizing her to seize goods worth 600 crowns from other Bretons.[15] At about the same time, widow Margery Russell of Coventry and her son obtained a letter of marque against merchants in certain towns in the kingdom of Castille and León, to a value of £800, to compensate for goods that had been stolen from Margery by men from Santander.[16]

Other women, too, engaged in foreign trade during the fifteenth and early sixteenth centuries, though without such political muscle. Agnes

[13] For correction for inflation, see sect. 3, Ch. 4 above.
[14] Married women may, of course, have joined their husbands in ways we cannot observe. For examples from Edinburgh, see Ewan, "Mons Meg and Merchant Meg."
[15] PRO C 1/6/247.   [16] Fox, "Coventry Guilds."

Brightwell of London acted through her son-in-law William Gritford, described as "her attorney and merchant overseas," in her international dealings with William Rody, a mercer, in 1406.[17] During the early 1470s, Marion Kent, the widow of John Kent, a wealthy merchant of York, imported not only textile-related goods like cloth, flax, and madder (used as a dye) but also lead, wax, trenchers for food, and tables for playing games. In the later 1470s or mid-1480s, Isabel Benley, a widow of Newcastle upon Tyne, was deeply involved in the purchase and sale of unspecified foreign goods, involving other merchants from Newcastle and Middleburgh, Zealand.[18] Elizabeth Kirkeby traded with Spain during Henry VII's reign. Her agent there was George Bulstrode, a London draper, who claimed that during the course of a single year he had sent merchandise to Elizabeth from Seville whose value came in sum to £4,000. Even when one discounts for legal exaggeration, this was clearly a very large volume of business. By the later sixteenth century, however, one encounters fewer references to women active in import/export trade.

Among female sellers of goods within England, the most fortunate operated from some kind of an indoor shop (see the cover illustration). Open on a daily basis, shops made possible the safe storage of merchandise and provided a comfortable indoor setting for the sociability and leisurely bargaining that accompanied many transactions.[19] The *Dialogues in French and English* published by William Caxton around 1483 includes among its language lessons an amiable bargaining session between a female seller of cloth and a male purchaser, involving the quality of the cloth, the kind of clothing for which it was suited, the measures used to determine its size, and its price per ell.[20]

Shops in late medieval and early modern England commonly consisted of a ground-floor room that fronted directly onto the street. In cities and towns, shop buildings were sometimes multistoried, with a manufacturing or finishing workshop in the back and a living area for the proprietor's family above.[21] If a woman rented a shop that had living quarters attached, or used one room of her house as a shop, she could supervise her children and servants while also dealing with customers. In towns, shop windows were covered by shutters at night; during the day they could be swung down to function as an open counter, protected by an overhanging roof that sheltered clients from the weather. Most shops were furnished

---

[17] CPMRL, 1413–1437, p. 10. For below, see Goldberg, "Women's Work."
[18] PRO C 1/64/44. For below, see Abram, "Women Traders."
[19] See, e.g., PRO REQ 2/63/100, discussed in Ch. 9 below.
[20] *Caxton's Dialogues in French and English*, pp. 15–17. I am grateful to Martha Carlin for this reference. An ell contained 45 inches or 1.25 yards.
[21] Keene, "Shops and Shopping" and Carlin, "'What Will You Buy?'" for this and below.

principally with chests for storing goods and shelves for displaying them. After the plague, as urban landlords became anxious to attract tenants, some shops began to offer more space for display and decoration and occasionally even a fireplace. In London, buildings known as selds lay behind some of the shops that faced onto the street. Selds, described as off-street bazaars, were large structures subdivided into a number of very small trading stations or mini-shops.

Because setting up a shop required capital or credit to rent the space and buy furnishings for it, women were often at a disadvantage. In London, however, we see some businesswomen renting shops throughout the later medieval and early modern period.[22] Before her marriage to William Strokelady (an expressive name!), a London fishmonger, in the early 1370s, widow Matilda Spark took the lease of a shop and warehouse in St. Mary atte Bowe for an annual rent of £7 8s.[23] She was later charged with having allowed a wall to become so ruinous that her buildings were likely to fall down, bringing adjacent ones down with them. Women rented 7.4 percent of the shops/housing units leased out between 1460 and 1484 by the Bridgemasters who controlled the property whose income paid for maintenance of London Bridge.[24] In the late 1590s, Margaret Puncherdon, a widow, leased a shop in the Savoy, London, for a yearly rent of £4.

Equity court petitions make clear that that during the later fifteenth and earlier sixteenth centuries women – especially widows – were operating shops of middling size in many towns. They commonly offered a diverse array of goods whose total value rarely exceeded a few hundred pounds, with individual sales of not more than a few dozen pounds. John Byllyngton of London, draper, agreed in the mid-1510s to buy from widow Elizabeth Feror assorted wares worth £38 10s., including woad (a blue dye for cloth), alum (used in fixing dyes and preparing leather), and gunpowder.[25] Isabel Smyth of the small port of Southwold, Suffolk, sold iron and canvas, probably for use in shipping, to merchant Henry Joye at about the same time. A few years later, Margaret Blakyslok, a widow who ran a shop in London, sold assorted small wares worth 26s. 8d. to Thomas Askam when he was getting ready to go to sea.

Several petitions stemmed from a woman's decision to turn over her shop to a male relative or former servant. Anne Blakegrave, wife of Richard, a mercer of London, was trading as a "wife sole merchant"

---

[22] For other examples, see CEMCRL, 1298–1307, pp. 190–2.

[23] CPMRL, 1364–1381, pp. 152–3.

[24] Corporation of London Record Office, Bridge House Rental, as discussed in Hanawalt, "Medieval London Women as Consumers." For below, see PRO REQ 2/33/128.

[25] PRO C 1/413/45. For below, see C 1/363/19 and C 1/460/41.

at the sign of the Dove in the parish of All Hallows the Less until around 1530.[26] But when she conveyed her business to John Palmer, a girdler of London and kinsman of hers, his irresponsible actions brought her into trouble. In 1540, widow Alice Kayleway operated a shop in Salisbury containing mixed goods worth £200.[27] Because, however, she was elderly and sickly and wished "to live more quietly in her old age," she decided to rent the shop for three years to William Dean. William, previously a servant of hers, agreed to pay Alice 13s. 4d. each week for the shop plus the merchandise that was currently in it. This included cloth of many kinds (velvets and satin, woolen worsteds and says, and canvas), spices (pepper, saffron, cloves, and mace), and "all manner of grocery wares and haberdasher wares." At the end of the three-year lease, William was to return the shop to Alice plus wares worth £200. William later claimed, however, that after he had been in the shop for only four weeks, having duly paid his weekly rent, Alice broke into the premises and carried away goods valued at £60 as well as £60 in money; she took also the inventory that listed what merchandise he had received with the lease and the account books of debts and reckonings concerning the merchandise in the shop. As a result, William said, he had been damaged not only by the loss of money and goods but also because he was now unable to recover the debts owed to him. In her response to this charge, Alice said that the condition of the lease was that William was to act as her agent in the shop, making an accounting to her every week. As soon as he entered the business, however, he had a new lock installed and through "his negligence and lewd conversation and demeanor and also by his prodigal expenses hath greatly wasted, consumed, and diminished the said stock of goods and wares." Hence, she argued, it was appropriate for her to break into the shop to recover her own property and the account books.

During the early years of Elizabeth's reign, women were still running shops of many sizes. Edith Goddard of Southampton conveyed "diverse wares, merchandises, and goods" worth £200 on credit to Richard Daye, a local merchant who was courting her stepdaughter in the 1560s or 1570s.[28] Margaret Langthorne, widow of a London salter, maintained the retail side of her husband's business for a few years during the 1560s or 1570s. One of her customers was John Alsopp, a leather worker of Derby, who bought small amounts of flax, soap, and other items. A carpenter's widow in Romford supported herself in 1561 by selling diverse wares, including pieces of cloth, in her little shop.[29] By the later sixteenth

---

[26] PRO C 1/682/16. For *femmes soles*, see sect. 1, Ch. 2 above and McIntosh, "The Benefits and Drawbacks of *Femme Sole* Status."
[27] PRO REQ 2/9/123.   [28] PRO C 3/54/85. For below, see C 3/51/77.
[29] ERO D/AER 10, 142.

7. Women selling fruits and sausages in London's Grace Church market. The man on the right is offering pigs' heads and probably tripe

century, population rise and the growing emphasis on consumer goods increased the number of shops in towns. Many of these shops, whether run by women or men, probably hired girls to help wait on customers.[30] We do not know, however, how many of the sellers in this more competitive environment were women or what the size of their shops was.[31]

Down a notch from indoor shops were stalls in an outdoor marketplace. All cities, larger towns, and market centers had one or more designated market areas. In its basic form, a market consisted of a widening of a street or an open area where several streets intersected, within which stalls could be set up on market days and – in some cases – animals could be penned. The marketplace was usually surrounded by buildings, most of which contained a shop or a drinking/eating house at ground level in the front (see Illus. 7). In the cities a market might be held every day, but smaller market communities normally had one or two designated market days each week. On those days, buyers and sellers came from the surrounding countryside, joined perhaps by specialized dealers traveling a longer distance. The market area was regulated by local officials, with a

[30] For shop girls, see Ch. 9 below.
[31] By the period 1695–1725, 8 percent of a cross-section sample of working women in London were shopkeepers, as were 7 percent of London women who took out insurance policies, 1726–9 (Earle, "Female Labour Market," p. 339; Earle, *Making of the English Middle Class*, p. 170).

bell to indicate when buying could commence. Local ordinances specified which goods were to be sold where, what prices could be charged
for foodstuffs and drink, and who could sell during peak hours (usually
local men, sometimes just the "freemen of the borough" or people who
had bought a license to trade in that market).[32]

By the sixteenth century, at least two large towns had set aside a section of the market for shopping by women. In that area they would have
been protected from the crowding, smells, and jostling that must have
characterized the main market. The women's market may have been a
setting in which women were especially likely to sell as well. In Nottingham in 1531, Elizabeth Cost and several other people rented two parcels
of ground in "the Women Market" that had previously been held by
Elizabeth Candeler, but we do not know whether the market continued
in operation later.[33] References are somewhat more plentiful to a small
"housewives' market" in Leicester, which seems to have specialized in
foodstuffs. In 1587, the town ordered that no one should sell woolen or
linen cloth in the housewives' market but only in the section of the main
market reserved for sale of cloth.[34] By 1588 the shops in the women's
market were said to be "in foul decay"; the market was paved in 1608.
Female purchasers apparently offered tempting opportunities for petty
theft: in 1601 a woman suspected of stealing a purse claimed that she
was in that part of the market "to buy a pennyworth of salt," and in
1663 an official was named to "see after cut purses about the woman's
market."[35]

Women faced some obstacles as market-sellers. It might be difficult or
impossible to obtain a license to trade, if only freemen of the town were
eligible, and married women or widows faced a challenge in keeping
their households running while they were away selling at market. Renting
a market stall also required at least a little capital, and in some parts of
London, a substantial payment. In 1379, all eleven stalls at the Standard
in London's Cheapside market were leased to women by the city for
rents of 13s. 4d. annually; seven stalls outside the church of St. Michael
le Querne at the west end of Cheapside paid rents ranging from 6s. 8d.
to 10s.[36] Since these were considerable sums to spend on overhead, one

---

[32] For the Parliamentary mandate, the "Assize of Bread and Ale," which set standards for
the quality of those items, see Ch. 6 below.
[33] *Records of the Borough of Nottingham*, vol. III, pp. 368–72.
[34] *Records of the Borough of Leicester*, vol. III, p. 243. For below, see ibid., p. 240, and *Records
of the Borough of Leicester*, vol. IV, p. 98. Roberts' statement that the name suggested
women's control over the market ("Women and Work," p. 94) seems unlikely.
[35] *Records of the Borough of Leicester*, vol. III, p. 426, and vol. IV, p. 484.
[36] Barron, "Women in London."

assumes that the volume of trade and profits of the women who took the leases were comparably large.

Another type of sales involved travel, carrying goods between communities or between houses in rural areas as a peddler. Because of the risk of personal assault and theft faced by a woman who was on the roads alone, especially if she had valuable goods with her, few women moved about as a regular part of their selling activity unless accompanied by a husband or male partner.[37] In 1596, Agnes Payne, widow, joined William Bearemen of rural Middlesex in buying "certain parcels of wares" worth between £3 and £4 10s. as well as a horse for 27s.[38] The wares and horse were to be used for their business, which was apparently itinerant selling. During the 1580s, Grace Spooner of "Myrryhill," War., who nominally traded with her husband, Lawrence, made a weekly circuit of the markets in a region that straddled the border of Leicestershire, Warwickshire, Staffordshire, and Derbyshire, taking with her a packhorse laden with various kinds of cloth.[39]

For the poorest women, those able to make no investment at all in a specialized venue or a horse for the sale of whatever goods they handled, there were two remaining options: their own dwellings, or the streets. Some women produced goods and sold them from their homes. This had the obvious advantage that the woman had no costs for renting retail space, and she could attend to her domestic responsibilities as well. To operate a de facto alehouse or eating house, for example, she had only to place the required marker outside her door and offer drink and/or food whose quality and price met local requirements. (Food or ale could also be sold outside the door, to be taken home, but it was increasingly common to have an indoor room designated for this purpose, where people could consume what they had just purchased.) As expectations for the size and degree of comfort of the establishments that sold food and drink rose over time, however, few women could offer such facilities within their own living places, nor did local authorities encourage them to do so.[40]

Poor women who could not sell from their homes normally became what was known as a "huckster" (the feminine form of someone who hucks or haggles goods). These petty street vendors, sometimes called "tranters" or "regraters" in local records, offered wares they had bought from others or items they were handling on commission. To their buyers, hucksters offered low-priced goods in small batches, only what was

---

[37] The 1379 Poll Tax returns for rural areas of the West Riding of Yorkshire, for instance, list few female chapmen or peddlers: Goldberg, "Women's Work."
[38] PRO REQ 2/161/50.
[39] PRO E 134/30 Eliz/Hil 10, as discussed more fully in sect. 1, Ch. 8 below.
[40] See Chs. 6–7.

needed for daily use; in larger communities, they worked particularly in poorer neighborhoods. By the later fourteenth century, hucksters were probably present in all of England's larger communities.[41]

This was physically demanding and exposed work. Although a few hucksters had little tables or stalls set up alongside the street, and an occasional woman had access to a handcart, most transported their goods on their backs or in baskets carried on their arms or heads.[42] Many hucksters moved through the streets, probably calling out to announce what they were selling; others stopped at set locations where people congregated or knocked at the doors of regular customers. Some late medieval hucksters specialized in certain items, especially bread or ale, while others included yarn or textiles as well as foodstuffs.[43] By the Elizabethan years, some hucksters had expanded into such items as used clothing, domestic items like dishes or pots, and wood or coal for fuel.[44] Others concentrated on particular foodstuffs, like the "oyster-wives" who would later become emblematic of London street hawkers. Because hucksters operated on such a small scale but were essential to the transfer of goods from producer or wholesaler to consumer, they constituted the bottom layer of the distribution pyramid in most urban communities.

A slightly different situation pertained in late medieval London. There the term "huckster" was employed in a broader fashion, covering women who rented a stall in one of the formal markets as well as mobile vendors. During the fifteenth century, some of these women had a certain degree of occupational identity and may have earned a reasonable income: of the women described as *femmes soles* in local records, half were said to be hucksters.[45] Margaret Kampdon, wife of William, a shearman, traded sole "in the art of huckstery" in 1456, when she was sued for beer she had bought from a brewer for subsequent sale; Alice Norwell was likewise

---

[41] The Poll Tax listing for Southwark in 1381 includes twenty women given the occupational label of huckster as compared to four men, while the Oxford return from the same year lists three hucksters among the total of fourteen women and 131 men who dealt in victuals of some sort (Goldberg, *Women, Work, and Life Cycle*, pp. 90–1, Carlin, *Medieval Southwark*, p. 175, and Bennett, "Medieval Women, Modern Women").

[42] See the illustrations in *Hugh Alley's Caveat*, and cf. Corporation of London Record Office GLMS 87, passim.

[43] In the north of England, hucksters sold food, yarn, cloth, and tallow candles (Goldberg, "Female Labour"). Hucksters in Chester during the second half of the fifteenth century might be described as *femmes soles*, but in practice they dealt in little more than bread or ale (Laughton, "Women in Court"). In the early sixteenth century, yarn was sold door-to-door by hucksters (Swanson, "The Illusion").

[44] For used clothing, see sect. 1, Ch. 8 below; for sale of wood and coal, see *Court Leet Records [of Southampton]*, vol. I, pt. II, pp. 167, 229, and 266.

[45] Barron, "The 'Golden Age'."

described as a sole merchant "in arte huxsters."[46] By the later sixteenth century, however, most of London's hucksters, like those elsewhere, were poor.

The number of hucksters in any given place and period depended upon demographic and economic factors as well as changing patterns of distribution. The presence of many hucksters in a community suggests that other opportunities for unskilled employment were insufficient to meet the demand. In Shrewsbury, for example, during the unsettled decades immediately after the plague, newly immigrated, not-married hucksters bought bread, grain, vegetables, and fish and then retailed their goods in the streets.[47] Although local authorities frowned upon this practice, even the meager profits to be made from such activity attracted women who had not yet found work elsewhere. During the fifteenth century, increases in the scale of ale-brewing necessitated more retailers, some of whom were hucksters. As the population rose and poverty worsened in the later sixteenth century, street vending became the best available option for some women. Indeed, by the later Elizabethan and Jacobean periods, the pressure for employment of any kind had become so powerful in some urban centers that men were willing to work as street vendors, threatening the ability of women to secure even these minimal positions.

Normally, women worked as hucksters only if they had no other legitimate means of earning a living. Selling on the streets produced very little income: hucksters made only a tiny profit (or received only a tiny commission) for each item sold and had little ability to bargain for better terms. Further, hucksters' work was regarded with suspicion in several respects. Local authorities disliked this form of retailing even if they tolerated it: it was not subject to the normal market controls and was a potential threat to the licensed sellers who rented market stalls or kept shops. Hucksters were therefore subject to punitive regulations about where and when they could sell, arbitrary fines, and sometimes temporary prohibition of their work. Equally importantly, women moving about the streets were likely to be regarded as disreputable and sexually available, open to the view of all and perhaps selling more than just their nominal wares. By around 1600, London's hucksters were the target of "a register of gestures – nudging, poking, spitting, or 'hemming'" from men.[48] If they were harassed, no civic authority would listen to their complaints.

---

[46] Barron, "Women in London" and Lacey, "Women and Work." For below, see Gowing, "Freedom of the Streets."
[47] Hutton, "Women in Fourteenth Century Shrewsbury."
[48] Gowing, "Freedom of the Streets," p. 143.

2   Apprenticeship

In some trades and many skilled crafts, young people might be taken on as apprentices, receiving training while providing increasingly expert assistance to their master or mistress. By accepting an apprenticeship contract, which usually required a cash payment from their parents, boys or girls were legally bound to remain with their employer for more than the single year required of servants: a minimum of three years, more commonly seven, and sometimes longer still. Like servants, apprentices received room, board, and some clothing, but in addition they were supposed to get formal training in the designated trade or craft. Apprentices were usually boys but during the fourteenth and fifteenth centuries, a small number of girls in the major cities were apprenticed to craftspeople who taught them the skills needed to run their own shops as adults. These girls were generally at least fourteen years old when they signed their contracts, and some came from middling or even upper-level families (merchants or gentry) who apparently thought that investing in an apprenticeship for their daughter was a way of preparing her to generate a good income as an adult. By the later sixteenth century, however, apprenticeship was changing. Many girls were now apprenticed, most of them poor. They often began their work at a younger age, especially if they were placed into such positions by parish poor-relief officials. Further, most female apprentices were now hired primarily as domestic or agricultural workers; those apprenticed to craftspeople received scant instruction in anything beyond the simplest tasks. Nominal apprenticeships were thus becoming little more than extended periods of service.

Even in periods when girls might receive actual training in a craft, the long-term benefits of an apprenticeship were less pronounced than for boys. This stemmed from that fact that for men in many cities, apprenticeship was a prerequisite for membership in a craft guild, the latter in turn a requirement for office-holding in urban government. For girls, an apprenticeship rarely led to guild membership in their own right.[49] Although women could become regular members of most religious fraternities, they were not usually admitted as independent members of the craft guilds unless they inherited a position from their father or husband. Even in those settings where women could join a guild in their own right, they were excluded from the offices that controlled the organizations and made decisions about economic matters. In no instance did women qualify for office in city or town governments. The wider benefits of apprenticeship were thus muted for girls.

[49] Barron, "Women in London."

Apprenticeship contracts, which may often in practice have been negotiated by the girl's parents, specified the terms of the agreement. The
master/mistress was to train, supervise, and, if necessary, chastise the
apprentice; if the employer did not fulfill the conditions of the apprenticeship agreement, the girl (or her relatives) could – at least in theory –
demand that she be freed from her obligation. The latter was more common during the later fourteenth and fifteenth centuries than later and
was more likely to happen if the parents of the apprentice were people
of some standing. In 1414, for example, Agnes Wawton, daughter of
Thomas Wawton, esquire, complained before the Mayor and Aldermen
of London against her mistress, Alice Virly.[50] Alice failed to appear
before the court after four summonses, and the sergeant of the Chamber
reported that she had moved away from the city. He said that she had left
"no one to provide for and teach her apprentice, nor had she assigned the
apprentice to any other person of the same mystery." Agnes was therefore
excused from her apprenticeship.

During the fourteenth and first half of the fifteenth centuries, female
apprenticeships were concentrated within the larger urban communities. London, with its independent craftswomen, naturally provided
many of the positions. The first surviving reference comes from 1276,
when Marion de Lymeseye was apprenticed to Roger Oriel, a maker of
rosaries.[51] In her thorough study of the London records, Caroline Barron
has found references to four female apprentices in the period 1300–50,
sixteen references in 1350–1400, and twenty-two in 1400–50. Girls were
apprenticed in many different occupations in London between 1300 and
1450. Of those masters or mistresses whose crafts are named, five were
silkworkers or embroiderers, four were involved in cloth production, two
made clothing, one was a rope-maker, and one a burnisher (= polisher
or finisher) of metals. Two girls were apprenticed to a notary public.[52]
Some of these young women lived in large households that included other
apprentices and servants, although few establishments were at the level
of Richard Somery's, a mercer who died in 1430.[53] Richard left bequests
to two female apprentices (one of whom received 40s., the other 100s.
"for her marriage"), three male apprentices, and one male servant, as
well as two men who had formerly been his apprentices and two female
ex-servants. Girls were rarely apprenticed in most other late medieval
communities. York had a large population of female servants but only
an occasional female apprentice.[54] In Coventry, two early apprenticeship

---

[50] CPMRL, 1413–1437, p. 12. Alice's craft is not specified.
[51] Barron, "Women in London," for this and below.
[52] Abram, "Women Traders."   [53] Barron, "Women in London."
[54] Goldberg, *Women, Work, and Life Cycle*, p. 191. For below, see Fox, "Coventry Guilds."

indentures for girls – to learn the craft of making leather purses – come from 1336 and 1345, but references are then scant until the later sixteenth and seventeenth centuries.

In London, female apprentices seem to have disappeared around the middle of the fifteenth century. This is probably because opportunities for them to run their own establishments as adults had declined. Barron has encountered not a single reference to girls as apprentices in the London records between 1450 and 1500 and only a few scattered ones later.[55] Similarly, Ben-Amos found that between 1580 and 1640 no female apprentices were mentioned in the records of fifteen of the major craft guilds in London.

During the late sixteenth century, girls began to be apprenticed in communities throughout the country, but the nature of these positions had changed. Apprenticeship now had a different meaning, and the background and age of the girls was different. The requirement that a female apprentice should receive training in a particular craft had weakened or been abandoned entirely. Instead, many girls were expected to do housework or agricultural labor, in addition to – or sometimes instead of – assisting in the unskilled stages of craft production. Since it did not take many years of training with no reward other than room, board, and clothing to learn the specified tasks, it seems clear that these girls were being used primarily as cheap labor. Although the language of apprenticeship was still used and young women still had to commit in their contract to an extended period (at least seven years) of residence with their master or mistress, apprenticeship was thus becoming equivalent to domestic or agricultural service. Yet apprenticeship carried a double disadvantage: the girl had to commit to a long period of living with an employer, without the freedom enjoyed by servants of changing masters each year; and whereas servants were paid cash wages, apprentices were generally not. Learning all the skills needed to run a household in early modern England certainly required instruction and supervision, but these were skills that many adult women could have taught, and it did not take seven years to learn them. By the early seventeenth century, most female apprentices were evidently working as de facto servants who received no wages.

We see this transition away from skilled craft training in many settings. Even when girls were apprenticed in areas where female crafts were practiced, they commonly worked in stages of the process that required considerable labor but little formal training. In Coventry, for example, a listing from 1595 mentions twelve female apprentices as well as others whose sex cannot be determined, girls who Fox thinks were associated

[55] Barron, "Women in London." For below, see Ben-Amos, *Adolescence and Youth*, p. 135.

with the workrooms of the many spinsters (= female spinners) working in the city.[56] In Romford, a female apprentice named Margaret was the primary cook for William Copeland's inn in 1594. Neither spinning nor basic cooking needed three to seven years of skilled instruction to master. Some apprenticeship contracts now specified a mixture of domestic training and craftwork. In Salisbury in 1612, for example, Elizabeth Deacon was bound as apprentice to a tailor and his wife in "the mystery and sciences of housewifery and flaxdressing," while Mary Gunter was apprenticed in the art of "housewifery and knitting."[57] Mendelson and Crawford have found that housewifery and "husbandry" (= agricultural labor) were the most commonly mentioned occupations in female apprenticeship indentures of the later sixteenth and seventeenth centuries.

Bristol provides an interesting picture of the changing meaning of apprenticeship for girls. This city had adopted the custom of *femme sole* trading from London, which probably expanded opportunities for women as heads of craft shops and hence as apprentices during the fifteenth century. But movement away from this model had already begun by 1530 and reached its peak in the early seventeenth century. During the first half of the sixteenth century, relatively few girls were apprenticed in Bristol (an average of five per year in the 1530s), but some of them were still receiving training in craftwork.[58] Between 1532 and 1552, for example, 31 percent worked for "sempstresses and tailors," learning to sew clothing, while 18 percent worked in the distributive and foodstuff trades. Another 41 percent accepted employment with women to be taught as "housewives and sempstresses," and the remainder were apprenticed to manual laborers. By the early seventeenth century, although more girls were entering apprenticeships in Bristol (nine or ten per year between 1617 and 1635), the type of work had shifted. During the 1610s–20s, 35 percent were hired solely as domestic maids, another 50 percent were to work as a servant plus helping with knitting or spinning, and a few were to do domestic service plus sewing or shopkeeping. Only 11 percent were taken on to work in craft areas alone, and those were mainly poorly paid but labor-intensive activities like spinning, lace making, and stocking knitting.

[56] Fox, "Coventry Guilds." For below, see ERO D/AER 17, 107.

[57] Wright, "Churmaids." For below, see Mendelson and Crawford, *Women in Early Modern England*, pp. 328–9. Lane provides little information prior to 1700 but notes that most girls were apprenticed to housewifery, agriculture, or the female fashion trades: *Apprenticeship in England*, esp. pp. 38–42.

[58] For this paragraph, see Ben-Amos, *Adolescence and Youth*, pp. 136–9. Girls formed 3 percent of all apprenticeships between 1542 and 1552 and 2–3 percent between 1617 and 1628.

The language and contracts used for craft apprenticeship often persisted even when there was no intent that the girl would actually receive any occupational training. At a borough court held in the Devizes, Wilts., in December 1594, Joan Bruer, the daughter of a local widow, enrolled the apprenticeship agreement in which she contracted to work for Richard Adlington, a brasier (= brass worker), for eight years.[59] Her contract does not say that Joan was to be taught the skills associated with Richard's craft or, for that matter, any other skills. Although she committed herself to stay with him for a long period, her reward was to be only lodging, food, drink, and suitable apparel, without money payment. Joan thus received considerably less remuneration than a servant who signed up for a series of single-year contracts. We do not know how old Joan was or whether she herself or her mother had worked out this arrangement with Richard. It seems clear, however, that only someone eager to find a secure living arrangement, with guaranteed food and clothing, would have accepted such an agreement.

Tied to this change in the nature of apprenticeships was a shift in the backgrounds and ages of the young women who accepted such positions. By the later sixteenth century, prosperous parents no longer thought it worthwhile to pay for an apprenticeship for their daughters, since it did not lead to future economic independence for them. Instead, most female apprentices now appear to have come from poorer families. This pattern became more pronounced after the passage of the 1598/1601 Poor Laws, which allowed parish officials to place pauper girls into apprenticeship, with no expectation they would receive any training except in domestic or agricultural work. These contracts said that the girl was to receive room, board, and clothing (but no wages) in return for a lengthy period of labor, often eight to ten years. Further, poor girls were commonly apprenticed at a younger age: in their early teens, if by parents, or at ten to twelve years if by parish officials.

Female apprenticeship was thus evolving into a system that took advantage of the need of poor young women to find employment away from home.[60] Few female apprentices by around 1600 gained marketable skills that would allow them to support themselves in the future. During a labor glut, young people from poor families could not afford to be choosy about what kind of residential employment they accepted. The importance of an

---

[59] Wiltshire Record Office G 20/1/16. I am grateful to Jennifer McNabb for this information.

[60] Although this shift was particularly marked for girls, some young men faced a comparable situation: several male apprentices in Tudor and Stuart Salisbury described themselves in testimony before the church courts not just as weavers or pewterers but also as domestic servants (Wright, "Churmaids").

abundance of workers within this changing pattern is emphasized by what happened within the London craft guilds after the plague and great fire of 1665–6, which caused a great drop in population and shortage of labor. Although there had been only a tiny number of female apprentices during the first half of the century, the number rose noticeably after the mid-1660s (though they were still few in comparison with male apprentices).[61] The Weavers' Company, for example, had previously taken strong action against women weavers, but in 1664 it began to accept female apprentices. During the next forty years, at least 125 women were registered as apprentices, a few of whom completed their terms, became free members of the company, and trained apprentices themselves.

Adult women who ran their own establishments could take on apprentices, thereby becoming responsible for both their occupational training and their social and religious upbringing. This practice seems to have been confined mainly to craftwork. Of the female apprentices mentioned in London between 1300 and 1450, two-thirds had female mistresses.[62] The crafts pursued by these women (who were obviously operating on a sufficiently large and long-term basis to make it profitable to take on an apprentice who had to be trained before she could become useful) included making and working silk, producing purses, doing embroidery, making calendars, and finishing metals.[63] Silkwomen, the only craftswomen in late medieval London to display some degree of collective identity and activity, regularly had apprentices. Two fifteenth-century apprentice contracts, for example, record the placing of young women from Yorkshire and Lincolnshire with London citizens and their wives, to learn the craft of the wife, both silkwomen.[64] An exceptionally late contract from London, in 1519, bound Margaret, the daughter of John Savage, to Katherine, the wife of goldsmith Robert Udale, to learn the craft of a silkwoman.

In late medieval London, craftswomen of various marital situations had apprentices. Singlewomen and widows could take apprentices in their own names. An unmarried woman who was evidently an artist had a female apprentice, to whom she left some of the copies and equipment she used in painting pictures, with a chest to keep them in.[65] A successful fifteenth-century silkwoman, widow Alice Claver, ran a large household including a female apprentice, several male apprentices, two servants, and

---

[61] Paul Seaver, personal communication. For below, Joseph P. Ward, personal communication, and see his *Metropolitan Communities*, p. 136.
[62] Barron, "Women in London."   [63] Ibid., and Lacey, "Women and Work."
[64] Dale, "London Silkwomen." For below, see Barron, "Women in London."
[65] Abram, "Woman Traders." For below, see Sutton, "Alice Claver," and Barron, "The 'Golden Age'."

a little boy and girl whom she took in out of charity. Widows were also entitled to keep any apprentice(s) who had been placed with their husbands, provided they continued the young person's training. Although widows often transferred such apprentices to a man working in the same craft, they sometimes retained the youngsters in their own household and occasionally passed them on to their new husband upon remarriage, if he was in the same occupation as their previous husband.[66] A married woman whose husband practiced a different occupation could likewise take her own apprentices. In 1378, for instance, Margaret Bishop of Sleaford, Sussex, bound herself to Burga, the wife of John Prichet of London, probably a toll collector, to learn Burga's craft of making tents or pavilions.[67] When Maud Picot decided to apprentice her son so he would learn tailoring skills, she chose Isabel Sampson of London as his mistress; Isabel was a tailoress, while her husband Robert worked as a cordwainer.

During the sixteenth century, trades- and craftswomen in other communities, too, sometimes hired male apprentices. In Coventry, during the 1540s and 1570s, women who worked as carpenters and drapers (probably continuing their former husband's businesses) took on apprentices, while in sixteenth-century Oxford, apprentices were hired by widows working in trades involving food and drink, leather (mostly glove- and shoemaking), and clothing (mostly tailoring), as well as a few in distributive occupations.[68] In sixteenth-century Bristol, widows frequently operated their husbands' workshops and trained their male apprentices, but they rarely took on new apprentices in their own right: in the 1540s, only 2 percent of beginning apprentices were bound to widows. With this discussion as background, we turn to women's involvement in the specific types of trade and craftwork.

---

[66] E.g., PRO REQ 2/60/21.

[67] Barron, "Women in London." For below, see her "The 'Golden Age'," which gives this and other examples of boys apprenticed to craftswomen but does not provide a date for this one. A cordwainer was a shoemaker.

[68] Fox, "Coventry Guilds," and Prior, "Women and the Urban Economy." For below, see Ben-Amos, *Adolescence and Youth*, pp. 145–6.

6   Drink work

Women's participation in the drink trades underwent considerable change across these centuries. Ale was the standard drink for most families, since water was not safe unless it had been boiled. Brewing and/or selling ale was done almost entirely by women until around 1500, and drink work was probably the most common single form of market involvement for women in the early fourteenth century.[1] By the fifteenth century, however, ale-brewing had increased in scale and become more commercialized. This created favorable opportunities for some women of intermediate rank but drove out many of the smaller, occasional brewers, including most not-married women. Other women retailed ale they had not produced themselves. With the introduction of beer and sweet wines, the demand for ale declined. The way beer was brewed and distributed excluded almost all women from participation, nor did they normally operate the taverns that sold wine. By 1620, female involvement in the drink trades was limited to poor women who hawked drink on the streets, a few widows allowed to run small alehouses or taverns, and the women who worked as employees within the larger public houses.[2]

Our ability to study the activities of women in the drink and food trades during the later medieval years stems from unusually good local court records. Making and selling ale or bread were already regulated in England by the later thirteenth century. "The Assize of Bread and Ale" as authorized by Parliament required that each batch of ale or bread be inspected before it was sold, with specified standards for its quality, size, and the price charged for it.[3] Brewers were to set out an "alestake" in front of their houses on days when they had ale to sell, and they and bakers were expected to use approved measures of specific sizes in selling their beverage (see Illus. 8). Locally chosen aletasters, always male,

---

[1] For a fuller discussion, see Bennett, *Ale, Beer, and Brewsters*; for Scottish female brewers, see Ewan, "For Whatever Ales Ye."

[2] A public house was an establishment that sold drink and sometimes food, shortened in modern usage to "pub."

[3] Bennett, *Ale, Beer, and Brewsters*, ch. 6.

8. A woman outside her alehouse, identified by its alestake, serving drink to a man

supervised the work of brewers, bakers, and sometimes other foodsellers, reporting offenders to the public court of that community. By the later fourteenth century, the names of specific offenders against the assize had been replaced in most court records by lists of all (or nearly all) people making and selling ale or bread, who were fined a small amount in what constituted a de facto local licensing procedure.[4] We therefore know more about workers in these trades than in other occupations. In this and the next chapter, detailed material from the five market centers will be set alongside general patterns.[5]

When using court rolls to study people working in these occupations, one immediately encounters the question of how the aletasters reported the work of women and hence how the clerks of the courts recorded it. Two possible methods were employed.[6] The first reported individually the names of the people who actually did the work. This system, used in Ramsey and Havering (dominated by its market town of Romford) and certain other places at least until around 1500, allows us to distinguish between men and women.[7] Figure 6.1 displays the proportion of all brewers and alesellers who were reported as female in those communities.[8] Here we see the preponderance of women in most decades

---

[4] For what information was entered, in what form, and how thoroughly it listed those people working in the drink trades, see the Appendix to ibid.

[5] For the methods and records used, see App. 1.1 below.

[6] Among the sixteen villages studied by Bennett, four reported individual names, seven used the household reporting system, and five alternated or changed between the two systems; two of her market centers used the individual method, one the household system, and two changed (Appendix to *Ale, Beer, and Brewsters*).

[7] For description of the five market centers, see sect. 1, Ch. 2 above.

[8] This graph and the next are based upon average number of people reported per year, including both brewers and alesellers. The two types of work are combined here since they followed very similar patterns. In some places and periods, however, alesellers are not reported as distinct from brewers; occasionally one or the other list is missing. In those cases, the percentage is for the single list. For the numbers, see Figs. 6.3 and 6.4.

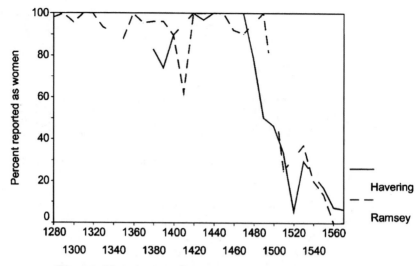

Fig. 6.1. Havering and Ramsey, percentage of brewers plus alesellers reported as women.
Based on average number reported per year. See Figs. 6.3 and 6.4.

prior to the late fifteenth century, with a sharp drop thereafter. Within the individual reporting method, there were two variations. In Ramsey, the clerk described women by their own first and last names, which does not allow us to separate married from unmarried women. Havering's clerks described married women as the wife of a named man but listed single-women and widows under their own first and last names while also labeling the latter as widows. This method is the most helpful for historians.

The other general approach, used prior to around 1470 in Tamworth, Northallerton, Minehead, and many other communities, listed the name not of the individual worker but rather of the head of the household within which the food or drink trade was being practiced.[9] This method was encouraged by the legal requirement that the principal figure within a household was responsible for the activities of all of its members and for any fines levied by the court as the result of work done within that unit. We can use an example from Minehead to illustrate how a married woman's work might appear under the household reporting format. Alice Corior

---

[9] This pattern was used in some of the cities as well. In York, for instance, only 13 of 221 people listed as brewers or alesellers in local court records in 1450–1 were female (Swanson, *Medieval Artisans*, p. 21). Yet other evidence makes clear that in many, probably most, of those households, the trade was in the hands of women (Swanson, "The Illusion"). The thirteen women listed under their own names were probably singlewomen or widows who headed their own households.

Toky's first husband was Steven Corior, a local fisherman and part-time farmer who entered his land in 1405.[10] As well as a cottage, three acres of arable land, and one acre of salt meadow, he held a fishing weir in the sea and an acre of harborside land next to the boathouses. Starting in 1407, Steven was reported regularly as a brewer, an entry which meant that brewing was taking place within his household. There is no indication from private suits that he brewed himself. Although Steven died in 1418, he (clearly now Alice) continued to be fined for brewing over the next few years. In December 1422, William Toky paid the substantial fine of 30s. to marry Alice and enter the land she had inherited from Steven.[11] William was then listed as a brewer from 1423 through 1436, though he had not been mentioned for drink work previously. After his death in 1437, Alice regained title to the land she had brought from her first marriage.[12] During the next five years she was reported for brewing, now identified individually for the first time, as William Toky's widow. If we assume that she was perhaps twenty to twenty-five years old at the time she started brewing in 1407, she would have been fifty-five to sixty by 1442. It seems clear that across that span she was the primary and perhaps the only brewer within two marriages as well as during periods of widowhood.[13]

When a male was named, we cannot distinguish between three possibilities on the basis of the listings themselves: the man was indeed doing the food/drink work; he was involved but had help from his wife or other women in his household; or he was engaged in an entirely different occupation and was named by the aletasters only in a titular sense. Other evidence suggests that brewers were generally women, at least until the late fifteenth century, while bakers could be either men or women. When a clerk using the household method listed a woman in her own name, she was nearly always the head of a domestic unit and hence either a singlewoman or a widow. Thus, what appears on the rolls to be a contrast between male vs. female workers is actually a distinction between men or married women vs. not-married women. As Fig. 6.2 displays, however, around 1470–80 the courts in the three communities that had previously used the household system began to report women individually, in their own names. This probably reflected an effort on the part of local officials to supervise drink traders more closely.[14]

---

[10] SRO DD/L P 26/6, court held 4 August, 6 Henry IV. For below, see DD/L P 26/5, rent roll from 8 Henry IV.

[11] SRO DD/L P 27/10, 1 Henry VI.   [12] Ibid., summer, 15 Henry VI.

[13] Alice was not reported for brewing during the eleven years that remained until her death in 1453, though there is no indication that she remarried: it is not clear how she supported herself in her old age (SRO DD/L P 27/11, autumn, 31 Henry VI).

[14] See sect. 4 below.

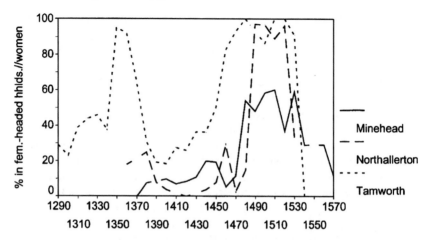

Fig. 6.2. Minehead, Northallerton, and Tamworth, percentage of brewers plus alesellers who lived in female-headed households or were reported as women.
Based on average number reported per year. See Figs. 6.3 and 6.4.

Throughout this and the next chapter, we need to remember that many people worked in several drink and/or food trades simultaneously or moved around between them. By considering each type of work on its own, we are separating out strands that were in practice often intertwined. We may use our market centers as an illustration. Between the 1348–9 plague and 1469, people who engaged in drink/food work in Ramsey, Tamworth, Minehead, and Havering participated in an average of 1.1–1.5 such trades, depending upon the place. Presumably many of them had other kinds of income-generating activities as well.

In thinking about multiple activities, we encounter one of the ways in which evidence from these market centers during the post-plague generations complicates accepted wisdom. It is often said that because women engaged in various types of work at the same time, they were less involved and less successful than men. It is certainly true that men who were trained in a skilled craft, like being a dyer or tanner, were in a position to earn a reasonable living through that activity alone, without doing other kinds of work, and that women were generally unable to become the heads of their own craft operations. But a different pattern pertained among the drink and food trades, which offered less financial reward. Here participating in multiple trades was not a sign of economic weakness. To the contrary, people who brewed their own beverages and baked their own

bread to sell in their alehouse would probably be able to reap higher profits than those who merely retailed one type of item, especially if they had
to purchase their stock from someone else. It is thus interesting that in
Ramsey, Tamworth, and Minehead during the period after the plague,
male drink and food workers engaged in a larger average number of these
trades than did women.[15] It was only because of the unusually favorable
economic position of Havering's women that their average was slightly
higher than men's.

1   Brewing ale

The first step in making ale was to malt the grain that would be brewed
together with water. Malting was therefore of considerable economic
importance in later medieval and early modern England. Large-scale
production and sale of malt were, however, usually in male hands. In
late medieval Chester, for example, supplies of malt were controlled
by some of the town's wealthiest male citizens, who stored grain in big
quantities and owned the malt-kilns.[16] Although much of that malt was
used for commercial brewing in establishments run by men, some was
sold to the many women who were brewing on a smaller scale. During
the post-plague generations, women occasionally produced or marketed
malt. Agnes, wife of William del Launde of Nottingham, was hired by
William Prior to make malt for him for a full year in 1365, and Exeter
women sold malt to brewers during the later fourteenth century.[17] In
1513–14, when royal servants came to East Yorkshire to buy provisions
to be shipped to Newcastle for the king's northern army, they bought large
amounts of malt from several groups of women, as well as from men.[18]
The women were probably operating as intermediate traders, purchasing
the malt from individual producers. By the mid-sixteenth century, one
finds few references to women within the malt trades.

---

[15] The numbers are: Ramsey, 1348–1469, an average of 1.50 drink/food occupations for
men, 1.11 for women; Tamworth, 1348–1469, 1.27 drink/food occupations for men,
1.14 for women; Minehead, 1379–1469, 1.35 drink/food occupations for men, 1.31 for
women; Havering, 1382–1469, 1.20 drink/food occupations for men, 1.25 for women.
During these generations many more women than men worked in the drink and food
trades in all four places. Assessments of the property of drink and food workers for
Ramsey and Havering in the Subsidies of 1523/5 were likewise higher if the men worked
in several of these trades, not just one: App. 11 to the on-line version of CRRamHB and
PRO E 179/105/150.

[16] Laughton, "The Alewives."

[17] Foulds, "Women and Work," and Kowaleski, *Local Markets and Regional Trade*, p. 132.

[18] PRO E 101/56/28.

Brewing ale, by contrast, was a major provider of opportunities for some women in smaller and middling communities until around 1500.[19] In rural communities and smaller towns during the later thirteenth and early fourteenth centuries, when virtually all ale was brewed at home, many women sold little batches to their neighbors at least now and then. Only a smaller subset produced ale for sale more regularly, at a commercial or "by-industrial" level.[20] Local production of this kind was promoted by the fact that ale could not be kept for more than a few days, so frequent brewings were needed, and it must have been fostered by high population pressure and extensive poverty, encouraging women to supplement their household's income by brewing. Further, the equipment needed for making ale was limited. Singlewomen and widows (or abandoned wives) were active participants in both village and urban settings. In Lincoln, about half of the women who paid a fee to sell ale during the 1290s appear to have been heads of their own households.[21] In this period, brewing probably involved a higher fraction of local residents than did the food trades.[22]

That pattern had already started to change in market centers and towns by the time of the 1348–9 plague, though it lasted longer in rural communities. Many of the occasional brewers, especially not-married women, dropped out as the remaining brewers moved into more commercialized production.[23] During the later fourteenth and fifteenth centuries, the scale of ale brewing increased still further due to a rising per capita demand for alcoholic beverages, part of a general improvement in standards of living after the plague and related to the growing popularity of alehouses.[24] Some married women who could afford the equipment, supplies, and labor costs were now able to bring in a significant income as brewers and sellers. Many worked independently of their husbands, men

---

[19] For a fuller discussion, see Bennett, *Ale, Beer, and Brewsters.*

[20] In Redgrave, Suffolk, 457 people were reported for selling ale between 1259 and 1293 (Smith, "A Periodic Market," for this and below). Of these, 192 (= 42 percent) were fined only a single time, while another 106 (= 23 percent) were named two to four times during that span. People who sold ten times or more, who were presumably commercial brewers, accounted for just 22 percent of the total. In the adjacent rural manor of Rickinghall, the proportion of occasional brewers between 1259 and 1293 was even higher and the proportion of frequent sellers even lower: 49 percent sold only once, and a mere 12 percent sold ten times or more.

[21] Bischoff, "Late Thirteenth-Century Urban Commuting." I am grateful to Dr. Bischoff for letting me have a copy of this paper.

[22] In late medieval Halesowen, Worcs., a market center with a population of around 600 people in 1300, twenty-five brewers were fined in the court rolls annually as compared with only four or five bakers; in the weekly market held at Botesdale in Redgrave, Suff., sixty to seventy brewers/sellers of ale were fined each year between 1260 and 1295, as compared with eight to ten bakers (Smith, "A Periodic Market").

[23] Bennett, *Ale, Beer, and Brewsters.*   [24] Dyer, *Standards of Living.*

engaged in other occupations. In urban communities of all kinds, some of these women came from respectable families, married to men who held local office, and they often worked in their trades for decades on end.

This shift is clearly visible in the larger towns and cities by the later medieval period. In Chester, commercial brewing was done largely by women of intermediate or upper social rank. In households where the husband was a craftsman, his wife and other female relatives brewed, whereas in wealthy families the job was assigned to female servants working under the supervision of their mistress. Even elite wives engaged in such activity. Alice le Armerer, wife of a man who was mayor of Chester six times during the 1380s and 1390s and herself a member of the prestigious Trinity Guild of Coventry, controlled a sizeable brewing operation.[25] After her husband's death in 1396, Alice continued to send malt to be milled and to employ servants in her own right for another twenty years. Brewsters in York came typically from the more substantial craft households. In Exeter, where a high fraction of all households brewed at least occasionally during the late fourteenth century, commercial brewing was common in households that enjoyed local wealth and political status and that hired a large number of servants.[26] Ale brewers in Colchester, most of them female, covered a wide socio-economic range during the later fourteenth century.[27] In addition to some very poor women, the wives of leading officials in the town were regularly named for violating standards for the quality or price of the ale they brewed. Of the women listed as brewers at one court session in 1377, six were married to men who had been or would be bailiffs of Colchester, plus three wives of men who represented the town in Parliament. As the author of Colchester's late medieval history notes, "An offence of which so many estimable women were guilty cannot have carried any social stigma."[28] But the expanding scale of ale-brewing and selling, which made possible more sizeable profits, brought some men in London and the larger towns into the trade, often assisted by female labor. In 1354, brewer William Barbour contracted with Robert le Waterleder of Nottingham that Matilda, Robert's wife, would carry water by the bushel for William's brewing.[29] Christina Tappester of Nottingham was employed in 1374 by Roger Masson, a tavern keeper and mayor of the town, and his wife Margaret to brew ale for their establishment for a six-month period.

Within the five market centers, too, the later fourteenth and fifteenth centuries offered unusual opportunities for some women to work as

[25] Laughton, "The Alewives." For below, see Goldberg, "Female Labour."
[26] Kowaleski, *Local Markets and Regional Trade*, pp. 133–6.
[27] Britnell, *Growth and Decline in Colchester*, p. 89.
[28] Ibid., p. 90.   [29] Foulds, "Women and Work," for this and below.

long-term commercial brewers. In Havering, the seventy-eight women who began brewing between 1420 and 1449 worked over an average span of 11.3 years. Only 18 percent of them brewed in just a single year, while 41 percent worked for two to nine years. Those who worked for ten years or more and hence were operating on what other historians have defined as a commercial basis accounted for 41 percent of the total, and an exceptional 22 percent worked for twenty years or more.

Some of Romford's long-term married brewers probably used their earnings to invest in their family's wellbeing and in good opportunities for their children. Margaret Cappes illustrates this pattern.[30] After being widowed in her first marriage, she re-married early in the 1430s. Her second husband was Thomas Cappes, a husbandman (= small farmer) who held ten to twenty acres of land. Margaret was first reported for brewing in 1432 and continued to be named every year until 1474. Although we lack details about where and how she sold her ale, this longevity and her apparent prosperity suggest that she was operating an alehouse. During the first fourteen years some of her business proceeds may have gone towards helping Thomas buy additional land, which he did in 1434, 1445, and 1446.[31] Later, she and her husband arranged for the marriages of their three daughters to craftsmen from Maldon and Stondon, Essex, and from London. Perhaps to finance those alliances, which constituted a step upwards for the young women, Margaret added baking to her repertoire between 1464 and 1473. This involved buying or renting an oven, but she would then have been able to sell bread to go with her drink. Thomas was regularly named as a Chief Pledge (an officer in Havering's local government); during the 1440s–60s, he served occasionally as constable or woodward; and he was one of the commissioners who collected a national subsidy in 1468, though he was still described as a husbandman. Sometime in 1470–1, he was assaulted by the servants of another local man and died shortly thereafter.[32] Margaret continued brewing and baking for a few more years but then decided to move into London to live with a married daughter. In her will, written in 1478, she left a comfortable array of household goods and clothing to her children, including such luxuries as a feather bed, six silver spoons, twenty pewter vessels, a red worsted wall hanging, and some gold and silver jewelry.[33] These possessions exceeded what the wife of a small farmer was likely to have owned based simply upon her husband's income. Even if Margaret's contributions to her family's economy were secondary to her husband's

---

[30] All the information below comes from the Havering court rolls, c. 1430–75, unless otherwise noted: see App. 1.1.
[31] *Feet of Fines for Essex*, vol. IV, p. 19.   [32] *Calendar of the Fine Rolls*, vol. I, p. 232.
[33] Guildhall Library London MS 9171/6, fol. 218r–v.

economic role – and we do not know that they were – they were nonetheless significant.

An unusually interesting example of a female brewer/aleseller in Romford comes from the following generation. Joan Carowe conducted her trade as distinct from that of her husband Henry, who opened a butcher's shop in 1468 and remained in that occupation until his death in 1504.[34] Between 1474 and 1502 Henry sold fish as well as meat. Presumably in order to have land nearby on which to fatten cattle, he leased a large marsh meadow in 1474.[35] After sowing a few wild oats in the early 1470s (fined as a frequent player at cards and dice, illegal games accompanied by betting), Henry became a solid member of the community.[36] By 1489, he was starting to be described as a "yeoman" of Romford, no longer as a butcher. While serving as chief constable, he was stabbed with a knife in the course of duty in 1492 by the former priest of a religious fraternity in Romford chapel but survived the attack. In his 1504 will, Carowe left a great deal of cash to various individuals and causes, including a bequest for a painting in Romford church.[37] Henry was a predecessor of the urban yeomen who became more visible and numerous as money-lenders and market middlemen later in the sixteenth century.

Joan Carowe was meanwhile pursuing her own economic activities. In 1469 she began brewing and selling ale, activities she continued until 1509. Because she was sometimes reported for selling fish or victuals too, she was probably running a public house that sold food as well as drink. After Henry's death in 1504, Joan kept her own work going for another five years, but in addition she made the unusual decision to continue Henry's butchery. (To do so, especially as an older woman, she must have hired men to do the slaughtering and preparing of meat.) She ran the business until 1510, when it was taken over by their son John. John, who had received some education, became an important Romford yeoman, deeply engaged in credit dealings and land purchases, and was later the elected bailiff of the manor of Havering.[38] He sent his own son, Joan and

[34] All the material below comes from the Havering court rolls, 1466–1510 unless otherwise noted: see App. 1.1.

[35] New College, Oxford MS 3734.

[36] ERO T/P 71/2. Henry served as a Chief Pledge and chief constable for Romford, 1489–1502, and was a churchwarden in Romford parish, 1489–94. He acted as a trustee for a local religious chantry in 1482, arbitrated a dispute between two important Romford figures in 1489, and witnessed other people's wills (PRO E 135/5/2, m. 19, PRO SC 2/172/35, m. 3, and ERO D/AER 1, 120).

[37] ERO D/AER 2, 75. For urban yeomen, see McIntosh, *A Community Transformed*, pp. 139–44.

[38] Joan's daughters had married young men from Romford and the surrounding communities, several of them skilled craftsmen and one a prosperous butcher (ERO D/AER 2, 57).

Henry's grandson, first to New College, Oxford, and then to London to study law. The younger man, who as an adult was styled a gentleman, became the deputy steward of the Liberty of Havering and one of its Justices of the Peace as well as the steward of New College's Hornchurch estate. Joan's profits from the operation she ran for forty years must have contributed to this rise from food and drink work into gentry status across just three generations.

In Minehead, production of drink was affected by the demand for kegged beverages for use aboard ships. While some production was for local consumption, references to barrels or casks of drink as well as sales of higher value than found in the other communities suggest that these brewers were also stocking vessels.[39] In 1490, Thomas at Were, probably an immigrant who offered drink near the fishing weir in the harbor, refused to sell to his neighbors, only "to his customers."[40] The latter presumably included sailors and ships. Singlewomen and widows who brewed in Minehead were much more likely than their peers in the other market centers to have probable relatives who engaged in the same trade, suggesting that they may have been sharing equipment because they could not afford their own.[41] By the early sixteenth century, brewing and selling apparently functioned as stepping stones to more profitable economic activity for some Minehead women. When customs accounts list the owners of individual units within the total cargo of a ship, we find that women occasionally imported or exported goods. In some cases this was directly related to their work as providers of drink. In 1504, the ship called "the Mary of Minehead" came back into harbor, probably from France, with its hold filled with wine, owned by fifteen men and three women.[42] The latter were all married to men who were reported for brewing and/or selling drink, and one woman was named herself for such work: they were probably acquiring wine for their taverns. In 1527, Joan Daton, a widow who had been brewing and selling for nearly twenty years, was one of three owners of colored cloths known as "Dunsters" sent to the continent in the "Mary Walsingham." The money accumulated from her drink work may have helped to finance such an investment.

A different pattern is seen in Northallerton, the least prosperous and most unsettled of the five market centers during the later fifteenth and

---

[39] E.g., SRO DD/L P 26/8, court held c. St. Margaret 4 Henry V, and DD/L P 28/15, court held 3 January 7 Henry VII.

[40] SRO DD/L P 28/15, court held c. St. Luke Evangelist 6 Henry VII. In Minehead, newcomers, especially those with foreign names, were likely to be given new surnames based upon their occupation or where they lived/worked.

[41] For shared ovens, see sect. 1, Ch. 7 below. Probable relatives were assessed by the rough and incomplete measure of a common surname.

[42] PRO E 122/26/22. For below, see E 122/27/7.

early sixteenth centuries. As late as the 1530s, the last decade in which the court rolls report drink and food workers, these trades were less specialized than in the other communities. Many women worked on a small scale as both brewers and bakers, and some engaged in other economic activities as well.[43] Although married women continued to dominate brewing until around 1530, the equipment needed for commercial brewing was evidently too expensive for some to purchase individually. This led to a practice of renting equipment, whereby a wealthier person sold malted grain and sometimes fuel to another woman together with the right to use the seller's facilities for the actual brewing.[44] In January 1506, John Malthous, a relative newcomer to the community who had recently married one of Northallerton's longest-term brewers, entered an action of debt on behalf of his wife against Robert Founder, whose wife likewise brewed.[45] John claimed that the previous December Robert's wife had purchased five bushels of malted barley worth 3s. 9d. from his wife, to be paid for on Christmas Day, but she did not deliver the sum owed. The subsequent pleadings make clear that Robert's wife had used that barley for three brewings, done apparently at Mistress Malthous' house and using her equipment. Three years later Margaret Bland was twice sued by John Malthous and his wife, once for several purchases of malted barley worth 7s. 7d., the other time for malted barley worth 5s. 1d. plus coal or charcoal worth 3s. 4d.[46] The brewing for which both barley and fuel were bought again seems to have been done at the Malthous' house.

By around 1500, demand for ale in most parts of England was beginning to drop, due to the mounting popularity of beer and later of sweet wines. Especially in towns, ale was increasingly seen as a weak drink suitable for women and poor men. Within the diminishing ale trade, some women remained active. In Tamworth, a cluster of women named Endesore may have shared and/or passed along to their younger relatives the more expensive equipment now needed to compete: Christina was reported for ale-brewing in 1510, Elena between 1516 and 1531, Agnes

---

[43] While most listings do not even distinguish between the two trades, an atypically detailed report from 1503 includes ten women named for baking only, three for brewing only, and twelve for both baking and brewing (NYRO ZBD 52/29). Joan Yotson was reported for baking and/or brewing between 1483 and 1496, but at the time of her death around 1500 she was also selling coal, wool fells, and grain (Durham Univ. Libr., Archs. and Spec. Colls., 5 The College, DCD Loc.viii:5).

[44] Brewing equipment was rented elsewhere in somewhat earlier periods. In Nottingham, Catherine, wife of Richard of Chilwell, hired a brewing tun from Alice, John of Oakley's wife, in 1361, for making ale for Lenton Fair; Alice Wollaton was sued in 1375 for a mashing-vat (used in brewing) that she had leased but broken (Foulds, "Women and Work"). Lenton Fair was held annually just outside Nottingham.

[45] NYRO ZBD 53/4.   [46] NYRO ZBD 53/8.

in 1521, and Margery in 1530–1.[47] Even in the later sixteeenth century, an occasional woman still produced ale. Elizabeth Indey, wife of William Indey of King's Lynn, Norfolk, was said in 1580 to have been "very well known to be a common brewer of ale within the said town . . . by the space of twenty years now last past."[48] During that time Elizabeth produced ale, having "bought, bargained, borrowed, and adventured" for whatever "malt, corn, wood, or other such necessaries as she [had] occasion to use about her said trade," and she sold and delivered ale to her customers. But Elizabeth was an exception: what remained of the ale-brewing trade in larger communities was by then largely in the hands of male beer brewers who occasionally used their vats to make a batch of ale. Some women still brewed at home for their own family's consumption, others assisted their brewing husbands or were hired to help with commercial production, but they were seldom in charge of their own business operation.[49]

We are fortunate in having unusually detailed quantitative information about brewers – as well as other drink and food traders – from the five market centers. (Brewers are defined as including everyone who produced drink, whether or not they sold it as well.[50]) Computer-assisted analysis of all reports made by the aletasters allows us to trace changes in the number of workers over these centuries and to explore various features of their personal and working situations. Figure 6.3 shows the average number of brewers reported annually. This begins with a decline between the late thirteenth century and the middle of the fourteenth, similar to that described more generally by Bennett.[51] After limited growth during the decades around 1400, the numbers dropped further until around 1460. (For Minehead, we cannot tell whether the number of brewers would have been even higher around 1300 if we had complete figures or whether this community witnessed an atypical surge in numbers during the first half of the fifteenth century.) Between the later fifteenth and the mid-sixteenth centuries, the numbers continued to slide downwards.

---

[47] KUL T MSS Henry VIII, Rolls 3–10, passim.

[48] PRO REQ 2/26/145. All of her transactions were said to have been made on her own, with her husband's general approval but without his specific "privity, consent, and assent" for her individual decisions and dealings.

[49] During the first half of the seventeenth century, probate inventories show that 49 percent of Cornish households and 39 percent of Kentish ones had brewing equipment, most of it for ale (Whittle, "Gender Division of Labour," fig. 3). Of a sample of London women, 1726–9, 23 percent were engaged in the preparation or sale of some form of drink or ran an alehouse, tavern, or inn. Women did not commonly work together with their husbands: only fourteen of 256 married women in London, 1695–1725, worked jointly with their husbands in one of the drink or food trades (Earle, *Making of the English Middle Class*, p. 170, and his "Female Labour Market," pp. 338–9).

[50] For the methods and sources used in these analyses, see App. 1.1.

[51] In *Ale, Beer, and Brewsters*.

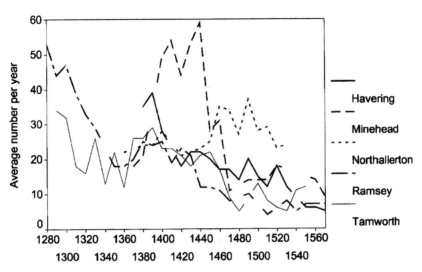

Fig. 6.3. Average number of brewers reported per year, women plus men.
See App. 1.1.

This stemmed from some combination of further increase in the scale of brewing, population changes within the market communities, and shifts in per capita demand for ale (as opposed to beer and/or sweet wines).

The sex or marital status of brewers as they were reported to the courts changed over time, as we saw in Figs. 6.1 and 6.2.[52] In Ramsey, virtually all brewers were female from the 1280s through the 1460s, with a lower fraction in the 1410s. That pattern resembles Romford/Havering's, where at least 80 percent of brewers were female between the 1380s and 1470s, apart from the 1390s. In Northallerton and Minehead, not-married women usually accounted for under 20 percent of the brewers between 1360 and the later fifteenth century, with slightly higher values in Northallerton during the 1380s and 1460s. By the late fifteenth century, when the five communities were reporting brewers in their own names, all were women. There was then a transition from male to female predominance among those listed on the court rolls as drink traders. We will explore below the historical puzzle of whether the dramatic drop in the proportion of women reflected an actual change in who was brewing

[52] For Havering and Ramsey, the percentages are for the fraction of women reported among all brewers. For Minehead, Northallerton, and Tamworth until around 1470 they represent the proportion of women reported in their own names, and hence presumably singlewomen or widows, as compared to those reported as men, and hence in most cases probably married women; thereafter it is the fraction of women reported.

or was merely a shift in reporting practices. During that transitional period, the market centers commonly contained a decade or two when some husbands and wives worked together, as Bennett has observed for London in the fifteenth century.[53]

Information from Tamworth allows us to refine Bennett's suggestion that the proportion of singlewomen and widows as compared to married women declined gradually between the late thirteenth and the early fifteenth centuries, due to the increasing scale and greater commercialization of brewing.[54] In Tamworth, where all brewers (and the few ale-sellers) seem to have been female throughout those years, the changing fraction of not-married women was evidently influenced by demographic and economic crises.[55] In normal times, most female drink workers were married, indicated by being reported under their husband's name. But during/after periods of high mortality, many widows or daughters who were left as household heads responsible for their family's support may have begun to brew for sale. As Fig. 6.2 displays, in the 1290s–1300s and again between the 1380s and 1430s, only 18–31 percent of the brewers were singlewomen or widows, while the rest were evidently married women. This may have been the basic later medieval pattern during ordinary conditions. The period between 1313 and the late 1330s, however, saw considerable disruption from harvest failures and resulting mortality crises. During those decades the proportion of not-married women who brewed in Tamworth rose to 39–46 percent. Their participation seems to have started dropping back down to its previous level during the 1340s, but it soared to 92–5 percent during the 1350s–60s, a period when many women found themselves responsible for the economic wellbeing of their families due to the death of male relatives from plague. The percentage of not-married women among Tamworth's brewers then returned slowly to its base level by around 1390.

Analysis of the size of fines paid each year by brewers in Tamworth supports the suggestion that singlewomen and widows sought a larger

---

[53] *Ale, Beer, and Brewsters.*

[54] Although Bennett too used Tamworth's records, her sampling technique – which was entirely appropriate to the purposes of her project – did not record these peaks. She looked at Tamworth's court rolls from 1289–90, 1319–22, 1370–3, 1419–22, 1470–1, and 1518–22. Because she used those particular years, she saw only a partial slice of the rise in the fraction of singlewomen and widows during the 1310s–20s and missed their huge increase during the 1350s–60s. Her statement for Tamworth says, "Not-married women accounted for roughly one-third of the presentments through the early fifteenth century" (*Ale, Beer, and Brewsters*, p. 184).

[55] Those fined for brewing in Tamworth in 1368 were termed "diverse women," and in the 1380s, brewers were cited with the female ending of the Latin term *braciatrix/ces* (KUL T MSS Edward III, Roll 45, and Richard II, Rolls 9 and 15); after the shift to individual name reporting in the 1470s, all the brewers reported were women.

income from their brewing during the immediate post-plague decades than did married women. (The fine was a reflection of how often and in what volume a woman brewed.) Whereas the average fines of married vs. not-married women were very close together between the 1290s and 1330s and again after 1390, during the generation between 1350 and 1379 the fines of singlewomen and widows were on average 1.5 to 3 times higher than those of married women.

For Havering, where we have exceptionally rich records of other kinds, we can explore the marital situation of women brewers and the relationship of their work to their husband's occupation.[56] This indicates that although nearly all late medieval brewers were married, they were not working merely as appendages to their husbands. Four-fifths of the female brewers between 1382 and 1469 were married.[57] Only a small fraction worked with their husbands: of 219 women, just 10 percent were married to men who also brewed, while the husbands of another 16 percent worked in a food trade. The remaining men worked in other crafts, farmed land, or were paid laborers. By the period 1470–1529, an even larger fraction of the brewers were married women.[58]

Evidence from the market centers helps us to scrutinize the suggestion that women commonly lacked sustained involvement with a given type of work and hence had little occupational identity. The span of years during which someone worked within the food/drink trades provides an indirect reflection of her or his level of engagement. For women in the market centers whose primary occupation was brewing, the average span was considerable.[59] Between the plague and 1469, 36 percent of Havering's female brewers and 39–41 percent of those brewers in Tamworth and Minehead who lived in male-headed households remained in the food/drink trades for ten years or more. This suggests a considerable proportion of commercial producers. Women who had a long history of brewing probably made a real contribution to their household's income, even if they were not the primary breadwinners, and they may well have been defined by others in occupational terms as brewers.

A way of testing Bennett's claim that brewing was seen as humble and low-status work is to examine the extent to which it was carried out

---

[56] To generate accurate information about marital status, I have noted a woman's marital situation for each year in which she was reported as a food/drink worker, thereby capturing changes in her marital status over time. A given woman might, for example, have five year-entries while married and another two as a widow.

[57] Of 1,083 year-entries between 1382 and 1469, 81 percent were married at the time, 18 percent appeared in their own names, and 1 percent were widows.

[58] Of 230 year-entries, 87 percent were married, 6 percent appeared in their own names, and 8 percent were widows.

[59] See App. 1.1 for the method used in assessing spans and App. 6.1 for the numbers.

in the households of people involved in local government.[60] The Chief Pledges (called the jurors in some places) were elected officials responsible for reporting upon public problems in their community's court. Leading members of their community, of solid economic standing (generally craftsmen, traders, yeomen, or substantial husbandmen), these men were well respected by their peers. If brewing was common among their families, the trade was obviously regarded as appropriate work for people of locally high status. Comparison of the names of Chief Pledges in the market centers with lists of those reported for brewing shows that a substantial fraction of these households produced and sold drink during the fourteenth and much of the fifteenth centuries. There is no sign here that brewing was held in low esteem. By the early sixteenth century, however, although some Chief Pledges were themselves now brewing, their wives no longer did so. The departure of these women from brewing presumably resulted from some mixture of being unable to compete economically and a mounting sense that drink work was not suitable for respectable women.

2   Aleselling

A different trajectory is seen among those who sold ale they had not made themselves. From the mid-fourteenth century onward, as the scale of brewing increased and the number of brewers declined, more sellers were needed to distribute their ale.[61] While alesellers were nearly all women during the later medieval years, men subsequently took over the higher end of this trade, wholesaling drink and running public houses. By the late sixteenth century, the main form of independent participation still open to women was hawking ale on the streets, though a few poor widows were allowed to run little alehouses and some women helped their husbands. These shifting relationships are nicely illustrated in Ramsey.[62] There, 90–105 people brewed ale during most decades between 1280 and 1329, nearly all of them women. But because most of them sold their beverages directly to customers, there were only one to five separate alesellers at work. During the decades between 1330 and 1439, the number of brewers (still predominantly women) was much lower, just thirty-three to sixty-four, due presumably to the commercialization of brewing. In that period,

---

[60] *Ale, Beer, and Brewsters*, as discussed in sect. 2, Ch. 2 above. See App. 1.1 for the method used here and App. 6.2 for the numbers. Because Ramsey's jurors were chosen from a wider social range, they were not included in this analysis.

[61] For this pattern in the market town of Battle, Sussex, see Mate, *Daughters, Wives and Widows*, pp. 62–3.

[62] CRRamHB, passim, as listed in App. 1.1.

the number of sellers (also heavily female) rose gradually to a peak of sixty-five to sixty-seven during the 1420s and 1430s. The combined total of 95–110 women who worked as brewers or sellers during the 1280s–1320s had thus risen slightly to a total of 110–25 during the 1420s–30s. From then on, however, the total number of women in the drink trades declined. During the period 1440–69, sixteen to twenty-four female brewers were at work in Ramsey each decade, and they were supported by only thirty-eight alesellers. The drop in the latter number suggests that more of the retailers too were now operating on a bigger scale, in some cases running alehouses, so fewer of them were needed. By the 1530s, men were starting to sell drink in Ramsey. During that decade, twenty-four of the thirty-nine reported sellers were male, and by the 1550s, twenty-six of twenty-nine were male, most of them probably running public houses. Some of these may have been assisted by their wives, but the man was now responsible for the business in legal and probably economic terms.

Of the two common methods of selling ale – within an alehouse or on the streets, as a huckster – the first covered a considerable range of size and respectability. Some alehouses were small and informal. They offered drink to people who brought their own vessels to be filled and taken home for consumption and to those who wanted to drink their ale there, using the owner's drinking pots. In Nottingham, Alice Skelton, probably a widow, bought two gallon pots, two quart pots, and four smaller pots from Martin Tankardmaker in 1371, enough equipment to allow her to sell ale at home on a small scale.[63] London women were fined in 1422 for selling ale in their houses, using illegally small or unauthorized measures.[64] The lesser alehouses in Chester, run by poor women, were thought to promote a variety of disorderly or immoral pastimes. Some houses, however, were operated by women of higher status. Between 1393 and 1419, the wife or mother of two of Chester's leading officials sold ale in their houses. Later, proprietresses of drinking houses might deliver beverages to people's homes. Around 1510, when Nicholas Wallewyn, a canon of Hereford, decided to put on a dinner party at his house, he bought ale worth £4 from Margaret Tayllour, a married alehouse keeper.[65]

In several of the market towns during the decades around 1500, larger alehouses required a husband-and-wife team or additional hired labor. In Northallerton, Laurence Hunter was reported as an alehouse keeper

---

[63] Foulds, "Women and Work"; for female keepers of small alehouses, see Hutton, "Women in Fourteenth Century Shrewsbury."

[64] CPMRL, 1413–1437, e.g., pp. 118–19 and 140. For below, see Laughton, "The Alewives."

[65] PRO C 1/364/64.

while his wife was listed for brewing and/or baking. In 1511, Laurence sued Thomas Henryson, a tailor, for 4½d. owed for ale bought from him and his wife together.[66] The only reference to an alehouse keeper in Northallerton who had to buy his drink from another person rather than producing it at home concerns one of the few men listed as running an alehouse who was not joined by a brewing wife. Keepers of the larger public houses commonly employed servants, often female, to serve their customers. John Hampton of Romford charged John Winter with trespass in 1491 for taking away both his servant and some food presumably intended for his customers.[67] Both men were brewers and sellers who worked with their wives. Richard Brigges, who ran an alehouse and later an inn, paid wages higher than those allowed by statute to six employees in 1493.

Although there was some hesitation about female alesellers even during the medieval period, opposition to women who operated on their own in this trade seems to have become more heated across the later fifteenth and sixteenth centuries.[68] To some extent, this resulted from demographic and economic pressure, which led to concern with employment for male household heads, and to the rising size of drinking houses, which made it hard for women to compete. In addition, during the later fifteenth and sixteenth centuries, authorities at both the local and the national levels of government became worried about disorderly drinking houses, part of a broader concern with social misbehavior.[69] Alehouses were seen as centers of wasteful expenditure on drinking and betting by young people and the poor, and the women who worked in them were commonly suspected of sexual availability.

Worry about unruly public houses is illustrated by Northallerton's experience during the decades around 1500, when alehouses, especially those frequented by the poor, were closely supervised by the borough court. Drinking beyond the legal deadline was a problem. In 1496, the jurors reported that John Shernake and John Rungton had spent the entire night drinking in the house of John Yotson (whose wife Joan was reported for brewing and baking in that period), despite the constable's order that they leave.[70] In spring, 1507, three men were fined for "sitting at ale in the house of Robert Brown in the middle hours of the night." Anxiety about alehouses increased if they permitted gaming or allowed vagrants or other undesirable outsiders to use their facilities. In 1487, Thomas

---

[66] NYRO ZBD 53/13. For below, see ZBD 52/18 (Thomas Medilton, 1495).
[67] PRO SC 2/172/36, m. 11v. For below, see SC 2/172/37, m. 5r.
[68] Bennett, *Ale, Beer, and Brewsters*, ch. 7.
[69] McIntosh, *Controlling Misbehavior*, esp. pp. 68–81.
[70] NYRO ZBD 52/18. For below, see ZBD 53/6.

Playsterer (whose wife was named for brewing/baking) was reported for giving hospitality to servants of local people at night, probably allowing them to play games for money, and was ordered to cease doing so, under the unusually large penalty of 6s. 8d.[71] Two years later he, along with three other men, was fined for receiving vagrants, suggesting that his establishment may have functioned as a hostelry as well as an alehouse.

Double-edged concern about the economic competition posed by female alehouse keepers as well as their unsupervised sexuality is visible in the steps taken by some of the larger communities to restrict the participation of women in this work unless they were older or widowed. In 1540, the town fathers of Chester acknowledged that alehouses and taverns in their town had previously been kept by young women, but they said that this custom was "otherwise than is used in any other places of this realm."[72] Noting that strangers to Chester thought this an "inconvenient use," the authorities ruled that no woman aged between fourteen and forty years would henceforth be allowed to keep an alehouse or tavern. Cultural evidence suggests resistance on the part of Chester's unusually powerful female brewers and sellers of ale against this order.[73] Early in Elizabeth's reign, York too moved to control brewing and alehouse keeping. Though the town's attention may not have been directed specifically against women – its goal was a tightly controlled, closely regulated, and easily taxed market in alcoholic drink – its new policies had an adverse effect upon female participation.[74] In that city, almost all recognized, commercial brewers of ale had remained female until around 1560. Those who paid the customary brewsters' fine in 1559 included many wives, some widows, and perhaps also a few singlewomen. However, when York instituted a formal licensing scheme in 1562 for brewers and alesellers, only fourteen women (mostly widows) were among the 139 people licensed as "honest citizens" permitted to work in these trades. Women's participation may well have continued as they assisted their husbands or employers, but, as Bennett has argued, the city's new policy had a significant impact. In practical terms, it made it difficult for women to continue in the trade on their own: male brewers were now labeled as more responsible and better able to hold a publicly recognized position. Further, women's contributions were devalued because their brewing was hidden from public view and because by implication they were no longer regarded as "honest citizens."

---

[71] NYRO ZBD 52/7.   [72] Clark, *The English Alehouse*, p. 79, for this and below.
[73] Wack, "Women, Work, and Plays." Most unusually, Chester's female alehouse keepers had their own guild in the early sixteenth century.
[74] Bennett, *Ale, Beer, and Brewsters*, pp. 109–11, for this and below.

Although local communities were primarily responsible for maintaining good order in drinking houses, Parliament provided some assistance. In 1495, it passed a statute that authorized any two Justices of the Peace to close down disruptive alehouses and demand a financial bond from the proprietors of other establishments guaranteeing that they would keep proper control.[75] In 1551–2, a further statute ruled that all drinking houses must be licensed; to get a license, a keeper had to post a bond promising to maintain good order, backed by secondary bonds from two creditable people.[76] Many women would have had difficulty in producing the necessary economic surety: not-married women seldom had sufficient assets of their own, and married women could not sign legal documents without their husband's participation.[77] Women were probably disadvantaged further by a growing social sense that they were incapable of maintaining good order in public houses.

By around 1600, the great majority of people licensed by the Justices of the Peace to run alehouses were male. The fraction of women among licensed keepers in Northampton in 1577, in Leicester in 1587, and in Norwich in 1587–96 ranged between 7 percent and 10 percent.[78] Of 901 keepers in rural parts of Kent, 1590–1619, only 9 percent were women; the proportion among urban keepers was virtually identical. Most of the licensed women were widows, and approval may have been granted in part so they would not have to be supported by publicly financed poor relief. Even the proprietors of unlicensed alehouses, generally smaller and with a poorer clientele than the authorized ones, were overwhelmingly male. Of sixty-six unlicensed alehouses in Nottingham in 1615, for instance, sixty-four were run by men, plus one widow and one woman who was probably married.[79]

Yet women must have continued to play a larger role in the actual operation of many alehouses than these numbers suggest. Married women might work together with their husbands, and in some cases they may have handled the day-to-day running of the establishment, even though it was listed in their husband's name. Of thirty-six alehouses licensed in

---

[75] 11 Henry VII, c. 2, modified slightly in 19 Henry VII: *Statutes of the Realm*, vol. II, pp. 569 and 697.

[76] 5 & 6 Edward VI, c. 25, *Statutes of the Realm*, vol. IV, pp. 157–8.

[77] Bennett has suggested that women were less likely than men to receive a license for three reasons: the female gender was associated in popular thought with disobedience and disruption; the legal situation of married women made it more difficult to call them to account in the courts; and the poverty of many of the female applicants undercut their ability to assume the civic responsibility that was implied by an official license (*Ale, Beer, and Brewsters*, pp. 107–8). For popular dislike of alewives, see Bennett, "Misogyny, Popular Culture."

[78] Clark, *The English Alehouse*, pp. 78–9 for this and below.

[79] *Records of the Borough of Nottingham*, Vol. IV, passim.

Rye in 1575, only two were run by women, both widows.[80] Yet twenty-three of the male proprietors were said to have another occupation as well. In those cases much of the actual work must have been done by their wives, probably assisted by female servants. In Salisbury during the later sixteenth and early seventeenth centuries, wives of alehouse keepers of various ranks worked alongside their husbands. The respectable Mrs. Boston hired labor for her husband's sizeable operation and helped to sell his ale, while lower down the scale, Henry Stocker testified in 1585 that he "chiefly liveth by selling and uttering [= making] ale, wherein he employeth his wife."[81] The female employees hired to serve drink in alehouses, sometimes called tapsters or tipplers, might develop a loyal clientele of customers. When Thomas Turke of Romford died as an elderly man in 1575, he left 3s. 4d. to "each of the maidens of the Cock and the Greyhound."[82]

In the other main pattern of selling, present to a limited extent during the later medieval years but becoming more common across the sixteenth century, women offered drink on the streets, either from temporary tables or as they moved about. Hawking the heavy liquid was physically taxing work, it brought little profit, and it left women open to official criticism and male advances. In London in 1386, Joan Garton bought ale from various brewers which she sold as a huckster.[83] Among those from whom she acquired her ale was John atte More, a brewer who sold ale both wholesale and retail in his own tavern. Later, however, Joan stopped buying from John because she found ale that suited her better elsewhere. John, already upset about that, was further angered when she sold much of her new ale on the streets near his tavern, offering unwanted competition. In recompense, he persuaded the beadle of her neighborhood to break into her house, alleging that she was hiding a married man there "for the purpose of illicitly sleeping with the same Joan." But for poor women in the cities, hawking ale might be the best possible option: it required no skills and little capital investment, since brewers were generally willing to let the sellers take drink and pay for it only upon their return.

The five market centers again offer more detailed information. (The people counted here as alesellers retailed drink they had not brewed themselves.) Figure 6.4 displays the average number of sellers reported per year, by decade. This shows a considerable increase in most places during the fifteenth century, with another rise during the 1530s–40s in Minehead, and then a decline by the mid-sixteenth century. When these figures are set against those for brewers (Fig. 6.3), we see that the rising

[80] Mayhew, *Tudor Rye*, pp. 152–3.   [81] Wright, "Churmaids," for this and below.
[82] ERO D/AER 13, 121.   [83] Goldberg, ed., *Women in England*, pp. 183–4.

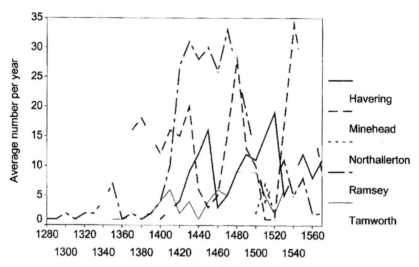

Fig. 6.4. Average number of alesellers reported per year, women plus men.
See App. 1.1.

number of alesellers offset much of the decline in number of brewers until the later fifteenth century. This was not an equivalent replacement, however, for aleselling was generally less profitable than brewing. We cannot distinguish between people who sold in alehouses and those who hawked drink, though it is likely that those who worked for many years had their own establishments.

Most of the alesellers in these communities were evidently female. In Havering and Ramsey, we can be sure that at least half and more commonly all of the reported alesellers were women until the early sixteenth century, when the proportion of women dropped. In Tamworth, the few sellers active in the 1350s–60s were either singlewomen or widows, resembling the pattern for female brewers. The proportion of not-married women was much lower during the first three-quarters of the fifteenth century, as was true in Minehead as well. After the change to individual name reporting, women remained active as alesellers in Tamworth and Northallerton into the first third of the sixteenth century; in Minehead their participation varied more markedly between decades, but was somewhat higher than seen elsewhere. In Havering, virtually all alesellers were married women into the early sixteenth century.[84] Prior to 1469, none of them had a husband in the same trade, though 15 percent were married

---

[84] During the period 1382–1469, 97 percent of the 333 year-entries were married, as were 95 percent of 262 year-entries between 1470 and 1529.

to men in another drink/food occupation. In the following two generations, women were more likely to sell ale together with their husbands, in
many cases probably within the setting of an alehouse, victualing house,
or inn.[85]

In Havering, Minehead, and Tamworth most people who sold ale
stayed in their work for relatively short periods of time, not surprising
given the negligible capital investment required if one were merely selling
drink on the streets.[86] The average span for both male and female alesellers was generally less than that of brewers. But during the period 1382–
1469, nearly a third of the women who sold ale in Havering remained in
food/drink work for ten years or more, a value that approached that of
brewers in the same period and suggests alehouse keeping.

3   Beer, wine, and taverns

During the second half of the fifteenth century, beer-brewing began to
spread outwards from the English ports, where it had been introduced
from the Low Countries and Germany, into communities of all sizes.[87]
Beer differed from ale in several respects. Because hops were used in
the brewing process, beer had more flavor. It could also be made with a
higher alcohol content than even the strongest ale; it lasted for a much
longer period of time, since the hops acted as a preservative; and it could
be kegged or barreled and then transported without affecting its quality.
Further, the process of brewing beer was more elaborate than that for
ale, requiring more expensive equipment and encouraging a larger scale
of production. The transition from ale to beer had a major impact upon
women.

Beer first appeared in the English port towns during the late fourteenth
and early fifteenth century, as an imported item brought from the Low
Counties and Germany. It was commonly followed by foreign-born beer
brewers who came to work in those same communities. By the middle of
the fifteenth century, Englishmen were themselves making beer in many
port towns. For example, in Colchester, beer was being imported from
the continent during the 1390s, but within a few decades beer brewers
were working in the town itself, some of them of Dutch background.[88]
By the 1450s, local men were brewing beer in Colchester. It was quickly

---

[85] Of 108 female alesellers between 1470 and 1529, 24 percent were married to men
reported for the same trade and another 19 percent had husbands in other food/drink
work.

[86] See App. 6.3.   [87] Bennett, *Ale, Beer, and Brewsters*, ch. 5.

[88] Britnell, *Growth and Decline in Colchester*, pp. 195–7. For the introduction of beer into
northern towns, see Goldberg, *Women, Work, and Life Cycle*, p. 114.

recognized that beer was ideally suited for use on ships, because it was more readily stored and transported than ale and probably because sailors welcomed the extra alcohol it provided. Provisioners for the royal navy were among the first to make the shift to beer.[89]

The chronology was a little later in smaller places. An ordinance from the southern port of Rye in 1456–7 makes clear that beer was being drunk in the town though it was still imported from elsewhere.[90] By the mid-1470s, however, a foreign, male beer brewer was at work in Rye, and by a century later, the ten English beer brewers comprised by far the wealthiest occupational group in the town. In Minehead, the presence of a man named William Beremaker on the lists of brewers from 1455 to 1472 implies both that he was a foreigner (since he was given an occupational surname) and that his drink was still sufficiently unfamiliar to warrant attention.[91] The Hans Corviser who brewed in 1462 and the Barlens Smyth active in 1474 had also probably come from the continent. Beer-brewing became an important activity in Havering too, sparked by demand from travelers moving along the main road to London and the proximity of the capital. The first mention of beer came in 1493, when Thomas Grayson, a recent arrival described as a gentleman, was reported as a "common seller of the drink called Bere."[92] The following year the nine men and two women fined for brewing ale were joined by Nicholas Taylour, expressly said to brew beer and probably the same man as the Nicholas Berebrewer reported in 1495–6.[93] By 1509, beer was sufficiently common, and sufficiently lucrative, that the Havering court ordered that a higher payment should be levied from those who brewed with "hoppys."

By the later sixteenth century, beer had become the drink of choice among many men, though it was slower to gain acceptance in rural communities and much of the north. Ale was increasingly relegated to an inferior position, consumed by poor men who could not afford beer and by women. Brewers of beer consequently replaced those who made only ale. They had the advantage of flexibility, for they could vary the strength of their beer and could easily produce ale as well when there was demand

---

[89] See, e.g., for 1413–22, PRO E 101/51/6; for the 1430s, E 101/53/5; for 1515, E 101/72/3, nos. 1064 and 1068; and for 1548–9, E 101/62/35. In April 1587, a London brewer set aside his normal schedule to produce special "ship beer for her majesty's ships," at an impressive rate of some 20–1 tuns per day (E 101/522/16). When a tun or barrel was used for liquids, it normally contained four hogsheads, or a minimum of 240 gallons.

[90] Mate, *Daughters, Wives and Widows*, p. 70.

[91] SRO DD/LP 27/11 and 28/13, passim. For below, see DD/LP 28/13.

[92] PRO SC 2/172/37, m. 5v.

[93] Ibid., m. 21v. For below, see PRO SC 2/172/40, m. 27v.

for it. Equipment for brewing ale, by contrast, was not adequate for making beer.

This shift in taste had a major impact upon women's involvement in the drink trades. Because of the technology and scale of beer production, brewers needed access to substantial capital and/or credit: for vats and pipes, for supplies of malt, hops, and fuel, for wooden kegs in which to store the beer, and for carts and animals with which to transport it. They had to travel to meet with suppliers and wholesalers, and they had to keep careful accounts that could be produced in court in case legal action arose from their transactions. Beer breweries also required more labor than a single individual or single household could provide. Because much of the work was physically demanding and often dangerous, men were more likely to be hired than women. Although the combination of these changes worked to exclude all small-scale producers from brewing beer, regardless of their sex, the new features placed women at a particular disadvantage.

Women generally appear in the expanding world of beer only if they were the wife, widow, or business partner of a male brewer. Among nine people reported as beer brewers in Norwich in 1564, only one woman was named.[94] By the late 1610s, a list of 204 brewers of beer in Middlesex includes 194 men working alone, three men who brewed with their wives, three widows (whose former husbands may have been brewers), and only a single woman who apparently brewed on her own. Nor were women commonly taken on as paid employees in breweries. During the 1480s, only four of the fifty-eight people hired by eight foreign-born operators of large brew houses in London were women.[95] In Romford, John Tyler, an immigrant from Wales, had three male servants assisting him in his brewery when he wrote his will in 1564, and two male employees in other establishments were scalded to death by falling into vats of brewing liquids in separate accidents during the 1560s.[96]

Widows who inherited beer breweries might seek a man to help run the operation. One way to do this was by marrying a brewer. A late Elizabethan widow named Joan inherited from her first husband the lease of a large brewery in the parish of St. Clement Danes, London, for which she paid a yearly rent of £100.[97] She soon married Vincent Windsor, and they ran the brewery together during the 1590s. After Vincent's death, she kept the establishment going until her marriage to Clement Calthorp, who took over the business. Alternatively, a widow might decide to take

[94] *The Records of the City of Norwich*, Vol. II, pp. 181–2. For below, see PRO REQ 2/420/161.
[95] Bolton, *The Alien Communities of London*, p. 19.
[96] PRO PROB 11/59, 35, PRO KB 9/604, pt. 2, no. 116, and KB 9/605, pt. 1, no. 70.
[97] PRO REQ 2/163/159.

on a male partner for her brewery. During the mid-1620s, Alice Squire of London tried – but failed – to operate a brewhouse in Thamestreet in the parish of St. Peter next to Paul's Wharf with John Hill, a brewer of the city.[98] Their heavy investment in renting and equipping the brewery emphasizes why women's handicaps in accessing credit were so damaging. The lease, which included the brewery itself, some rooms above it, a warehouse, and a yard, was valued at £13 6s. 8d. The brewhouse contained a great copper vat worth £35, a mash tub worth £8, and pumps at the waterside plus pipes of lead leading to the house valued at £15. This equipment, most of which was specified for beer but included a few items for making ale, came in sum to just under £100. To this was added the seven chaldrons (= 224–52 bushels) of coal they had in stock to fire the vats, worth £7. Alice and John also had various barrels and kegs worth nearly £15 for storing and transporting their beverages as well as three horses with harnesses and one drey for delivering them, worth £9 10s. In sum, their brewing-related equipment came to just over £130, while their personal possessions in their own homes amounted to only £73.

The shift from ale to beer harmed female sellers as well. The marketing of beer required a more elaborate chain of distributors than had been true for ale, but women rarely had either the financial creditworthiness to operate as wholesalers or the physical strength to handle the barrels. In addition, beer was normally sold from public houses, not on the streets, lessening the need for hucksters. While beer was still relatively unknown, some female alehouse keepers tried adding it to their drink list. Around 1480, Sibyll Wolley of London bought beer worth 40s. from retailer Michael Buk "for victualing of such guests as drew unto her house."[99] The wife of Richard Hudson, a pewterer of London, ran a small alehouse in the 1510s, to which she arranged that William Godard, a brewer of London, would deliver beer. Later, most female sellers appear to have specialized in small (= weak) beer, bought by other women and poor men. An account book kept by an unnamed beer brewer during the late 1570s and 1580s, probably someone working in London, shows that women were a minority of the keepers of drink/food establishments who were his customers.[100] This brewer produced different types of beer on various days. When he brewed and sold strong (= full strength) beer, his purchasers were normally men, though an occasional woman is listed. But when he made small beer, women were more likely to buy. As beer increasingly displaced ale across the later fifteenth and sixteenth

---

[98] PRO C 239/96/80, identified through Carlin's valuable handlist, *London and Southwark Inventories*.
[99] PRO C 1/64/1115. For below, see C 1/414/7.   [100] PRO E 101/522/16.

centuries, women were cut out from all but the bottom layer of retailing within this potentially profitable trade.

Declining demand for ale was intensified by a growing taste for sweet wine across the sixteenth century. During the later medieval period, consumers of regular wine were generally aristocratic, for the beverage was expensive when compared with ale or even beer. Wine imports rose during the fourteenth century, with a peak probably reached around 1400. In Colchester, for example, merchants and shipowners began to import wine during the 1330s.[101] During the following century, they brought in wine from Gascony and Bordeaux, in return for locally produced cloth. Wine was available even in market centers like Tamworth, where the borough court ordered in 1383 that it had to be sampled and valued by the town's bailiffs before it could be sold.[102] Across the fifteenth century, however, wine imports declined, affected by disruptions in trade caused by the Hundred Years War.

Sweet wines had a different history. An increase in consumption may have started in the later fifteenth century and certainly rose during the sixteenth.[103] Served normally in taverns or inns and increasingly attractive to men of middling as well as higher social status, sweet wine's popularity helped to restrict the clientele of alehouses by the Elizabethan period. The genuine versions, like Malmesey, were fortified and sweetened in the continental country in which they were produced, but by the mid-sixteenth century English people were becoming adept at modifying less expensive ordinary wine. Sometimes this was done directly by consumers, before the wine was drunk. Thus, the purchases made sometime during Henry VIII's reign for the dinners and suppers of a group of unidentified people, probably visitors to London, included white and occasionally red wine, sack, and Muscadine; the latter were both strong but not sweetened wines.[104] To these, the drinkers added sugar and such spices as pepper, saffron, ginger, cinnamon, cloves, mace, and caraway seeds together with dried fruits like raisins and dates. The household account book of Thomas Hillary, who was living in Chelmsford, Essex, in 1548–9, lists charges for carrying and "hopping" sweet wine.[105] But later, responding to consumer demand, commercial wine distilleries opened in London: Isabella Whitney speaks of stores of wine in a "stillyard" in 1573.

During the later fifteenth and early sixteenth centuries, some women were involved in the importing or wholesaling of wine, including fortified versions. Around 1480, Elizabeth Anstell and Robert Wyllyngham

[101] Britnell, *Growth and Decline in Colchester*, pp. 19 and 63; for below, see ibid., p. 195.
[102] KUL T MSS Richard II, Roll 9.
[103] Dyer, *Standards of Living*, e.g., p. 67.   [104] PRO E 101/519/14.
[105] PRO E 101/520/5. For below, see Whitney, "The Manner of Her Will."

of Southampton jointly bought three butts (= around 378 gallons) of Malmesey wine that had just been imported into England on a carrack called the "Dragon," for a price of £14.[106] Elizabeth and Robert probably planned to sell the wine in smaller batches to tavern keepers. A decade later, Alice Chester of Bristol bought three pipes (= around 315 gallons) of wine worth £10 from Evan vabe Evan ap Rosser, of Breconok, Wales, drink she then sold to retailers.

Although vintners and keepers of the taverns where wine was sold were generally male, women had some secondary roles. They might be hired to serve drink, or they might work alongside their husbands in running an establishment.[107] In Minehead, for example, where references to taverns and wine begin in the 1460s, Tege Carpenter and his wife, immigrants from Ireland, were reported in 1485 for keeping their tavern open at illegal times and encouraging the servants of local people "to waste their goods" there.[108] Around 1510, Thomas Grey of London, a grocer, sold "certain tuns of wine" worth £20 to Henry Busby alias Thykked, an Oxford vintner and tavern keeper, and his wife Joan.[109] Daughters could likewise be important to the operation of a tavern. The will of John Davenant, a vintner and mayor of Oxford at the time of his death in the 1620s, said that his five sons were to inherit landed property, to be apprenticed to a London merchant, or to continue at school or the university.[110] His daughters, by contrast, were to be kept at home until their marriages, taking turns keeping the bar at his tavern called "the Crown" and doing the accounts each night.

A detailed account of wine-selling and drinking at a tavern in the market center of Spalding, Lincs., in the early 1590s shows that although the official proprietor of the house was present in it, his wife and a female servant were there to assist him. The statements provided by witnesses in an Exchequer suit filed against Edmund Domelaw provide a lively picture of how sweetened wine was prepared and consumed at his tavern during three winter months in late 1591/early 1592.[111] The nine witnesses, who covered a considerable social range, had all patronized Edmund's house at

---

[106] PRO C 1/64/281. For below, see C 1/107/96.
[107] In 1389–90 Joan Palfraymen sold wine in a tavern in Selby, West Yorks., owned by her cousin, a merchant in York (Swanson, *Medieval Artisans*, p. 22). The occasional women described as vintners in fourteenth-century Shrewsbury were probably carrying on their deceased husband's trade (Hutton, "Women in Fourteenth Century Shrewsbury").
[108] SRO DD/L P 28/15, court held c. St. Luke Evangelist 1 Henry VII; for the 1460s, see DD/L P 28/14, court held c. St. Luke Evangelist 2 Edward IV, and DD/L P 28/13, court held December 1467.
[109] PRO C 1/410/46.   [110] Prior, "Women and the Urban Economy."
[111] PRO E 134/35 Eliz/East 26. The suit revolved around the exact nature of the various wines sold by Domelaw in his tavern, some of which were subject to an import duty he had not paid.

least once during that period, four of them traveling from nearby parishes to do so.[112] While at his tavern they enjoyed sack and claret from Gascony or La Rochelle, served with added sugar and spices, plus already sweetened wines like Malmesey, Muscadine, and "Hullock." The witnesses were asked whether Edmund had served out the wine himself or told someone else to do it for him. One man replied that Edmund usually prepared the wine himself (adding sugar and spices), but sometimes his wife did so. Another said that his drink was brought to him "by a wench of the house and, as he thinketh, by the commandment of the defendant's wife." The women served out some startlingly large amounts to their guests. Two men each drank one quart of a claret wine, one drank a pint of Muscadine plus a pint of claret wine, one drank "a gallon of claret wine and sack," and – most ominously – one said "he cannot directly depose how much he hath drunk and what he did pay."

Beginning in the later Elizabethan period, the crown began to grant out the right to deal in sweet wines as a monopoly, in several cases to royal favorites. A wine seller henceforth had to pay to acquire a license from the monopoly holder or a person to whom the grant had been conveyed. These licenses could be sold from one person to another. Lists of the people who held wine licenses during the early seventeenth century suggest that women were more heavily involved in this trade than as alehouse keepers. Analysis of a sample of ten counties from a detailed list of people who paid for licenses to sell wine in 1623 shows that 13–29 percent of the licensees in most counties were women, with an average of 21 percent for the full group.[113] That was about twice the proportion of women among keepers of alehouses during the 1580s–90s.

Several disputes over wine licenses that came before the equity courts involved married couples who ran drinking establishments. Between the early 1590s and 1607, a patent "for drawing wine within the towns of England," apparently a sub-grant of one issued initially to Sir Walter Raleigh, was held first by Francis Atkinson and then by Reginald Dobson

---

[112] His customers included several men from Spalding itself: two yeoman, aged twenty-one and thirty-five years; a thirty-year-old sadler; a thirty-two-year-old gentleman, and a thirty-two-year-old servant. In addition, coming from rural communities were a forty-year-old husbandman from Fleet, a fifty-year-old husbandman from Gedney, and two yeomen, one aged twenty-two years from Moulton, the other aged thirty-eight years from Weston.

[113] PRO E 101/526/27. The sample included counties starting with B through E. Two outliers were excluded from the range but not the total average, both counties with very small numbers of wine licensees: only 8 percent female in Cumberland but 47 percent female in Durham. Because all women were listed with first and last names, their marital status cannot be determined. The ambiguous names of Francis/Frances and Christian were excluded from consideration.

and his wife Elizabeth, who ran a tavern or alehouse in Barnard Castle, Durham.[114] After Reginald's death, Elizabeth continued to hold the license until her marriage to William Barnes, whereupon they used it together. In Bawdeswell, Norfolk, James Jeckes held a license "for drawing and selling of wine" beginning Michaelmas, 1607, for which he paid £5.[115] When he later decided to move away from Bawdeswell, he conveyed his license to John Beales for £9. Beales in turn subcontracted part of the license to Richard Hase and Francis his wife, who ran an inn in Bawdeswell called "the sign of the Crown," for an annual payment of £4.

4   **A historical puzzle: were women displaced from the drink trades around 1500?**

While Bennett has described in general terms the disappearance of women from the drink trades during the fifteenth and sixteenth centuries, we lack detailed studies of how this occurred within particular communities.[116] Further, the factors she rightly suggests as contributing to this change are longer-term forces: increased commercialization in ale production, brewers' guilds run by men, the new technology of beer-brewing, and growing regulation of drink sellers, all accompanied by mounting patriarchal concern about women. Although she does not provide dates for the disappearance of women from the drink trades, she implies that this was a gradual process, extending over the second half of the fifteenth century and into the sixteenth. To gain a better picture of how the broader influences she identified interacted with the specific demographic, economic, and social pressures that operated within individual settings, we need local studies.

Information from our market centers indicates that an apparent and perhaps a real transition from female to male preponderance among brewers and sellers as reported in local court records occurred more abruptly than Bennett's discussion suggests. As we have seen, women continued to dominate ale brewing and selling through the later fifteenth century and sometimes a few decades longer: in four of the communities virtually all reported drink workers were women during the 1480s–90s, as were about half in Minehead (see Figs. 6.1 and 6.2). There was then an apparent transition to male dominance, beginning sometime between 1480 and 1530 in each of these five towns. The married women who had been

---

[114] PRO REQ 2/391/34. For the widow of a tavern-keeper who felt into debt because Queen Elizabeth voided the wine patent granted to Sir Walter Raleigh in May 1593, on the basis of which her husband had run a wine tavern in Saffron Walden, Essex, see REQ 2/401/31.
[115] PRO REQ 2/295/90.   [116] In *Ale, Beer, and Brewsters*.

brewing and/or selling ale prior to this shift, some of whom had engaged in commercial activity for many years, were replaced by people – in most cases men – who were new to such work and often new to the community. The transition from female to male names happened surprisingly quickly, completed within a single generation in four of the places and within four decades in Minehead. What makes this a historical puzzle is that we cannot be sure whether women were in fact displaced from the drink trades. Were the men reported after the shift the actual brewers/sellers, or were they merely heading the household in which women made and sold beverages, a return to the style of reporting practiced in many communities prior to around 1470? We will describe the evidence for a female-to-male transition and explore the possible explanations.[117]

Background to the transition

The shift from female to male domination among those reported was preceded in some settings by closer supervision of drink workers. In Minehead, Northallerton, and Tamworth, where married women had been reported under their husband's names during the fourteenth and much of the fifteenth centuries, the courts changed sometime between 1460 and 1500 to the pattern of listing drink and food workers in their own names (see Fig. 6.2). This change occurred in each community during a time of social turbulence marked by misbehavior in alehouses, taverns, and inns, by problems with poor people, and by heightened local violence.[118] The Chief Pledges/jurors of the local courts, the men responsible for reporting on public problems, apparently decided that as part of their attempts to maintain order, people engaged in the drink trades needed to be controlled more carefully. If, for instance, there was trouble at a public house, the constable had to know who its actual keeper was. This meant that drink workers must be named individually in the aletasters' reports to the court. We can examine the shift in reporting practices within the three settings, noting what else was going on at that time.

In Tamworth, the change began during the 1450s–60s, when the court went back and forth between the two patterns of reporting, but by the

---

[117] The possible displacement of women must be distinguished from the decreasing number of brewers/sellers reported to the courts. The ongoing decline seen in Figs. 6.3 and 6.4 resulted primarily from increases in scale prior to around 1550, but after that time the courts were probably not naming all workers. Because the Parliamentary statute of 1551–2 required that drinking houses be licensed and transferred responsibility for their supervision to the Justices of the Peace, people reported to the local courts thereafter may in many cases have been smaller brewer/sellers who ran unlicensed houses.

[118] For inns, which served food and drink to local people as well as to those who lodged there, see sect. 3, Ch. 7 below.

late 1470s only the actual brewer or seller was named. Across the next sixty years, the proportion of women in these trades did not drop below 90 percent. The shift occurred during a period of social tension, when the leading men who ran the local court were clearly trying to clamp down on disruptive behavior. Between 1456 and 1462, Tamworth's Chief Pledges reported illegal gaming in drinking houses, badly run alehouses and inns, and sexual misbehavior.[119] It fined poor people who took wood from hedges to use as fuel (known as "hedgebreaking"). The level of violence appears to have been high, with an exceptionally large number of people – many of them young – reported for fighting and assaults. The Chief Pledges may have been especially sensitive to problems with order at that time due to conflicts between the Ferrers and Buckingham families, an early phase of the power struggles known as the Wars of the Roses.[120]

In Northallerton, the shift to individual name reporting took place in the 1480s. During the 1460s and 1470s, at the end of the era of household reporting, ten presumably unmarried women and fifty-six men or their wives were reported for brewing/selling ale and/or baking.[121] By the 1490s, when the individual name reporting system was fully in place, seventy women (= 97 percent) and just two men were listed. Northallerton's history was disrupted at the time of this change. Frequent outbreaks of disease in the community – plague in most cases – may well have contributed to an unusually high degree of turnover in food/drink workers between the 1470s and 1490s.[122] Poor harvests in the Northallerton area during the 1480s–90s compounded the broader economic decline of the north of England stemming from lost overseas markets and London's increasing capture of long-distance trade. These factors increased local poverty and sent more poor people onto the roads. Between 1475 and 1485 Northallerton's court addressed problems with hedgebreaking, vagrants, and poor newcomers, focusing upon Scots during the 1490s.[123] Local officials were worried about the community's lesser alehouses and inns (the first was mentioned in 1476); they reported gaming, excessive drinking, and sexual misconduct between 1475 and 1496. The community was disrupted by a large riot involving outsiders in 1485 and was the centerpoint of a rebellion against the crown in 1489.[124]

[119] KUL T MSS Henry VI, Rolls 45 and 47–51.
[120] Carpenter, *Locality and Polity*, pp. 426–7 and 453–4.
[121] Brewing/selling was not distinguished from baking in most Northallerton listings.
[122] Newman, *Late Medieval Northallerton*, pp. 70–92.
[123] NYRO 221658, ZBD 51/1, 52/5, 52/7, 52/11, 52/14, 52/18, 52/21, and 52/25 for these and below.
[124] NYRO ZBD 52/3, Newman, "Order and Community in the North," and Hicks, "The Yorkshire Rebellion."

Minehead too changed its reporting system during the 1480s. During the 1470s, while household listings were in use, 9 percent of the brewers and alesellers were not-married women, the rest being men/married women; with the shift to the individual name method, women's participation rose to 49 percent in the 1490s and to 62 percent in the 1500s. Once again there are signs of social disturbance. The familiar cluster of concern with misbehavior and poverty flared up: permitting wrongdoing in one's public house, sexual misconduct, and hedgebreaking.[125] In this community there was also considerable immigration, including Irish and Welsh people. During the 1480s–90s, some of the newcomers took work in the drink trades. We can assess this change only crudely, by examining surnames.[126] Of 135 people reported as brewers/sellers during the 1490s, ninety-one (= 67 percent) had names not found among traders of any kind reported to the court during the 1470s. Many of these were apparently new arrivals to the community. Further, unlike the pattern during the 1460s, when only 8 percent of the drink workers had Irish or Welsh surnames or the first name Tege, during the 1490s the figure jumped to 31 percent for male drink traders and 21 percent for women, with more Irish than Welsh names.[127] A rising number of new and especially foreign brewers/sellers probably heightened local leaders' sense that their work needed to be overseen more carefully.

Evidence of a transition

In all five market centers, women's names among the drink workers listed by the local courts were almost entirely replaced by men's across a time span ranging from one to four decades some time during the late fifteenth or first half of the sixteenth centuries. Because sudden changes involving economic, social, and cultural processes are inherently unlikely, one

---

[125] All these issues appear in SRO DD/L P 28/15, passim.

[126] This method of establishing probable family relationships, the only one possible in the absence of fuller demographic data, obscures ties through maternal lines and may create false ties by counting people as related who shared the same surname but not a family link.

[127] The surnames counted as probably Irish or Welsh (based upon regional surname dictionaries and omitting others that are possible but less certain) were: Casy, Coule, Davy, Dennis, Donell, Hassan, Heny, Howell, Iver, Ketegan, Lewelyn, Lymryk, Maddok, Moris, Mourghan, Owen, Phelip, Power, Quyrk, Suly, Tege, Thomas, Walshe, and Waterford. Tege, an anglicized version of the Irish equivalent of Timothy, was found only during the 1490s. Of people active during the 1490s, only those named Donnell and Power had been preceeded in drink work during the 1460s by someone with the same surname, and though they were not counted here as newcomers, they were not necessarily relatives since those were common names in southern Ireland. I am grateful to Mr. Alfred O'Brien of University College Cork for his assistance.

might assume that this was merely a shift back to the older pattern of reporting married women workers under their husband's name. There are, however, few cases in which a woman brewer/seller prior to the transition was replaced on the lists by a husband-and-wife team or by a man alone who had the same surname. This suggests strongly that the earlier drink workers, most of them female, left their trades entirely, with their businesses taken up by people who appear to have been unrelated to them. Further, many of those who began brewing or selling after the transition, most of them men, seem to have been recent immigrants to the community, people whose names do not appear in earlier records. In examining these changes, we will begin with Romford/Havering, where the evidence is particularly rich.

The transition in Romford began during the 1480s and was largely accomplished within thirty years. (It is not surprising to find a new pattern emerging early here, for the community was precocious in many social and economic respects.[128]) We will look at the shift in stages, remembering that women had been listed in their own names as far back as the surviving records extend. Between 1464 and 1481, the last of the pre-transitional years, fifty-one people had been reported by the local court as brewers/sellers of ale and twenty-one as sellers only. Of these, seventy were women (= 97 percent) and two were men. Of the women, 93 percent were married, but none of their husbands worked in the drink trades; four were widows, and one was listed in her own name. After a seven-year gap in the records, 1482–8, only nine of those women (= 13 percent) and one of the men were still active. This mass exodus from the drink trades stands in contrast to the greater degree of continuity seen among drink workers between 1440–57 and 1464–81.[129] The change did not stem from a shift to the household method of reporting, which would have led to the substitution of a husband's name for his previously listed wife: in only six cases were the husbands of former drink workers reported after 1489, and in two of them husband and wife were both named, suggesting that they were actually working together in these trades.

The early transitional period, 1489–97, saw a remarkable influx of new people into Romford's drink trades. Although only around twenty brewers and twelve alesellers were reported in most years, the turnover among them was very high, resulting in a total of 120 people engaged in drink work sometime during those nine years. Of these, just 31 percent were women reported without their husbands, while 57 percent were married

---

[128] As discussed in McIntosh, *Autonomy and Community*.

[129] Of the drink workers active in 1464–81, 39 percent had been listed in 1440–57 and another 19 percent followed someone with the same surname; 43 percent were newcomers to the trade.

couples and 13 percent were men listed without their wives. For the men who were named on their own about whom we have occupational evidence from other sources, all were described as brewers. Some of the male drink traders were solid members of the community, continuing to hold the types of local office that the husbands of their predecessors had filled, including serving as Chief Pledge. This group included the new large-scale brewers of beer who had just arrived in Romford. But at the opposite end of the spectrum were nine brewers/alehouse keepers (seven of them joined by their wives) and two innkeepers who were frequently reported to the Havering court for entertaining undesirable outsiders, keeping bad rule, fighting, or permitting illegal gaming or sexual misconduct within their establishments.[130] By 1498, eight of these lesser public house keepers, all recent arrivals to Havering, had been banished from the community.

During Romford's late transitional period, 1499–1520, 170 brewers and sellers were reported, but only 21 percent were women operating without their husbands. Further, all of those not-married women were retailing other people's ale, generally a much less profitable activity than brewing. The fraction of married couples had dropped to 40 percent, while men working without their wives now formed 39 percent. There was again limited continuity between periods: only 18 percent of the women and 37 percent of the men who worked between 1489 and 1497 were still active after 1499. We can use Romford's tax assessments in 1524–5 to examine the future economic standing of the drink workers based upon whether they were working independently or with a spouse in 1499–1520.[131] The wealthiest group consisted of men who operated without their wives. They were rated at a range of levels but included an exceptional 32 percent who were assessed at the very high level of £20 or more. The latter included the large-scale beer brewers who were now setting up operation in Romford. The assessments of men who headed a couple in which both brewed were concentrated in the lower (under £2) or middling (£2–9) range, whereas married women who worked in the drink trade without the participation of their husbands were almost all poor. If we look ahead to the post-transitional years, between 1530 and 1559 no women were reported for brewing. Of the few female alesellers, just over half were widows and the rest married women.

The apparent disappearance of women from the drink trades in Ramsey followed a similar pattern, though the change began slightly later. Ramsey, whose court had listed women in their own name since at least the 1280s, underwent most of its shift from female to nominal male dominance

[130] McIntosh, *Autonomy and Community*, pp. 255–61.   [131] PRO E 179/108/150.

between 1490 and 1520, though we cannot pinpoint the dates because the court rolls are missing for much of that period.[132] Between 1491 and 1518–19, the proportion of women among reported brewers and alesellers dropped sharply, from 100 percent to just 17 percent. In the surviving rolls we find many new people within these trades rather than substitution of a husband's name for his wife's. Of the twenty-six women listed in 1491, all of whom worked independently of their husbands and some of whom had brewed and sold ale for several decades, only one was still active in the 1510s, while another was replaced by a man with the same surname (perhaps her son, but not her husband). The other nine male drink workers active in the later 1510s came from families that appear to have had no previous connection with these occupations. The proportion of women reported recovered partially during the 1530s, due in part to some spousal teams (seven of the twenty married women were joined by their husbands in the same trade); thirty-one of the thirty-three men reported were either new arrivals in Ramsey or came from older families that had not worked in these trades during the 1510s. During the 1540s and 1550s just 10–12 percent of the reported drink workers were women.

The transition from female to male names began during the 1530s in Tamworth, Northallerton, and Minehead. In Tamworth, the shift among brewers happened very quickly. (We cannot trace the change among alesellers, since they were not reported after 1540.) Until the early 1530s, all the brewers listed by the court were female. Of the thirty women who had been reported for brewing sometime between 1510 and 1531, five had husbands who worked in other aspects of the food and lodging trades. Eleanor Brone, for instance, reported for brewing between 1510 and 1521, was married to John Brone, named as an innkeeper between 1511 and 1520. But the remaining twenty-five female brewers were apparently operating on their own. Of those thirty women, not one was listed as still active between 1540 and 1551: all reported brewers were now male. Nor did this change result from a return to household reporting. None of the women active prior to 1531 was listed under her husband's name after 1540, and only three had the same surname as a man who brewed between 1540 and 1551. Of the nineteen male brewers reported in the later period, sixteen bore names not found previously in the food/drink trades.

Northallerton's shift likewise began abruptly, though we can observe only its opening stage because the court rolls no longer name drink

---

[132] Between 1473 and 1530, records survive only from 1491, 1501 (which does not list drink workers or social problems), and 1518–19.

workers after 1537. Between 1526 and 1531, forty-four of the forty-six people reported in the drink trades had been women (= 96 percent), whereas in 1533–7, only eleven of forty-seven (= 23 percent) were female. Of the women in the earlier period, 86 percent were married, and just one had a husband who also worked in the drink trades.[133] Only six of those women were still reported in 1533–7, but another eleven had evidently been replaced on the rolls by their husbands or another relative with the same surname and may have continued working behind the scenes. The remaining twenty-seven women active in the earlier period (= 61 percent) left the drink trades entirely after 1531 and were followed by no probable relative. That is a high dropout rate across just two years, especially since many of the previous workers were long-term participants. Of the thirty-six men active in 1533–7, twenty-five (= 69 percent) had surnames not borne by anyone who had worked in these trades between 1526 and 1531, and most do not appear in earlier records at all. If Northallerton's court rolls had survived beyond 1537, we might well have witnessed a further drop in the fraction of women reported.

In Minehead, the transition from female to male preponderance was less pronounced, both because more men had been listed in the drink trades during the decades around 1500 and because the decline in women's apparent involvement was spread over a longer interval. Between the 1480s and the 1530s, the fraction of women brewers and alesellers had never exceeded around 60 percent, and a diminution of their share to below 20 percent was not reached until 1565–71. Here again our ability to delineate the exact chronology is limited by lost court rolls.[134] Of the seventy-five people named as brewers in the 1520s or as alesellers in the 1530s, 47 percent were women, whereas of sixty-four alesellers in the 1540s, only a third were female. When records of both occupations resume, 17 percent of the forty-two people named in 1565–71 were women, mostly widows. By that time, however, the listings may not have been complete.

Possible interpretations of this evidence

The information presented above can be explained along two lines, one stressing how material was recorded on the court rolls, the other arguing

---

[133] This may have been a northern pattern. Married women likewise remained heavily involved in brewing in the market town of Wakefield, West Yorks., and some of the rural villages around it into the 1530s (Walker, "The Burgess Courts, Wakefield," and *The Court Rolls of the Manor of Wakefield from 1537 to 1539*, e.g., pp. 69, *bis*, and 85).

[134] We have information about brewers through 1526, with a gap from then until 1565; for alesellers, we have lists through 1544 but a hole until 1565.

that real changes occurred in who was working in the drink trades. Either answer to this historical puzzle is legitimate, though the author finds the second more persuasive.

Interpretation 1: Changes in data entry. This approach emphasizes that the entries on the court rolls should not be taken at face value, that they do not necessarily give the names of the person who was actually brewing or selling. During the later fifteenth or first half of the sixteenth century, such an interpretation would conclude, the clerks of these courts shifted away from the system of individual name reporting, which reveals first female dominance and then some husband-and-wife partnerships, to a house-hold system of reporting, listing married female drink workers under their husband's name. Such a clerical change would have produced the fairly rapid apparent transition seen in four of the market centers. To make this interpretation persuasive, one would need to explain why certain courts that during the central medieval period had used the household system of reporting shifted to the individual name method sometime between 1460 and 1490 and then reverted to the older form a generation later. Further, a shift in clerical procedure would have to be recognized as distinct from whatever pressures led most of the women who had previously dominated drink work in their communities to abandon their trade. One would also need to add to the equation the arrival of many newcomers who moved into such work, regardless of whether it was a man or woman who was actually making/selling drink within those households.

Interpretation 2: A real change in who was doing the brewing and selling. A second explanation argues that the shift reported on the court rolls reflected a real change in who was brewing and selling. When a man was reported after the transition, this approach accepts that he was indeed engaged in and in charge of the operation, though his wife or female servants may have participated. As certain types of drink work became more profitable, especially those involving beer and wine, they became attractive to men. The period of husband-and-wife partnerships would by this reading have been a stage between female and male dominance within the drink trades.

The context within which the transition occurred in these market centers was marked by demographic, economic, and/or social dislocations similar to what was noted for the shift from household to individual reporting during the fifteenth century. In the three places that had previously changed their record-keeping practices, life had been more tranquil during the intervening decades, with less instability and little anxiety about wrongdoing.[135] But at the times when female drink workers were

---

[135] This was a common pattern during the later fifteenth and first half of the sixteenth centuries: see McIntosh, *Controlling Misbehavior.*

being replaced by male names on the court rolls, we encounter a set of similar pressures in all five communities. If this explanation of the evidence is correct, those factors should be added to the ones suggested by Bennett to explain more precisely why the female-to-male transition occurred when it did.

The first is demographic. A high fraction of the existing drink workers in most of the communities disappeared at the start of the transitional periods, opening up niches that would be filled at least nominally by men. The departure of the earlier brewers and sellers may have been due in part to disease. High turnover was visible in Havering during the 1480s, Northallerton during the 1520s (when plague was specifically mentioned), Tamworth during the 1530s, and perhaps Ramsey between 1490 and the early 1530s. Research on the monks of Christ Church Priory in Canterbury and Westminster Abbey shows a series of mortality peaks between around 1480 and 1530.[136] Westminster, for example, had two or three unusually bad years each during the 1480s, 1490s, and 1520s, and four bad years during the 1500s. Many of the outbreaks were described at the time as plague, but one at Canterbury in 1485 was said to be the new disease known as "sweating sickness," probably a form of influenza. Local studies indicate bouts of disease in the 1530s too. Although epidemics struck individual communities at different times, the years between 1480 and 1540 seem to have been unusually subject to virulent disease. People who worked in drinking houses in the market centers would have been particularly at risk, exposed not only by their regular patrons but also by travelers moving through the area. There is no suggestion that the diseases were gender specific, but most of the drink traders prior to the transition were women and therefore most likely to face contagion. The fact that local court rolls are frequently missing during the period when many previous drink workers vanished raises the possibility that an outbreak of disease and other local disruptions affected record-keeping as well.

A second possible trigger was an increased presence of poor people, whether outsiders or local residents. Worry about new arrivals and the disruption they introduced must have been heightened when they congregated in alehouses or inns. Havering's court worried about vagabonds and disorder in the local hostel for indigent strangers, issuing strict new rules for its conduct in 1492.[137] Ramsey too was concerned about poor outsiders, prohibiting the lodging of beggars in 1518–19. Local officials in Tamworth, Northallerton, and Minehead reported vagrants, some of them foreign, and/or fined those who received them during the period of

---

[136] Hatcher, "Mortality in the Fifteenth Century," and Harvey, *Living and Dying*, pp. 122–7.

[137] McIntosh, *Autonomy and Community*, pp. 238–9. For all the examples below, see App. 1.1 unless otherwise noted.

the transition in their communities. These concerns were tied to worry about poverty in the town. Ramsey, Tamworth, and Minehead were troubled by hedgebreaking, and Northallerton faced severe need during the late 1520s and 1530s due to bad harvests and other economic problems.[138] This is reflected in an order that all poor "undersettles" (= people who rented housing from another person) should be evicted. The situation was probably compounded in 1536 by the decision of many Northallerton people to participate in the Pilgrimage of Grace, a rebellion against the crown which led to deaths and confiscation of property.

Another factor seems to have been how and where drink was served to customers. During the decades when women's reported participation in the drink trades dropped sharply, we start encountering references to beer, wine, and inns. Romford's first inn, mentioned in 1464, was joined by several others during the 1480s, and beer was brewed locally from the 1490s onwards. In Ramsey, jurors during the early 1530s were worried about disorderly inns, including their use by servants and poor people. The difficulties faced by women as sole proprietresses of larger public houses must have been to some extent economic, but it was also probably harder for them to enforce good order among their employees and guests: if trouble broke out, a man's physical and social authority might be needed. Local officials may also have been troubled about having a woman in charge of a house where male guests congregated and sometimes spent the night.

A final probable influence was deep concern on the part of local leaders about order, good behavior, and control, issues commonly linked to poverty and gender. During the transition period in each of the market centers, the leading men were attempting to use their authority to maintain decency and security within their communities. The Chief Pledges/jurors reported on some or all of the forms of social misbehavior that had been visible during the earlier shift in reporting methods: men, especially servants, who squandered their limited resources playing illegal betting games; drunken and disorderly public houses; and sexually uncontrolled people.[139] Attention seems to have focused on the lesser alehouses, those that catered to a poorer, more mobile, and sometimes dishonest clientele. Gaming in public houses was addressed in Havering during the 1490s and 1510s, in Ramsey during the 1510s, and in Tamworth during that decade and the 1540s, when it was also ordered that no one should allow servants to come to their houses late at night, presumably for further gaming. All five places punished alehouse

---

[138] Newman, *Late Medieval Northallerton*, pp. 70–92, for this and below.
[139] For a fuller discussion, see McIntosh, *Controlling Misbehavior*.

keepers who did not maintain good rule (commenting sometimes upon the female tapsters who served drink) and all reported misbehavior that was either explicitly or implicitly sexual (e.g., men who kept women in their homes overnight or visited "suspect houses," or men or women who were "badly governed in their bodies").

This concern with the presence and possible sexual availability of women in public drinking places raises the possibility that Minehead's atypical pattern in shifting from women's to men's names among the drink workers (slower and less complete than in the other places) was influenced by the nature of the maritime economy. Because much of the demand for beverages in the port came from ships, women could produce and sell kegged drink on a private basis. Since they did not need to deal with customers in alehouses, they may have sidestepped concern about women's roles in public settings.

The history of women's drink work thus contains some significant changes over time. The pattern found around 1300, in which a large number of women brewed and sold a little ale at least occasionally, was modified by demographic and economic developments, including the increased commercialization of brewing. During the later fourteenth and fifteenth centuries, the market communities and towns provided fertile soil for married women from respected local families who made and sold ale on a commercial basis, sometimes for years on end and without the involvement of their husbands. This situation was temporary and fragile, however, vulnerable to ongoing increases in the scale of production, the introduction of beer and sweet wines, and growing discomfort about women's roles as keepers of public houses. By around 1600, women rarely functioned as independent brewers or proprietresses of drinking houses. Some married women helped their husbands in alehouses and taverns, other women worked in such establishments as servants or paid employees, and poor urban women hawked ale on the streets. A few widows were given permission by local authorities to operate alehouses, one suspects to keep them from asking for poor relief, or obtained a license to sell wine. While it is true that many women did low-status, poorly paid work within the drink trades throughout these centuries, we need also to acknowledge the importance of the unusual economic and social autonomy of some women during the post-plague generations.

7   The food trades and innkeeping

The food trades and innkeeping might seem natural types of work for women, since they could be regarded as extensions of their domestic skills. In practice, however, female participation was limited, due largely to women's handicaps in obtaining credit for equipment and supplies, hiring labor, traveling, and maintaining order. Opportunities for women as producers and sellers of food were concentrated at the bottom of the system. Baking and more lucrative forms of food work, such as dealing in imported goods, were normally in the hands of men in larger communities, though in market centers some women baked. The most common activity for women, selling food on the streets as hucksters, brought the usual problems faced by mobile female vendors. Inns, which provided food, drink, and lodging for their customers and let local people come in to eat and drink, became larger and more complex during the later fifteenth and sixteenth centuries.[1] They now served increasingly as centers for business dealings as well as providing better food and more comfortable accommodations for their guests. Although relatively few women had run inns on their own during the later medieval period, as inns expanded it became more difficult for them to act as sole proprietresses, though some worked with their husbands or provided labor as servants. In this chapter we will look first at baking, a type of activity well documented since it was subject to the regulations of the Assize of Bread and Ale, and then at other foods and innkeeping.[2]

1   Baking

Bread, the staple of most people's diet, was generally baked in ovens, though in some places and periods the poor had to make do with flat bread cooked on a pan or griddle. Various grades of oven-baked bread

---

[1] Inns are considered here rather than under drink or service work because provision of food was a major component of their diverse functions.
[2] For the Assize, see Ch. 6 above.

were available, with wheat bread at the high end of the spectrum, "black" bread (made of rye and/or oats) sometimes mentioned in the middle, and "horse bread" (made of beans and peas, nominally produced as animal fodder but sometimes eaten by poor people too) at the bottom. During periods of high grain prices, people commonly shifted downwards in the type of bread they purchased. Baking required an oven, which was expensive to purchase and maintain, so only the wealthiest families baked their own bread in these centuries. Anyone who owned an oven was likely to keep it in use as much as possible, promoting a larger scale of commercial production and the use of family or paid labor. Difficulty in obtaining capital and controlling labor must have been deterrents for many women who might otherwise have become bakers. It is therefore not surprising that most bakers were men throughout these centuries, especially in the larger communities, and that the male fraction evidently rose over time, due probably to increases in the scale of baking. When women did bake, they often produced the less expensive kinds of bread. Retailing bread baked by others was commonly done by poorer women, especially hucksters.

A detailed glimpse into the physical setup of a bakery is provided by the inventory of Elizabeth Wilcox, a Tamworth widow who described herself as a baker in her 1598 will and seems also to have been making cheese.[3] Her father-in-law and husband had been bakers, and Elizabeth was planning to continue her husband's trade until her second son, Henry, who was under age and still living at home at the time of her death, was old enough to take over the business. The kitchen and a separate bolting house (for sifting flour) contained a molding board, two kneading troughs, a bolting unit with two tubs, one chest for bread, seven "peales" (= a baker's shovel), five barrels, a bread grater, two baskets, three dozen trenchers, various sacks and bags, a churn, four cheese vats, two sutters (= the board placed between the cheeses in the press), and one cheese ladder (= the board placed over the cheese to collect the fat while it is being squeezed). The "kylnhouse" presumably included the baking oven as well as a cheese press, though the former is not mentioned specifically. Elizabeth left all that equipment to Henry, together with wood, coal, and the rest of the term remaining on the lease of the house and shop in which she and her husband had lived and worked.

Her inventory indicates that the bakery-cum-cheesemaking operation had supported a fairly comfortable style of life. At the time of her death

---

[3] Lichfield Joint Record Office wills, 1598, Elizabeth Wilcox, Tamworth. Her maiden name was Blewe, and several female Blewes had worked in the food/drink trades during the decades around 1500.

Elizabeth lived in a large house with her three sons and three daughters. She had leased out part of the building to another couple, perhaps to bring in extra income after her husband's death. Of the six rooms she used for her own family, the largest was the main hall, which seems to have functioned as both dining room and shop. It was wainscoted with wooden panels and decorated with painted cloths. The chamber over the hall contained three beds, chests, and tables, while the parlor held two more beds and other personal items. Chambers over the parlor and kitchen were used for storage. The kitchen was well stocked with cooking equipment, and she had thirty-two pieces of pewter as well as other dishes for serving and eating. Elizabeth had also two cows and two calves, probably related to her cheesemaking. The total value of all her goods came to £22 18s., while the time remaining on her lease of the house and working buildings was assessed at £3 6s. 8d. Her possessions therefore fell within the same general range as several Tamworth men of her generation who engaged in what are commonly described as more skilled crafts: tanner John Harrison who died in 1585 (whose goods were valued at £15), and shoemaker William Baron who died in 1587 (with goods worth £33 16s. 6d.).[4]

Since an oven and other equipment for baking formed a substantial part of a family's investment in living/working space and often had to be taken on long leases, Elizabeth Wilcox and her family were not alone in operating a bakery over successive generations. In another Tamworth example, William Irpe was reported as a baker between 1458 and 1470. Matilda Irpe, probably his widow or daughter-in-law, kept the bakery going between 1488 and the early sixteenth century, followed by her son John, who baked from 1504 to 1512. He was succeeded by Henry Irpe, who ran the bakery from 1519 until at least 1531. Henry lived in Lichfield Street with his wife Alice and nine children and/or servants in the early 1530s, and it is likely that the family's bakery had been located there for multiple generations.[5]

In poorer communities, where paying for and maintaining an oven might be too expensive for a single person, several methods provided access to a shared oven. In some manors, there was a communal oven, provided by the lord but under condition that all the tenants use it for their baking and pay a fee for doing so. A related pattern is visible in Northallerton during the early sixteenth century, where one person owned an oven and charged others for its use, similar to the arrangements made for brewing. Thus, Thomas Prest's wife, reported as a baker (and probably

[4] *Probate Inventories of Tamworth*, pp. 6–7.
[5] See the Tamworth court rolls (App. 1.1), and Kettle, "A List of Families." I am grateful to Philip Morgan for the latter reference.

a brewer) from 1505 through 1515, did not have her own oven: in 1509 she was accused of non-payment of the charge she owed for baking her bread in another person's house.[6]

As early as the decades around 1300, the financial demands imposed by baking had given an advantage to men and probably to married women as opposed to singlewomen and widows. Of fifteen bakers from villages near Lincoln who paid a fine during the 1290s to sell bread in the urban market, only two were women, and they may both have been married.[7] In York around 1301, a list of bakers of black bread, an inexpensive version that was more likely to be made by women, includes ten men but just two women. The difficulties faced by singlewomen who wanted to bake are illustrated by the history of Agnes ad Fontem at the fair of St. Ives, held annually near Ramsey. During the earlier 1290s, Agnes retailed bread baked by others.[8] Successful in that role and apparently looking for greater profit, she decided to start baking on her own. But although she became known as Agnes le Baker, she was unable to stay afloat financially. She was excused from a court fine in 1300 because she was destitute, and the following year she was reported for running a brothel, renting rooms to prostitutes.

Male domination of commercial baking probably intensified during the later medieval years.[9] When a large household (we do not know whose) bought bread in several communities to the south and west of London sometime between 1320 and 1350, the nine sellers – all apparently bakers themselves, not retailers – were male.[10] In Exeter, where most baking during the later fourteenth century was done by men, the few female bakers worked at the fringes of the trade, making and selling oat or horse

---

[6] NYRO ZBD 53/8, and cf. ZBD 53/6, a suit concerning items bought from her. For shared brewing equipment, see Ch. 6 above.

[7] Bischoff, "Late Thirteenth-Century Urban Commuting." For below, see Goldberg, ed., *Women in England*, p. 187. Bennett has suggested that the participation of rural women as bakers may have increased between the late thirteenth century and the 1340s, based upon her evidence from Brigstock (*Women in the Medieval English Countryside*, pp. 190–1).

[8] Moore, "Aspects of Poverty."

[9] In 1379–81 there were no women bakers but four men in (King's) Lynn, five men in Lichfield, twenty-eight men in Oxford, one woman plus five men in Southwark, one woman plus seven men in Rotherham, and one woman plus thirty men in York (Goldberg, *Women, Work, and Life Cycle*, pp. 88–92). We do not know the marital status of Margaret Stoke, who lived in Lombard Street, London in 1375 and ran a sufficiently large bakery that she employed a "freinshbaker" as her ovenman (CPMRL, 1364–1381, p. 187). Coventry was atypical, for in the fifteenth and sixteenth centuries, women could be admitted into the Bakers' Guild. Fox does not indicate with what frequency this actually occurred, but Alice Grene, Cakebaker, was ordered to pay 12d. annually to the guild in 1536 ("Coventry Guilds").

[10] PRO E 101/510/8. The purchases were made in Kingston, Carshalton, Southwark, and Croydon.

bread.[11] We cannot tell, however, to what extent wives and female servants were assisting in the work. Goldberg has noted the frequency with which the latter were found in bakers' households in the late medieval north.[12] The widows and married women who occasionally supplied "biscuit" for military expeditions during the first half of the sixteenth century were probably acting as middlemen.

In urban areas, large-scale bakers after the late fifteenth century sold primarily to retailers, not directly to consumers. The purchasers were often proprietors of victualing houses (= establishments that sold cooked food) or inns.[13] Southwark, Surrey, located just across the river from London, was home to many hostelries and victualing houses for travelers coming into the city. Elizabeth Peryn owned and supervised a bakery in Southwark in 1530, probably one she had inherited from her deceased husband.[14] She hired John Bokatte alias Boggyn to "serve her in the office of Baker," including the job of making deliveries to her regular customers (themselves all retailers) in a number of nearby communities. On a particular day in May, for instance, John took bread to the following customers: five dozen loaves to William Baitte at Walsworth, Surrey; three and a half dozen to John Dowes at Paris Garden; ten dozen to William Angell in Peckham, Surrey; fifteen dozen to William Halle of St. Margaret's parish, Middlesex; two dozen to William Wylde at Westminster; and four dozen to Hugh Welthen, place unstated. For all these sales, the retailers were charged 1s. per dozen, but John did not collect their payments at the time, telling them they could pay later on a system of running credit. Some urban governments passed measures to protect bakers from the competition of inns. York, for example, ordered in 1503 that no innkeepers should bake horsebread for their own customers but instead buy it from bakers; bakers in turn were prohibited from keeping hostelries.[15] In Canterbury, Kent, in 1512 and in Dover, Kent, in 1522, it was similarly ruled that innkeepers should not bake certain kinds of bread for sale at their own establishments.

For larger bakers, maintaining one's line of retailers could be imperative. Around 1530, John Bordman, a barber-surgeon of London then living in Southwark, operated a bakehouse with his wife Isabel.[16] After

[11] Kowaleski, *Local Markets and Regional Trade*, p. 139.
[12] Goldberg, "Female Labour." For below, see PRO E 315/4, account 3, for 1513–14, and PRO E 101/62/35 for 1549.
[13] See sects. 2 and 3 below.
[14] PRO C 1/728/27. Martha Carlin, who is working on a study of food in later medieval England, kindly gave me this reference.
[15] *York Civic Records*, vol. II, p. 182. For below, see Mate, "The Rise of Beer-Brewing." I am grateful to Dr. Mate for letting me see this chapter from her forthcoming book.
[16] PRO C 1/799/11.

working for some time and building up a stable of regular distributors, the Bordmans decided to leave baking. John planned to return to work as a barber, and Isabel intended to make starch, used for stiffening clothing (especially ruffs) and linen flatware. The Bordmans therefore rented their bakehouse to Lawrence Gowman, baker, and gave him, in return for a further payment, the names of "all such customers as were accustomed to sell their bread," together with the Bordmans' commitment that they would do no further baking themselves. Lawrence claimed, however, that the Bordmans later set up another oven and started to bake again. Not only did they try to get the business of their old customers away from him, they "gave to them 13 for every 12" loaves, what we know as a baker's dozen. Their actions cut Lawrence's profits so severely that he could not pay the debts he had incurred in setting up the bakery and buying wheat. It is interesting that neither John nor Isabel Bordman had a fixed occupational identity as a baker: he was actually a member of a different London guild, and she was willing to give up baking in order to try out the newly expanding "project" of starch making.

By the Elizabethan and Jacobean periods, the women who worked as bakers were generally found at the bottom of the range. In Southampton in 1602, for example, one woman and four men were charged with burning cheap fuel in their bakehouses, thereby causing a fire danger to others: they used shrubby bushes rather than real wood.[17] The handicaps women faced on economic grounds were compounded in some cases by urban efforts to protect male bakers. York not only prohibited female participation in baking but went so far as to order in 1567 that bakers' wives were not even to come to the grain market to buy supplies for their husbands.[18] Conversely, in wealthier areas of the country, women of middling and upper rank may have been supervising baking within their own households during the seventeenth century.

We can examine changes among bakers more quantitatively in the five market centers. Evidence from Ramsey and Tamworth (as displayed in Fig. 7.1) shows many more bakers at work each year during the 1290s–1310s than during the 1330s–40s. Since the population is thought to have declined by no more than around 10 percent during the bad harvests of the 1310s, this suggests that the scale and commercialization of baking rose during the half century before the plague, as has been observed in brewing. As business was consolidated into fewer hands, poorer men

---

[17] *Court Leet Records [of Southampton]*, vol. I, pt. II, p. 368.

[18] *York Civic Records*, vol. VI, p. 131. For below, see Whittle's analysis of inventories, which shows that 34 percent of households in the wealthy county of Kent had baking equipment between 1600 and 1650. In poorer Cornwall, by contrast, very few households baked in their own ovens ("The Gender Division of Labour," fig. 3).

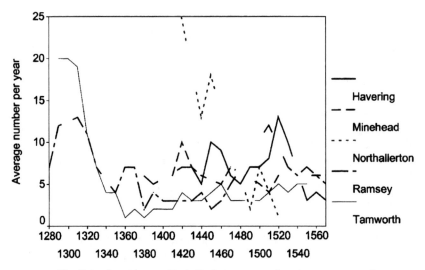

Fig. 7.1. Average number of bakers reported per year, women plus men. See App. 1.1.

and women were driven out. The number of bakers then varied within a fairly narrow range in all four communities until the late fifteenth century. Northallerton displays a parallel drop in numbers but not until the first half of the fifteenth century, consistent with the continuation of older patterns we observe in all food and drink areas. The increased number of bakers in Havering and Ramsey during the early decades of the sixteenth century probably stemmed from demographic growth, as there is no reason to think that individual bakers were producing less.

Women did not dominate late medieval baking as they did brewing and aleselling. (We are assessing here the proportion of bakers who were reported as women for Ramsey and Romford throughout and for all places in the late fifteenth century, and those who headed their own households for Minehead, Tamworth, and Northallerton in earlier periods.) In most decades before 1348–9, a quarter to a half of Ramsey's bakers were women; in Tamworth no more than a quarter of the bakers were singlewomen or widows.[19] The proportion of female bakers in Ramsey was higher immediately after the plague, presumably because some widows or daughters inherited a bakery and kept it going to support their households, but then declined sharply over the next half-century. In Tamworth, the remaining not-married women dropped out of baking entirely during the second half of the fourteenth century; bakers were

[19] See App. 7.1 for the figures, and Ch. 6 for the two methods of reporting women.

referred to collectively as men in 1368.[20] In most decades during the fifteenth century in Ramsey and Havering, no more than 40 percent of all bakers were women, and those values declined across the sixteenth. During the 1460s–70s, however, women moved heavily into baking in Havering. Interestingly, these were almost all women who had been reported for brewing and selling ale for some time, suggesting that they were now adding baking to their other work, perhaps triggered by the growing demand for food as well as drink in alehouses, eating houses, and inns.[21] Northallerton displayed a very different pattern, probably due to the lack of differentiation in its food/drink trades and ongoing use of shared ovens. Here all bakers were women as late as the decades around 1500. But even in this less commercialized world, not-married women evidently found it hard to compete: between 1498 and 1528, 85 percent of the female bakers were married.

In Havering, where we can explore marital status and relation to husband's work, five-sixths of the limited number of female bakers between 1382 and 1469 were married.[22] They were even more dominant during the period 1470–1529. A minority of the married women operated bakeries jointly with their husbands, and only a few of the men engaged in other food/drink occupations.[23] The rest did unrelated kinds of work.

If the span of years worked provides a rough indicator of the degree of occupational involvement, we find that bakers were heavily engaged with their trades. The investment required to lease and equip a bakery probably discouraged casual participation in this occupation. Up until 1470, bakers reported as male and any female bakers living in male-headed households were likely to remain in food/drink work for a slightly longer time than their counterparts whose primary activity was brewing and for considerably longer than alesellers.[24] From 1470 onwards, the average span for male bakers was shorter in Havering than for male brewers, many of whom were now producing beer, but longer in Minehead and Tamworth.

---

[20] KUL T MSS Edward III, Roll 45.

[21] Most of these women continued brewing/selling/baking until they disappeared from the records during the 1480s: see sect. 4, Ch. 6 above.

[22] Of a total of 110 year-entries prior to 1470, 84 percent were married women, 12 percent were listed in their own name, and 5 percent were widows. For below, of 70 year-entries, 91 percent were married, 1 percent were listed in their own name, and 7 percent were widows.

[23] Of the eight women who started their baking careers prior to 1470, three were married to bakers; of the twelve women who took up baking in 1470 or later, just two had baker husbands. Only two husbands before 1470 and two thereafter worked in other food/drink trades.

[24] See App. 7.2 as compared with Apps. 6.1 and 6.3.

In some towns women sold bread they had not baked themselves. Bread for home consumption was commonly handled by hucksters, not directly by the baker or large intermediate retailers, so women found opportunities in this poorly paid and physically exposed work. In Winchester in 1299–1300, twelve bakers were accused of selling bread directly from their houses before noon, but more than forty women were fined for having come to the bakers' houses before that time to fetch bread to be retailed.[25] Fourteenth-century Shrewsbury had few bakers, and very few women bakers, but many hucksters who carried bread for sale. Some hucksters were married to bakers: in April 1527, six men were reported as bakers in the market center of Alfriston, Sussex, while five of their wives were named as "hucksters of bread and beer."[26]

Town governments and craft guilds differed widely in their response to the sale of bread by hucksters. In some cases the role of women in retailing bread was accepted. Bristol ordered in 1474–5 that no baker was to keep a shop in which he sold bread himself but should instead deliver his goods to "the hucksters of Bristow, there to be sold as it hath been of old time used and customed."[27] The bakers' ordinances of Hull from 1598 provided for the marketing of loaves by poor women, who were to be given thirteen for the price of a dozen by the bakers. More common, however, were efforts by guilds and town governments to stop or at least to control the sale of bread by hucksters.[28] The borough of Beverley, East Yorks., for example, ordered in 1596 that no huckster should buy bread from a baker, intending to sell it again.

2   Other foods

Although most types of food were prepared, cooked, and served by women within the domestic context, these tasks were divided between men and women in commercial settings. Men generally controlled the import/export of foodstuffs and worked as middlemen within England's distribution system. In London, even during the periods most favorable to female participation, women were rarely found among large-scale retailers of food. In 1383, of 128 members of the Grocers Company, people who

[25] Keene, *Survey of Medieval Winchester*, p. 255. For below, see Hutton, "Women in Fourteenth Century Shrewsbury," pp. 94–5. Likewise in medieval London, only a few women had bake-houses of their own, but a larger number bought bread from bakers and sold it door-to-door, sometime using a cart to carry their wares (Abram, "Women Traders").

[26] Mate, *Daughters, Wives and Widows*, pp. 67–8.

[27] *The Great Red Book of Bristol*, Text, pt. III, pp. 102–3. For below, see Roberts, "Women and Work."

[28] Goldberg, *Women, Work, and Life Cycle*, pp. 110–11. For below, see *Beverley Borough Records, 1575–1831*, pp. 65–6.

dealt primarily in imported and exported goods, just one was a woman.[29] Any women functioning at this level were likely to be relatives of wealthy grocers, as was Rose de Burford, the daughter of one extremely successful London grocer and widow of another during the 1320s. Although Rose had evidently operated a high-status embroidery shop of her own while married, after her husband's death she maintained his business and took on a male apprentice.

Most women involved in food work were sellers, and generally at lower levels. When a large group of visiting Frenchmen spent ten days at Blackfriars in London sometime between 1399 and 1413, five of the forty-six people who sold provisions to them were women.[30] Two of the ten sellers of poultry-related wares were women, one of whom sold a range of items for a total price of 14s. 6d., the other just some gelatine for 4d. Margery Feld received 8s. for "1000 fruit" of unspecified type, and Christine Mortymer sold rushes for the floor. Only Joan Chichele, described as a spicer and presumably a member of the important London merchant family of that name, was paid a larger sum for a variety of high-value items: sugar, rice, pepper, saffron, and cloves, for a total of 49s. 7d. Other women sold food on the streets, a pattern that became more common during the later sixteenth century, as the population of London and many of the other major cities grew through immigration of poor people. Because the housing available to the urban poor seldom included cooking facilities, the demand for ready-to-eat food rose, providing work for more hucksters and sidewalk sellers.[31] Since the exact role of women varied with the type of food, we will look at each category separately.

Butchers, who slaughtered animals and sold meat, were almost invariably male, apart from a few widows who probably functioned through male employees. As was true of most of the communities for which we have Poll Tax returns from 1379–81, all the butchers reported at any time in Minehead, Northallerton, and Ramsey were male; Tamworth and Romford listed an occasional widow of a butcher who kept the trade going for a year or two.[32] We cannot tell to what extent this very strong gender division was due to practical considerations – the physical strength required to handle and slaughter animals, especially cattle – as opposed to

[29] Lacey, "Women and Work." For below, see Barron, "Women in London," and additional information kindly supplied in a personal communication. In 1317, Rose had sold to Queen Isabella for 100 marks an embroidered cope which was to be given to the Pope.
[30] PRO E 101/512/33.   [31] See Ch. 9 below.
[32] In the Poll Taxes, all nine butchers in rural Howdenshire, East Yorks., were male, as were Pontefract's eight, Southwark's four, Worcester's four, and York's twenty-nine; seventeen of Oxford's eighteen butchers were male, as were eleven of twelve in Canterbury (Goldberg, *Women, Work, and Life Cycle*, pp. 88–92).

a culturally defined sense that the work was too rough or nasty for women. In some cases, however, the wives of butchers may have assisted in the business (see Illus. 9). In fourteenth-century Shrewsbury, butchers' wives were frequently presented for leaving dung and entrails in the streets.[33] Women sometimes used meat by-products obtained from butchers to make sausages or meat puddings, and in Leicester butchers' wives were allowed to sell cooked meat.

An activity closely associated with butchery was chandlery (= literally making or selling candles, though it came to mean a shop carrying assorted small supplies for households and later for ships). Unlike beeswax candles, expensive and almost always made by men, tallow candles made from animal fat were sometimes produced by women, especially those who had access to slaughtered animals. In late medieval York, for example, some butchers' wives made candles.[34] But women appear more frequently as sellers of candles that they had not produced themselves, often retailing assorted foodstuffs and miscellaneous small wares as well.[35] Tamworth included chandlers in its reports of offenders under the Assize of Bread and Ale from the 1390s onwards, describing them generally as sellers of candles plus oatmeal, salt, flour, and/or other victuals.[36] In 1404 they were said to retail candles they had bought from others. They thus resembled the hucksters of diverse wares mentioned in many other communities. During the period when Tamworth's aletasters reported food/drink workers under the name of the household head, between a quarter and three-quarters of the chandlers in most decades were single-women or widows. A listing from 1368 mentions money received "from diverse women" for selling meal, apparently referring to chandlers.[37] From 1470 until the 1510s, at least two-thirds of the chandlers were female.

Although women rarely fished for commercial purposes, they are frequently found as sellers in larger communities.[38] Some female fishmongers operated through the formal market. In Norwich, for example,

---

[33] Hutton, "Women in Fourteenth Century Shewsbury," p. 95. For below, see Goldberg, *Women, Work, and Life Cycle*, p. 109, and *Records of the Borough of Leicester*, vol. I, p. lvii.

[34] Goldberg, "Female Labour," and for late medieval London, see Abram, "Women Traders."

[35] Hutton, "Women in Fourteenth Century Shrewsbury," Kowaleski, *Local Markets and Regional Trade*, p. 167, and her "Women's Work."

[36] Tamworth court rolls: see App. 1.1. For below, see KUL T MSS Henry IV, Roll 4. The "hucksters" reported in Tamworth during the 1370s were later replaced on the rolls by chandlers and alesellers.

[37] KUL T MSS Edward III, Roll 45.

[38] E.g., the Poll Tax returns of 1381 show that seventeen of Oxford's eighteen fishermen were male, as were all twenty-four fishers in York (Goldberg, *Women, Work, and Life Cycle*, pp. 90–2).

9. A woman collecting blood from a pig recently slaughtered by a butcher

between the late fourteenth and early sixteenth centuries, the fraction of fishmongers' stalls in the market that were leased by women ranged from 10 to 35 percent.[39] London's Chamberlain paid 2s. 6d. to a joiner in 1584 for making a wooden "table" for one of the markets (probably a plaque to be hung on the wall), bearing the city's crest and displaying the regulations concerning fishwives. This suggests not only that fish sellers were commonly female but also that some of them could read. An illustrated critique of the city's markets prepared in 1598 shows women selling fish from shops along New Fish Street.[40] In the market centers, however, fishmongers were generally male. In Romford, nearly all fishmongers were men until around 1460; the occasional woman named thereafter usually worked together with her husband. In Northallerton and Tamworth, all the fishmongers reported were men.

In the cities, many women retailed fish less formally, hawking it on the streets. We generally learn about this activity because of the illegal means through which they acquired or sold their wares: either buying from fishermen before the fish reached the official market (= "forestalling"), or buying from market sellers but then retailing the fish at higher prices to consumers (= "regrating"). (See Illus. 10.) In York around 1301, the fish sellers reported for forestalling included five or six men and three or four women.[41] Five fishwives bought fish at Colchester's pier in 1311 which they then sold in smaller quantities. These women, who were named because their fish were old and smelling by the time they were offered for sale, were joined by female sellers of more salubrious fish, many of whom were the wives of stallholders in the market. In fourteenth-century Shrewsbury, female fish sellers were generally married to fishermen.[42] London's fishwives sold fish on the streets from at least the fourteenth century, crying out to advertise their wares.[43] By the Elizabethan period, London officials were becoming concerned about both the number and the nature of the city's female fish sellers. A mayor's order from 1595 spoke of the "exceeding great number of lewd and wicked women called fishwives, which swarm about in all parts of this city, liberties, and suburbs . . . [and] be of such vile behaviour and condition as is not fit any longer to be suffered."[44] After taking a survey of fish and fruit sellers in the wards, the Common Council ordered that there should be only 160

[39] Ibid., p. 108. For below, see *Chamber Accounts of the Sixteenth Century*, p. 24.
[40] *Hugh Alley's Caveat*, p. 55.
[41] Goldberg, ed., *Women in England*, p. 188. For below, see Britnell, *Growth and Decline in Colchester*, p. 37.
[42] Hutton, "Women in Fourteenth Century Shrewsbury."
[43] Abram, "Women Traders," and see *Calendar of Letter-Books*, p. 297, *Memorials of London*, p. 367, and CPMRL, 1413–1437, pp. 137–8.
[44] Gowing, "Freedom of the Streets," for this and below.

10. A huckster leaving London's New Fish Street market, with baskets of fish on her head and in her hand. A dog, looking hopeful, and a boy follow her

such sellers in total, all of them wives or widows of freemen, "of honest fame and behaviour and every of them to be of the age of thirty years at the least."

In some settings, the various types of fish were handled by different people. In late medieval York, dealers in freshwater fish included many local fishermen and sellers, whereas the saltwater fish trade was international and hence dominated by the merchant class.[45] In Tamworth by the

[45] Swanson, *Medieval Artisans*, pp. 18–20.

early fifteenth century and in Northallerton by the later part of that century, many of the outside sellers – men who lived elsewhere but brought their wares in to the local markets – likewise focused on either freshwater or saltwater fish.[46] Women seem to have been less likely to specialize than men, perhaps because they usually operated on a smaller scale. In Lincolnshire, Agnes, wife of William Sadelere of the port of Louth, was fined in 1375 for buying salt and fresh fish before it came to the market and then selling it in nearby communities.[47] In later fourteenth-century Exeter, some women sold both fish and shellfish (including oysters and mussels), which they may have harvested in the Exe estuary just south of the city.

Producing and selling poultry and dairy products were key areas of economic activity for women. It is not surprising that women played an important part in at least the lower levels of these trades, for raising poultry and running the dairy were female concerns within the domestic economy.[48] Nor was much capital investment required to make butter or simple cheese and bring these items and/or poultry wares to market; the income must have provided a welcome addition to the household's resources for some rural and small-town housewives. Among the purchases made in 1473–4 for the household of Henry Langley in several market centers in northwest Essex or southern Suffolk were many eggs and occasional chickens and geese bought from women, almost all of them married.[49] These purchases were in very small units, with most payments ranging between 1d. and 18d. (the latter for six geese).

In cities and larger towns, where most of the full-time sellers of poultry and dairy products were male, women worked typically on a smaller scale.[50] In some cases they sold items they had produced themselves.

[46] E.g., KUL T MSS Henry IV, Roll 1, Henry VI, Rolls 14 and 40, and Edward IV, Roll 1; NYRO ZBD 221658, 52/26, 53/2, and 53/4.

[47] Goldberg, ed., *Women in England*, pp. 188–9. For below, see Kowaleski, *Local Markets and Regional Trade*, p. 139. These women, who usually hawked their wares, were rarely the heads of households.

[48] During the first half of the seventeenth century, domestic production of butter and cheese was high. Whittle's analysis shows that 59 percent of Cornish households and 55 percent of Kentish ones had equipment for these types of dairying activity ("Gender Division of Labour," fig. 3).

[49] PRO E 101/516/9.

[50] Thus, of thirty-seven poulterers named in York in or shortly after 1301, only five were women (Goldberg, ed., *Women in England*, p. 187). When butter was bought on a large scale for Queen Elizabeth's household in 1588–9, all the eleven sellers were male, as were five of six sellers of poultry (PRO E 101/432/9). Larger female suppliers sometimes employed male agents. John Raymond, a London poulterer, claimed that he bought "diverse and sundry kinds of poultry wares" at various times in 1590–1 from Margaret Gandy, through the hands of Richard Wiseman, "her servant and factor" (PRO REQ 2/164/140).

11. Women selling a duck and weighing butter on a scale in London's Leaden Hall market

The hens, eggs, capons, geese, and partridges offered by women in late medieval Winchester had often been raised in their own gardens in this under-populated city; others were brought to market from nearby villages.[51] By the late sixteenth century, the wives of dairy farmers in Middlesex were said to come into London's markets two or three times each week, bringing butter, eggs, milk, cheese, and bacon.[52] (See Illus. 11.) But much of the retailing was carried on by hucksters who bought their supplies from others. Female sellers of hens, capons, geese, pigeons, butter, cheese, and/or eggs were reported for forestalling or regrating the market in Colchester in 1310, in Norwich in 1391, in Nottingham in 1395, and in London in 1305, 1372, and 1422.[53]

Mobile sellers came under closer scrutiny by urban officials after the mid-sixteenth century. In 1560, "butter maids" and "butter wives" were reported for selling their wares in Southampton, the two terms reflecting the unusual concern of that particular city's authorities with the activities

[51] Keene, *Survey of Medieval Winchester*, p. 262.
[52] Everitt, "Marketing of Agricultural Produce."
[53] *Court Rolls of the Borough of Colchester*, vol. I, pp. 1–15, *The Records of the City of Norwich*, p. 381, *Records of the Borough of Nottingham*, vol. I, pp. 276–7, CEMCRL, 1298–1307, p. 234, Lacey, "Women and Work," and CPMRL, 1413–1437, pp. 137–8.

of singlewomen as opposed to wives and widows.[54] Complaint was made in Southampton in 1572 that the hucksters "are so many that the butter, eggs, and other victuals which is brought to the market to be sold is scarce able to serve their turn"; it was ordered that these sellers should henceforth be limited in number and be required to buy their wares outside the town, not in the market, unless permitted by the mayor's proclamation late in the market day "when other householders shall be [already] served."

The sale of vegetables, herbs, fruits, and spices offered some opportunities for women. We have little information about the commercial availability of locally grown items, but chance references suggest that medieval women were involved as producers and sellers. Garlic and onions were sold by Hawisia Row for a mayoral feast in Leicester in 1307–8, and four women were charged in Colchester in 1311 with forestalling apples and pears as well as dairy products.[55] Alice le Garlicseller of Nottingham was in Melton Mowbray, Leics., in 1359 when her horse and chattels were seized by a Nottingham man, and a herbwife is mentioned in late medieval London. Onions were being produced in some volume, apparently for market sale, in Ramsey from at least the 1440s.[56] The hucksters who hawked garlic, onions, and fruit around the streets of late fourteenth-century Exeter commonly lived on the edge of poverty and were often part-time workers.[57] In ports, vegetables may have been a welcome supplement to the sailor's normal diet of bread, beer, and salted fish or meat. The holding of John Roche of Minehead, an important local shipmaster in 1517–18, contained not only a house, a close containing two acres of land, and a boathouse, but also six gardens; we do not know, however, whether John or his wife did the trading in vegetables.[58] Spices, a high-value commodity transported over substantial distances by specialized male importers, were generally sold by men as well.[59] But a few women worked as spicers in fourteenth-century Shrewsbury, and in 1490, Edy Lucas, a widow of Salisbury, was retailing pepper, saffron, oil, and other wares on a fairly large scale at fairs within her region of the country.

---

[54] Froide, "Single Women, Work, and Community." For below, see *Court Leet Records [of Southampton]*, vol. I, pt. I, pp. 76–7.

[55] *Records of the Borough of Leicester*, vol. I, pp. 258–9, and *Court Rolls of the Borough of Colchester*, vol. I, pp. 15–61, passim. For below, see Foulds, "Women and Work," and Abrams, "Women Traders."

[56] PRO SC 2/179/63, m. 5r, and BL Add. Roll 39665.

[57] Kowaleski, *Local Markets and Regional Trade*, pp. 142–3.

[58] SRO DD/L P 28/16, the rent roll.

[59] All five spicers listed in Pontefract in the Poll Tax of 1379 were male, as were Oxford's six spicers and York's twelve in 1381 (Goldberg, *Women, Work, and Life Cycle*, pp. 88–92). For below, see Hutton, "Women in Fourteenth Century Shrewsbury," and PRO C 1/100/73.

By the late sixteenth century, commercialized market gardening was becoming an active enterprise around London and other major cities, under Dutch and Flemish influence, but it was largely under male control.[60] Although much of the fruit sold in cities by around 1600 was similarly brought in from more distant orchards or even imported from overseas, not grown on nearby farms, some suburban women nonetheless brought their own vegetables and fruit into city markets. In 1623, Elizabeth Wilson of West Ham, a smaller community just to the east of London, said that she came into the city regularly to sell her family's produce, apparently in one of the markets.[61] After completing business for the day, she and her female friends went to the King's Head tavern near Leadenhall market to drink a pint or two of wine before leaving for home.

Alongside the more specialized traders were women who retailed a variety of different foodstuffs and sometimes drink and other items as well, often as hucksters. Women sold eggs, cheese, shellfish (oysters, whelks, and mussels), grain, and charcoal at excessive price in Winchester in 1372, while Nottingham's female sellers in 1395 offered flour, salt, garlic, poultry, butter, eggs, tallow candles, and coal.[62] Small-scale sellers of diverse foodstuffs were found in the market centers as well. In 1400, Agnes, the wife of William Wodeward of Ramsey, was reported for a variety of offences, all made worse by unpleasant behavior to her neighbors in the marketplace (she had been "contrary").[63] She sold candles, wax, oat flour, specialty bread, and other groceries for too high a price when compared to what she paid for them wholesale or what her neighbors charged; she forestalled cheese, butter, and eggs; she sold only eight herring for the price of 1d., whereas her neighbors sold ten herring for 1d.; and she bought "Thornbacks [= a type of fish, probably a ray or skate] and other victuals and merchandise" that were being brought into Ramsey and resold them at excessive prices. In Northallerton, women sold several kinds of inexpensive foodstuffs during the early sixteenth century: beans, bean meal, fish meal, rye, and oats.[64]

While the producers and sellers considered thus far handled food that would be taken home for cooking and eating, a few people in the cities

---

[60] Everitt, "The Marketing of Agricultural Produce," pp. 510–11, for this and below.

[61] Capp, "Separate Domains?" She described herself as a "market-woman."

[62] Keene, *Survey of Medieval Winchester*, pp. 390 and 262; *Records of the Borough of Nottingham*, vol. I, pp. 270–3 and 276–7.

[63] BL Add. Roll 39639r.

[64] NYRO ZBD 53/8 (a plea of debt from 1509 nominally involving Thomas Prest and Thomas Dale but almost certainly stemming from the activity of their wives, both of whom were food/drink dealers), and ZBD 54/28, Simon Prest vs. widow Agnes Herryson, and vice versa, 1536.

prepared and sold hot items.[65] Their customers could either eat the food on the spot or take it away with them. Most of these public cooks appear to have been men, though some wives may be hidden behind their husband's name. In late medieval London and its suburbs, female cooks sometimes sold meat, game, or poultry but seem more commonly to have dealt in specialty foods: cheesecakes and puddings made of eggs, bread, and cheese, or pasties of meat and fish.[66] In or around the High Street in Westminster between 1376 and 1391, one or two women commonly joined the four to six men fined for selling cooked meat or cooked fish that had gone bad or was overpriced; from 1393 through the early fifteenth century, plain cooks were joined by several people called "potcooks" who boiled food rather than roasting or baking it, a group that included a few women.[67] At the end of the fifteenth century, three women and six men from Westminster were indicted before the king's court for selling cooked beef, mutton, and poultry for excessive prices.[68] By the early sixteenth century, however, the cooks selling on Westminster's streets were all said to be male.

Women may have assisted men as public cooks in other urban settings too.[69] The borough ordinances of York from around 1301 refer to cooks as men, not women; of the thirty-five cooks reported for violating those ordinances, only three were women.[70] But the ordinances of York's guild of cooks from 1424 imply that the wives or female servants of male cooks helped with the preparation of food: they state that women lacking full skills did much of the actual work. Women cooks were found likewise in mid-fourteenth-century Shrewsbury, some of them singlewomen but others married to men who were themselves cooks.[71] In smaller communities, women cooked and sold food from their own homes. In Minehead, Edith Cartere, an unmarried woman, sued John Ralie in 1405–6 for 20s.

---

[65] This section considers women who were involved with cooking as a trade, selling the food that was produced. For women working as cooks for another household on a waged basis, see sect. 3, Ch. 3 above.

[66] Carlin, "Fast Food."

[67] Westminster Abbey Muniments 50707–50709, 50711–50712, 50714–50715, 50720, Views of Frankpledge; 50737, 50732, 50734, and 50745, Views of Frankpledge. These references and the ones below were generously provided by Martha Carlin.

[68] PRO KB 9/183/6. Two of the women were married and one not; none was given an occupational designation as a cook, though four of the six men were. For below, see Westminster Abbey Muniments 50772, View of Frankpledge, 1507.

[69] The Poll Tax returns for 1381 show seventeen male cooks and no women in Oxford and three female cooks among a total of 137 men and women in all the victualing trades in Southwark. For the purchase of pre-cooked food by poor women, see Ch. 9 below.

[70] Goldberg, ed., *Women in England*, pp. 186–8. For below, see Carlin, "Fast Food."

[71] Hutton, "Women in Fourteenth Century Shrewsbury." For below, see Goldberg, *Women, Work, and Life Cycle*, pp. 90–1, and Carlin, *Medieval Southwark*, p. 175.

due for "his table" (= meals) and other victuals he had bought from her.[72] In 1413 someone in the household of John White (probably his wife) prepared four meals worth 16d. for John Bremsterte during the time of the purification of his wife after she had given birth.

It is possible that the general discomfort visible during the later medieval years with the qualifications and products of cooks may have become more specifically focused on women during the early sixteenth century. If so, this would parallel the shift described by Bennett concerning the representation of brewers.[73] The male cook in Chaucer's *Canterbury Tales* was said to be skilled at boiling chickens with marrowbones, making soup, baking pies, and using flavors and spices.[74] But, the author notes in his naive "Chaucer-the-pilgrim" voice, the cook had an ulcerous sore on his shin. According to urban rules, that health problem should have disqualified him from cooking publicly. In a satirical work published around 1545, John Heywood's Pardoner describes a commercial cook named Margery Coorson who went to Hell but did such a terrible job of cooking meat over a spit that the devils and damned souls sang and rang their chains for joy when she was taken back to England.[75] This change may have been part of broader cultural anxiety about women's participation in economic activities that offered competition to male workers and placed women into public view.

From the later fifteenth century, cooked food was increasingly available from victualers or at victualing houses. The occupational title of victualer had previously been used to describe a seller of various foodstuffs, with no indication that it was ready to eat. It was presumably in that sense that Tamworth and Ramsey reported men and women, married and not-married, as victualers between the late thirteenth and the late fourteenth centuries. From the mid-fifteenth century onward, however, the term increasingly came to mean someone who offered cooked food. When the term "victualing house" was employed, it suggests that customers had the option of consuming the food (and often drink) they had purchased on the premises of what was in effect a restaurant. Among the foods offered in Southwark victualing houses during the late medieval years were meat and poultry, dairy produce, bread, and fruit.[76] Because many eating houses sold drink as well as food, the distinction between them

---

[72] SRO DD/L P 26/6, court held January 1406. For below, see DD/L P 26/8, court held c. St. Andrew Apostle 1 Henry V.

[73] In her "Misogyny, Popular Culture" and *Ale, Beer, and Brewsters*, pp. 123–30; see also Hanna, "Brewing Trouble."

[74] Chaucer, "General Prologue" to *The Canterbury Tales*, description of the Cook.

[75] *The Play Called the Four PP*, not paginated but pp. 30–1 of the text. I am grateful to Martha Carlin for this reference.

[76] Carlin, *Medieval Southwark*, pp. 191–2.

and alehouses or taverns was not sharp. In London, Elizabeth Bate ran an unsuccessful victualing house around 1540, working independently of her husband, Cuthbert, a clothworker.[77] For her establishment she bought not only meat, bread, and other food but also ale. In 1615, Jarvis Smith and his wife Agnes operated a victualing house in London: they hired a man to draw beer and ale for their customers, but Agnes was in charge of the receipts.

The official proprietors of the victualing houses reported in Ramsey, Havering, and Minehead during the later fifteenth and sixteenth centuries were nearly all men, but in many cases their wife or female servants probably helped prepare and serve the food. In Ramsey, Richard Eynsworth was reported for running a victualing house during the 1590s. Since, however, he appears to have been a fisherman as well (he owned two boats and considerable fishing equipment at the time of his death), it was probably his wife Joan who took charge of the eatery.[78] After Joan was widowed in 1597, she continued to run the eatery, which may have formed part of the building in which they lived on the High Street, for at least another year. Food-related work continued to engage some women into the early eighteenth century.[79]

3   Innkeeping

The transformation of inns that began during the later fifteenth century and gained momentum across the later sixteenth and early seventeenth centuries magnified the problems faced by women who might wish to run them. So long as inns were small establishments that offered simple overnight accommodation plus food and drink for travelers and their horses, they could be operated by an individual woman, perhaps assisted by a male servant who took care of the stables. Progressively during the Elizabethan and Jacobean periods, however, many inns in the country's market centers and larger towns changed nature. Their accommodations became more comfortable; the food and drink they offered became more varied; and they became centers for conducting business. An inn of that style required major capital investment in the building, its furnishings,

[77] PRO C 1/958/25. For below, see PRO REQ 2/388/38.
[78] His will is Huntingdon Archdeaconry Wills, vol. XVI, fol. 22r, a transcript of which was kindly supplied by the DeWindts.
[79] Of a cross-sectional sample of London women, 1695–1725, 9 percent worked in catering/victualing, while another 7 percent were hawkers or carriers, many of whom probably dealt in food. Of a group of London businesswomen who bought insurance policies, 1726–9, 16 percent produced or sold food of some kind (Earle, "Female Labour Market"; percentage calculated from figures in Earle, *Making of the English Middle Class*, p. 170).

and supplies, and it demanded a sizeable staff. It seems clear that contemporaries concerned about maintaining good order thought that such an establishment needed a man as its keeper.

During the later fourteenth and fifteenth centuries, most inns in all but the larger cities were fairly modest places. Even then, their proprietors were commonly male, at least for official purposes.[80] Of the women who operated hostelries in their own names in late medieval London and York, some but not all were the widows of innkeepers.[81] But many of the men described on occupational lists as hostelers in York and Exeter were engaged in other trades at the same time, suggesting that they relied upon the labor of their wives, daughters, and/or servants to run their establishments.[82] We know that the wives of some innkeepers in other settings brewed the drink their husbands served, and hostel keepers frequently had female servants who worked as chambermaids or tapsters.

In the later fifteenth century, some inns in market centers and larger towns began to serve a wider clientele of travelers and to offer food and drink to local people as well. In that period of early expansion, wives commonly assisted their husbands in preparing ale and sometimes bread for their house. In Northallerton, Thomas Carlton and his wife Isabel were reported in 1506 as innholders, probably at "the Swan."[83] Isabel had been listed since 1497 as a brewer and/or baker, and Thomas joined her in 1502. In Romford, John Clerk worked as a baker during the 1450s, but by 1464 he was described as the keeper of "the Swan" inn, for which his wife did the brewing. Innkeeper Richard Brigges likewise relied upon his wife's brewing for their ordinary drink, but he purchased a butt of Malmesey wine in 1496 for 60s.[84] In Tamworth, the first person described

---

[80] Of the communities that named hostelers (later to be known as innholders or innkeepers) in the Poll Taxes of 1379–81, all of Oxford's twelve were men, as were all of York's twenty; five of six in (King's) Lynn were male, twelve of thirteen in Pontefract, and twenty-two of twenty-four in Southwark (Goldberg, *Women, Work, and Life Cycle*, pp. 88–92). Earlier periods may have seen more female innkeepers. York for instance, listed ten women hostelers as well as thirty-three men in 1301 (Goldberg, ed., *Women in England*, p. 188).

[81] Abram, "Women Traders," and Swanson, "The Illusion." Alice atte March of London ran an inn in 1375, hiring Richard Counfort as her ostler or stableman (CPMRL, 1364–1381, pp. 203–4).

[82] Swanson, *Medieval Artisans*, pp. 23–4; Kowaleski, *Local Markets and Regional Trade*, p. 144. For below, see Mate, "The Rise of Beer-Brewing," and Goldberg, "Female Labour."

[83] NYRO ZBD 53/6. In 1507, Joan Turner of Deighton, a village a few miles to the north of Northallerton, sued the Carltons for debt. Joan alleged that Isabel had hired her as a servant, to work from the first week of Lent through Michaelmas 1506, for wages of 4s., but had paid her only 2s. 11d.

[84] PRO SC 2/172/38, m. 8v. For below, see KUL T MSS Henry VI, Rolls 27–52 and Edward IV, Rolls 1–4.

as an innkeeper was Richard Dalton, a man whose parents had been in the food/drink trades and who had himself been brewing since 1444. In 1456, however, he was reported as a hosteler, and thereafter he appeared as an innkeeper and sometimes a baker of human and/or horse bread until 1470, assisted at first by his wife Joan. The fines paid by Tamworth's innkeepers from the 1470s onwards were unusually large, suggesting a profitable occupation. As with taverns and victualing houses, a woman might be in charge of the bookkeeping side of an inn. When the Warden of the Cinque Ports, Sir Richard Guildeford, spent two days in Rye during the 1480s, it was the innkeeper's wife who was reimbursed for providing his supper and dinner one night and his breakfast and dinner the next day.[85] During the 1520s, John Grene, a glover of York who kept a stable of packhorses and saddles for his use when traveling, owed money to "the wife at the Bell" inn in Doncaster.

In the decades around 1500, smaller inns, whether run by men or women, were frequently viewed by local leaders as potential centers of disorder. In Northallerton, Thomas Bates, who ran some kind of inn or boarding house in the poor section of town known as "the Backsyde" and whose wife was regularly named for brewing/baking and selling ale, was reported nine times between 1495 and the mid-1510s for allowing bad people, especially whores and vagabonds, to stay in his house and for allowing misrule in it.[86] Three suspected prostitutes living in his establishment were ordered out of town in 1498, and Bates was said to employ Scots – who were scorned and hated – as servants in 1499. Ramsey's court passed a series of orders in the 1530s prohibiting the playing of illegal games by servants or poor people in hostelries as well as the reception of "any stranger called 'Veyfaryng [= wayfaring] Folke'" without warrant from the constable.[87]

Some inns may have been unsafe for travelers. In the early 1480s, Sir John Boole, the parish priest of Falley, Hants., was asked by the Vicar of "Claryburgh" to come to Newport, on the Isle of Wight, to talk with him.[88] While there, John lodged with Joan Elton, widow, "at the sign of the George," taking his meals with her as well as sleeping there. According to his later equity court petition, Joan asked him at supper one evening whether he could give her any money with which to buy malt, to which he answered he had only 20s. That night, Joan summoned to her house

---

[85] Mate, *Daughters, Wives and Widows*, p. 70. For below, see Swanson, *Medieval Artisans*, pp. 59–60.

[86] Newman, *Late Medieval Northallerton*, pp. 132–3 and 138, and NYRO ZBD 52/24–5.

[87] BL Add. Roll 34377R, BL Add. Rolls 39662, 34377R, 39663, and 39664A.

[88] PRO C 1/61/379. The place may have been Burghclere, Hants. See also the Deloney story below.

"10 or 12 mischievous disposed men" who "took him in his bed fast asleep and there said plainly they would cut his throat without [= unless] he would deliver them all his money and there they took all that ever he had." When he reported the theft the next morning to the constables and other men of the town, "they made but a mock and a scorn therof."

By the later Elizabethan period, most communities that had a market or lay along a main road contained at least a few big inns that offered good food/drink, agreeable rooms, and storage facilities for animals and goods. These inns functioned as business centers. In them producers, sellers, and middlemen met to arrange deals; in them contracts were signed, credit was arranged, and money-lending took place. As Alan Everitt has said, the inn "was the hotel, the bank, the warehouse, the exchange, the scrivener's office, and the market-place of many a private trader."[89] An example of these comfortable inns, with their private chambers for transacting business, is the one run by James Pearsall of Rye, Sussex, who died in 1593.[90] His inn was of only intermediate size, but it was much better appointed than would have been true fifty years before. For the use of his guests, he had eight joined bedsteads and two trundle beds placed in five sleeping chambers and a little parlor; his linen included thirty-seven pairs of sheets, thirty-three table cloths, thirty-two towels, and 112 napkins, plus pillow covers and other types of cloths and towels. In the kitchen were equipment for making bread and a "limback" (= a type of still used to fortify sweet wines). For preparing and serving food, James's inn had thirty-one brass cooking utensils, two brass andirons, three brass chafing dishes, and six brass candlesticks, as well as iron andirons and other equipment for fireplaces. The main public rooms for the use of his guests were the hall and great parlor downstairs, which were furnished with such luxuries as painted cloths on the walls, cushions made of leather or decorated with needlework, and curtains for the windows. The more private chambers upstairs were graced by oil paintings, chairs with cushions and stools of needlework, and bed curtains made of fancy colored cloth.

In Elizabethan Romford, innkeepers were among the leading men in the town. Most were holders of top local offices and donors to charitable causes, and some advanced their sons into higher social status through

---

[89] "The Marketing of Agricultural Produce," p. 559. The use of inns as the settings for commercial exchange had begun earlier in some of the major centers: for London in 1298 and 1350, see CEMCRL, 1298–1307, pp. 12–13, and CPMRL, 1323–1364, p. 233; for late fourteenth-century Exeter, see Kowaleski, Local Markets and Regional Trade, pp. 143–4.

[90] Mayhew, Tudor Rye, pp. 183–7.

extensive formal education. The households of the innkeepers included on a list of communicants in the parish church in 1562 had an average size (omitting children under age thirteen) of 5.6 people, the largest of any of the urban occupations and exceeded only by the area's knights and gentlemen.[91] All the innkeepers' households contained servants, some female; and their average of 2.6 servants was larger than that of other occupations apart from the urban yeomen (with 3.0) and the knights and gentlemen (with 4.6).

Although larger inns were almost always operated by men, they required substantial amounts of female labor. It was women who changed the beds, cleaned the rooms, did the laundry, ironed the linens, and in many cases prepared and served food and drink. These tasks were performed by the wife or other relatives of the male proprietor, residential servants, and/or paid employees. When women appear as innkeepers, they were usually widows who had smaller houses. In Norwich, for example, only one widow was found among thirty-eight innkeepers in 1564.[92] In Elizabethan Romford, the sole female innkeeper was Margaret Thunder, who ran an inn for twenty years. Already in her second widowhood when she first appeared as a brewer in 1554, she was reported from 1560 through the 1570s as both a brewer and an innkeeper. On the 1562 communicant listing, she was accompanied by three minor children from a former marriage, and at her death in 1585 she left only a few items to her two sons and her married daughter; the inventory of her goods came to just £14 2s. 7d., a small amount by local standards.[93] In Manchester, two widows who died during the early 1590s appear to have kept modest inns, each featuring three sleeping chambers and two parlors plus equipment for cooking, brewing, and serving food and drink.

Several equity court petitions provide glimpses into inns run by widows around 1600. Ursula Dove of Duxford, Cambs., was the proprietress of a little inn at Wicheford Bridge during the early seventeenth century.[94] One of her guests was Thomas Lisson of Bury St. Edmunds, a carrier who often stopped at her place on his way to and from London. Ursula claimed that between 1615 and 1619 he racked up a total bill of £13 for his own food and lodging plus food for his horses. In his response, Thomas acknowledged that he used to stay at Ursula's inn on a weekly basis and that he did not pay cash on the spot, but he denied that he owed the sums specified in her complaint. He countered that her legal action

[91] McIntosh, *A Community Transformed*, tables 1.11 and 1.14.
[92] *The Records of the City of Norwich*, vol. II, pp. 181–2.
[93] ERO T/R 147/1, last 11 pp., and D/AER 15, 16. For below, see Willan, *Elizabethan Manchester*, p. 94.
[94] PRO REQ 2/396/21.

was vexatious, brought at the instigation of her son John, who owed him money. Anne Mallyson, a widow who lived on the edge of the market center of Blyth, Notts., in 1613, ran what she described as a victualing house, though it also offered overnight accommodation.[95] In her petition she claimed that she had "no other means whereby to live and maintain her credit, children, house, and family but by entertaining such of his Majesty's loving subjects as shall repair to [her] house for their necesssary provision of meat, drink, and lodging." Apparently fearing that her legal credibility would be weakened by her occupation, Anne emphasized that her guests included "men of the best rank of esquires, gentlemen, and others." To obtain the coal she needed for her house, Anne agreed with a local husbandman that in return for the use of two barns of hers, with standing room for cattle, he would go to some coal pits eight miles away from Blyth and bring back to her four wagonloads of "sea coals," each load containing four quarters (= 32 bushels).

An occasional woman was able to profit from the emerging role of inns as commercial centers. In 1614, widow Julianne Brigges operated a hostelry at "the sign of the George" in Farnham, Surrey, where she played a recognized role in transmitting money from one person to another.[96] Richard Hawsted of Petersfield, Hants., a mercer, bought certain wares from Roger Knight, a chapman from Berkshire, for which he owed Roger £5 17s. They agreed that Richard would give the money to John Strouder, who would deliver it to Julianne at her inn. She would then keep it until Roger's next arrival, since he was a regular guest of hers. In a petition submitted the following year, Richard charged that although the money was given to Julianne, who agreed to deliver it to Roger, she had not handed it over to him. In her response, Julianne said that on the day that John was alleged to have given her the money, she was "very busy about her house in entertaining her guests and looking to her other businesses." When John told her he wanted to give her some money to be delivered to Roger, she told him that Roger would be at her inn that very night, so John could give it to him directly. In support of her claim that she never received the money from him, she noted that "she did many times receive moneys of her guests and friends that came to her house, which was there left to be paid and delivered to others to whom the parties that so left the same appointed it." She was careful, however, always to record the receipt of every sum in a book she kept for that purpose; she also always gave a note in writing to the person who left money in her hands. Since she had no note in her book of having taken money from John and he had no receipt for it, she argued that Richard's charge was false.

[95] PRO REQ 2/416/75.   [96] PRO REQ 2/395/32.

A remarkably vivid – though remarkably negative – portrayal of a female innkeeper comes from Thomas Deloney's proto-novel, *The Pleasant History of Thomas of Reading, or The Sixe Worthie Yeomen of the West.*[97] This set of loosely intertwined stories, probably written around 1599, suggests some ambivalence about women's participation in the market economy. It also contains a dramatic warning about the dangers of women who dominated their husbands within a business partnership. Deloney, a London weaver who supported himself by writing during his frequent periods of unemployment, set his story nominally during the twelfth century. It is, however, replete with references to the circumstances and attitudes of his own world, the lower and middling levels of which he knew well.

The episodes of interest focus upon the hostess of "the Crane" inn in Colnbrook, Berks., who manipulated and distorted her normal female roles to control her husband and gain wealth by murdering rich men. Named only as "Jarman's wife," she had devised an ingenious method of killing guests and stealing the money they had with them. At her direction, though with the approval of her husband, who was the official keeper of their inn, a carpenter built a trap door into the floor of their best bedroom, which was located directly above the kitchen. Once a wealthy visitor had fallen aleep, the Jarmans pulled out the iron pins that held the trap door closed, the door was released and "downe would the man fall out of his bed" into a boiling and "mighty great caldron, wherein they vsed to seethe their liquor when they went to brewing." The victim, "being suddenly scalded and drowned . . . was neuer able to cry or speake one word." The Jarmans then used a ladder to climb into the locked chamber above, where they took the murdered man's money. After they had disposed of the body and destroyed the victim's clothing, the husband removed his horse to a safe hiding place. In this travesty of hospitality, the negative potential of women's income-producing work was underlined, for the kitchen was culturally defined as female space and the brewing done within it as a characteristically female enterprise.

The protagonist of the story is Thomas Cole of Reading, a clothier.[98] His substance, Deloney notes approvingly, "was exceeding great: he had daily in his house an hundred men seruants and xl. Maids; he maintained [in work] beside aboue two or three hundred people, spinners and carders, and a great many other housholders." A paragon of capitalistic manufacture, Thomas traveled frequently into London on business, stopping for the night on several occasions at the Jarmans' inn in Colnbrook.

---

[97] *The Works of Thomas Deloney*, pp. 211–72. The episode described below is on pp. 254–60: individual page references will not be provided. Another set of incidents from this text is discussed in Ch. 9 below.

[98] For clothiers, see sect. 1, Ch. 8 below.

During his initial visits, he was saved from the Jarmans' evil plans, once by "a great fray that hapned in the house betwixt a couple that fell out at dice." (This accentuates the hosts' failure to maintain the good order mandated for licensees of inns and to ensure that no illegal betting games were played in their establishment.)

Eventually, however, Thomas succumbed to Mistress Jarman's wiles. After his arrival at the inn one evening, she plied him with hot spiced wine and had "certaine musitians of the towne" come to play for him. When he was virtually insensible, she performed the distorted wifely role of warming a kerchief for his head and putting him to bed in the rigged room. Once Thomas was soundly asleep and the rest of the plot should have been put into action, her husband lost his nerve: "By my consent (quoth he) the matter should passe, for I thinke it is not best to meddle on him." Mistress Jarman, however, had a stiffer spine. "What man (quoth she) faint you now? haue you done so many and doe you shrinke at this?" She then urged her husband on through a mixture of simple greed and class antagonism. "Shewing him a great deale of gold" which Thomas had put into her keeping overnight, she said, "Would it not grieue a bodies heart to lose this? hang the old churle, what should he doe liuing any longer? he hath too much, and we haue too little: tut husband, let the thing be done." In the end, "her wicked counsell was followed." After Thomas had dropped into the boiling vat and died, the Jarmans carried out their usual clean-up actions to make "all things as it should be." When, however, Jarman went to the inn's stable to fetch the hired horse that Thomas had been riding, the animal escaped and was later recognized by its owner. The musicians, who returned to the inn in the morning to serenade Thomas, likewise inquired about his absence, as did his wife when he failed to return home as planned. Finally a local Justice of the Peace was notified of Thomas's disappearance and the subsequent disappearance of Jarman. Mistress Jarman, who had stayed behind, confessed, and Jarman was later discovered hiding in Windsor Forest. They were both hanged for their crime.

Although many women probably assisted their husbands in producing and selling foodstuffs or innkeeping, these trades offered limited opportunities for women to operate on their own above the level of retailing their wares in the market or on the street.

8 Women's participation in the skilled crafts

In most of the specialized crafts, those that required both an investment in equipment and training in the necessary skills, women were generally involved only as paid or unpaid workers, not as independent heads of their own establishments. We know that married women, daughters, female servants, and/or hired employees carried out certain aspects of craft production, but it is difficult to assess their exact contributions, for the records normally give only the name of the head of the operation. Some women were paid by the item (or "piece") for work done at home, hired as needed by male craftsmen and receiving low pay. By the early seventeenth century, a growing variety of piecework was available to poor women. During the periods around 1300 and again around 1600, the relatively few women who played more autonomous roles in craft production were generally widows who kept their husband's business going at least temporarily. The later fourteenth and fifteenth centuries, however, appear to have provided a somewhat greater range of opportunities for women, especially in London. We can explore these patterns by looking first at production and sale of textiles, especially manufacture of woolen cloth, where female labor was essential in the initial stages. After examining women's roles in making and selling clothing and accessories, we turn to other crafts, where women rarely ran their own workshops.

1   Cloth and clothing

Women were involved in some aspects of the manufacture and sale of textiles. Woolen cloth production was England's primary industry during these centuries, for nearly all clothing – except for the very wealthy – was made from woolen fabrics.[1] Whereas around 1300 most English wool was exported to the continent in its raw form, to be made into cloth there,

---

[1] See, e.g., Bolton, *The Medieval English Economy*, Bridbury, *Medieval English Clothmaking*, and Kerridge, *Textile Manufactures*.

manufacture within the country increased sharply across the fourteenth century. After some disruption during the economic downswing of the mid-fifteenth century, cloth production reached new heights after 1480 and continued to grow during the sixteenth century. Increasingly, however, it followed a "boom and bust" pattern, interrupted by wars on the continent that shut down foreign trade. Although some cloth was made in towns, and trading in cloth was generally urban based, much of the production occurred in rural regions. During the fifteenth century, the leading areas were East Anglia (Norfolk, Suffolk, and Essex) and parts of the southwest; cloth was made in the north too, though usually of lower quality due to the types of wool available there. Cloth manufacture brought great prosperity to some communities. Lavenham, Suffolk, for example, was just a small village in the early fifteenth century, but by the 1520s it ranked thirteenth in wealth among all English communities, above many of the larger towns.

The main fabrics produced until the sixteenth century were large and heavy woolen cloths, well suited to cold climates. Some of these were used within England, but many were exported. Beginning in the middle of the sixteenth century, immigrants from the continent brought with them the techniques for making lighter-weight cloths, suitable for export to warmer regions. These "new draperies" enabled English manufacturers to tap into emerging markets in the Mediterranean, Caribbean, Africa, and Asia. Other types of cloth were made from linen, hemp, or silk, and smaller items might be knitted.

Woolen cloth production occurred through a series of separate stages, each of which was typically carried out by different workers. The raw wool had first to be carded or combed, to align the strands, after which it was spun into yarn. The yarn was then used to weave cloth, on a loom. Before the cloth could be made into consumer goods, it had to be "finished." These processes usually involved dyeing, fulling (impregnating the raw cloth with a special kind of clay and then beating it to join the strands of yarn into a more uniform texture), stretching it on a square frame to give it a regular shape, and shearing its surface to a uniform depth. Clothiers functioned as middlemen, hiring weavers to make cloth, sometimes taking it to finishers, and selling the final product. Mercers were large-scale dealers in cloth, often importing/exporting it and sometimes dealing in other goods as well.

Although the making of cloth and clothing depended upon women's labor, the particular tasks assigned to them demanded little capital investment but also paid little. They carded and spun wool and by the early seventeenth century they knitted woolen stockings or made lace, but they rarely headed their own weaving or finishing establishments.[2] Women's textile-related activities could be picked up during spare moments and integrated on a secondary basis with other economic activities and domestic responsibilities. Because the work was often sedentary, it was well suited to old women who were no longer able to carry out more physically demanding labor. Opportunities at middling and occasionally even upper levels of the system of producing cloth and clothing were somewhat greater during the generations after the plague. In late fourteenth-century Exeter, for example, while many women did menial work such as preparing yarn or stitching clothing together, some were weavers, tailors, makers of hose, or dressmakers, and a few widows successfully pursued their late husbands' business as cloth merchants.[3] Late medieval London offered the greatest range of opportunities to women in textile work for several reasons: the demand for a wider range of luxury goods that offered more specialized opportunities for women workers; the encouragement given to widows to keep their husbands' operations going; and London's custom of allowing a married woman to trade on her own (as a *femme sole*) if she was working independently of her husband.[4] By the sixteenth century, however, women's work was heavily concentrated at the bottom levels.

Textile manufacture

The stages of cloth production that employed the most women involved conversion of the wool cut from sheep into the yarn used in weaving. To support the output of a single loom, considerable preliminary labor was required. Carders or combers used two hand-held wooden racks with metal pins set into them to untangle the wool and smooth its strands (see Illus. 12). Spinning was done during the central medieval period with a distaff and spindle but by the later fourteenth and fifteenth centuries increasingly with a wheel. Combing, carding, and spinning were all usually done by women who worked at home on a part-time basis.

Records from the later fourteenth and fifteenth centuries give some indication of the importance of women in the preparation of yarn. The Poll Tax listings of 1379–81 for Oxford and Southwark include a few people described occupationally as "kempsters," women who combed wool.[5]

[2] For a fuller discussion, see Kerridge, *Textile Manufactures*.
[3] Kowaleski, "Women's Work."
[4] Lacey, "Women and Work," Barron, "Women in London," and Hanawalt, "Dilemma of the Widow." But see McIntosh, "The Benefits and Drawbacks of *Femme Sole* Status," for why women might choose not to declare themselves as *femmes soles*.
[5] Bennett, "Medieval Women, Modern Women." For below, see Hutton, "Women in Fourteenth Century Shrewsbury."

12. Women smoothing, carding, and spinning wool (using a distaff and spindle)

In fourteenth-century Shrewsbury, women were combers and spinners, though carders were often male. In Nottingham during the 1350s and 1360s, several disputes concerned cards that had been loaned, pawned, or stolen by women; married women were hired on a private basis to spin wool for others; and a woman was paid to wash 38 leas of yarn before spinning.[6] The larger textile producers in Exeter commonly hired female

[6] Foulds, "Women and Work." A lea was a variable measure for yarn.

13. A woman spinning, using a hand-turned wheel

servants or piecework employees to card and spin for them.[7] During the
decades around 1400 in Winchester, combing was done primarily by
women, and combs were sometimes hired.

Spinners, too, were usually women.[8] (The term "spinster" prior to
around 1500 meant a female spinner, with no reference to her marital status.) In late medieval London, spinsters were likewise common;
Winchester clothiers hired spinners to work on particular assignments
at home.[9] A partial transition away from use of the traditional distaff
and spindle to the newer and more productive spinning wheel took
place during the later fourteenth and fifteenth centuries (see Illus. 13).
Archaeological evidence from Winchester notes fewer spindle whorls or
weights, used with a distaff, presumably reflecting an increased number
of spinning wheels in that period.[10] A woman living at Bishopthorpe,
just south of York, was called "Isabella Whelespynner" in 1379, suggesting that wheels were not yet common.[11] In 1395/6 the wife of a poor
townsman in Colchester, Essex, leased a spinning wheel for 10d. but
failed to pay what she owed for it. By the fifteenth century, wheels were
mentioned more frequently, especially in towns. Inventories from York

[7] Kowaleski, *Local Markets and Regional Trade*, p. 153. For below, see Keene, *Survey of
Medieval Winchester*, pp. 299–300.
[8] Poll Tax evidence shows that in (King's) Lynn, all ten people identified as spinners/
spinsters were female, as were all thirty-nine in Oxford and all twenty-six in Southwark
(Goldberg, *Women, Work, and Life Cycle*, pp. 88–92).
[9] Lacey, "Women and Work"; Keene, *Survey of Medieval Winchester*, pp. 299–300.
[10] Keene, *Survey of Medieval Winchester*, p. 300.
[11] Goldberg, *Women, Work, and Life Cycle*, p. 145. For below, see Britnell, *Growth and
Decline in Colchester*, p. 102.

show that craftsmen who engaged in a variety of employments, including foundry work and making armour, had spinning wheels in their house, used presumably by their wives, daughters, or female servants; a brewer who died in 1481 had a separate spinning house in which he probably hired female workers to produce yarn on a commercial scale.[12] The shift to wheels may have worked to the disadvantage of poor women who could not afford to buy or even rent such equipment, and it probably lowered piecework rates for all types of spinning, since a wheel enabled a woman to produce more yarn in a given period of time.

The importance of such work for women depended upon their marital as well as their economic status. For a married woman, combing/carding or spinning might provide a helpful augmentation of the household's income, to be done as circumstances permitted. Thus, Katherine, wife of James Sadler of York, was said in 1393 to work in "kempstercraft," or combing, but she also assisted her husband in his leatherwork; Marion de Walde, wife of a York potter, worked at a spinning wheel when she had time.[13] But because the pay was low, not-married women in most settings and periods were barely able to support themselves through these kinds of activities.[14] In Beverley, East Yorks., Alice of Bridelyngton, a singlewoman, lived with a woman in 1367 who had allegedly left her husband; both worked as spinsters. Isabella Foxhole, the daughter of a peasant from Houghton, East Yorks., came to York after being in service with an uncle in Pontefract: she was said in 1418 to earn a meager living by carding and spinning wool. Several of the textile entrepreneurs in late medieval York left bequests of a few pence each to the poor carders and spinners they employed. But some spinsters, like many other workers, profited from the demand for labor that followed the plague of 1348–9, allowing them to bargain for wages higher than those allowed by statute. This was true in Yorkshire and Somerset, where seventy-two of the 121 women (= 60 percent) presented to the Justices of Labourers in 1358 worked as spinners, some of them engaged in other activities as well.[15]

During the later Elizabethan period, as poverty – and official concern about it – mounted, carding and spinning were seen as appropriate employments for needy women. Of the 726 adult women recorded in Norwich's Census of the Poor of 1570, 76 percent were engaged in some kind of spinning, almost all working on a part-time basis in their own dwellings.[16] The spinners included women in their seventies who were

---

[12] Swanson, "The Illusion."

[13] Goldberg, "Female Labour," and his *Women, Work, and Life Cycle*, p. 118.

[14] E.g., Goldberg, *Women, Work, and Life Cycle*, p. 119. For below, see his "Women's Work."

[15] Ibid. and Penn, "Female Wage-Earners."

[16] *Norwich Census of the Poor*, p. 99. For below, see Pelling, "Old Age."

blind, weak, or lamehanded. A fine illustration of the idea that spinning was suitable work for poor women was offered in a pageant presented to Queen Elizabeth when she visited Norwich in August, 1578: a
tableau representing good order in the commonwealth, with living actors,
featured women engaged in spinning.[17] When the clothmaking town of
Hadleigh, Suff., set up a "taskhouse" in the 1580s and 1590s in which
the idle poor were forcibly housed while being taught to work, the town
furnished cards, spindles, and spinning wheels for their training, and the
leading clothiers contributed wool.[18] By the first half of the seventeenth
century, some households were spinning for their own use.[19]

Because yarn was produced by multiple spinners, middlemen sometimes bought it up and sold it to weavers. Although women were generally at a disadvantage within distribution systems that required the
outlay of capital and an ability to travel freely, we know of at least one
mother/daughter pair in the north of England who dealt in yarn. In 1612,
Henry Cowborne of Blackrod, Lancs., described himself as "a very poor
man and a webster [= weaver] and having a wife and 3 children and little
means to keep himself in work whereby to relieve himself and his wife and
children."[20] In his petition against Margaret Hogley of Wheatley, Lancs.,
Henry charged that Margaret and her daughter Ann, knowing him to
be eager to get supplies for his weaving, offered to sell him yarn worth
£5. The condition of this sale was that he pay 20s. right away and the
remaining £4 at the end of a year; the Hogleys agreed further to bring him
additional yarn before the year was over, "whereby he should be better
able to pay the said sum of £4." On those terms, Henry signed a written obligation for £4. But because the yarn the Hogleys delivered to him
"proved very bad and naught," he was not able to pay his debt, nor did
they bring him any additional yarn. Instead, having lured him to a house
in Wigan after his payment was due, they fetched a sergeant who arrested
him and held him in prison for five days. This not only impoverished his
wife and children but also placed him at risk of his "utter undoing . . .
being an artificer and workman and having nothing to uphold him but
his credit."

---

[17] *Progresses and Public Processions*, vol. II, pp. 143–5.
[18] Hadleigh Borough MS 4/1, e.g., fols. 122, 197, and 248, and MS 21/27, as discussed in
McIntosh, "Networks of Care."
[19] Of probate inventories from Cornwall, 38 percent mentioned spinning equipment, as
did 46 percent from Kent (Whittle, "Gender Division of Labour," fig. 3). We cannot
determine what fraction of this yarn was used for weaving within those same households and how much was sold. By the early eighteenth century, spinning had almost
disappeared as an occupation for London working women, only 1 percent of whom still
described themselves as spinners (Earle, "Female Labour Market").
[20] PRO PL 6/2, 19 September 1612.

The next stage in the cloth-making process, weaving, required a loom. Because many looms were large and expensive even by 1300 and became more elaborate with the passage of time, this occupation was out of reach for most women. Unless they had financial support from their husband, they could probably not afford the cost of buying or renting a loom; unless they lived in a large house with many residents, they might not have space in their dwelling for such a bulky object or enough labor to keep it in regular and profitable use (see Illus. 14). In late medieval listings that give the occupation of the head of the household, most people identified as weavers in larger towns were men.[21] In Yorkshire, however, female clothmakers were atypically active during the second half of the fourteenth century: a quarter of all weavers in market communities were women, and their role was even more pronounced in rural parts of the West Riding.[22] The records of a tax paid on cloth purchased in Yorkshire in 1394–5 indicate that 25–39 percent of those who sold cloth – who were in many cases weavers – were women, but they sold fewer and smaller cloths on average than did male producers.[23] In Winchester's tax accounts for the same year, only eleven of 159 sellers (= 7 percent) were women, two of whom were widows of a weaver and a fuller; here too the women sold less than half as many cloths as men.[24] In London, relatively few women appear to have worked independently as weavers, and they were generally married. Isabella Yerdele, wife of John but operating as a *femme sole*, was said in 1382 to have made thirteen woolen cloths worth 102 marks (= £68) which she delivered to Simon Gardiner to be fulled.[25] Some of London's female weavers focused on lower-value cloths, for which equipment and supplies were less expensive and which could be made more quickly. Rose Thorne, who took a female apprentice in 1445 but did not instruct her adequately, was described as a "coarseweaver."

But other evidence suggests strongly that women who were not designated formally as weavers were making use of the looms in their houses. In some cases a wife, daughter, or female servant might assist the male

---

[21] The Poll Taxes of 1379–81 show, for instance, that in (King's) Lynn, none of the ten weavers was female, true also for the thirty-four weavers in Oxford and not far different from the two women out of seventy-two weavers in York (Goldberg, *Women, Work, and Life Cycle*, pp. 88–92). Nottingham had one female weaver in 1478–9: *Records of the Borough of Nottingham*, vol. II, pp. 298–303.

[22] Four of sixteen weavers were female in Pontefract, three of twelve in Ripon, and two of seven in Wakefield; in rural areas, 39 percent were women (Goldberg, *Women, Work, and Life Cycle*, pp. 88–92).

[23] Swanson, *Medieval Artisans*, pp. 35–6, gives the higher figure and Goldberg, "Women's Work," the lower one.

[24] Keene, *Survey of Medieval Winchester*, pp. 309–10 and 389.

[25] CSPML, 1381–1412, pp. 19–20. For below, see CPMRL, 1437–1457, p. 65.

14. A woman weaving cloth on a loom controlled by foot treadles

weaver or work alongside him, if the loom required two people to operate. Women hired to work in weaving were among those reported for taking excess pay in Somerset and Herefordshire during the labor shortage of the 1350s and 1360s.[26] In fourteenth-century Shrewsbury, male weavers were commonly assisted by female members of their households; in fifteenth-century York, a few widows continued their husbands' weaving, including keeping their apprentices, which implies that they had learned the necessary skills while married.[27] In other cases, wives apparently borrowed their husband's loom. In Nottingham, Rose, the wife of Henry le Chaloner (= a weaver of blankets), agreed on 25 June 1351 to weave eleven ells (= 13.75 yards) of woolen cloth for William of Radford, shoemaker, and to deliver the cloth to him "well-dressed" four weeks later.[28]

As many of England's larger towns began to face a difficult combination of economic downswing and continued immigration of women sometime during the fifteenth century, they commonly attempted to restrict women's participation in weaving. A series of orders starting at the beginning of the century and gaining momentum after 1450 suggests that women workers were now seen as a threat to the livelihood of male weavers. In York, an ordinance of 1400 ruled that no women should henceforth be allowed to weave in the city unless they had been properly trained and were "sufficiently knowledgeable to work in the craft."[29] Use of female workers on broadlooms in Coventry was said in 1453 to be "against all good order and honesty." In Bristol in 1461, a civic ordinance criticized male weavers who hired "their wives, daughters, and maidens."[30] In a fine rhetorical sweep, this practice was said to cast into destitution male workers who might be required for military service and therefore needed to be kept in good physical condition. (Kingston-upon-) Hull prohibited women in 1490 from any work connected with weaving; women were barred entirely from looms in Norwich in 1511, as were boys under the age of fourteen, both groups ostensibly on the grounds that they lacked the strength to produce decent cloth.[31]

An occasional woman was still operating her own weaving establishments during the first half of the sixteenth century. Katherine Brede, a widow of Devizes, Wilts., agreed in the 1540s to provide to Thomas

---

[26] Penn, "Female Wage-Earners."
[27] Hutton, "Women in Fourteenth Century Shrewsbury"; Swanson, *Medieval Artisans*, pp. 35–6.
[28] Foulds, "Women and Work."
[29] Cited by Swanson, *Medieval Artisans*, p. 36. For below, see Roberts, "Women and Work."
[30] Swanson, *Medieval Artisans*, pp. 35–6, and Roberts, "Women and Work."
[31] Ladd, "Thomas Deloney"; Roberts, "Women and Work."

Daungerfelde of Gloucestershire, a clothier, diverse "long and broad woolen cloths colored white, of her own making, with her usual mark woven in the same cloths."[32] When Thomas came to Katherine's home to collect those cloths, she contracted to produce another twenty cloths for him within the next three months in return for £60 which Thomas promised to pay her. The arrangement specified that the cloth should be of the same quality as those she had woven for him previously and include her mark. Thomas sold the first batch of cloth to William Mannynge, a London mercer, who liked it so much that he asked to buy Katherine's next twenty cloths too. When, however, Thomas and William rode to Katherine's house to pay her the promised £60 and pick up the new cloths, Katherine refused to hand them over to Thomas or give him the writings that documented their agreement. Since she was apparently producing twenty broadcloths within a three-month period, virtually impossible for a single worker, and since the cloths all had her own mark woven into them, suggesting that they had been made in her workshop, she was probably hiring other people to help with the weaving.[33]

In the finishing crafts, women might assist the male head of the business but seldom had their own craft operation. The fullers' guild of Lincoln ordered in 1297 that no one should "work at a wooden bar [= for fulling] with a woman unless with the wife of the master or her handmaid," while in the late medieval north dyers employed female servants to wash cloth preparatory to dyeing.[34] Only an occasional woman worked in her own right as a fuller, dyer, or shearer in fourteenth-century Shrewsbury, late fourteenth-century Exeter, and late medieval York, and most of these were probably widows of men who had previously run the craftshop.[35]

Finishing work often required physical strength to work with wet, heavy cloths, and it demanded a considerable investment in equipment. Elizabeth Martendale and Robert Hawkeswell were dyers of inexpensive fustian cloth in London during the early 1540s, before they went deeply

---

[32] PRO C 1/1214/5–8.

[33] The normal output for a two-person loom in the later medieval period has been reckoned at forty cloths/year, with an optimum output of fifty cloths per year (Swanson, *Medieval Artisans*, p. 34).

[34] Leyser, *Medieval Women*, p. 163; Goldberg, "Female Labour."

[35] Hutton, "Women in Fourteenth Century Shrewsbury," Kowaleski, *Local Markets and Regional Trade*, pp. 154–5, and Swanson, *Medieval Artisans*, pp. 42–3. The Poll Tax returns show no women among the six dyers and fourteen fullers in Oxford, among the three dyers and three fullers in Worcester, among the five dyers in Pontefract, or among the eighteen dyers in York (Goldberg, *Women, Work, and Life Cycle*, pp. 88–92). Ripon was atypical, with two women among four dyers, as was Doncaster, with four women among seven fullers.

into debt.[36] (Dyeing may have been Elizabeth's former husband's craft, which she was trying to keep going by taking another man as a partner.) Together they held a twenty-six-year lease of a property called "The White Rose" in White Cross Street in the parish of St. Giles without Cripplegate. Their establishment contained a workhouse with twenty-one better quality vats for "dyeing liquors" and thirty-five poorer vats, together worth nearly £13. Two other vats and four barrels held slip, and six brakes (= mechanical devices) were used to wring the cloths. Outside in the yard were 100 drying racks. But this was a modest operation, for all their equipment amounted only to around £20.

References to cotton in several equity court petitions from the north of England during the second half of the sixteenth century or early seventeenth probably allude to two distinct substances. In the first, woolen cloth was frizzed or "cottoned" by rubbing it until it acquired a soft, fluffy nap.[37] Cottoned cloth was then used for petticoats, waistcoats, and the linings of cloaks and coats. This is probably the meaning in a case from Radclyffe, Lancs., in the 1550s. Before her marriage to a local carpenter, Ellen Madder delivered "one pack of cloths called cottons" to James Harier of Bury, Lancs., to be taken to London and sold.[38] She paid him 3s. 4d. for his services but later claimed that he had failed to give her the £8 he received for the cloths. But we also find mention of "cotton wool," apparently referring to the vegetable fiber which by the later sixteenth century was being imported into England from the southern and eastern Mediterranean.[39] In 1608, Robert Warberton of Moston, Lancs., a linenweaver, delivered 7 lbs. of cotton wool worth 10s. 6d. to Margery Pendleton of Eccles, Lancs., spinster, "to spin and make into thread" for him, but she failed either to produce the thread or to return the cotton. Though the raw material was new, spinning remained women's work.

By the second half of the sixteenth century, the manufacture of linen cloth, made from flax, provided employment for some women. Linen, a more expensive cloth than wool, was used for clothing and bed or table coverings by the wealthy during the medieval years, but during the Elizabethan and Jacobean periods it was increasingly purchased by people of middling and occasionally even lower status as well.[40] Before English (and later Irish) flax-growing had expanded to fill local demand, some was imported from the continent. In the mid-1510s, Margaret Dene of

---

[36] PRO C 239/11/72. The inventory is damaged in places, with a few of the later valuations missing.
[37] Kerridge, *Textile Manufactures*, p. 19.   [38] PRO DL 1/46/M5.
[39] Kerridge, *Textile Manufactures*, p. 141. For below, see PRO PL 6/2, 21 August 1613.
[40] For changes in consumption, see Spufford, *The Great Reclothing*.

London, trading as a sole merchant (her husband William was a leatherseller), bought three packs of flax from Edgar van Kempen, a merchant of the Hanse, for £21 13s. 4d.[41] Preparation of linen yarn was labor-intensive, for the flax had to be soaked in water and beaten in small batches, after which the strands could be removed and readied for spinning. While men sometimes handled the heavy work of soaking and beating, the preparation of thread was generally assigned to women.[42]

In the market center of Retford, Notts., where both wool and flax were prepared for weaving during the sixteenth century, male wills include references to larger spinning wheels for wool and smaller ones for flax.[43] The men in whose households spinning was done all had other occupations, so it was probably women who actually carried out the work. Local regulations of 1600 assumed that many of these workers would be women, and it is clear that the term "flax spinster" still meant a female spinner, since two of the women so designated were married. Female servants may also have been hired to help with these activities. In 1632, John Carberton, a yeoman, bequeathed to his servant Ann Otter all the flax and hemp (used to make canvas, but prepared in similar ways) in his house, both spun and unspun. Poor women in Retford were likewise left charitable bequests of flax, which they could spin and sell.

Linen cloth was woven on special looms, smaller than those used for woolen broadcloth. Although this might have facilitated a higher degree of involvement by women, some male weavers of woolen cloth simply expanded into linen as well: in fifteenth-century York, some weavers had both woolen and linen looms, as was true also in Shrewsbury.[44] A few female clothmakers were able to tap into the luxury demand in late medieval London. Agnes Shepster and another woman made 159 sheets of Holland linen cloth which they sold to the royal household within an eighteen-month period.[45] As linen production became better established within England, middlemen emerged, working between the producers of flax thread and the weavers. In 1608, two linen weavers in the northwest, widows Joan Walmisey of Salmesbury, Lancs., and Margaret Hoole of Marton, Lancs., bought flax worth 23s. and 15s. respectively from men

[41] PRO C 1/403/52.

[42] In Halesowen, Worcs., four women and two men were fined as early as 1300 for soaking flax in the lord's fishpond (Hilton, "Lords, Burgesses"). These women were not merely helping their husbands, for the latter worked in different occupations. During the 1550s, five husbandmen of Carcroft and Crofton, West Yorks., were reported for wetting flax and hemp in "Burne Wroo": PRO DL 1/58/F12.

[43] Marcombe, *English Small Town Life*, pp. 102–4 for the rest of this paragraph. No wills survive for women.

[44] Swanson, *Medieval Artisans*, pp. 36–7.

[45] Lacey, "Women and Work," which does not provide an exact date for this activity.

who described themselves as "occupied in buying and selling of flax or linen and other wares."[46] That wording suggests that the dealers would also have sold the weavers' cloth for them.

At first glance, silkworking appears to offer an atypical pattern, for it was an almost exclusively female craft during the later fourteenth and fifteenth centuries. In London, silkwomen and their female employees provided both management and labor for this area of luxury production.[47] Manufacture of cloth and other items, like ribbons and lace, from imported silk thread had begun in England by around 1300 but became common over the course of the following century. At first, women in a variety of towns engaged in this activity. In Nottingham during the 1350s, when occupational surnames were still in use, Joan le Silkesewer burned two kerchiefs belonging to Hamon of Ireton, while Christina le Silke-seuere sued Simon Ball for her wages.[48] In York, two wealthy silkwomen were working in the 1430s, and as late as the 1490s, Alys Hordell, "sylke-woman," was active in Coventry. These women may all have trained in London, for young women are known to have come there from other parts of the country to be apprenticed with silkwomen.[49]

By the mid-fifteenth century, silkworking had become overwhelmingly concentrated in London, and its female practitioners were regarded as members of a craft distinct from those of their fathers or husbands. They included wealthy owners of large shops that employed a number of female apprentices and servants. The wills of five late medieval silkwomen proved in London's Commissary Court included some considerable estates as well as charitable bequests to prisoners, hospitals, the poor, parish churches, and religious fraternities.[50] Many of the married silkwomen traded as *femmes soles* as they dealt with foreign merchants and imported and sold goods of high value, sometimes including expensive fabrics other than silks. Thus, Cecily Walcote, a silkwoman of London married to mercer John Walcote, agreed around 1480 to buy several types of Venetian luxury cloth worth £152 from Barnard de Via Cava, a Genoese merchant.[51] Cecily's husband was probably a useful

---

[46] PRO PL 6/1, nos. 65 and 74.

[47] Abram, "Women Traders," Dale, "London Silkwomen," and Lacey, "Women and Work."

[48] Foulds, "Women and Work." For below, see Goldberg, *Women, Work, and Life Cycle*, p. 123, and Fox, "Coventry Guilds."

[49] Dale, "London Silkwomen."

[50] As described in Hanawalt, "Medieval London Women as Consumers." The wealthiest woman, widow Beatrice Filer, left £140 as well as silver spoons and other goods to her five children: Guildhall Library London MS 9171/6, f. 272v. See also McIntosh, "The Benefits and Drawbacks of *Femme Sole* Status."

[51] PRO C 1/110/125.

business connection for her, for silk workers normally bought their supplies either from London mercers or from Italian merchants in London. At the lower end of the scale, Isabel Norman, an apparently unmarried silkwoman of London, bought "gold of Cyprus on pipes" (probably gold thread wound around a tube) from Ivo Catayne for £8 in 1422; silkwoman Catherine Butteler of London bought just £4 worth of "stuff and wares" in the 1470s from John Porter of London.[52] Alice Claver's history is particularly well documented. Thoroughly trained in silkworking, almost certainly through a formal apprenticeship, she became the second wife of Richard Claver, a well-to-do mercer, sometime before his death in 1456.[53] During Richard's life she practiced her own craft, and after his death she did not remarry but continued to operate as a silkwoman and to raise their young son. By the 1480s, she was managing a substantial workshop, supplying silk cloth, ribbons, and laces to the household of Edward IV and making elaborate ornaments for the coronation mantles of Richard III and his queen.

London's silkwomen acted as a group on several occasions during the later fourteenth and fifteenth centuries, suggesting a degree of occupational identity that was unique among English women. They collectively petitioned the mayor in 1368 against a Lombard merchant who was trying to corner the market in raw and colored silks, and in 1455 and 1482 they petitioned Parliament against foreign competition.[54] The latter efforts may have had some impact, as five acts were passed between 1455 and 1504 forbidding the importation of certain silk goods for periods ranging from four to twenty years. Yet London's silkwomen never organized into a formal guild and never gained the kind of control which male craft organizations exercised over standards of production, wages, and the training of apprentices. Nor did they play any role in the government of London. Hence they were vulnerable when male workers started moving into the craft during the second half of the fifteenth century. Whereas the petition of 1455 was sent by the "Silkwomen and Throwsters [= those who wove the fabric] of the craft and occupation of silkwork," the petition of 1482 referred to the "men and women of the whole craft of silkwork of the City of London." The latter document said that continental silkmakers had forced many men as well as women out of work.

It was indeed true that the silk crafts were by then declining within England, outpriced by foreign-made goods. By the sixteenth century, silk items were generally imported, often by London merchants, especially mercers. Silkworking had decayed so markedly that suggestions

[52] CPMRL, 1413–1437, p. 146; PRO C 1/64/808.
[53] Sutton, "Alice Claver."   [54] Dale, "London Silkwomen," for this paragraph.

were made for introducing Italian silkweavers into England to teach the craft.[55] Women now traded in silk only as widows or if acting with a male member of their family. Between 1602 and 1606 Petronella Samyne, a London widow, acted as the English representative for her two sons, importers of silk who spent most of their time in Verona, Italy.[56] Their business required very heavy investment: in 1602–3 alone her sons sent eleven bales of silk to England, to a total value of around £2,500. Early in the seventeenth century, a change in fashion among wealthy women created new but poorly paid opportunities for women and men who knitted silk stockings. Although the hosiers who coordinated this trade were usually male, Anne Tatsall, another London widow, maintained her husband's business in the early 1620s. She was said to be a "dealer in the trade of dressing, making, turning, buying and [selling] of silk stockings," assisted by several female servants and a man who had previously been an apprentice and journeyman with her husband.[57]

Sale of textiles

Cloth was sold at a variety of levels, ranging from major shipments that were exported to or imported from the continent, through the activity of wholesale distributors within England, down to the shops, market-sellers, and peddlers who offered cloth directly to customers. Some women, especially widows, imported and exported cloth during the generations between 1348–9 and the early sixteenth century, but opportunities at this level were limited to those urban women with unusual access to cash, credit, and international connections. Around 1480, Clemence Waldyngfeld, a widow probably of London who was trading cloth with the continent, owed £18 to William Brynyng, a London mercer.[58] He asked her to repay her debt not in money but rather by ordering her agent, Robert Holbech, to deliver Flemish cloth of that value to him at Bruges. At about the same time, Elizabeth Lobbe and her husband James, who evidently lived in London, bought from merchant Lowys Gerbray at an unstated place on the continent "as much merchandise of linen cloth and other wares" as came to the sum of £35 13s. 4d. Dame Elizabeth Stokton, widow, was heavily invested in the overseas cloth trade around 1500.[59] She delivered to Sebastian Giglis, a merchant

---

[55] Ibid.   [56] PRO REQ 2/407/29.
[57] PRO REQ 2/392/39. By the period 1695–1725, large-scale production of silk wares was entirely in male hands. A sample of London working women shows that they now participated only as "silk-winders," those who prepared the raw silk for weaving. These low-status workers constituted the largest group within the category of textile manufacture in a sample of working women (Earle, "Female Labour Market").
[58] PRO C 1/64/143. For below, see C 1/64/525.   [59] PRO C 1/137/33.

of Lucca then in London, twenty-one "fine and coarse woolen cloths of diverse colors" which he was to have "fulled, rowed, barbed, dressed, and shorn" and then carried from London to Venice to be sold. For that work plus the cost of transport, customs duties, and subsidies on the cloth, she gave Sebastian £27 18s. in money. Around 1530, Agnes Thornton, wife of William but trading as a *femme sole* merchant in London, bought several packs of canvas worth £30 14d. from Peter Malyarde, a merchant of Rouen.[60] But after around 1560 the increasing scale of international trade made it increasingly difficult for women to compete.

Dealing in cloth within England was a more feasible option, since it required less capital investment or credit and less travel. In the 1440s, Julian Mermean, a female trader in Somerset, sent a servant to carry one pack of her goods – almost certainly cloth – to Sir John Lane in Wells.[61] When the servant arrived, he stayed at a local inn, where he displayed Julian's wares to Sir John and two visitors from Bridgewater, Som., one of them a mercer. After Sir John left, the Bridgewater men invited the servant to drink with them, and when he became "overset with drink," they broke open Julian's pack and persuaded him to accept just £5 for the goods, which they then sold to another man for a higher price. Around 1510, Margaret Parkar of Faringdon, Berks., sold cloth worth £383 12s. 10d. to Avery and Christopher Rawson, London mercers.[62] This was certainly more cloth than she could have made herself, suggesting that she was working as an intermediary in her area, a center of clothmaking at that time.

Other women sold cloth directly to consumers from a shop. During the later fourteenth and fifteenth centuries, some of the women described as mercers or drapers were probably widows carrying on the work of their husbands.[63] Later too, an occasional widow maintained a business previously run by her husband. Isabel Tipping, an Elizabethan widow, was described as "perhaps the richest woman in Manchester" thanks to her success in continuing her husband's trade in linen yarn and cloth.[64] Some widows, however, did not even try to run the shop they had inherited. Around 1535, Philippa Sale was left a widow through the death of her husband George, a merchant tailor of London. In a later legal action Oliver Tatam, who had apparently been George's apprentice, claimed that Philippa agreed to lease to him George's shop located in Watling Street, London, on a yearly basis; with the lease went the woolen cloth

[60] PRO C 1/657/33.   [61] PRO C 1/15/85.   [62] PRO C 1/353/25.
[63] Abram, "Women Traders," and Hutton, "Women in Fourteenth Century Shrewsbury."
[64] Willan, *Elizabethan Manchester*, p. 93. For below, see PRO C 1/908/4.

currently in the shop, valued at £100. Oliver took over the shop and made a heavy initial investment in additional cloth. But, he claimed, shortly after his entry into the shop, Philippa expelled him from it and granted it to someone else, seizing the cloth that was in the shop and suing him in a common law court.

Married women, too, sold textiles, working either on their own or as partners/assistants to their husbands. In London, Maud, wife of Robert le Brokettour, received a large woolen cloth from Thomas Dogget around 1305 which he asked her to sell for 12s. 6d.[65] Anne Blakegrave, the wife of Richard Blakegrave, a London mercer, traded independently during the early 1530s. She bought some imported linen cloth worth £59 9d. for sale in her shop called "The Dove," held of the Dyers' Company in the parish of All Hallows the Less. Thomas Staunton sold cloth and other "mercery wares" in his shop in Bury St. Edmund, Suffolk, during the Elizabethan period.[66] Yet when a customer came in to buy some grogram cloth, his wife was present in the shop with him, and before he set a price on the cloth, he consulted with her. Mary Cooke of Westminster was apparently a more active partner in a cloth and clothing business run with her husband Thomas, said to be a gentleman.[67] In 1619, Mary received from Henry Deane, a London esquire who was temporarily low on cash, twenty yards of luxury cloth ("hair colored and russet wrought silk grogram") worth £10 and one petticoat made of green and white tufted taffeta with a silver border worth £4, which he asked her to sell for him. She then displayed his items to a female servant of William Horewood of the Inner Temple, gentleman, who said that her master might want to buy them as a gift for his fiancée. One notes that there was a fine line between giving goods to a retailer who would then find a buyer for them, as Henry alleged he had done, and pawning the same goods for an immediate cash loan, which seems closer to the facts in this case.[68]

An even more prominent part within a nominally husband-and-wife business was played by Grace Spooner, married to Lawrence of "Myrry-hill," War. The Spooners were accused of having sold cloth on 27 March 1585 in the open market at Tamworth.[69] This violated local ordinances because Spooner was not a freeman of the borough. An officious local man seized the cloth they offered, marked it to the queen's use, and notified the royal Exchequer, presumably hoping for an informer's share of the goods as a reward from the crown. This led to a complicated legal

[65] CEMCRL, 1298–1305, p. 210. For below, see PRO C 1/904/18–20.
[66] PRO REQ 2/63/100. For a fuller discussion of this case, see Ch. 9 below.
[67] PRO REQ 2/424/43.
[68] For pawning, see sect. 3, Ch. 4 above.   [69] PRO E 134/30 Eliz/Hil 10.

action. For our purposes, the information given by the witnesses interviewed in the case provides some fine detail about a small-scale, mobile, cloth-retailing business.

The Spooners specialized in linen and other kinds of cloth. The items offered for sale at Tamworth market on the day in question, which came to a total value of £127 15s., included Holland linen of various qualities, several grades of cambric and lawn, fine canvas for dublets called "Brown Holland," plain canvas, and "housewife's flax cloth." The lengths of the individual pieces of cloth ranged from 20 to 80 ells each (1 ell = 45 inches). The physical volume of the Spooners' goods was limited by the need to fit them into a pack that could be carried by a horse, but they offered some variety of cost, with prices extending downward from 12s. per ell for fine lawn to 18d. per ell for housewife's flax. One witness estimated that the Spooners "turn[ed] yearly in linen cloth the sum of £200." Lawrence and Grace were said to have traveled widely to purchase their cloth, going to London, Coventry, Sturbridge Fair near Cambridge, and Lenton Fair near Nottingham.

Rather than having a fixed shop in one particular community, the Spooners (or, more accurately, Grace) traveled in a regular circuit among the weekly markets in their part of the west Midlands. None of these places alone probably offered enough customers to sustain the Spooners' business, but in series they did. Grace apparently rode on one horse and led the second, laden with her cloth. In the schedule described by witnesses, which sounds almost prohibitively grueling, she started her week at Hinkley, Leics., on Monday morning, going then to Atherstone, War., for the Tuesday market there, to Lichfield, Staffs., on Wednesdays, Burton (upon Trent), Staffs., on Thursdays, Derby on Fridays, and Tamworth on Saturdays. Because markets opened early in the day, Grace would have needed to sell her wares each morning and then ride on to the next town in the afternoon. Quite surprisingly, she had managed to maintain this pace of life for sixteen to twenty years. Since the circuit required that she travel a total of about 120 km between Monday and Saturday, plus getting to and from her own house on the weekends, it is possible that she did not in fact go to every market every week.[70]

The division of labor between Thomas and Grace within their business was by no means equal. Although Thomas was named as the defendant in the Exchequer case, because he was the person whose standing as a freeman of Tamworth was in question (Grace as a woman was not eligible), his actual participation seems to have been minimal. Although

---

[70] Because of the scheduling of the weekly markets, Grace could not take the most efficient route between them.

all the witnesses refer to the cloth and the "standing" or stall in the market as belonging to the Spooners, in the plural, there is no indication that Thomas was present at Tamworth on the day in question. Witnesses saw *Grace* standing in the shop, and they said that *she* made the weekly circuit. The only point at which they speak about both Spooners is when describing where they bought their cloth, suggesting that Thomas was involved in their purchasing trips to the larger cities and fairs. One can only hope that Thomas was working equally hard on whatever his primary occupation was while Grace was slogging around the countryside with her pack of goods.

Making and selling clothing and accessories

During these centuries new clothing was not purchased ready-made off the rack. Instead wealthier customers went to a tailor or dressmaker to arrange for an item to be made specifically for them. In towns, where most tailors of both women's and men's clothes were men, the customer and tailor would discuss the design of the piece of clothing and the fabric(s) to be used, the size and cost, and the schedule for completion.[71] The cloth could either be supplied by the tailor or brought in by the customer after purchase from a textile seller. The tailor normally carried out the most skilled single stage of work on the project himself: laying out and cutting the fabric, where an error might mean that a new piece of cloth had to be purchased. Thereafter, however, he generally gave the material to a seamstress to sew according to his instructions.[72] Early in 1599, Mistress Anne Constable contracted with tailor John Allan of the Strand, just outside the city of London, to make three gowns, two petticoats, and other clothing for her, at a total cost of £17 5s. 11d.[73] As arranged, the pieces John had prepared were sewn together by women he hired, and he delivered the items to Anne a few months later. Especially in smaller communities, some women worked independently as dressmakers, completing all stages of the process themselves. The village of

---

[71] Prior, "Women and the Urban Economy," pp. 110–11. The Poll Tax returns of 1379–81 show that all eighteen tailors in (King's) Lynn were male, as were the six tailors in Worcester and the seventy-three in York; Oxford had one woman among fifty tailors, Shrewsbury had one among ten, Pontefract had two among eighteen, and Southwark had four among forty-five (Goldberg, *Women, Work, and Life Cycle*, pp. 88–92).

[72] For a similar distinction in seventeenth-century France, see Crowston, *Fabricating Women*.

[73] PRO REQ 2/60/61. What makes this situation unusual was that her husband, Robert, was currently being held prisoner in Ireland, hardly a time, one might have thought, for Anne to be ordering expensive clothing.

Udimore, Sussex, for example, had an unmarried female dressmaker in 1379.[74]

Because one tailor might employ multiple seamstresses (commonly called "sempsters" or "shepsters" in medieval records), women in towns frequently found work of this kind.[75] It required little capital and basic sewing did not require much training, but the wage paid per item was low. In fourteenth-century Shrewsbury, no women worked as tailors, but many poor women were seamstresses.[76] Records from late medieval London likewise show women assisting in the manufacture of clothing, described as threadwomen, needlewomen, or sempstresses. Westminster, a London suburb that concentrated upon retailing, contained many male tailors, enabling some women – often unmarried – to maintain a fragile economic existence by sewing for them and other customers.[77] Anastasia Barnwell, a singlewoman who did sewing at home, received an order in 1508 from the guild of the Assumption of the Virgin Mary to make three dozen "liveries" to be worn at a feast, for which she was paid 3s. In late medieval York, too, sempsters were unmarried women.[78] Some seam-stresses worked in the tailors' shops, but many were hired on a piecework basis, doing the sewing in their own homes.[79]

Clothing was sold in a different fashion to the poor. Upholders, uphol-sters, or furbishers were traders in secondhand goods, especially used or cast-off clothing: they cleaned, repaired, and/or re-worked their wares into more attractive items before selling them to the bottom of the urban con-sumer market. A dozen women were licensed as upholders in Canterbury over the course of the fifteenth century, as was a widow in Nottingham in 1478–9.[80] When sixty-eight Londoners were convicted in 1321 for selling used clothes at the evening markets held at Cornhill and in Cheapside

---

[74] Mate, *Daughters, Wives and Widows*, p. 45.

[75] Oxford's Poll Tax listing for 1381 includes eleven seamstresses among eighty-eight female household heads; in Southwark's return for the same year, ten seamstresses were joined by three specialized makers of clothing among 137 women who headed households: Bennett, "Medieval Women, Modern Women," and Carlin, *Medieval Southwark*, p. 175.

[76] Hutton, "Women in Fourteenth Century Shrewsbury," pp. 92–3. For below, see Abram, "Women Traders," and Lacey, "Women and Work."

[77] Rosser, *Medieval Westminster*, p. 198, for this and below.

[78] Goldberg, "Female Labour."

[79] Women remained involved in clothing work into the early eighteenth century, though only minimally in cloth production. Of a cross-section of London women, 1695–1725, just 5 percent were engaged in textile manufacture, while 20 percent made or mended clothes; of a sample of businesswomen who bought insurance policies, 1726–9, 31 percent dealt with textiles or clothing, but nearly all were sellers of cloth or makers of clothing (Earle, "Female Labour Market," and his *Making of the English Middle Class*, p. 170).

[80] Goldberg, *Women, Work, and Life Cycle*, pp. 132–3; *Records of the Borough of Nottingham*, vol. II, pp. 298–303.

(a practice forbidden by civic regulation probably because it was then too dark to examine the goods properly), fourteen were women.[81] Although most of the women engaged in this trade were poor, Agnes Hill, upholder, bought "the freedom of the city of London," bringing advantageous trading rights, for the considerable sum of 100 marks in 1448.

By the later sixteenth century, used clothing was commonly sold on the streets of larger communities by hucksters. This practice was linked to pawning, for some sellers were willing to accept other items as pawns if cash was not available. In 1573, the government of Leicester noted that women who sold used clothing and household goods, "hawking abroad from house to house," were willing to take goods on credit and were indeed called "pledge women."[82] A similar connection was seen in Salisbury in the early seventeenth century. Official discomfort about these sellers and their wares was sometimes explained in terms of possible contagion. In 1582, jurors in Cornhill, London, complained against "the vagrant women such as commonly go up and down in the streets carrying and selling of apparel, whence the same cometh is not known, but suspected to come from houses which have been visited [with disease], whereby the common people are in danger of infection."[83]

New or expanded production of several secondary types of clothing provided additional employment for poor women in the later sixteenth and early seventeenth centuries. Among these was knitting caps or stockings. During the fourteenth and most of the fifteenth century, caps had been made out of woven cloth, work done occasionally by women.[84] But during the later fifteenth century knitted caps were introduced, using a system of four or five needles.[85] This kind of knitting was usually done by women, at home and on a piecework basis. By the 1520s and 1530s, the male cappers in York who organized this trade were becoming wealthy thanks to the female labor they hired, and by the Elizabethan period poor women all over the country were making caps.[86] A similar process was used in knitting wool stockings, which by the early seventeenth century had become standard articles of apparel. Thirsk has estimated that around 10 million pairs of stockings were needed annually, production that would have employed about 100,000 people for fifty weeks

---

[81] Barron, "Women in London," for this and below.

[82] *Records of the Borough of Leicester*, vol. III, p. 147. For below, see Wright, "Churmaids."

[83] Guildhall Library London MS 4069/1, fol. 33, as cited by Gowing, "'Freedom of the Streets'," pp. 141–2.

[84] In the 1381 Poll Tax return for Southwark, for example, four of the 137 female household heads were cappers (Carlin, *Medieval Southwark*, p. 175).

[85] Swanson, *Medieval Artisans*, p. 51, and see *Records of the Borough of Nottingham*, vol. II, pp. 298–303.

[86] Swanson, *Medieval Artisans*, pp. 50–1.

per year, if each worker knitted two pairs of stockings per week as by-employment.[87] As early as 1570, Norwich's Census of the Poor included forty-seven women who did plain knitting and ten knitters/makers of hose; poor women were shown knitting hose in the pageant of the ideal commonwealth produced for Queen Elizabeth in Norwich in 1589.[88] Knitting stockings was likewise among the occupations that Winchester's Elizabethan House of Correction planned to offer to its female inmates.[89]

Growing demand for decorative items like lace and buttons created further poorly paid work for women. These finicky, repetitive tasks were well suited to the smaller hands of some women and children. The most important was the trim known as "bone lace," in which the thread, normally linen, was held on bobbins made of bone. Bone lace was just coming into fashion as of 1570, when Norwich's Census of the Poor listed fifteen plain lace makers but only one bone-lace maker.[90] By 1596, the Collectors of the Poor in the rural parish of Eaton Socon, Beds., were paying 2d. per week to a woman "that teacheth the poor children to work bone lace." Given the low pay received by lace makers, this may appear to have been a sure way to constrain those children to a lifetime of poverty, but it was popular with other poor-relief officials too. In Salisbury, thirty women were employed in 1625 to teach the crafts of spinning, knitting, or making bone lace to poor children.[91] The following year, Salisbury ordered that no children be allowed to beg; instead, "all the children of the poor that are not able to relieve them[selves shall] be set to sewing, knitting, bone-lace making, spinning of woolen or linen yarn," or other similar tasks. Button-making too provided work commonly done by women and children.[92] Not surprisingly, button-making was on the list of occupations considered suitable for the poor in Salisbury in the 1620s.

Elements of clothing made from leather or fur were normally produced in shops operated by male craftsmen like glovers or hatmakers. But although labor was frequently provided by women, the work was supervised by men.[93] In late medieval York, much of the sewing of gloves

---

[87] Thirsk, *Economic Policy and Projects*, pp. 5–6.

[88] *Norwich Census of the Poor*, p. 99; *Progresses and Public Processions*, vol. II, pp. 143–5.

[89] Thirsk, *Economic Policy and Projects*, pp. 65–6.

[90] *Norwich Census of the Poor*, p. 99. For below, see Bedfordshire Record Office P 5/12/1.

[91] Wright, "Churmaids." For below, see ibid., p. 102.

[92] Thirsk, *Economic Policy and Projects*, pp. 14 and 66. For below, see ibid., p. 66.

[93] In Shrewsbury in the mid-fourteenth century, a few women were described as glovers, and the Southwark Poll Tax of 1381 includes one glover among 137 female household heads (Hutton, "Women in Fourteenth Century Shrewsbury"; Carlin, *Medieval Southwark*, p. 175). For craftspeople who made heavy goods from leather, like saddles and shoes, see sect. 2 below.

was done by women, and in a rare exception, one woman was actually admitted as a master of the glove-makers' craft.[94] In Norwich during the first half of the fourteenth century, women were paid to line the mayor's hat with beaver fur. Catherine Pikto, a London widow, was apparently working as a hat maker in her own right when she accepted William Marcham as a bound apprentice in the 1470s.[95] He completed his seven-year term with her and later became a "hatter-merchant" himself.

Especially in London, with its greater demand for luxury goods, women found opportunities for skilled employment in decorative work. Embroidery was a traditionally female art form in England, dating back to the early medieval years. Used in some cases on wall hangings or covers for furniture and sacred objects, embroidery was also added as trim on religious or secular clothing. In late medieval York, where relatively little embroidery was done, widow Alice Legh was owed the substantial sum of 26s. 8d. by her male employer, a vestment-maker, for "fine hemming of [em]broidery."[96] In London during the later fifteenth century, some female embroiderers ran their own shops and hired labor, enabling them to work on a large scale and earn high prices for their creations. Alice Darcy and Thomas Guydichon sold a piece of embroidered cloth to the Earl of Lincoln for 300 marks (= £200), and Alice was preparing another piece that was estimated at the same price.[97] A few London women worked as jewelers, even when their husbands were in different trades, and they were found as "wiredrawers" of gold and silver, producing thin strands of these precious metals for use in decorating clothing and making jewelry.[98] Around 1480 Anne Hille, a singlewoman working in her craft of "tiremaker" (= producer of decorative headdresses), was asked by a servant of Henry Cote, goldsmith, to make "a pair of fine tires" for his master, to be "wrought with fine damask gold."[99] The cover to this book shows an English woman with an elaborate hairstyle selling in a shop that provided hairdressing supplies and perhaps perfumes. Her customer, a monk whose hair has been shaved into the required tonsure, is looking longingly at a mirror or a picture of a person with long curly locks.

---

[94] Swanson, *Medieval Artisans*, p. 60. For below, see Goldberg, *Women, Work, and Life Cycle*, p. 130.

[95] PRO C 1/61/540.   [96] Goldberg, *Women, Work, and Life Cycle*, p. 123.

[97] Abram, "Women Traders," which does not provide an exact date.

[98] Lacey, "Woman and Work," and CPMRL, 1458–1482, pp. 112–13.

[99] PRO C 1/64/1161. Cote later sued her in a London court, where, Anne alleged, he invited the trial jurors who were to hear the case to come to a dinner at his expense; there they they consented to decide against her.

2   Other crafts

Women rarely ran other kinds of leather or metal craftshops on their own. The exceptions were either widows or daughters of men who had pursued these occupations (a pattern found especially during the later fourteenth and fifteenth centuries) or women employed in a few specific areas that required good small-muscle coordination. Yet even in some of the most male-dominated crafts, the occasional records that provide more detail indicate that married women or daughters sometimes helped the head of the workshop and that singlewomen might be hired as servants or paid assistants.

In the leather crafts, women almost never appear as skinners, tanners, tawyers, saddlers, or shoemakers heading their own operations.[100] If they worked in these crafts, either as family members or paid employees, they were generally engaged in the finer, more specialized processes. Thus, they might skin leather or make purses from it but did not do the heavier work of tanning or turning cured leather into saddles or shoes.[101] The leathersellers' gild of London expressly permitted wives and daughters to work for a male craftsman even though they had not been formally apprenticed to that trade.

A few widows continued their husband's work. In mid-fourteenth-century Shrewsbury, all the shoemakers and saddlers were men, but an occasional tanning yard was run by a widow.[102] During the earlier fifteenth century, London widow Matilda Penne was unusual in keeping the skinner's shop of her husband William going for more than twelve years after his death. She must have acquired some training either as a younger woman or during her marriage, for she took on her own apprentices. They evidently served as her agents overseas in buying and/or selling skins, some of which were supplied by Hanseatic merchants from Germany and the Baltic areas. Although her work was not always up to the highest standards, she was a good enough businesswoman to see that her debts were well secured. When Anne Bursell of St. Martin's the Great was left

[100] Tanners prepared heavy, stiff leather, such as would be needed for shoes or saddles; tawyers produced thin, supple leather for such purposes as gloves. The Poll Tax listings of 1377–81 show no female household heads in the leather crafts in (King's) Lynn or York, one woman out of twenty-six in Pontefract, West Yorks., and one out of ninety-four in Oxford. Only Southwark had a higher proportion, with five women out of fifty-nine (three skinners, one saddler, and one shoemaker): Goldberg, *Women, Work, and Life Cycle*, pp. 88–92. Fourteenth-century Exeter had no female leatherworkers (Kowaleski, *Local Markets and Regional Trade*, pp. 156–61).

[101] For leather goods as clothing, see sect. 1 above. For below, see Abram, "Women Traders."

[102] Hutton, "Women in Fourteenth Century Shrewsbury." For below, see Veale, "Matilda Penne."

a pregnant widow in 1610 after the death of her husband, a cordwainer (= shoemaker), she realized that she could not maintain the shop on her own.[103] Working through a male friend, she persuaded Richard Andrews, another cordwainer, to leave his own business, bringing his wares and equipment to Anne's house and shop. This arrangement was linked to their proposed marriage. Some leather craftsmen who were facing death thought their widow would be better off with a rental income.[104] They therefore bought real estate rather than expecting that the women would keep the business going.

Women also traded in furs. Sanche Akent, wife of John, was approached sometime around 1500 by a London skinner, who asked her to sell for him "3 furs of black shanks and 6 furs of black lamb."[105] In a practice similar to the upholstering of clothing, used furs too could be refurbished. Agnes, wife of William de Bury of London, was charged in 1344 with buying worn-out white and light-colored furs which she sent off to be dyed black. She then sold the goods at Cornhill as if they were "good and proper" furs. Around 1480 Alice Ban . . . a London widow, brought certain "peltry ware" worth £12 to William Langton, skinner, telling him to repay her when he could.[106] Later, however, she asked him to choose "one of the best and finest gray among all the said peltry" and use it to fur a cloak for her.

In the wood and large metal crafts, we again find suggestions of female involvement behind the scenes.[107] The guild of metal founders in York ordered in 1390 that masters were allowed to instruct their wives, and one master was allowed a second apprentice because he had no wife to assist him.[108] In late medieval York, Beverley, and London, a few women, mainly widows, worked as brick manufacturers, tilers, carpenters, coopers, shipwright, armorers, or makers of spurs. An interesting reflection of how tasks could be broken down by gender is provided by the will of Adam Heche, a York amorer, who in 1404 left to a son his instruments for making heavy plate armor; he bequeathed to a daughter, however, his

---

[103] PRO REQ 2/416/6.   [104] Keene, "Tanners' Widows."

[105] PRO C 1/113/76. For below, see CPMRL, 1323–1364, p. 213.

[106] PRO C 1/61/343. The document is damaged, with a few words missing.

[107] The Poll Tax listings of 1377–81 show low proportions of women in the building and metal trades: one out of twenty-two for Pontefract, three out of 114 for Oxford, and three out of 215 in York; slightly higher fractions are recorded in (King's) Lynn (three of thirty-three) and Southwark (three of forty-eight): Goldberg, *Women, Work, and Life Cycle*, pp. 88–92. Exeter in the late fourteenth century recorded no women in these trades, but women smiths are mentioned in the 1379 Poll Tax return for the West Riding of Yorkshire (Kowaleski, *Local Markets and Regional Trade*, pp. 161–7, Goldberg, "Female Labour," and his "Women's Work").

[108] Goldberg, *Women, Work, and Life Cycle*, p. 128. For below, see ibid., and Abram, "Women Traders."

tools and materials for making chain mail, which required the preparation and integration of many small pieces of metal.[109]

Several exceptional London women achieved some success as architects/masons or bell-founders during the later fourteenth and fifteenth centuries. Agnes Ramsey, daughter of the famous London architect/mason William Ramsey and wife of Robert Hubard, another mason, ran her father's business after his death in 1349.[110] Sometime during the 1350s, she drew up a contract with Queen Isabella, widow of Edward II, for construction of her tomb at the London Greyfriars at a cost of over £100. Agnes continued to collect her father's debts and engage in property transactions until 1399. In the parish of St. Botolph Aldgate, outside London's walls, two widows continued their husbands' bell-founding workshops during the middle years of the fifteenth century.[111] Joan Hill, widow of Richard Hill, sustained his business for about a year after his death in 1440, retaining three of Richard's four apprentices and taking on a new one of her own. During that time, her workshop cast twelve bells, all marked with Richard's shield modified by the addition of a lozenge containing a floret, a heraldic indication of womanhood. At the time of her death, Joan's household included the four apprentices plus two female servants and the daughter of a fellow bell-founder, six male servants, a skilled bellmaker, a clerk, and four other men whose jobs were not specified in her will. The Hills' bellfoundry then came into the hands of John Sturdy, who operated the establishment until his death sometime between 1456 and 1459. It was at that point taken over by his widow Joan, under whose direction at least fourteen more bells were cast.

Women were more likely to be employed in the small metal trades. During the fifteenth century and even more so during the sixteenth, two types of fine metalwork were strongly associated with women: making the cards used for combing wool and cloth, which contained small metal pins set into a wooden backing; and making pins for use in clothing and hair. Female cardmakers were found in fifteenth-century Bury St. Edmunds, while in York a tailor paid 3s. 4d. in 1454–5 in order that his wife might operate independently as a cardmaker, working with her servants.[112] Both cities were located in regions of cloth production. In Bristol, ordinances concerning wiredrawers and cardmakers in 1469–70 exempted the wives and daughters of burgesses from their prohibition of working in these crafts without sufficient training.[113] The sad plight of Agnes Tykhyll, daughter of William, a saddler of London, reflects the importance of

[109] Goldberg, *Women, Work, and Life Cycle*, p. 128.
[110] Barron, "Women in London," for this and below.   [111] Barron, "Johanna Hill."
[112] Swanson, "The Illusion," and Goldberg, ed., *Women in England*, p. 189.
[113] Fleming, *Women in Late Medieval Bristol*, p. 7.

female labor, in this case child labor, in preparing the wire needed for pins and cardmaking.[114] On Christmas Day 1410, while she was still a child, Agnes was apprenticed for the exceptionally long term of fourteen years to William Celler, a London wiredrawer. Six or seven years later, however, well before the end of her apprenticeship, William moved away from the city (probably because of financial problems), leaving Agnes – who had "an insufficient knowledge of the trade" – in the custody of his wife. When Mistress Celler was ordered to bring the girl before the Mayor's Court and explain the situation, she claimed that Agnes had been under the legal age of apprenticeship when she signed her first contract with them. On Christmas Day 1416, however, the girl had been re-apprenticed to both Cellers together, this time "to learn the art of a cardmaker." When Agnes was examined separately, the court found that the written documents setting up the newer apprenticeship had been signed only recently, and that she was still under age. Agnes claimed that she had "sealed the indentures under threats of a beating and that she would rather go back to her father." The court ruled that she should be freed from both indentures.

By the late sixteenth century, pinmaking offered greatly expanded piecework employment for women thanks to the rising desire for elaborate dress and hair styles among women of middling and upper status.[115] One of the projects designed to advance England's consumer demand and economic self-sufficiency, pins were normally made in the female worker's home.[116] Here, again, such work was recognized as a way to train the poor to support themselves: in 1626, making pins or cards was described as a suitable activity for children in Salisbury, to keep them from begging.[117]

This discussion indicates that although some women were involved in the skilled crafts, their work was usually done either as an unpaid contribution to the household economy or on a for-pay basis by those who had no better way to bring in a little income. Whereas running a workshop that handled one of the major stages in cloth production or that made

---

[114] CPMRL, 1413–1437, pp. 53–4.
[115] Swanson, "The Illusion," Goldberg, "Female Labour," and his *Women, Work, and Life Cycle*, p. 129.
[116] Thirsk, *Economic Policy and Projects*, esp. pp. 65–6. For below, see Wright, "Churmaids."
[117] Women's involvement in the male-dominated crafts was to remain low into the early eighteenth century. Of a cross-section of London women between 1695–1725, only 2 percent were engaged in "miscellaneous manufacture" that included crafts of the kind discussed in this section; of a sample of more prosperous London women who took out life insurance between 1726 and 1729, just 4 percent worked in areas like being a pewterer, a wheelwright, a turner, or a glass-seller (Earle, "Female Labour Market," and his *Making of the English Middle Class*, p. 170).

goods of leather or metal normally offered an adequate living for a man, the kinds of employment available to women provided limited income, useful as a supplement to a man's earnings but barely enough to support a woman on her own at even the most modest level. This was true even though the country's most important single industry could not have functioned without the preliminary labor supplied by women. Opportunities for independent action at middling or upper levels of the craft world were usually open only to the widows of craftsmen and merchants, and then mainly in London during the later fourteenth and fifteenth centuries.

9   Turning the coin: women as consumers

In a role we have thus far ignored, virtually all women throughout the centuries under discussion must have bought goods at least occasionally. Involvement with most of the income-generating activities considered above forced women to become purchasers. Servants were sent to buy things for their employers, women who took in boarders needed bedding, candles, and food, landladies had to maintain their property in adequate repair, and all producers bought raw materials and equipment for their work. But even women who were not directly engaged in the market economy purchased food, clothing, or household goods for their own family's consumption. No households in England were entirely self-sufficient: even the poorest rural families needed to buy salt, cooking pots, and either clothing or the textiles from which to make it. Poor women in towns and all women of middling and higher status were probably regular purchasers of some of the food eaten by their families and at least occasional purchasers of clothes and household items.

The study of consumption differs from examination of how services or goods were provided. Asking a distinct set of questions associated with the standard of living, this field draws also upon different sources. Because it is an emerging area within late medieval and early modern history, we do not yet have a full understanding of consumption patterns, nor are we sure who was responsible for purchasing which items within households.[1] It is likely, however, that men were the buyers of supplies needed for their work and were expected to maintain the physical structure of the family's dwelling place, while the responsibility for purchasing food, clothing, and household goods fell primarily upon women's shoulders. Whether they did so in person or through an agent depended upon the socio-economic status of the family and upon the type of items needed.

Credit was obviously of vital importance in consumer relationships. Because prices were not fixed, bargaining took place between seller and

[1] For valuable early contributions, see Dyer, "The Consumer and the Market," his *Standards of Living*, esp. ch. 6, Muldrew, *The Economy of Obligation*, esp. chs. 1–2 and 7, and the works cited below.

prospective buyer about what was to be bought, how much was to be paid, and when. This included an evaluation of the economic honesty and creditworthiness of both parties as well as an assessment of the quality of the wares. Further, many female consumers – like many male ones – allowed payments for purchases to accumulate before paying a larger lump sum, so they became enmeshed in outstanding obligations. But to keep their right to extended credit, they had to maintain a good economic reputation. If a vendor became worried about a woman's ability to pay, if he heard that she or her family was struggling financially, he might demand immediate payment of the sums owed to him. That in turn could force the woman to call in whatever debts were owed to her, perhaps jeopardizing her good credit with those people.

This final chapter turns the coin by offering a brief and preliminary account of the money women spent, not the money they earned. The evidence now available suggests that while women were buyers throughout these centuries, a new pattern was appearing by the late sixteenth century. Women, especially those of middling rank, were coming to be valued as potential purchasers of the non-essential items of clothing and household goods that were increasingly available in England. A more aggressive attempt to persuade women as well as men to buy such wares may be regarded as the beginnings of a consumer society. In talking about purchasing, we will start at the top of the social hierarchy and move downwards.

The wealthiest women normally participated in shopping only indirectly. Routine purchases, like staples for their households, were made through a domestic officer to whom such tasks had been assigned.[2] Women might, however, place more personal orders for their own luxury goods. When Edward II's widow, Isabelle of France, was living just north of London in 1357–8, she sent frequently to the city for such items as tapestries, embroidery work, jewelry, furs, lampreys, and spices.[3] Some women based in the countryside had an agent in the capital who shopped for them. Between 18 March and 31 August 1401, Elizabeth, Lady Zouche, a widow living in Eaton Bray, Beds., wrote at least four times to John Bore, her receiver in London, asking him to buy expensive items for her, including damask and silk cloth, a gold rosary with a paternoster that she wanted to give to her mother, and a pipe (= four barrels) of white wine. If elite women needed to view an item they were considering buying, it might be brought to them for inspection. At the very beginning of the sixteenth century, Ellen Peryn and her husband

---

[2] For a general discussion, see Harvey, "The Aristocratic Consumer."
[3] Carlin, "'What Will You Buy?'" for this and below.

William, who were making and selling jewelry in London, received 33s. 4d. as an advance payment for a gold frontlet (= an ornament worn across the forehead) for Dame Edith, wife of Sir John St. John, a knight of the body to Henry VII.[4] The condition of this trial purchase was that the frontlet would be taken to Dame Edith's house, but if she did not like it, it would be returned to the Peryns.

Some noble and gentry families came to London in person once or more each year to purchase goods for their homes in the countryside as well as for political, legal, and social reasons.[5] During the later medieval period, the wealthiest of them had houses in London at which they stayed during these visits; some also acquired separate storehouses or wardrobes in the capital for storage of recently purchased bulky goods until they were needed at one of the family's houses. Women were among the lay aristocrats who enjoyed these London visits. In the 1390s, Alice de Briene came frequently to the London house given to her by her father-in-law, where she would spend a week at a time accompanied by a large retinue of servants and twenty horses. While there, she bought cloth for the livery of her household as well as seeking medical advice and transacting legal business. In 1387–8, Mary de Bohun, wife of Henry of Derby, came to London with her husband for the meeting of the "Merciless" Parliament. Since the family's own house had been burned during the uprising of 1381, they stayed at the London residence of the bishop of St. David's. Mary went shopping in Bread Street with her sister Eleanor, Duchess of Gloucester, and visited her mother, who was staying in London at the time, before giving birth to her second son; she rewarded Joan, the *obstetrix*, with a gift of £2.

At middling levels in both urban and rural areas, women let servants handle much of the routine daily shopping but bought more specialized goods themselves, where they needed to be sure of the quality and appropriate price. Further, since all sales were accompanied by bargaining or haggling, shopping offered an element of sport as well.[6] Equally importantly, shopping provided an opportunity to visit with friends among the sellers and other buyers and to catch up on the latest news.[7] (See Illus. 15.)

A petition to the Court of Requests from Elizabeth's reign describes the sociability that could accompany a purchase. A widow named Agnes lived in Bury St. Edmunds, Suffolk, where she was close friends with

[4] PRO C 1/253/57.
[5] Barron, "Centres of Conspicuous Consumption," for this paragraph.
[6] See *Caxton's Dialogues* and sect. 1, Ch. 5 above.
[7] Masschaele, "The Public Space of the Marketplace."

15. Women chatting while buying vegetables and grain at a market

Thomas Staunton, mercer, and his wife.[8] They were neighbors, Thomas was a friend of her former husband's, and Agnes often "kept company with him and his wife." The Stauntons were also providers of "all such mercery wares as she needed." One day she went to their shop in Bury to chat with the Stauntons and look at fabric for a gown to be made of black grogram. Thomas showed her a piece of suitable cloth which, after discussion with his wife, he offered to sell to Agnes at the rate of 6s. per yard. Then, however, they fell into what Agnes later described as a joking discussion of an alternative way of paying for the fabric: Thomas "pleasantly and familiarly demanded of [Agnes] whether she would take so much of the said grogram as would serve her for a gown . . . and pay him ten

<hr />

[8] PRO REQ 2/63/100.

pounds for it at the day of [her] marriage." Agnes, who was not thinking of remarrying, answered "in like merry sort that she durst adventure to give one hundred pounds for the same at the day of her marriage." They then returned to more sober negotiations, leading to Agnes' agreement to purchase 11½ yards of the cloth (either she was an extremely ample woman or it was going to be an unusually heavy, elaborate gown) at the rate of 6s. per yard. Since she did not pay for the cloth at the time, Thomas entered the contract into his book of accounts for the shop, "amongst other things that [she] had bought of him upon credit." Later, however, Thomas told someone else that he had sold the 11½ yards to Agnes for £100, to be paid on the day of her marriage. When that statement was reported back to Agnes, she confronted Thomas, asking what he meant by saying such a thing. He replied hastily that he had made the statement only in jest and did not intend to suggest any such contract. But after her later marriage to Edward Walwyn, a London merchant, Thomas brought suit against Agnes for £100.

For poor women in towns, shopping had to be fitted in around their income-generating activities. Their purchases were normally made in very small units, just enough to supply immediate needs, and commonly took place not in formal shops but from small-scale retail traders on the streets, many of whom were themselves women. If they could not pay for food or other necessities, they might have to pawn goods of their own. Such women usually had limited – or no – cooking facilities in their lodgings (analyses of the goods mentioned in London women's wills, 1393–1415 and 1514–47, show that poor testators seldom possessed cooking or even eating equipment), and they probably lacked money to buy fuel.[9] Hence any cooked food they ate had to be purchased, probably from booths or baskets along the streets. Carlin's study of the location of stalls that sold hot, ready-to-eat food in late medieval London indicates they were concentrated in the poorest neighborhoods.[10] She suggests that the major purchasers of such food were the local poor, often working women living alone or supporting a small household who stopped on the way home each evening to pick up for a few pennies what they would eat that evening and the next morning. Any clothing or household supplies bought by poor women were likely to be used, not new. Further, because they usually worked themselves during the daytime, their buying probably occurred later than the standard shopping hours. They may, for example, have

[9] Robert Wood, "Poor Widows," Carlin, "Fast Food," and Pennell, "Great Quantities of Gooseberry Pye."
[10] "Fast Food." Wealthy residents were likely to have kitchen staffs of their own, while travelers ate where they lodged.

frequented the evening markets at Cornhill and in Cheapside in 1321, where used clothing was on sale.[11]

Though shopping was thus part of the economic world of nearly all women, it occurred within a cultural context that saw some danger in women's roles as consumers. Medieval moralists emphasized the spiritual dangers of greed and luxury, warning women against vain display or using up their husband's wealth to no productive purpose.[12] The marketplace, regarded as a site particularly conducive to female sartorial excess, enticed women into spending too much money and time there.[13] During the Elizabethan and Jacobean periods, the negative impact of markets and consumerism upon women was forcefully articulated by some male authors. Clergymen who wrote about the ideal Christian household and the roles of each person within it encouraged women to remain quietly at home, living simply and supervising the godly (yet efficient) operation of their household.[14] In the semi-serious rhetorical attack launched by Joseph Swetnam "the woman hater" and others during the 1610s, prominent among female sins was an eagerness to display themselves in public, clad in new and stylish clothing.

But alongside that formulation, a new set of pressures was beginning to emerge in the late sixteenth century. As early capitalism developed, fortified later by colonial expansion and mercantilism, consumers were vital. England was now producing a wider array of non-essential items, some of them the result of deliberate attempts to expand national wealth through such manufacture and the employment it provided.[15] Imported goods, unfamiliar and exotic items brought from all over the world, began to flood into English markets and shops. For this system to work, someone needed to buy the goods, which were generally luxury items: either elements of dress or personal ornamentation that enhanced one's appearance but were not necessary to it, or domestic possessions that made life more comfortable or convenient but were not needed for the basic operation of the household. Men controlled the production or importing and sometimes the sale of the new consumer goods, but the economy relied upon the willingness of both women and men to buy them. It was

---

[11] Barron, "Women in London."

[12] See, e.g., *Jacob's Well* and *Mirk's Festial*, and cf. the figure of Lady Mede in Piers Plowman (Langland, *Piers Plowman An Edition of the C-Text*, ed. Pearsall).

[13] E.g., "How the Good Wijf Taughte Hir Doughtir," the mid-fourteenth-century original of a poem that remained popular through the sixteenth century. Henry of Lancaster's *Livre de Seyntz Medicines*, written in 1354, comments allegorically that foolish women come into markets "more elegantly adorned than on Easter day" (p. 119).

[14] See examples in Aughterson, ed., *Renaissance Woman*, for this and below.

[15] Thirsk, *Economic Policy and Projects*.

generally the female head of the household who bought fabric and arranged to have it made up into clothing for herself, her children, and the servants of the household; it was she who determined when new equipment was needed for cooking or dining and when existing furnishings needed to be replaced or brought up to date. As merchants and shops began more energetic efforts to persuade people to buy their goods, women were included among the targets.

The impact of this early consumerism was probably felt differently by women on the basis of their rank. The wealthiest women had always been consumers, able in most cases to spend money on goods that displayed their status, not just those essential to their household's operation. For them the new emphasis on consumption only reinforced a pattern already present.[16] Poor women may have looked longingly at the tempting array of unfamiliar goods displayed in shop windows or offered by itinerant sellers, but they would seldom have been able to afford more than a few mild luxuries like an apron, ribbons, or hair pins.[17] It was women of the middling levels who were most actively exposed to the new range of consumer goods and who could in many cases afford some of them. This group included the wives, widows, and daughters of merchants, professional people, and substantial craftsmen in the towns and cities as well as the female members of gentry and prosperous yeomanry households who came into urban areas to shop.

Not surprisingly, London was in the forefront of the growing consumer ethic, extending its role as the undoubted center of England's trade during the later fifteenth and sixteenth centuries.[18] In a 1573 poem, Isabella Whitney mockingly listed her bequests to London at the time she was forced by a financial crisis to depart from the city, where she had been working as a servant.[19] She mentions the types of cloth available on several streets and the wares of the goldsmiths and other sellers of luxuries, but these are placed alongside references to prisons and poorhouses. The emphasis on consumption had become more pronounced by the time of an addition made by John Stow early in the seventeenth century to his

---

[16] It should be noted, however, that during the seventeenth century some wealthy but "pious" women chose to live frugally, in deliberate simplicity, promoting what Sara Mendelson has termed "inconspicuous consumption": "Seventeenth-Century Women: Patterns of Consumer Behavior," unpublished paper given at the North American Conf. on British Studies, Toronto, November 2001. I am grateful to Dr. Mendelson for letting me have a copy of this paper.

[17] For the increasing range of items of dress and decoration carried by seventeenth-century peddlers, see Spufford, *The Great Reclothing*.

[18] For the classic statement, see Fisher, "The Development of London as a Centre of Conspicuous Consumption."

[19] Whitney, "The Manner of Her Will."

popular *Survey of London*.[20] There he describes in rich verbal colors the better shopping districts of the city. "The very gay Shew" of the shops, he says, the range of foreign commodities with which they were furnished, and the pleasure of purchasing led not only Londoners but other English people too "to spend extravagantly." Though Stow points out that "the graver Sort" disapproved of this excess, his own stance was more ambivalent. He comments, for example, that around 1550 there had been no more than a dozen milliners' shops making and selling ladies' hats in all London; yet by around 1580 "every street became full of them," from the city of Westminster to London itself. Stow then provides a long and rather dazzling list of the luxury goods offered by London's merchants, many of them imported, but he ends less positively, noting that these "made such a Shew in the Passengers Eyes, that they could not but gaze on them, and buy some of the knicknacks, though to no Purpose necessary."

Stow's hesitations about this new world, including his resistance to artful display of unessential goods, are reflected in Deloney's *The Pleasant History of Thomas of Reading, or The Sixe Worthie Yeomen of the West*, written around 1599.[21] In a series of episodes, Deloney portrays the wives of six country clothiers who came to London and experienced its market for the first time (the events occurred nominally in the twelfth century but clearly reflected contemporary patterns and tensions). During their visit, the women were invited to the homes of London merchants' wives, whose attire, "most daintie and fine," was so different from their own simple dress; on outings with their hostesses, they saw "the commodities of the Cittie." On a visit to Cheapside, for example, "with great wonder they beheld the shops of the Goldsmithes; and on the other side, the wealthy Mercers, whose shoppes shined with all sorts of coloured silkes: in Watlingstreet they viewed the great number of Drapers: in Saint Martins Shoomakers." Upon their return home, the wives tried to persuade their husbands to buy them more elegant clothing, using – among other arguments – appeals to their rights as Christians and English citizens: "Are not we Gods creatures as well as [the] Londoners? and the Kings subjects, as well as they? then finding our wealth to be as good as theirs, why should we not goe as gay as Londoners?"

Drawing upon an older ethic, the leading figure among the husbands, Simon of Southampton, reproved his wife. "Good woman, be content,

[20] Stow, *A Survey of the Cities of London and Westminster* (London, 1755), 11, fol. 4Av, as cited by Newman, "City Talk," pp. 181–2, for this and the quotations below. Newman offers linguistic evidence for her suggestion that this description was added in an edition of the early seventeenth century.

[21] *The Works of Thomas Deloney*, pp. 211–72. All the following quotations are taken from pp. 234–40. For this text, see also sect. 3, Ch. 7 above.

let vs goe according to our place and abilitie: what will the Bailiffes [leading officials of Southampton] thinke, if I should pranke thee vp like a Peacocke, and thou in thy attire surpasse their wiues? they would either thinke I were madde, or else that I had more mony than I could well vse." Pointing out that "Mens coffers are iudged by their garments," he warned that he might be taxed more heavily if his wife dressed extravagantly. The values they had held before the ill-fated London trip, as reflected in their simple clothing, were still valid, Simon claimed: "Gray russet, and good hempe-spun cloath doth best become vs; I tell thee wife, it were as vndecent for vs to goe like Londoners as it is for Londoners to goe like courtiers." His wife responded sulkily that the only reason she and the other wives were not given fine clothing was that "our husbands be not so kind as Londoners: why man, a Cobler there keepes his wife better than the best Clothier in this countrey [= county]: nay, I will affirme it, that the London oyster-wiues, and the very kitchin-stuffe cryers, doe exceed vs in their Sundaies attire."

In a statement with which Stow would probably have agreed, Simon appealed to the city's distinctive place in government and its symbolic importance: "But wife you must consider what London is, the chiefe and capitall Cittie of all the land, a place on the which all strangers cast their eies; it is (wife) the Kings chamber and his Maiesties royall seate: to that Cittie repaires all nations vnder heauen. Therefore it is most meete and conuenient, that the Citizens of such a Citie should not goe in their apparell like Peasents, but for the credit of our countrey, weare such seemely habits, as do carrie grauity and comeliness in the eyes of all beholders." When his wife's predictable response that they should move to London failed, she feigned sickness approaching death until Simon promised to buy her a gown made of elegant cloth bought in Cheapside and tailored by a craftsman there. At the end of the episode, when the other husbands had likewise capitulated to their wives' appeals, Deloney concludes, "So that euer since, the wiues of South-hampton, Salisbury, of Glocester, Worcester, and Reading, went all as gallant and as braue as any Londoners wiues."

As Deloney suggests, the desire for fashionable new clothing had become intertwined with the problem of maintaining visual markers of status. Defining dress in accordance with one's rank had been the goal of a long string of later medieval and sixteenth-century sumptuary laws regulating what women and men of various socio-economic levels were allowed to wear.[22] But now things were getting worse, as new sources of

---

[22] Sumptuary laws began in the later fourteenth century, became common during the later fifteenth, and continued during the sixteenth (for early versions, see, e.g., *Statutes of the Realm*, 13 Richard II, c. 13, 3 Edward IV, c. 5, and 22 Edward IV, c. 1).

wealth broke down traditional social gradations. Philip Stubbes, in his *The Anatomy of Abuses*, first published in 1583, fulminates that "this canker of pride" for stylish new apparel had affected not just the wealthy but also the daughters of rural yeomen, husbandmen, and cottagers.[23] Even if their parents were already £100 in debt, young women were determined to get their luxury items "by hook or crook . . . whereby it cometh to pass that one can scarcely know who is a noble woman, who is an honourable, or worshipful woman, from them of meaner sort."

Stubbes was right. The emerging consumer culture did indeed force a reassessment of how to define individual women's credit. In the new pattern, respectable women had to be able to go shopping and to display through their purchases their family's standing and their own good taste. But could a woman maintain an honorable reputation under these circumstances? If she appeared on the streets wearing stylish clothing, did that raise questions about her sexual conduct? As Karen Newman notes, "Consumption is presented as a female preoccupation and pastime in the discourses of Jacobean England, and women are both consumers and commodities."[24] The situation was even more complicated for the young women who worked in shops. Shop girls became more numerous and acquired new functions within the consumer-directed model. They were, of course, still expected to assist customers with their purchases, but now they were also required to offer an attractive appearance, stylish dress, and cosmopolitan manners. Their appeal was directed at male as well as female customers. A work published in 1619 commented that London's shops "with pretty wenches swarm, / Which for thy custome are a kind of charme / To Idle gallants."[25] At the same time, any young woman earning her own money, especially when well dressed and on public display, was potentially suspect.[26] Women might be encouraged to go into the public world of the shops, as buyers or employees, but there was anxiety that their appearance might suggest that they were themselves objects that could be given a price and bought.

Uneasiness about the linkage between female consumerism and female sexuality was reflected by contemporary commentators. King James I on several occasions attacked the country gentry who, at the instigation of their wives or daughters, abandoned their duties at home and flocked into London to buy the "new model and fashion."[27] The women, he

[23] As excerpted in Aughterson, ed., *Renaissance Woman*, p. 76.
[24] "City Talk." For a more general discussion, see Appadurai, ed., *The Social Life of Things*.
[25] Pasquin's "Palinodia," as cited by Newman, "City Talk," p. 181.
[26] But for several morally upright shop women, see Thomas Heywood's "The Fair Maid of the Exchange."
[27] As cited by Newman, "City Talk," p. 188: original source not given.

noted sourly in 1608, "if they were unmarried, marred their reputations, and if married, lost them." The popular "city comedies" of the Jacobean period included as stock figures the wives of merchants or craftsmen eager to display their costly but inappropriate clothing and to seek substitutes for their sexually unsatisfying husbands.[28] Thomas Dekker, addressing the city of London as a woman in 1602, warned, "Thou art the goodliest of thy neighbours, but the proudest; the wealthiest, but the most wanton. Thou hast all things in thee to make thee fairest, and all things in thee to make thee foulest: for thou art attired like a bride, drawing all that look upon thee, to be in love with thee, but there is much harlot in thine eyes."[29]

To overcome these problems, efforts were made to provide a safe and pleasant environment in which women could shop without fear that their reputations would be damaged. The Royal Exchange was built in London during Elizabeth's reign expressly as a comfortable and sheltered setting for business, but it soon became a male space. Women walking there might be accosted, and it was used at night by prostitutes and by mothers looking for a place to abandon newborn babies.[30] A setting better suited to the shopping of respectable women was the large structure opened by the Earl of Salisbury in 1609, originally called Britain's Burse but later known as the New Exchange.[31] This "Renaissance shopping mall" had arcades and galleries on the ground floor for shops carrying a wide variety of luxury goods; smaller rooms upstairs were intended for private meetings and conversation. While women had thus interacted with the market as buyers throughout these centuries, the emergence of a consumer society was beginning to create new possibilities and new problems for them by 1620.

---

[28] See, e.g., Leinwand, *The City Staged*, esp. ch. 5.
[29] Thomas Dekker, "Induction" to *The Seven Deadly Sinnes of London* (London, 1606), as cited by Gowing, "'Freedom of the Streets'," p. 131.
[30] Gowing, "'Freedom of the Streets'."
[31] Newman, "City Talk," for this and below.

Conclusion

This study has expanded our understanding of women's work in England between 1300 and 1620 in several respects. In offering wide coverage of the ways that women generated some income of their own, it has made clear that their activities were of key importance not only to themselves and their families but also to the performance of the country's economy. Women offered essential services for pay and played a vital role in the production of certain goods and the sale of many commodities. Success in their work depended upon credit, both their individual social and economic standing, and their ability to access the forms of financial credit. By spanning the transition between the later medieval and early modern periods, we have been able to trace changes in the types of work open to women as related to the demographic, economic, and social world around them. We have shown that patterns in the north of England differed in interesting ways from those found in the better studied south and have used detailed information from five market centers to investigate women's work in the drink and food trades. Throughout the study, we have gained human insight into the reality of women's work from the narrative petitions submitted to royal equity courts after 1470, which add life to information drawn from simple lists of taxpayers, the names of workers in certain occupations, or parties in private suits.

The book has demonstrated that, despite their contributions, the range of options for women who needed or wanted to generate some income of their own between 1300 and 1620 was generally quite restricted. Although women were involved in many different economic sectors, they were concentrated at lower levels. They provided services, mainly those that took place within a domestic context, but their freedom to do so resulted from the fact that such work was seen as undesirable by men. They loaned money and took part in pawning transactions, but they were rarely found in the top ranks of the expanding credit system of the later sixteenth and early seventeenth centuries. As producers and sellers of goods, they were clustered within activities related to their work at home (dealing with food, drink, and cloth/clothing), and they normally operated on a small scale. They brewed and sold ale but not beer, the more profitable drink that became common after around 1500; they prepared the yarn used in textile manufacture and later did piecework like making lace or pins but rarely took part in more lucrative crafts. During most periods, the women who appear at higher levels of business were typically the widows of merchants or craftsmen whose operation they were maintaining temporarily.

The limited set of choices for women within the market economy derived from multiple handicaps stemming from contemporary gender definitions based upon patriarchal assumptions. Throughout these centuries, women's work was seen as secondary to the needs of male household heads, the natural breadwinners. Any activities they pursued to generate some income had to be accommodated to their biological, economic, and social roles within the domestic context. Women were disadvantaged economically as compared to men, rarely able to compete on equal terms, for practical, legal, and cultural reasons. Their own creditworthiness was assessed in ways that differed from men's: it mattered whether they were married and what their husband's economic situation was. Women faced problems in hiring and controlling labor, and specialized training through apprenticeships or other means was rarely open to them. According to the common law, married women had no legal identity distinct from that of their husbands. Unless they had been awarded *femme sole* status in a few of the cities, they were not able to sign contracts or prosecute court cases on their own. Women who participated in the cash-based economy in their own right might be perceived as inappropriately independent, unrestrained by a husband or father and free to indulge in verbal or sexual excess. Given these factors, it is unsurprising that most women's involvement with the market economy involved patching together a variety of part-time, unskilled or semiskilled, and poorly paid kinds of work. Insofar as this study highlights the disadvantages faced by all women and the continuity of many features of women's work, it agrees with the position advocated most forcefully by Bennett.[1]

Yet the types and level of women's economic involvement were not static over the course of these three centuries. We know relatively little about the earlier fourteenth century, but the evidence presented here indicates that the atypical demographic conditions that pertained between 1348–9 and around 1500 allowed (or forced) some women to take a more active and independent part in the public economy than was to be true by 1620 and than had probably been true in 1300. Women were

---

[1] See sect. 2, Ch. 2 above for a discussion of that argument and those mentioned below.

especially important in those communities and periods when the local economy was strong but there was a shortage of men to fill the available niches. Although poor women continued to work on a piecemeal and diversified basis during the post-plague generations, some women from respected families in market centers and larger towns engaged in commercialized production or sale at middling economic levels. Most stayed in types of work considered appropriate to women, making/selling drink, textiles, or clothing. Some were married, pursuing an activity distinct from their husband's work, while others were widows or daughters who found themselves responsible for supporting their own households due to high mortality from ongoing outbreaks of plague. Not-married women might either run their own enterprises or continue the business of their late husband or father. A few operated at high economic levels or entered types of production not usually regarded as female. Some of these women remained in a given line of work for many years and may have acquired a measure of occupational identity. They were present in the public world of the marketplace and perhaps participated in some of its discussions. While this study does not go as far as Barron and Goldberg in stressing the favorable features of the period after 1348–9 (it does not claim that these years were a "Golden Age" for urban women, in the sense of enjoying rough equality with male workers), it differs from Bennett's assessment by highlighting the unusual opportunities and agency enjoyed by some women during the 100–150 years after the first major outbreak of plague.

Beginning in the later fifteenth century, and developing across the sixteenth, a cluster of conjoined demographic, economic, and cultural changes made it more difficult for women to engage in profitable economic activities. Although a larger proportion of all women may have been working to generate an income in 1620 than during the fifteenth century, they were generally found within just two categories. Those women active in trades or craftwork were usually wives or daughters who assisted their male relatives in running a business. Even if a woman in fact contributed most of the labor, the business was now owned and controlled by the man in economic and legal terms. This constituted a real loss as compared to the degree of independent authority held by some late medieval women. The second group of working women were obliged to bring in an income due to the widespread poverty of the decades around 1600, stemming from population pressure, crop failures, and other economic problems. A growing proportion of girls and young women competed for poorly paid positions as servants (some labeled misleadingly as apprenticeships), while other women did piecework at home, worked in alehouses/inns, or sold goods on the streets, rendering them vulnerable to sexual advances and social disapproval.

Women were almost entirely excluded from the higher economic activities that were emerging by the early seventeenth century. Expanded manufacturing, growing international trade, and the burgeoning system of formalized credit all accentuated the disabilities women had long faced. They could not compete in this new top stratum of the economy because of their problems in signing contracts, obtaining loans or other kinds of credit, utilizing land as a security, arranging to transport capital within the country or overseas, traveling, and using the courts to pursue debtors. The few women operating at this level were either wives working in partnership with a well-placed husband or widows working under the inherited good name and financial standing of their deceased husband. Women of middling status appear to have been gaining value as consumers by 1620, but coming into the marketplace as shoppers rather than as producers/sellers relegated them to a secondary economic role. Comparison of the opportunities for working women during the decades around 1400 with those around 1600 suggests that choices for women had indeed narrowed and that it is indeed legitimate to stress the importance of change across the late medieval/early modern transition.

Appendices

1.1. Methods and manuscripts: equity court sample and five market centers

1.2. Equity court sample, 1470–1619: types of female activity in the market economy

1.3. Equity court sample: marital status of women

1.4. Equity court sample: regional distribution of cases

6.1. Brewers: average span worked and percentage who worked for ten or more years

6.2. Percentage of Chief Pledges/jurors and their wives/households that brewed

6.3. Alesellers: average span worked and percentage who worked for ten or more years

7.1. Bakers: percentage reported as female or lived in female-headed households

7.2. Bakers: average span worked and percentage who worked for ten or more years

Appendix 1.1
Methods and manuscripts: equity court sample and five market centers

---

1 Selection of the equity court sample

I wanted to obtain a sample that offered the widest possible chronological and regional coverage of the kinds of economic activities considered in this book. To do so, I first used printed calendars of the central equity courts' records and handwritten lists available at the Public Record Office in Kew (London) to identify cases that appeared to involve women's own economic activities.[1] Since those entries do not describe the type of legal problem in detail, I used two selection criteria in deciding which suits to examine: (1) the case had to have a female complainant or respondent (the equity court equivalents of plaintiff and defendant), whether she was acting alone or with one or more other people, of either sex; and (2) the description needed to suggest that the woman was involved in an activity covered in this project. To maintain a focus on women's own activities in the market economy, I excluded suits that concerned landholding, those involving inheritances, and those where a woman was acting on behalf of a male relative or carrying out the terms of her deceased husband's will.

---

[1] To obtain cases, I used the following procedures. For the court of Chancery, class C 1, I went through the printed calendars, looking at the first sixteen bundles out of each fifty bundles throughout the set (bundles 1–1549). For Chancery class C 2, I used the early nineteenth-century printed calendars, which are arranged alphabetically by surname of the complainant, looking at letters A–E and N–P for Elizabeth and N–P for James I. For Chancery class C 3, I used the handwritten list at the PRO, doing the first six out of every fifty bundles for bundles 1–299, which went through 1616. For the court of Requests, class REQ 2, I used the printed calendars for bundles 1–136 and the handwritten lists at the PRO for later ones. I did all bundles from 1–35; the first six out of every twenty bundles for 40–125; bundles 1–6, 10–16, and 30–6 out of every 40 bundles for 160–245; the first 10–16 out of every 20 bundles for 150–194; and all bundles 295–311 and 387–424. For the court of the Exchequer, class E 134, I used the handwritten lists at the PRO for Elizabeth and James I. The lists varied considerably in the amount of detail given about the nature of the complaint. Some gave a full sentence, while others used only brief terms like "money matters," "land," "complaint against lesser court," or "inheritance." When the latter system was in use I looked at all cases involving money matters or complaints against a court if a woman was a party but not at those concerned with land or inheritances.

Promising manuscripts were then examined to see if they were indeed relevant.

In generating this sample, I tried to obtain roughly equal numbers of cases within four sub-periods, to reveal possible changes over time beginning with the later fifteenth century when the records become sufficiently numerous: 1470–99, 1500–59, 1560–99, and 1600–19. My initial selection process yielded 229 suits that described the economic pursuits of 231 women. Since, however, few of the cases came from the north of England, I used the same criteria with respect to the records of the equity courts of Lancaster and Durham, adding another fifty-four cases from 1540–1619 and gaining a better geographic distribution.[2]

2   Selection and methods used for the five market centers

These small communities were chosen because of their diverse locations and economic patterns and because suitable records have survived. To trace changes over time one needs a long run of manor or borough court rolls that list people who worked in the food and drink trades and that document other local concerns, recorded through private suits and jury reports about public issues. The places selected all have good records for the later fourteenth and fifteenth centuries, with variable coverage before and after that time. Tamworth's court rolls list drink and later food workers for most years between 1290 through 1551, as do Ramsey's from 1280 through 1588. The manor court rolls for Havering, which include the market town of Romford, start in 1382 and continue to list at least some workers in these trades through 1616; those for Minehead stretch from 1379 through 1603. In order to include a northern community, where late medieval records are less well preserved, I had to settle for a somewhat shorter period and more interrupted sources: Northallerton's borough court rolls run in interrupted sequence from 1362 through 1537. Because listings of food/drink traders after 1580 are almost certainly incomplete, quantitative analysis of the number of people working per year and their gender runs only through the 1570s. The records used in the numerical analyses are listed below.

In working with the reports of drink and food workers, I entered into SPSS software every person named at every surviving court session as a producer or seller of food or drink, together with information about that person's sex, marital status, the nature of each mention of her/his

---

[2] For the Duchy of Lancaster class DL 1, I used all published calendars for Henry VII–Elizabeth and went through DL 1/249–250 and DL 1/272 for 1611–13 and 1617–18. For the Palatinate of Lancaster, I went through PL 6/1–2 for 1473–1611 and 1612–13. For the Palatinate of Durham, I went through DURH 2/1–2 for 1576–1601 and 1605–6.

work by the court, and the fine imposed. After regularizing surnames to a single spelling for each, I consolidated the individual entries for a given person into a single combined entry per year, with a summary notation of how many times that person had been named, for what reasons, and how much total fine was paid. That resulted in data bases of no more than c. 6,000 annual person-entries per community. I was then able to utilize SPSS to generate some of the numerical analyses and graphs but had to establish linkages with other types of records by hand. The graduate students named in the acknowledgements did much of that work. For each court roll I also took text-based notes in Nota Bene software on economic, social, and political/legal issues. For Havering/Romford, I had extensive notes from an earlier project.

Doing the data entry required a series of decisions about how to categorize and analyze the material. The first question concerned classification of the types of drink and food work done, recognizing that in many cases it was carried out on a part-time basis and/or pursued in addition to other economic activities. Because many men and women engaged in multiple kinds of work even within the drink/food occupations, I have counted people under the trade for which they were most often reported but have noted other kinds of activity as well. Analyses based on primary occupation were possible for only four of the communities. Northallerton's food/drink designations are too unspecific to permit such an examination (people were reported generically for brewing/baking).

To assess how long food/drink workers remained in these trades, I have measured the total span between a given person's first and last appearance in any of the occupations. Here I counted the first and last dates as years, so someone who worked from 1389 to 1391 would be entered as having a span of three years. I then categorized that person under the activity for which she or he was most commonly listed and calculated average spans by occupation and period for each place. I used spans rather than the number of years reported, as has been done in some other studies, because in most of these market centers the rolls have not survived for every single year. If, for example, we have records for 1437, 1441, 1442, and 1445 and a woman was listed as a brewer in all four, it seemed more useful to describe that as a span of nine years than to count her as having been reported four times.

In exploring the extent to which the households of Chief Pledges or presentment jurors brewed, I took the names of these local officials from two court sessions in each decade, chosen wherever the records permitted from sessions near the middle of the decade. There were twelve to forty-one men/session, depending upon the place and period. The Chief Pledge names were then compared against the lists of all brewers to see how many of those men were themselves engaged in this trade, had a wife who was, or were the head of the household in which brewing was done. Brewing within five years of the time when the man was listed as a Chief Pledge was counted as a yes. The figures were then expressed as percentages of the number of Chief Pledges per decade. Although I have used only a sampling of all Chief Pledge lists, there is no reason to think that the results are skewed since the list of brewers is fairly complete: a larger number of Chief Pledges would not necessarily have produced a higher fraction engaged in such work. Ramsey was excluded from this analysis since its jurors were drawn from a wider social range and hence are not necessarily reflective of high local status.[3]

3   **Court rolls used for quantitative analysis of drink/food traders in the five market centers**

a   *Havering (Romford), Essex, 1382–1618*

	Location and reference	
Years	Public Record Office	Essex Record Office
1382–9		D/DU 102/1–5, D/DSgM31, D/DHt M191
1389–91	SC 2/172/27	
1392–8		D/DU 102/6–10, D/DHt M192
1396–9	SC 2/172/28	
1399–1402	SC 2/172/29	
1405–6	SC 2/172/30	
1408		D/DU 102/3A
1414–18		D/DU 102/11–2
1422, 1426–8		D/DU 102/13–20
1430–9		D/DU 102/21–29
1437–9	SC 2/172/31	
1440–9		D/DU 102/29–39
1443–5	SC 2/172/32	
1450–6		D/DU 102/38, 40–46
1464–9		D/DU 102/47–54
1470–5		D/DU 102/54–58
1477–83	SC 2/172/33	
1479–80	SC 2/172/34	
1488–91	SC 2/172/35	
1491–8	SC 2/172/36–38	
1498–1502	SC 2/172/39	
1502–3		D/DU 102/59–60

[3] I am grateful to Anne and Edwin DeWindt for this information.

(cont.)

	Location and reference	
Years	Public Record Office	Essex Record Office
1503–9	SC 2/172/40	
1509–14	SC 2/173/1	
1514–18	SC 2/173/2	
1518–21	SC 2/173/3	
1529–30	SC 2/173/4	
1538		D/DU 102/61
1551–9		D/DU 102/62–6
1560, 1563–9		D/DU 102/66–71
1570–9		D/DU 102/71–8
1580–9		D/DU 102/78–84
1590–9		D/DU 102/84–94
1600–9		D/DU 102/94–104
1610–18		D/DU 102/104–10
1590–1, 1597–8,		
1599–1600, 1602–3,		
1608–9, 1611–16		
(estreats only)	LR 11/58/847 E-I	
	LR 78/904.	

Note: For a listing of each roll individually, see McIntosh, *Autonomy and Community*, App. III, and her *A Community Transformed*, App. G.

b   *Minehead, Somerset, 1379–1603*

Years	Reference at Somerset Record Office, DD/L P
1379–81	26/4
1405–13	26/6
1407–22	26/8
1422–38	27/10
1439–56	27/11
1462–82	28/13
1462–4, 1483–5	28/14
1485–1509	28/15
1516–46	29/25
1566–72	29/31
1581–5	29/32
1576–1602, passim	29/40
1603	30/48

c   *Northallerton, North Yorkshire, 1362–1537*

Years	Reference at North Yorkshire Record Office, ZBD
1362–3	49/15
1369	49/17
1385–6	49/18
1391	50/1
1407–8	50/6
1425	50/22
1445–6	51/5
1447–8	51/7
1451–2	51/11
1456–7	51/14
1462	51/16
1475	51/20
1483	52/1
1487–8	52/7
1491	52/14
1496	52/18
1497	52/21
1498	Microfilm 410, copy of PRO SC 2/211
1499–1500	52/24–25
1502	52/26
1503	52/29
1503–4	53/2
1505	53/4
1506	53/6
1510	53/13
1513	53/15
1514	53/17
1515	53/19
1526	54/9
1528	54/17
1531–2	Old ref. 189464
1533	54/26
1534–7	54/28

d *Ramsey, Huntingdonshire, 1280–1588*

Years	British Library Add. MSS Roll	Public Record Office
	Location and reference	
1280, 1287, 1289	39595–6	Just.Itin.1/351b, m. 3r
1294–5, 1297	39597–8, 39562	
1304, 1306–9	39599, 34361, 39699, 34359, 39702, 34770, 34342	
1311–12, 1316–17	34362, 34768, 34360, 34345	SC2/179/16, 179/18
1320–1, 1325–9	39600A–B 39601–2	SC2/179/19, 179/22, 179/24
1333, 1335, 1337, 1339	34363, 34363A, 39603–4, 34364–5	
1350, 1352–4, 1356–9	39605–12, 34366	
1360–3	39613–6, 39703	
1370, 1372, 1377–8	39617–20, 39704	
1380–8, 1386–9	39621–8, 39700, 39705	
1390–9	39629–38	
1400–2, 1408	39639, 34367, 34921	SC2/179/47
1410–12, 1414	39640–1, 39644–5	
1422–3, 1425–6, 1428–9	34368–70, 39643, 39745	SC2/179/59
1430, 1433–6	39646–9, 34371	
1440, 1443	39650	SC2/179/63
1452, 1456–9	39652–3	
1460–2, 1464–5, 1468	39653–5, 34372–4	
1473	39656	
1491	39656	
1518–19	34376	SC1/179/84
1531, 1533–8	39659–64, 34377	
1542–4, 1547–9	39665–7, 34314, 34379I–J	
1551–6	34379A–G, 39567	
1562, 1564, 1567–9	34316–7, 34380–4, 39568–9	
1570–1, 1573, 1576, 1578–9	34385–91, 39570–2 39667	
1580–2, 1584–8	34392–4, 34396–402, 34843–4, 39573–4, 34318, 33413	

Note: For a more detailed listing, see CRRamHB. I have used these transcriptions together with the listings of food/drink traders generously supplied to me by Edwin and Anne DeWindt.

e   *Tamworth, Staffordshire, 1290–1551*

Years	Reference at Keele University Library, Tamworth MSS
1290–9	Edward I, Rolls 3–14
1304–6, 1309	Edward I, Rolls 17–24; Edward II, Rolls 1–2
1310–19	Edward II, Rolls 3–18
1320–9	Edward II, Rolls 17–26; Edward III, Rolls 1–3
1331–8	Edward III, Rolls 4–13
1342–9	Edward III, Rolls 14–19
1354–9	Edward III, Rolls 21–34
1360–9	Edward III, Rolls 34–49
1370–9	Edward III, Rolls 50–64; Richard II, Rolls 1–6
1380–9	Richard II, Rolls 7–21
1390–8	Richard II, Rolls 21–9
1402–4, 1408–9	Henry IV, Rolls 1–4
1410–19	Henry IV, Rolls 4–7; Henry V, Rolls 1–8
1420–9	Henry V, Rolls 9–16; Henry VI, Rolls 1–14
1430–9	Henry VI, Rolls 15–24
1440–9	Henry VI, Rolls 24–32
1450–9	Henry VI, Rolls 33–50
1460–2	Henry VI, Rolls 51–2; Edward IV, Rolls 1–2
1470–1	Edward IV, Rolls 3–4
1488–9	Henry VII, Rolls 1–2
1500–9	Henry VII, Rolls 5–13; Henry VIII, Rolls 1–2
1510–19	Henry VIII, Rolls 3–8
1520–1	Henry VIII, Roll 8
1530–1	Henry VIII, Roll 10
1546–7	Henry VIII, Roll 12
1550–1	Edward VI, Roll 1

Appendix 1.2
Equity court sample, 1470–1619: types of female activity in the market economy

	Central equity courts sample				Northern equity courts sample	
	1470–1499	1500–1559	1560–1599	1600–1619	1540–1599*	1600–1619
Producing/selling goods						
Food	1 = 2%	3 = 6%	1 = 2%	2 = 3%	0	0
Drink	6 = 11%	8 = 15%	5 = 8%	6 = 10%	1 = 5%	1 = 3%
Cloth/clothing	11 = 21%	10 = 19%	4 = 6%	7 = 11%	2 = 11%	5 = 14%
Other (including mining) / type unknown	7 = 13%	7 = 13%	4 = 6%	2 = 3%	2 = 11%	3 = 9%
Total	25 = 47%	28 = 53%	14 = 23%	17 = 27%	5 = 26%	9 = 26%
Borrowing/lending money or pawning goods	15 = 28%	10 = 19%	25 = 40%	24 = 38%	11 = 58%	20 = 57%
Boarding/residential nursing	7 = 13%	6 = 11%	7 = 11%	5 = 8%	1 = 5%	3 = 9%
Service/apprenticeship	5 = 9%	8 = 15%	5 = 8%	11 = 17%	1 = 5%	1 = 3%
Leasing buildings or rooms	1 = 2%	0	5 = 8%	4 = 6%	1 = 5%	2 = 6%
Other†	0	1 = 2%	6 = 10%	2 = 3%	0	0
Total	53	53	62	63	19	35

* Includes two cases from before 1560 and seventeen from 1560–99.
† Includes non-residential nursing, transport, holding patents, and provision of water.

Sources: See App. 1.1.

Appendix 1.3
Equity court sample: marital status of women

	Central equity courts sample				Northern equity courts sample	
	1470–1499	1500–1559	1560–1599	1600–1619	1540–1599*	1600–1619
Marital status						
Widowed	25 = 47%	22 = 42%	25 = 40%	23 = 37%	11 = 58%	13 = 37%
Married	16 = 30%	16 = 30%	19 = 31%	23 = 37%	1 = 5%	7 = 20%
Single	6 = 11%	9 = 17%	11 = 18%	14 = 22%	4 = 21%	14 = 40%
Own name	6 = 11%	6 = 11%	7 = 11%	3 = 5%	3 = 16%	1 = 3%
Total	53	53	62	63	19	35

* Includes 2 cases from before 1560 and 17 from 1560–99.

Sources: See App. 1.1.

Appendix 1.4
Equity court sample: regional distribution of cases

	Central equity courts sample				Northern equity courts sample	
	1470–1499	1500–1559	1560–1599	1600–1619	1540–1599†	1600–1619
Region of the country*						
L/LS = London and immediate suburbs	32 = 60%	25 = 47%	19 = 31%	25 = 40%	1 = 5%	0
SE = Southeast and East Anglia	8 = 15%	10 = 19%	16 = 26%	17 = 27%	1 = 5%	1 = 3%
SW = Southwest, South, and West	7 = 13%	12 = 23%	12 = 19%	9 = 14%	0	0
EC = East Central and Midlands	1 = 2%	3 = 6%	8 = 13%	10 = 16%	1 = 5%	1 = 3%
N = North and Northwest	1 = 2%	0	4 = 6%	1 = 2%	16 = 84%	33 = 94%
No information	4 = 8%	3 = 6%	3 = 5%	1 = 2%	0	0
Total	53	53	62	63	19	35

* The regions have been defined here to include the following counties. Southeast and East Anglia: Berks., Cambs., Essex, Hants., Herts., Kent, Middx., Norfolk, Suffolk, Surrey, and Sussex; Southwest, South, and West: Cornwall, Devon, Dorset, Glos., Hereford, Shropshire, Som., Staffs., Wilts., and Worcs.; East Central and Midlands: Beds., Bucks., Derby, Hunts., Leics., Lincs., Northants., Notts., Oxon., Rutl., and War.; North and Northwest: Chesh., Cumb., Durham, Lancs., Northumb., Westm., and Yorks.

† Includes two cases from before 1560 and seventeen from 1560–99.

Sources: See App. 1.1.

Appendix 6.1
Brewers: average span worked and percentage who worked for ten or more years*

| | Havering | | | | | | Minehead | | | | | | Tamworth | | | | | |
| | Men | | | Women | | | Men/married women to 1469; men from 1470 onwards | | | Non-married women to 1469; all women from 1470 onwards | | | Men/married women to 1469; men from 1470 onwards | | | Non-married women to 1469; all women from 1470 onwards | | |
Periods#	No.	Mean span of years	Span 10 years or more	No.	Mean span of years	Span 10 years or more	No.	Mean span of years	Span 10 years or more	No.	Mean span of years	Span 10 years or more	No.	Mean span of years	Span 10 years or more	No.	Mean span of years	Span 10 years or more
Pre-1348	–	–	–	–	–	–	–	–	–	–	–	–	260	4.4	13%	217	3.0	6%
1348–1469	32	3.6	9%	219	9.7	36%	442	11.1	41%	77	6.6	25%	166	9.7	39%	263	6.0	23%
1470 onwards	85	6.5	27%	52	5.0	5%	123	3.0	7%	87	3.8	14%	17	3.2	0	43	4.2	9%

* This includes people whose primary occupation was brewing. Primary occupation is defined as the one for which the person was reported most often in the listing of drink/food workers in the court rolls. Gender classifications are based on how people were reported in the records.

The dates for which we have information for each place are:
    Havering: 1382–1469, 1470–1618
    Minehead: 1379–1469, 1470–1603
    Tamworth: 1290–1347, 1348–1469, 1470–1551

Sources: See App. 1.1.

Appendix 6.2
Percentage of Chief Pledges/jurors and their wives/households that brewed

Decade	Havering			Minehead		Northallerton*		Tamworth	
	No. of Chief Pledges	% of Chief Pledges who brewed	% of wives who brewed	No. of Chief Pledges	% of households who brewed	No. of Chief Pledges	% of households who brewed	No. of Chief Pledges	% of households who brewed
1330s	–	–	–	–	–	–	–	19	37
1340s	–	–	–	–	–	–	–	19	32
1350s	–	–	–	–	–	–	–	18	17
1360s	–	–	–	–	–	–	–	15	60
1370s	–	–	–	–	–	–	–	17	65
1380s	28	21	36	–	–	–	–	18	89
1390s	31	17	26	–	–	–	–	15	73
1400s	31	6	19	–	–	–	–	14	79
1410s	–	–	–	18	94	–	–	16	56
1420s	–	–	–	19	89	–	–	15	40
1430s	37	0	19	21	71	–	–	16	31
1440s	36	0	39	16	75	12	33	15	60
1450s	35	0	34	21	67	21	43	15	67
1460s	28	0	39	20	60	12	33	14	29

Decade	Havering			Minehead			Northallerton*			Tamworth		
	No. of Chief pledges	% of Chief Pledges who brewed	% of wives who brewed	No. of Chief Pledges	% of Chief Pledges who brewed	% of wives who brewed	No. of Chief Pledges	% of Chief Pledges who brewed	% of wives who brewed	No. of Chief Pledges	% of Chief Pledges who brewed	% of wives who brewed
1470s	31	0	23	14	43	0	12	17	8	19	5	32
1480s	39	13	15	18	33	6	21	29	33	16	0	19
1490s	41	34	24	20	20	5	26	15	58	–	–	–
1500s	29	31	21	20	30	5	22	0	55	20	0	40
1510s	29	3	0	16	19	0	26	4	42	14	0	57
1520s	–	–	–	18	11	0	16	13	13	16	0	31
1530s	21	19	0	22	5	0	15	20	7	17	6	12
1540s	–	–	–	24	4	0	–	–	–	16	25	0
1550s	–	–	–	–	–	–	–	–	–	18	28	0
1560s	23	4	0	–	–	–	–	–	–	–	–	–
1570s	30	3	0	–	–	–	–	–	–	–	–	–

* Because Northallerton's court rolls are more interrupted, some decades (those with fewer than 20 people shown) are based on only one list of Chief Pledges/jurors, not the normal two.

Sources: See App. 1.1.

Appendix 6.3
Alesellers: average span worked and percentage who worked for ten or more years*

| | Havering | | | | | | Minehead | | | | | | Tamworth | | | | | |
| | Men | | | Women | | | Men/married women to 1469; men from 1470 onwards | | | Non-married women to 1469; all women from 1470 onwards | | | Men/married women to 1469; men from 1470 onwards | | | Non-married women to 1469; all women from 1470 onwards | | |
Periods#	No.	Mean span of years	Span 10 years or more	No.	Mean span of years	Span 10 years or more	No.	Mean span of years	Span 10 years or more	No.	Mean span of years	Span 10 years or more	No.	Mean span of years	Span 10 years or more	No.	Mean span of years	Span 10 years or more
Pre-1348	–	–	–	–	–	–	–	–	–	–	–	–	2	1.0	0	–	–	–
1348–1469	1	1.0	0	62	8.7	32%	82	7.0	24%	31	4.0	10%	81	6.3	20%	61	4.0	10%
1470 onwards	98	4.7	15%	108	4.0	12%	159	4.8	18%	134	5.6	23%	3	1.0	0	59	3.4	10%

* This includes people whose primary occupation was aleselling. For Tamworth, alesellers includes those described as "Tranters." Gender classifications are based on how people were reported in the records.
# The dates for which we have information for each place are:
  Havering: 1382–1469, 1470–1618
  Minehead: 1379–1469, 1470–1603
  Tamworth: 1290–1347, 1348–1469, 1470–1551
Sources: See App. 1.1.

Appendix 7.1
Bakers: percentage reported as female or lived in female-headed households*

Decade	Havering	Minehead	Northallerton	Ramsey	Tamworth
1280s	–	–	–	57	–
1290s	–	–	–	58	15
1300s	–	–	–	–	20
1310s	–	–	–	38	16
1320s	–	–	–	27	18
1330s	–	–	–	86	14
1340s	–	–	–	–	25
1350s	–	–	–	75	0
1360s	–	–	–	100	0
1370s	–	–	–	57	0
1380s	17	–	–	50	0
1390s	0	–	–	25	0
1400s	0	–	–	0	0
1410s	–	33	–	0	0
1420s	14	40	8	0	0
1430s	0	29	–	0	0
1440s	40	50	8	0	33
1450s	30	0	22	0	0
1460s	100	20	–	0	20
1470s	100	14	–	40	0
1480s	40	–	–	–	33
1490s	14	0	100	–	–
1500s	14	0	100	–	33
1510s	13	0	100	17	0
1520s	0	0	100	–	0
1530s	10	0	–	29	0
1540s	–	–	–	17	0
1550s	0	–	–	29	0
1560s	25	33	–	17	–
1570s	0	17	–	20	–

* For Havering and Ramsey, percentages are for those reported as women. For Minehead, Northallerton, and Tamworth, percentages prior to 1470s are for female-headed households; from 1470 onwards, they are for those reported as women. These figures are based on the average number per year.

Sources: See App. 1.1.

Appendix 7.2
Bakers: average span worked and percentage who worked for ten or more years*

| | Havering | | | | | | Minehead | | | | | | Tamworth | | | | | |
| | Men | | | Women | | | Men/married women to 1469; men from 1470 onwards | | | Non-married women to 1469; all women from 1470 onwards | | | Men/married women to 1469; men from 1470 onwards | | | Non-married women to 1469; all women from 1470 onwards | | |
Periods#	No.	Mean span of years	Span 10 years or more	No.	Mean span of years	Span 10 years or more	No.	Mean span of years	Span 10 years or more	No.	Mean span of years	Span 10 years or more	No.	Mean span of years	Span 10 years or more	No.	Mean span of years	Span 10 years or more
Pre-1348	–	–	–	–	–	–	–	–	–	–	–	–	148	7.6	28%	48	3.4	13%
1348–1469	41	5.9	20%	8	7.4	25%	12	11.3	33%	12	6.5	25%	33	10.3	39%	3	3.0	0
1470 onwards	63	5.0	16%	12	2.2	0	55	4.5	15%	7	1.6	0	15	9.5	27%	1	18.0	100%

* This includes people whose primary occupation was baking. Gender classifications are based on how people were reported in the records.
# The dates for which we have information for each place are:
    Havering: 1382–1469, 1470–1618
    Minehead: 1379–1469, 1470–1603
    Tamworth: 1290–1347, 1348–1469, 1470–1551
Sources: See App. 1.1.

Bibliography

PRINTED PRIMARY SOURCES

Aughterson, Kate, ed. *Renaissance Woman: A Sourcebook*. London, 1995.
Beverley Borough Records, 1575–1831. Ed. J. Dennett. Yorkshire Archaeological Society, Record Series, LXXXIV, 1933.
Calendar of Early Mayor's Court Rolls Preserved Among the Archives of the Corporation of the City of London at the Guildhall, A.D. 1298–1307. Ed. A. H. Thomas. Cambridge, 1924.
Calendar of the Fine Rolls, Vol. I, 1461–71. London, 1949.
Calendar of Letter-Books Preserved Among the Archives of the Corporation of the City of London at the Guildhall, Letter-Book G. Ed. Reginald R. Sharpe. London, 1905.
Calendar of Plea and Memoranda Rolls [of the London Mayor's Court, 1323–1484]. Ed. A. H. Thomas and P. E. Jones. 6 vols. Cambridge, 1926–61.
Calendar of Select Pleas and Memoranda of London, 1381–1412. Ed. A. H. Thomas. Cambridge, 1932.
Caxton, William. *Caxton's Dialogues in French and English*. Ed. Henry Bradley. Early English Text Society. London, 1900.
Chamber Accounts of the Sixteenth Century. Ed. Betty R. Masters. London Record Society, vol. 20. London, 1984.
Chaucer, Geoffrey. "General Prologue." In *The Canterbury Tales*. Any modern edition.
Court Leet Records [of Southampton]. Vol. I, pts. 1 (1550–77) and 2 (1578–1602). Ed. F. J. C. Hearnshaw and D. M. Hearnshaw. Southampton Record Society Publications. Southampton, 1905–6.
Court Rolls of the Borough of Colchester. Vol. I. Ed. I. H. Jeayes. Colchester, 1921.
The Court Rolls of the Manor of Wakefield from 1537 to 1539. Ed. Ann Weikel. Yorkshire Archaeological Society, Wakefield Court Rolls Series, vol. IX. 1993.
The Court Rolls of Ramsey, Hepmangrove, and Bury, 1268–1600. Ed. and transl. Edwin B. DeWindt. Toronto, 1990.
Deloney, Thomas. *The Works of Thomas Deloney*. Oxford, 1967.
Early English Meals and Manners: The Babees Book. Ed. F. J. Furnivall. Early English Text Society, orig. ser. no. 32. London, 1868.
Feet of Fines for Essex, Vol. IV. Colchester: Essex Archaeological Society, 1964.
Goldberg, P. J. P., ed. *Women in England, c. 1275–1525*. Manchester, 1995.
The Great Red Book of Bristol. Text, pt. III. Ed. E. W. W. Veale. Bristol Record Society, 1951.

Heywood, John. *The Play Called the Four PP*. Ed. T. C. and E. C. Jack. Orig. publ. 1545; New York, 1970.

Heywood, Thomas. "The Fair Maid of the Exchange" (1607). Ed. Peter H. Davison and Arthur Brown. Oxford, 1963.

"How the Good Wijf Taughte Hir Doughtir," in *Early English Meals and Manners: The Babees Book*. Ed. F. J. Furnivall. Early English Text Society, orig. ser. no. 32. London, 1868.

Hugh Alley's Caveat: The Markets of London in 1598. Ed. Ian Archer, Caroline Barron and Vanessa Harding. London, 1988.

Jacob's Well: An English Treatise on the Cleansing of Man's Conscience. Ed. Arthur Brandeis. Early English Text Society, O.S. vol. 115. London, 1900.

Lancaster, Henry of. *Le Livre de Seyntz Medicines. The Unpublished Devotional Treatises of Henry of Lancaster*. Ed. Emile Jules Arnould. Anglo-Norman Texts, vol. II. Oxford, 1940.

Langland, William. *Piers Plowman: An Edition of the C-Text*. Ed. Derek Pearsall. Berkeley, 1979.

Liverpool Town Books: Proceedings of Assemblies, Common Councils, Portmoot Courts, 1550–1862. Vol. I, 1550–1571; vol. II, 1571–1603. Ed. Jesse Alfred Twemlow. Liverpool, 1918/1935.

London and Southwark Inventories, 1316–1650: A Handlist of Extents for Debts. Ed. Martha Carlin. London, 1997.

Memorials of London and London Life in the 13th, 14th, and 15th Centuries. Ed. Henry Thomas Riley. London, 1868.

Mirk, John. *Mirk's Festial: A Collection of Homilies*, pt. 1. Ed. Theodor Erbe. Early English Text Society, extra ser. vol. 96. London, 1905.

"Noah's Flood." In *The Chester Mystery Cycle*, play III. Ed. R. M. Lumiansky and David Mills. Early English Text Society, supp. ser. no. 3. London, 1974.

The Norwich Census of the Poor, 1570. Ed. John F. Pound. Norfolk Record Society, vol. 40. Norwich, 1971.

Probate Inventories of Tamworth. Staffs. County Council Education Committee Source Book, 1978.

The Progresses and Public Processions of Queen Elizabeth. Ed. John Nichols. 3 vols. London, 1823.

Records of the Borough of Leicester. Vol. I. Ed. Mary Bateson. London, 1899; vol. III. Ed. Mary Bateson. Cambridge, 1905; vol. IV. Ed. Helen Stocks and W. H. Stevenson. Cambridge, 1923.

Records of the Borough of Nottingham. Vol. I. London, 1882; vol. II. London, 1883; vol. III. London, 1885; vol. IV. London, 1889.

The Records of the City of Norwich. Ed. William Hudson and J. C. Tingey. Vol. I. Norwich, 1906; vol. II. Norwich, 1910.

Statutes of the Realm. 12 vols. London: Record Commission, 1810–28.

The Stonor Letters and Papers, 1290–1483. Ed. C. L. Kingsford. Camden Soc. 3rd ser., vols. XXIX–XXX. London, 1919.

Whitney, Isabella. "The Manner of Her Will, and what she left to London and to all those in it at her departing." In *The Longman Anthology of British Literature*. Vol. I (New York, 1999), pp. 1002–10.

Wilson, Thomas. *A Discourse upon Usury*. Ed. R. H. Tawney. London, 1925.

Wiltshire Extents for Debts, Edward I–Elizabeth I. Ed. Angela Conyers. Wiltshire
    Record Society, vol. XXVIII, 1972.
York Civic Records. Vol. II. Ed. Angelo Raine. Yorkshire Archaeological Society,
    vol. 102, 1941; vol. VI. Ed. Angelo Raine. Yorkshire Archaeological Society,
    Vol. 112, 1948.

SECONDARY SOURCES

Abram, A. "Women Traders in Medieval London." *The Economic Journal* 26
    (1916): 276–85.
Adair, Richard. *Courtship, Illegitimacy and Marriage in Early Modern England.*
    Manchester, 1996.
Allison, K. J. "An Elizabethan Village 'Census'." *Bulletin of the Institute of Historical
    Research* 36 (1963): 91–103.
Anglin, Jay P. *The Third University: A Survey of Schools and Schoolmasters in the
    Elizabethan Diocese of London.* Norwood, Pa., 1985.
Appadurai, Arjun, ed. *The Social Life of Things.* Cambridge, 1986.
Bailey, Mark. "Demographic Decline in Late Medieval England." *Economic
    History Review,* 2nd ser. 49 (1996): 1–19.
Bardsley, Sandy. "Women's Work Reconsidered: Gender and Wage Differentia-
    tion in Late Medieval England." *Past and Present* 165 (1999): 3–29.
Barron, Caroline M. "Centres of Conspicuous Consumption: The Aristocratic
    Town House in London 1200–1550." *London Journal* 20 (1995): 1–16.
    "The Education and Training of Girls in Fifteenth-Century London." In
    Courts, Counties and the Capital in the Later Middle Ages, ed. Diana E. S.
    Dunn. New York, 1996, pp. 139–54.
    "The 'Golden Age' of Women in Medieval London." *Reading Medieval Studies*
    xv (1989): 35–58.
    "Johanna Hill (d. 1441) and Johanna Sturdy (d. c. 1460), Bell-Founders." In
    Medieval London Widows, 1300–1500, ed. C. M. Barron and A. F. Sutton.
    London, 1994, pp. 99–112.
    "Women in London: The 'Golden Age' Revisited." Forthcoming.
Barron, C. M., and A. F. Sutton, eds. *Medieval London Widows, 1300–1500.*
    London, 1994.
Beattie, Cordelia. "The Problem of Women's Work Identities in Post Black
    Death England." In *The Problem of Labour in Fourteenth-Century England,* ed.
    P. J. P. Goldberg, James Bothwell, and W. M. Ormrod. York, 2000, pp. 1–20.
Ben-Amos, Ilana K. *Adolescence and Youth in Early Modern England.* New Haven,
    Conn., 1994.
    "Gifts and Favors: Informal Support in Early Modern England." *Journal of
    Modern History* 72 (2000): 295–338.
Bennett, Judith M. *Ale, Beer, and Brewsters in England: Women's Work in a Changing
    World, 1300–1600.* New York, 1996.
    "Medieval Women, Modern Women: Across the Great Divide." In *Culture and
    History 1350–1600,* ed. David Aers. London, 1992, pp. 147–75.
    "Misogyny, Popular Culture, and Women's Work." *History Workshop* 31 (1991):
    166–88.

"Theoretical Issues: Confronting Continuity." *Journal of Women's History* 9, no. 3 (Autumn 1997): 73–94.

"Ventriloquisms: When Maidens Speak in English Songs, c. 1300–1550." In *Medieval Woman's Song*, ed. Anne L. Klinck and Ann Marie Rasmussen. Philadelphia, 2002, pp. 187–259.

"Women and Men in the Brewers' Gild of London, ca. 1420." In *The Salt of Common Life*, ed. Edwin Brezette DeWindt. Kalamazoo, Mich., 1995, pp. 181–232.

Women in the Medieval English Countryside. Oxford, 1987.

Bennett, Judith M., and Amy M. Froide, eds. *Singlewomen in the European Past, 1250–1800*. Philadelphia, 1999.

Biller, Peter. *The Measure of Multitude: Population in Medieval Thought*. Oxford, 2000.

Binding, Hilary, and Douglas Stevens. *Minehead: A New History*. Minehead, 1977.

Bischoff, Paul. "Late Thirteenth-Century Urban Commuting: Urban Influence and Commercialization." Unpublished paper delivered at the Anglo-American Medieval Historical Geography Conference, Cardiff, July 1995.

Bolton, J. L. *The Alien Communities of London in the Fifteenth Century*. Stamford, 1998.

The Medieval English Economy, 1150–1500. London, 1980.

"'The World Upside Down'. Plague as an Agent of Economic and Social Change." In *The Black Death in England*, ed. W. M. Ormrod and P. G. Lindley. Stamford, 1996, pp. 17–78.

Boose, Lynda E. "Scolding Brides and Bridling Scolds: Taming the Woman's Unruly Member." *Shakespeare Quarterly* 42 (1991): 179–213.

Bridbury, A. R. *Medieval English Clothmaking: An Economic Survey*. London, 1982.

Briggs, Chris. "Empowered or Marginalized? Rural Women and Credit in Later Thirteenth- and Fourteenth-Century England." *Continuity and Change* 19 (2004): 13–43.

Britnell, R. H. *Growth and Decline in Colchester, 1300–1525*. New York, 1986.

Brodsky, Vivien. "Widows in Late Elizabethan London." In *The World We Have Gained*, ed. Lloyd Bonfield, R. M. Smith, and Keith Wrightson. Oxford, 1986, pp. 122–54.

Campbell, Bruce M. S. "Commercial Dairy Production on Medieval English Demesnes: The Case of Norfolk." *Anthropozoologica* 16 (1992): 107–18.

Capp, Bernard. "The Double Standard Revisited: Plebian Women and Male Sexual Reputation in Early Modern England." *Past and Present* 162 (1999): 70–100.

"Separate Domains? Women and Authority in Early Modern England." In *The Experience of Authority in Early Modern England*, ed. Paul Griffiths, Adam Fox, and Steve Hindle. New York, 1996, pp. 117–45.

When Gossips Meet: Women, Family, and Neighbourhood in Early Modern England. Oxford, 2003.

Carlin, Martha. "Fast Food and Urban Living Standards in Medieval England." In *Food and Eating in Medieval Europe*, ed. Martha Carlin and Joel T. Rosenthal. London, 1998, pp. 27–52.

Medieval Southwark. London, 1996.

"'What Will You Buy?' Shopping and Shopkeeping in Pre-Modern London." Unpublished paper presented at the Pre-Modern Towns Conference. Institute of Historical Research, 22 January 2000.

Carney, Patricia. "Social Interactions in Early Modern England: Cheshire and Essex, 1560–1640." Ph.D. thesis, University of Colorado, 2002.

Carpenter, Christine. *Locality and Polity: A Study of Warwickshire Landed Society, 1401–1499*. Cambridge, 1992.

Clark, Alice. *Working Life of Women in the Seventeenth Century*, ed. Amy Louise Erickson. Orig. publ. 1919; London, 1992.

Clark, Elaine. "Debt Litigation in a Late Medieval English Vill." In *Pathways to Medieval Peasants*, ed. J. A. Raftis. Toronto, 1981, pp. 247–79.

"Medieval Labor Law and English Local Courts." *American Journal of Legal History* 27 (1983): 330–53.

"Some Aspects of Social Security in Medieval England." *Journal of Family History* 7 (1982): 307–20.

Clark, Peter. "The Alehouse and the Alternative Society." In *Puritans and Revolutionaries*, ed. Donald Pennington and Keith Thomas. Oxford, 1978, pp. 47–72.

The English Alehouse: A Social History, 1200–1830. London, 1983.

Clark, Peter, and Jennifer Clark. "The Social Economy of the Canterbury Suburbs: The Evidence of the Census of 1563." In *Studies in Modern Kentish History*, ed. A. Detsicas and N. Yates. Maidstone: Kent Archaeological Society, 1983, pp. 65–86.

Cressy, David. *Travesties and Transgressions in Tudor and Stuart England*. Oxford, 2000.

Cross, Claire. "Northern Women in the Early Modern Period: The Female Testators of Hull and Leeds 1520–1650." *Yorkshire Archaeological Journal* 59 (1987): 83–94.

Crowston, Clare. *Fabricating Women: The Seamstresses of Old Regime France, 1675–1791*. Durham, N.C., 2001.

Cunningham, Carole. "Christ's Hospital: Infant and Child Mortality in the Sixteenth Century." *Local Population Studies* 18 (1977): 37–42.

Dale, Marion K. "The London Silkwomen of the Fifteenth Century." *Economic History Review*, 1st ser., 4 (1933): 324–35.

Davis, Natalie Zemon. "Women in the Crafts in Sixteenth-Century Lyon." In *Women and Work in Preindustrial Europe*, ed. Barbara A. Hanawalt. Bloomington, Ind., 1986, pp. 167–97.

DeWindt, Anne Reiber. "The Town of Ramsey: The Question of Economic Development, 1290–1523." In *The Salt of Common Life*, ed. Edwin Brezette DeWindt. Kalamazoo, Mich., 1995, pp. 53–116.

Dyer, Christopher. "The Consumer and the Market in the Later Middle Ages." *Economic History Review*, 2nd ser., 42 (1989): 305–27.

Making a Living in the Middle Ages. New Haven, Conn., 2002.

"Small Places with Large Consequences: The Importance of Small Towns in England, 1000–1540." *Historical Research* 75 (2002): 1–24.

"Small Towns." In *The Cambridge Urban History of Britain, Vol. I, 600–1540*, ed. David M. Palliser. Cambridge, 2000, pp. 505–40.

Standards of Living in the Later Medieval Ages: Social Change in England, c. 1200–1520. Cambridge, 1989.

Eales, Jacqueline. *Women in Early Modern England, 1500–1700.* London, 1998.

Earle, Peter. "The Female Labour Market in London in the Late Seventeenth and Early Eighteenth Centuries." *Economic History Review*, 2nd ser., 42 (1989): 328–53.

The Making of the English Middle Class: Business, Society, and Family Life in London, 1660–1730. Berkeley, 1989.

Erickson, Amy Louise. *Women and Property in Early Modern England.* New York, 1993.

Erler, Mary C., and Maryanne Kowaleski, *Gendering the Master Narrative: Women and Power in the Middle Ages.* Ithaca, N.Y., 2003.

Everitt, Alan. "The Marketing of Agricultural Produce." In *The Agrarian History of England and Wales*, vol. IV (1500–1640), ed. Joan Thirsk. Cambridge, 1967, pp. 466–592.

Ewan, Elizabeth. "For Whatever Ales Ye: Women as Consumers and Producers in Late Medieval Scottish Towns." In *Women in Scotland, c. 1100–c. 1750*, ed. Elizabeth Ewan and Maureen Meikle. East Linton, 1999, pp. 125–36.

"Mons Meg and Merchant Meg: Women in Later Medieval Edinburgh." In *Freedom and Authority: Scotland c. 1050–1650*, ed. Terry Brotherstone and David Ditchburn. East Linton, 2000, pp. 131–42.

"Scottish Portias: Women in the Courts in Mediaeval Scottish Towns." *Journal of the Canadian Historical Association*, new ser., 3 (1992): 27–43.

Farmer, Sharon. *Surviving Poverty in Medieval Paris: Gender, Ideology, and the Daily Lives of the Poor.* Ithaca, N.Y., 2002.

Finlay, Roger A. P. "Population and Fertility in London, 1580–1650." *Journal of Family History* 4 (1979): 26–38.

Finn, Margot. *The Character of Credit: Personal Debt in English Culture, 1740–1914.* Cambridge, 2003.

Fisher, F. J. "The Development of London as a Centre of Conspicuous Consumption in the Sixteenth and Seventeenth Centuries." *Transactions of the Royal Historical Society*, 4th ser., 30 (1948): 37–50.

Fleming, Peter. *Women in Late Medieval Bristol.* Bristol Branch, The Historical Association, Local History Pamphlet no. 103. Bristol, 2001.

Fletcher, Anthony. *Gender, Sex and Subordination in England, 1500–1800.* New Haven, Conn., 1995.

Foulds, Trevor. "Women and Work in Nottingham After the Black Death, 1351–76." Unpublished paper.

Fox, Levi. "The Coventry Guilds and Trading Companies: with Special Reference to the Position of Women." In *Essays in Honour of Philip B. Chatwin.* Oxford, 1962, pp. 13–26.

Foyster, Elizabeth. *Manhood in Early Modern England.* London, 1999.

French, Katherine L. "Maidens' Lights and Wives' Stores: Women's Parish Guilds in Late Medieval England." *Sixteenth Century Journal* 29 (1998): 399–425.

"'To Free Them from Binding': Women in the Late Medieval English Parish." *Journal of Interdisciplinary History* 27 (1997): 387–412.

"Women in the Late Medieval English Parish." In *Gendering the Master Narrative*, ed. Mary C. Erler and Maryanne Kowaleski. Ithaca, N.Y., 2003, pp. 156–73.

Froide, Amy M. "Marital Status as a Category of Difference: Singlewomen and Widows in Early Modern England." In *Singlewomen in the European Past, 1250–1800*, ed. Judith M. Bennett and Amy M. Froide. Philadelphia, 1999, pp. 236–69.

"Single Women, Work, and Community in Southampton, 1550–1750." Ph.D. thesis, Duke University, 1996.

"Surplus Women and Surplus Money: The Role of Singlewomen as Creditors in Early Modern England." Paper given at the 1999 meeting of the North American Conference of British Studies.

Goldberg, P. J. P. "Coventry's 'Lollard' Programme of 1492 and the Making of Utopia." In *Pragmatic Utopias: Ideals and Communities, 1200–1630*, ed. Rosemary Horrox and Sarah Rees Jones. Cambridge, 2001, pp. 97–116.

"Female Labour, Service and Marriage in the Late Medieval Urban North." *Northern History* 12 (1986): 18–38.

"'For Better, for Worse': Marriage and Economic Opportunity for Women in Town and Country." In *Woman Is a Worthy Wight: Women in English Society, c. 1200–1500*, ed. P. J. P. Goldberg. Stroud, 1992, pp. 108–25.

"Marriage, Migration, Servanthood and Life-Cycle in Yorkshire Towns of the Later Middle Ages." *Continuity and Change* 1 (1986): 141–69.

"Pigs and Prostitutes: Streetwalking in Comparative Perspective." In *Young Medieval Women*, ed. Katherine J. Lewis, Noel James Menuge, and Kim M. Phillips. New York, 1999, pp. 172–94.

"The Public and the Private: Women in the Pre-Plague Economy." In *Thirteenth Century England III*. Woodbridge, 1991, pp. 75–89.

"Women in Fifteenth-Century Town Life." In *Town and Townspeople in the Fifteenth Century*, ed. John A. F. Thomson. Wolfeboro Falls, N.H., 1988, pp. 107–28.

Women, Work, and Life Cycle in a Medieval Economy: Women in York and Yorkshire c. 1300–1520. Oxford, 1992.

"Women's Work, Women's Role, in the Late-Medieval North." In *Profit, Piety and the Professions in Later Medieval England*, ed. Michael Hicks. Wolfeboro Falls, N.H., 1990, pp. 34–50.

Goose, Nigel. "Household Size and Structure in Early-Stuart Cambridge." *Social History* 5 (1980): 347–85.

Gowing, Laura. *Domestic Dangers: Women, Words, and Sex in Early Modern London*. Oxford, 1996.

"'The Freedom of the Streets': Women and Social Space, 1560–1640." In *Londonopolis*, ed. Paul Griffiths and Mark S. R. Jenner. Manchester, 2000, pp. 130–51.

"Gender and the Language of Insult in Early Modern London." *History Workshop Journal* 35 (1993): 1–21.

Griffiths, Paul. "'Waxey Words': Meanings of Crime in London, 1560–1660." Unpublished paper given at the North American Conference on British Studies, Toronto, Canada, November 2001.

Haigh, C. A. "Slander and the Church Courts in the Sixteenth Century." *Transactions of the Lancashire and Cheshire Antiquarian Society* 78 (1975): 1–13.

Hajnal, John. "Two Kinds of Preindustrial Household Formation System." *Population and Development Review* 8 (1982): 449–94.

Hanawalt, Barbara A. "At the Margins of Women's Space in Medieval Europe." In her *'Of Good and Ill Repute.'* New York, 1998, pp. 70–87.

"The Dilemma of the Widow of Property in Late Medieval London." In *The Medieval Marriage Scene: Prudence, Passion, and Policy*, ed. Cristelle Baskins and Sherry Roush, Arizona Center for Medieval and Renaisssance Studies, forthcoming.

"The Host, the Law, and the Ambiguous Space of Medieval London Taverns." In her *'Of Good and Ill Repute.'* New York, 1998, pp. 104–23.

"Medieval London Women as Consumers." Unpublished paper given at Medieval Congress, Kalamazoo, Mich., May 2003.

"Peasant Women's Contribution to the Home Economy in Late Medieval England." In *Women and Work in Preindustrial Europe*, ed. Barbara A. Hanawalt. Bloomington, Ind., 1986, pp. 3–19.

"Remarriage as an Option for Urban and Rural Widows in Late Medieval England." In *Wife and Widow: The Experiences of Women in Medieval England*, ed. Sue Sheridan Walker. Ann Arbor, 1993, pp. 141–63.

"Separation Anxieties in Late Medieval London: Gender in 'The Wright's Chaste Wife'." In her *'Of Good and Ill Repute.'* Oxford, 1998, pp. 88–103.

The Ties That Bound: Peasant Families in Medieval England. Oxford, 1986.

"The Widow's Mite: Provisions for Medieval London Widows." In *Upon My Husband's Death: Widows in the Literature and Histories of Medieval Europe*, ed. Louise Mirrer. Studies in Medieval and Early Modern Civilization. Ann Arbor, 1992, pp. 21–45.

Hancock, F. *A History of Minehead in the County of Somerset*. Taunton, 1903.

Hanna, Ralph, III. "Brewing Trouble: On Literature and History – and Alewives." In *Bodies and Disciplines*, ed. Barbara A. Hanawalt and David Wallace. Minneapolis, 1996, pp. 1–18.

Harris, Barbara J. "Women and Politics in Early Tudor England." *The Historical Journal* 33, no. 2 (1990): 259–81.

Harvey, Barbara. "The Aristocratic Consumer in England in the Long Thirteenth Century." In *Thirteenth Century England VI*. Woodbridge, 1997, pp. 17–37.

Living and Dying in England, 1100–1540. Oxford, 1993.

Hatcher, John. "Mortality in the Fifteenth Century." *Economic History Review*, 2nd ser., 39 (1986): 19–38.

Plague, Population and the English Economy, 1348–1530. London, 1977.

"Understanding the Population History of England, 1450-1750." *Past and Present* 180 (2003): 83–130.

Helmholz, R. H. "Usury and the Medieval English Church Courts." *Speculum* 61 (1986): 364–80.

Hettinger, Madonna J. "Defining the Servant: Legal and Extra-Legal Terms of Employment in Fifteenth-Century England." In *The Work of Work: Servitude, Slavery, and Labor in Medieval England*, ed. Allen J. Frantzen and D. Moffat. Glasgow, 1994, pp. 206–28.

Hicks, M. A. "The Yorkshire Rebellion of 1489 Reconsidered." *Northern History* 22 (1986): 39–62.

Hilton, R. H. *The English Peasantry in the Later Middle Ages*. Oxford, 1975.

"Lords, Burgesses and Hucksters." *Past and Present* 97 (1982): 3–15.

"Medieval Market Towns and Simple Commodity Production." *Past and Present* 109 (1985): 3–23.

"Women Traders in Medieval England." *Women's Studies* 11 (1984): 139–55.

Holderness, B. A. "Credit in a Rural Community, 1660–1800." *Midland History* 3 (1975): 94–115.

"Credit in English Rural Society before the Nineteenth Century, with Special Reference to the Period 1650–1720." *Agricultural History Review* 24 (1976): 97–109.

"Widows in Pre-Industrial Society: An Essay Upon Their Economic Functions." In *Land, Kinship and Life-Cycle*, ed. Richard M. Smith. Cambridge, 1984, pp. 423–42.

Honeyman, Katrina, and Jordan Goodman. "Women's Work, Gender Conflict, and Labour Markets in Europe, 1500–1900." *Economic History Review* 44, no. 2 (1991): 608–28.

Howell, Martha C. *Women, Production, and Patriarchy in Late Medieval Cities*. Chicago, 1986.

Hutton, Diane. "Women in Fourteenth Century Shrewsbury." In *Women and Work in Pre-Industrial England*, ed. Lindsay Charles and Lorna Duffin. London, 1985, pp. 83–99.

Ingram, Martin. "Ridings, Rough Music and the 'Reform of Popular Culture' in Early Modern England." *Past and Present* 105 (1984): 79–113.

"'Scolding Women Cucked or Washed': A Crisis in Gender Relations in Early Modern England?" In *Women, Crime and the Courts in Early Modern England*, ed. Jenny Kermode and Garthine Walker. London, 1994, pp. 48–80.

Jenner, Mark S. R. "From Conduit Community to Commercial Network: Water in London, 1500–1725." In *Londonopolis: Essays in the Cultural and Social History of Early Modern London*, ed. Paul Griffiths and Mark S. R. Jenner. Manchester, 2000, pp. 250–72.

Jones, Ann R. "Maidservants of London: Sisterhoods of Kinship and Labor." In *Maids and Mistresses, Cousins and Queens: Women's Alliances in Early Modern England*, ed. Susan Frye and Karen Robertson. New York, 1999, pp. 21–32.

Jones, Norman. *God and the Moneylenders: Usury and Law in Early Modern England*. Oxford, 1989.

Jordan, William Chester. *Women and Credit in Pre-Industrial and Developing Societies*. Philadelphia, 1993.

Karras, Ruth Mazo. *Common Women: Prostitution and Sexuality in Medieval England*. New York, 1996.

"The Regulation of Brothels in Later Medieval England." *Signs* 14 (1989): 399–433.

Keene, Derek. "Shops and Shopping in Medieval London." In *Medieval Art, Architecture, and Archaeology in London,* ed. Lindy Grant. Oxford: British Archaeological Association, 1990, pp. 29–46.

Survey of Medieval Winchester. Winchester Studies 2. Oxford, 1985.

"Tanners' Widows, 1300–1350." In *Medieval London Widows, 1300–1500,* ed. C. M. Barron and A. F. Sutton. London, 1994, pp. 1–27.

Kent, D. A. "Ubiquitous but Invisible: Female Domestic Servants in Mid-Eighteenth Century London." *History Workshop* 28 (1989): 111–28.

Kenyon, Nora (Ritchie). "Labour Conditions in Essex in the Reign of Richard II." *Economic History Review* 4 (1934): 429–51.

Kermode, Jennifer I. "Money and Credit in the Fifteenth Century: Some Lessons from Yorkshire." *Business History Review* 65 (1991): 475–501.

Kerridge, Eric. *Textile Manufactures in Early Modern England.* Manchester, 1985.

Kettle, Ann J. *A List of Families in the Archdeaconry of Stafford, 1532–3.* In *Collections for a History of Staffordshire.* Staffordshire Record Society, 4th ser., vol. VIII, 1976.

"Ruined Maids: Prostitutes and Servant Girls in Later Medieval England." In *Matrons and Marginal Women in Medieval Society,* ed. Robert R. Edwards and Vickie Ziegler. Woodbridge, Suffolk, 1995, pp. 19–31.

Kowaleski, Maryanne. "The Expansion of the South-Western Fisheries in Late Medieval England." *Economic History Review* 53 (2000): 429–54.

Local Markets and Regional Trade in Medieval Exeter. Cambridge, 1995.

"Port Towns in Medieval England and Wales, 1300–1540." In *The Cambridge Urban History of Britain,* vol. I (600–1540), ed. D. M. Palliser, pp. 467–94. Cambridge, 2000.

"Singlewomen in Medieval and Early Modern Europe: The Demographic Perspective." In *Singlewomen in the European Past, 1250–1800,* ed. Judith M. Bennett and Amy M. Froide. Philadelphia, 1999, pp. 38–81.

"Women's Work in a Market Town: Exeter in the Late Fourteenth Century." In *Women and Work in Preindustrial Europe,* ed. Barbara A. Hanawalt. Bloomington, Ind., 1986, pp. 145–64.

Kussmaul, Ann. *Servants in Husbandry in Early Modern England.* Cambridge, 1981.

Lacey, Kay E. "Women and Work in Fourteenth and Fifteenth Century London." In *Women and Work in Pre-Industrial England,* ed. Lindsay Charles and Lorna Duffin. London, 1985, pp. 24–82.

Ladd, Roger A. "Thomas Deloney and the London Weavers' Company." *Sixteenth Century Journal* 32 (2001): 981–1002.

Lane, Joan. *Apprenticeship in England, 1600–1914.* London, 1996.

Laslett, Peter. "Mean Household Size in England since the Sixteenth Century." In *Household and Family in Past Time,* ed. Peter Laslett and Richard Wall. Cambridge, 1972, pp. 125–58.

Laughton, Jane. "The Alewives of Later Medieval Chester." In *Crown, Government, and People in the Fifteenth Century,* ed. Rowena E. Archer. New York, 1999, pp. 191–207.

"Women in Court: Some Evidence from Fifteenth-Century Chester." In *England in the Fifteenth Century*, ed. Nicholas Rogers. Harlaxton Medieval Studies 4, 1994, pp. 89–99.

Laurence, Anne. *Women in England, 1500–1760: A Social History.* New York, 1994.

Leinwand, Theodore B. *The City Staged: Jacobean Comedy, 1603–1613.* Madison, Wisc., 1986.

Theatre, Finance, and Society in Early Modern England. Cambridge, 1999.

Lemire, Beverly. "Petty Pawns and Informal Lending: Gender and the Transformation of Small-Scale Credit in England, circa 1600–1800." In *From Family Firms to Corporate Capitalism: Essays in Business in Honour of Peter Mathias*, ed. Kristine Bruland and Patrick O'Brien. Oxford, 1998, pp. 112–38.

"Women, the Informal Economy and the Development of Capitalism in England, 1650–1850; or, Did Women Get Credit?" Unpublished paper presented at the 1999 North American Conference on British Studies, Boston, Mass., 1999.

Leyser, Henrietta. *Medieval Women: A Social History of Women in England, 450–1500.* New York, 1995.

Marcombe, David. *English Small Town Life: Retford, 1520–1642.* Nottingham: Department of Adult Education, University of Nottingham, 1993.

Masschaele, James. "The Public Space of the Marketplace in Medieval England." *Speculum* 77 (2002): 383–421.

Mate, Mavis. *Daughters, Wives and Widows after the Black Death: Women in Sussex, 1350–1535.* Woodbridge, 1998.

"The Rise of Beer-Brewing." Unpublished chapter from her book *Trade and Economic Development, 1450–1550*, forthcoming.

Women in Medieval English Society. Cambridge, 1999.

Mayhew, Graham. *Tudor Rye.* Brighton: Falmer Centre for Continuing Education, University of Sussex, 1987.

McIntosh, Marjorie K. *Autonomy and Community: The Royal Manor of Havering, 1200–1500.* Cambridge, 1986.

A Community Transformed: The Manor and Liberty of Havering, 1500–1620. Cambridge, 1991.

"The Benefits and Drawbacks of *Femme Sole* Status in England, 1300–1630." *Journal of British Studies* 44:3 (2005), forthcoming.

Controlling Misbehavior in England, 1370–1600. Cambridge Studies in Population, Economy and Society in Past Time. Cambridge, 1998.

"The Diversity of Social Capital in English Communities, 1300–1640 (with a Glance at Modern Nigeria)." *Journal of Interdisciplinary History* 29 (1999): 459–90. Reprinted in *Patterns of Social Capital*, ed. Robert I. Rotberg. Cambridge, 2001, pp. 121–52.

"Local Responses to the Poor in Late Medieval and Tudor England." *Continuity and Change* 3 (1988): 209–45.

"Money Lending on the Periphery of London, 1300–1600." *Albion* 20 (1988): 557–71.

"Networks of Care in Elizabethan English Towns: The Example of Hadleigh, Suffolk." In *The Locus of Care: Families, Communities, Institutions, and the*

Provision of Welfare Since Antiquity, ed. Peregrine Horden and Richard Smith. London, 1998, pp. 71–89.

"Response." In a special issue devoted to her book, *Controlling Misbehavior in England*, *Journal of British Studies* 37 (1998): 291–305.

"Servants and the Household Unit in an Elizabethan English Community." *Journal of Family History* 9 (1984): 3–23.

"Women, Credit, and Family Relationships in England, 1300–1620." *Journal of Family History* 30:2 (2005), forthcoming.

McNabb, Jennifer. "Constructing Credit in Early Modern England: Debt, Insult, and Authority in the Market Towns of Middlewich and Devizes, 1540–1610." Ph.D. thesis, University of Colorado, 2003.

Meldrum, Tim. *Domestic Service and Gender, 1660–1750*. Harlow, Essex, 2000.

Mendelson, Sara. "Seventeenth-Century Women: Patterns of Consumer Behaviour." Unpublished paper given at the North American Conference on British Studies. Toronto, Canada, November 2001.

Mendelson, Sara, and Patricia Crawford. *Women in Early Modern England, 1550–1720*. Oxford, 1998.

Moore, Ellen Wedemeyer. "Aspects of Poverty in a Small Medieval Town." In *The Salt of Common Life: Individuality and Choice in the Medieval Town, Countryside, and Church*, ed. Edwin Brezette DeWindt. Kalamazoo, Mich., 1995, pp. 117–56.

The Fairs of Medieval England. Toronto, 1985.

Muldrew, Craig. "Credit and the Courts: Debt Litigation in a Seventeenth-Century Urban Community." *Economic History Review* 46, no. 1 (1993): 23–38.

The Economy of Obligation: The Culture of Credit and Social Relations in Early Modern England. London, 1998.

"'Hard Food for Midas': Cash and Its Social Value in Early Modern England." *Past and Present* 170 (2001): 78–120.

"Interpreting the Market: The Ethics of Credit and Community Relations in Early Modern England." *Social History* 18 (1993): 163–83.

"'A Mutual Assent of Her Mind?' Women, Debt, Litigation and Contract in Early Modern England." *History Workshop Journal* 55 (2003): 47–72.

Newman, Christine. *Late Medieval Northallerton: A Small Market Town and Its Hinterland, c. 1470–1540*. Stamford, 1999.

"Order and Community in the North: The Liberty of Allertonshire in the Later Fifteenth Century." In *The North of England in the Age of Richard III*, ed. A. J. Pollard. Stroud, 1996, pp. 47–66.

Newman, Karen. "City Talk: Women and Commodification." In *Staging the Renaissance*, ed. David S. Kastan and Peter Stallybrass. London, 1991, pp. 181–95.

Palliser, D. M., and A. C. Pinnock. "The Markets of Medieval Staffordshire." *North Staffordshire Journal of Field Studies* 2 (1971): 49–63.

Palmer, Charles Ferrers. *The History of the Town and Castle of Tamworth*. Tamworth, 1845.

Pelling, Margaret. "Nurses and Nursekeepers: Problems of Identification in the Early Modern Period." In her *The Common Lot: Sickness, Medical*

Occupations and the Urban Poor in Early Modern England. London, 1998, pp. 179–203.

"Old Age, Poverty, and Disability in Early Modern Norwich." In *Life, Death, and the Elderly: Historical Perspectives*, ed. Margaret Pelling and Richard M. Smith. London, 1991, pp. 74–101.

"Older Women: Household, Caring and Other Occupations in the Late Sixteenth-century Town." In her *The Common Lot: Sickness, Medical Occupations and the Urban Poor in Early Modern England.* London, 1998, pp. 155–75.

"Trade or Profession? Medical Practice in Early Modern England." In her *The Common Lot: Sickness, Medical Occupations and the Urban Poor in Early Modern England.* London, 1998, pp. 230–58.

Pelling, Margaret, and Charles Webster. "Medical Practitioners." In their *Health, Medicine and Mortality in the Sixteenth Century.* Cambridge, 1979, pp. 165–235.

Penn, Simon C. "Female Wage-Earners in Late Fourteenth-Century England." *Agricultural History Review* 1987 (1987): 1–14.

Pennell, Sara. "'Great Quantities of Gooseberry Pye and Baked Clod of Beef': Victualling and Eating Out in Early Modern London." In *Londonopolis: Essays in the Cultural and Social History of Early Modern London*, ed. Paul Griffiths and Mark S. R. Jenner. Manchester, 2000, pp. 228–49.

Phythian-Adams, Charles. *Desolation of a City: Coventry and the Urban Crisis of the Late Middle Ages.* Cambridge, 1979.

Pinchbeck, Ivy. *Women Workers and the Industrial Revolution, 1750–1850.* New York, 1930.

Poos, Lawrence R. *A Rural Society After the Black Death: Essex, 1350–1525.* Cambridge, 1991.

"The Social Context of Statute of Labourers Enforcement." *Law and History Review* 1 (1983): 27–52.

Postles, David. "An English Small Town in the Later Middle Ages: Loughborough." *Urban History* 20, no. 3 (April 1993): 7–29.

Prior, Mary. "Women and the Urban Economy: Oxford, 1500–1800." In *Women in English Society, 1500–1800*, ed. Mary Prior. London, 1985, pp. 93–117.

Putnam, Bertha H. *The Enforcement of the Statutes of Labourers during the First Decade after the Black Death.* New York, 1908.

Riddle, John M. *Eve's Herbs: A History of Contraception and Abortion in the West.* Cambridge, Mass., 1997.

Riddy, Felicity. "Looking Closely: Authority and Intimacy in the Late-Medieval Urban Home." In *Gendering the Master Narrative*, ed. Mary Erler and Maryanne Kowaleski. Ithaca, N.Y., 2003, pp. 212–28.

"'Women Talking about the Things of God': A Late Medieval Sub-Culture." In *Women and Literature in Britain, 1150–1500*, ed. Carol M. Meale. 2nd edn., Cambridge, 1996, pp. 104–27.

Rigby, S. H. *English Society in the Later Middle Ages: Class, Status, and Gender.* New York, 1995.

Roberts, Michael. "'Waiting Upon Chance': English Hiring Fairs and their Meanings from the 14th to the 20th Century." *Journal of Historical Sociology* 1 (1988): 119–60.

"Women and Work in Sixteenth Century English Towns." In *Work in Towns, 850–1850*, ed. Penelope J. Corfield and Derek Keene. Leicester, 1990, pp. 86–102.

"'Words They Are Women and Deeds They are Men': Images of Work and Gender in Early Modern England." In *Women and Work in Pre-Industrial England*, ed. Lindsey Charles and Lorna Duffin. London, 1985, pp. 122–80.

Rosser, Gervase. "Going to the Fraternity Feast: Commensality and Social Relations in Late Medieval England." *Journal of British Studies* 33 (1994): 430–46.

Medieval Westminster, 1200–1540. Oxford, 1989.

Rotberg, Robert I. "Social Capital and Political Culture in Africa, America, Australasia, and Europe." In *Patterns of Social Capital: Stability and Change in Historical Perspective*, ed. Robert I. Rotberg. Cambridge, 2001, pp. 1–18.

Sharpe, J. A. *Defamation and Sexual Slander in Early Modern England: The Church Courts at York*. Borthwick Papers, no. 58, 1980.

Shepard, Alexandra. "Manhood, Credit, and Patriarchy in Early Modern England, c. 1580–1640." *Past and Present* 167 (2000): 75–106.

Slack, Paul A. *Poverty and Policy in Tudor and Stuart England*. London, 1988.

Smith, Richard M. "Geographical Diversity in the Resort to Marriage in Late Medieval Europe: Work, Reputation, and Unmarried Females in the Household Formation Systems of Northern and Southern Europe." In *Woman is a Worthy Wight: Women in English Society, c. 1200–1500*, ed. P. J. P. Goldberg. Stroud, 1992, pp. 16–59.

"The Manorial Court and the Elderly Tenant in Late Medieval England." In *Life, Death, and the Elderly: Historical Perspectives*, ed. Margaret Pelling and Richard M. Smith. London, 1991, pp. 39–61.

"A Periodic Market and Its Impact Upon a Manorial Community: Botesdale, Suffolk, and the Manor of Redgrave, 1280–1300." In *Medieval Society and the Manor Court*, ed. Zvi Razi and Richard Smith. Oxford, 1996, pp. 450–81.

Spicksley, Judith. "The Early Modern Demographic Dynamic: Celibates and Celibacy in Seventeenth-Century England." Ph.D. thesis, University of Hull, 2001.

Spufford, Margaret. *The Great Reclothing of Rural England*. London, 1984.

Stretton, Tim. *Women Waging Law in Elizabethan England*. Cambridge, 1998.

Studd, Robin. *The Tamworth Court Rolls: An Introduction*. Tamworth, 1987.

Sutton, Anne F. "Alice Claver, Silkwoman (d. 1489)." In *Medieval London Widows 1300–1500*, ed. C. M. Barron and A. F. Sutton. London, 1994, pp. 129–42.

Swanson, Heather. "The Illusion of Economic Structure: Craft Guilds in Late Medieval English Towns." *Past and Present* 121 (1988): 29–47.

Medieval Artisans: An Urban Class in Late Medieval England. Oxford, 1989.

Thirsk, Joan, ed. *The Agrarian History of England and Wales*. Vol. IV (1500–1640) of *The Agrarian History of England and Wales*, ed. H. P. R. Finberg. Cambridge, 1967.

Economic Policy and Projects: The Development of a Consumer Society in Early Modern England. Oxford, 1978.

Tilly, Louise A. and Joan W. Scott. *Women, Work, and Family*. New York, 1978.

Tittler, Robert. "Money-Lending in the West Midlands: The Activities of Joyce Jeffries, 1638–49." *Historical Research* 67 (1994): 249–63.

Todd, Barbara J. "The Crown and the Female Money Market, 1660–1700." Unpublished paper presented at the North American Conference of British Studies, Chicago, Ill., 1996.

"Small Sums to Risk: Women's Investments in the Age of the Financial Revolution." Unpublished paper presented at the North American Conference of British Studies, Boston, Mass., 1999.

Tonkinson, A. M. "The Borough Community of Tamworth and Its Courts at the End of the Thirteenth Century." M.A. thesis, University of Keele, 1985.

Underdown, David. "The Taming of the Scold: The Enforcement of Patriarchal Authority in Early Modern England." In *Order and Disorder in Early Modern England*, ed. Anthony Fletcher and John Stevenson. Cambridge, 1985, pp. 116–36.

Veale, Elspeth. "Matilda Penne, Skinner (d. 1392/3)." In *Medieval London Widows 1300–1500*, ed. C. M. Barron and A. F. Sutton. London, 1994, pp. 47–54.

Wack, Mary. "Women, Work, and Plays in an English Medieval Town." In *Maids and Mistresses, Cousins and Queens*, ed. Susan Frye and Karen Robertson. New York, 1999, pp. 33–51.

Walker, Garthine. "Expanding the Boundaries of Female Honour in Early Modern England." *Trans. Royal Historical Society*, 6th ser., 6 (1996): 75–106.

Walker, J. W. "The Burgess Courts, Wakefield." *Yorkshire Archaeological Society Record Series* 74 (1929): 16–32.

Ward, Joseph P. *Metropolitan Communities: Trade Guilds, Identity, and Change in Early Modern London*. Stanford, Calif., 1997.

Webster, Charles, ed. *Health, Medicine and Mortality in the Sixteenth Century*. Cambridge, 1979.

Whittle, Jane. *The Development of Agrarian Capitalism: Land and Labour in Norfolk, 1440–1580*. Oxford, 2000.

"The Gender Division of Labour: The Skills and Work of Women in Rural Households, England, 1450–1650." Unpublished paper.

"Servants in Rural England, c. 1450–1650." In *The Marital Economy in Scandinavia and Britain, 1400–1900*, ed. Maria Agren and Amy Erickson. Aldershot, 2004.

"Women, Servants, and By-Employment in English Rural Households, 1440–1650." Paper delivered at Royal Historical Society, April 2004; forthcoming in *Transactions of the Royal Historical Society*.

Wiesner, Merry. *Working Women in Renaissance Germany*. New Brunswick, N.J., 1986.

Willan, T. S. *Elizabethan Manchester*. Manchester: The Chetham Society, 1980.

Willen, Diane. "Women in the Public Sphere in Early Modern England: The Case of the Urban Working Poor." *Sixteenth Century Journal* 19, no. 4 (1988): 559–75.

Wood, Andy. *The Politics of Social Conflict: The Peak Country, 1520–1770*. New York, 1999.

Wood, Henry. *Borough by Prescription: A History of the Municipality of Tamworth*. Tamworth, 1958.

Medieval Tamworth. Tamworth, 1972.

Wood, Merry Wiesner. "Paltry Peddlers or Essential Merchants: Women in the Distributive Trades in Early Modern Nuremberg." *Sixteenth Century Journal* 12 (1981): 3–13.

Wood, Robert A. "Poor Widows, c. 1393–1415." In *Medieval London Widows 1300–1500*, ed. C. M. Barron and A. F. Sutton. London, 1994, pp. 55–70.

Wright, Sue. "'Churmaids, Huswyfes and Hucksters': The Employment of Women in Tudor and Stuart Salisbury." In *Women and Work in Pre-Industrial England*, ed. Lindsay Charles and Lorna Duffin. London, 1985, pp. 100–21.

Wrightson, Keith. "The Puritan Reformation of Manners, with Special Reference to the Counties of Lancashire and Essex, 1640–60." Ph.D. thesis, University of Cambridge, 1973.

Wrigley, E. A., and R. S. Schofield. *The Population History of England, 1541–1871: A Reconstruction.* London, 1981.

Zell, Michael. *Industry in the Countryside: Wealden Society in the Sixteenth Century.* Cambridge, 1994.

Index

Adair, Richard, 66
adolescents, *see* service, domestic
ale, 146–52
  see also brewing
alehouses, 157–61, 202
  moral suspicion of, 158–60, 180–1
aleselling, 156–63, 269
alewives, moral suspicion of, 158, 159
apprenticeship, 29, 30, 41, 47, 133–9
  shifting meaning of (for women), 135–7
  under women, 138–9
architecture, 236
Assize of Bread and Ale, 16, 140–1

babies, 64
baking, 183, 184–5, 270, 271
  see also bread
barber-surgeons, 83
Bardsley, Sandy, 32
Barron, Caroline, 29–30, 31, 36, 37, 134, 135
beer, 163–5
  see also brewing
bellmaking, 236
Ben-Amos, Ilana Krausman, 135
Bennett, Judith, 32–4, 35, 36, 37, 152, 154, 155, 159, 170, 179, 201
boarders, 62–72
  as servants, 67, 68–9
boarding, 61–2, 71–2
bonds, 90–3
bread, 182–3
  production of, 183, 184–5, 270, 271
  retail of, 183, 186–7, 190
brewing, 266, 267–8
  gender patterns of, 153, 165–7, 170–1, 173–7, 178–81
  occupational identity in, 35, 155
  of ale, 146–52
  of beer, 163–5
  regulation/records of, 140–1
  status of, 155–6

butchering, 191–2
buttons, 232

candles, 192
Canterbury Tales, 201
capmaking, 231–2
carding (of wool), 212–13
cardmaking, 236–7
chandlery (candlemaking), 192
charwomen, *see* service, domestic
Chaucer, Geoffrey, 201
Chief Pledges (jurors), 155–6, 172, 257–8, 267–8
children, as boarders, 64–8
Clark, Alice, 28
cleaning, 75
cloth
  finishing of, 220–1
  manufacture of
    carding/combing, 212–13
    spinning, 212–16, 222
    weaving, 217–19, 220, 222–3
  trade in, 225–9
  types of, 210–11, 221–5
clothing, 229–33
  as visual marker of status/reputation, 247–9
  decoration of, 233
  types of
    leather/fur, 232–3
    second-hand, 230–1
  see also sumptuary laws
combing (of wool), 212–13
consumerism, 239–49
  credit (economic) in, 239–40
  gendered patterns of, 42, 239, 240, 244–5
  moral suspicion of, 244, 248–9
  socio-economic patterns of, 240–4, 245
  see also London
cooking, 73–5, 199–201
cotton, 221

courts, equity, 20–8, 50, 255–6, 263, 264,
        265
    petitions to, 91, 123–4, 126–7, 206–7
crafts and trades
    types of
        architecture, 236
        bell-founding, 236
        cloth-making, *see* cloth
        drink trades: aleselling, 156–63, 269;
            brewing, *see* alehouses, alewives,
            brewing; malting, 145; wine,
            167–70
        food trades: baking, *see* bread;
            butchering, 191–2; chandlery, 192;
            cooked foods, 199–201; dairying,
            196–8; fishmongering, 192–6;
            innkeeping, 202–9; poultry, 196–8;
            spices, 198; *see also* huckstering
        fur, 235
        leather, 234
        masonry, 236
        seamstressing, 229–30
        small metal, 236–7
        wood and large metal, 235–6
Crawford, Patricia, 36
credit, 120
    economic, 11, 12–13, 37–8, 49–50, 62,
        239–40
    personal, 9, 10–12, 27, 98–9
currency, changing value of, 102–3

dairying, 196–8
Davis, Natalie Zemon, 35
Dekker, Thomas, 249
Deloney, Thomas, 208–9, 246–7
disease, 26, 76–7, 83, 179

Eales, Jacqueline, 36
elderly, as boarders, 69–71
embroidery, 233
equity courts, *see* courts
Erickson, Amy, 21

femme couverte, 15
femme sole, 16, 24, 29, 35, 37, 105, 131,
        136
financial services, 9–10, 85–6, 120–1
    gendered patterns of, 41–2, 86–7, 95–7,
        112–14
    types of
        bonds, 90–3
        informal, 87
        money-lending, 86, 98–107, 112–14
        pawnbroking, 86, 107–14
        real estate, 86, 93–5, 114–16

fishmongering, 192–6
food
    types of
        bread, *see* baking
        butchering, 191–2
        cooked foods, 199–201
        dairy, 196–8
        fish, 192–6
        poultry, 196–8
        produce, 198, 199
        spices, 198
        see also huckstering
    purchases by poor, 243
fraternities, 40
Froide, Amy, 103
fur, 232–3, 235

gender patterns
    in brewing/selling of drink, 153, 165–7,
        170–1, 173–7, 178–81
    in cloth trades, 211–12
    in consumerism, 239, 240, 244–5
    in domestic service, 60–1
    in financial services, 37–8, 41–2, 86–7,
        95–7, 112–14
    in food trades/innkeeping, 182, 185–6,
        187, 188–9, 190–202, 270
    in weaving, 217–19
    in work, 3, 7–8, 31–7, 38, 40, 121–3
Goldberg, Jeremy, 30, 31, 36
Great Fire of London (1665–6), 137–8
guilds, 121, 133
    women as members of, 40

Hanawalt, Barbara, 35
Havering/Romford, Essex, 18
    boarding in, 63
    Chief Pledges in, 267–8
    concern over poverty in, 179–80
    concern over social misbehavior in,
        180–1
    disease in, 179
    drink trades in, 141–2, 148–50, 152–4,
        155, 158, 161–3, 165, 174–5, 266,
        267–8, 269
    food trades in, 188, 189, 191, 194, 202,
        270, 271
    innkeeping in, 180, 203, 205–6
    occupational identity (in food/drink
        trades) in, 144, 145, 189, 271
    records of, 178, 256, 258–9
    servants in, 50, 51–2, 55–6, 59, 60, 103
    sex work in, 77
    wet nursing in, 64
health care, 79

Heywood, John, 201
Hilton, R. H., 31
home, as location of marketing, 130
hospitals, 83–4
Howell, Martha, 35
huckstering (street vending), 130–2, 161,
    197–8, 199
  of bread, 183, 190

ill, boarding of, 80
innkeeping, 202–9
inns, 180, 202–9
  moral suspicion of, 204–5, 208–9
interest, 100–2

James I of England (James VI of Scotland),
    248–9
jewelry, 233

knitting, 231–2
Kowaleski, Maryanne, 31–2, 35

lace, 232
landladies, 114–16
laundering, 72–3
Laurence, Anne, 36
leather, 232–3, 234
lending, see money-lending
Leyser, Henrietta, 36
linen, 221–3
London
  as center of consumerism, 245–7
  hucksters in, 131–2
  New Exchange, 249
  Royal Exchange, 249

malting, 145
marketing, 123
marriage, patterns of, 8–9, 264
  in baking, 189
  in brewing, 153
  in cloth trades, 215
married women
  as cloth traders, 227–9
  as money-lenders/pawnbrokers, 105–6,
    112
  as servants, 49
masonry, 236
Mate, Mavis, 35, 36
McNabb, Jennifer, 66
Mendelson, Sara, 36
midwifery, 80–3
Minehead, Somerset, 18
  Chief Pledges of, 267–8
  concern over poverty in, 179–80

drink trades in, 142–3, 150, 152–4, 155,
    161–3, 168, 170–1, 173, 177, 181,
    266, 267–8, 269
food trades in, 191, 200, 202, 270, 271
occupational identity (in food/drink
    trades), 144, 145, 189, 271
records of, 178, 256
money-lending, 86, 98–107, 112–14
  by marital status, 103–7
  changing patterns of, 99
  collection of debts, 107
  interest, 100–2
  means of repayment, 102
  of inheritances, 104–5
moral suspicion
  of alehouses, 158–60, 180–1
  of alewives, 158, 159
  of consumerism, 244, 248–9
  of inns, 204–5, 208–9
  of prostitution, 77
  of women, 41
mortgages, 86, 95

Newman, Karen, 248
Northallerton, North Yorkshire, 18
  Chief Pledges of, 267–8
  concern over poverty in, 179–80
  disease in, 179
  drink trades in, 142–3, 150–1, 152–4,
    157, 158, 161–3, 171, 172, 176–7,
    267–8
  food trades in, 184, 188, 189, 191, 194,
    196, 270
  innkeeping in, 203, 204
  records of, 178, 256, 257, 260

occupational identity
  among bakers, 189
  among silkwomen, 138, 223–4

patriarchal attitudes, 4–5, 41, 251
pawnbroking, 86, 107–14, 243
peddling, 130
petitions, equity court, 20–8, 91, 123–4,
    126–7, 206–7
piecework, 42, 122, 210
  in cloth/clothing work, 215, 231
  in small metal crafts, 237
Pinchbeck, Ivy, 28
pinmaking, 236–7
plague, 8
  economic effects of, 9, 29, 30, 39, 57,
    126, 137–8, 154, 188, 215, 251–2
Poll Tax (1377–81), 14
poor relief, 71–2

population, patterns of, 8, 38–9, 40, 59
poultry, 196–8
poverty, 36, 40, 59, 179–80, 252–3
  employment of the poor, 41, 42, 46, 76,
      130–2, 198, 215–16, 232, 237
  food purchases of the poor, 243
  health care of the poor, 84
pregnancy, boarding during, 63–4
Prest, Wilfred, 21
produce, 198, 199
prostitution, 75–7

Ramsey, Huntingdonshire, 18
  concern over poverty in, 179–80
  concern over social misbehavior in,
      180–1, 204
  credit, personal, in, 12
  disease in, 179
  drink trades in, 141–2, 152–4, 161–3,
      175–6
  food trades in, 185, 187–8, 189, 191,
      198, 201, 202, 270
  inns in, 180
  occupational identity (in food/drink
      trades) in, 144, 145
  records of, 178, 256, 261
real estate, 93–5
  maintenance agreements, 94–5
  mortgages, 86, 95
  rental of, 114–16
  as surety for loans, 93–4
Romford, see Havering

seamstresses, 229–30
servants
  as boarders, 67, 68–9
  as money-lenders, 103–5
  see also service
service
  domestic, 24–7, 41, 67
    adolescent (life-cycle service), 46–7
    adult, 47–9
    duties of, 50–3
    employment patterns in, 53–4, 56–61
    master/mistress–servant relations in,
        55–6
    non-residential, 72–5
    payment of, 54
  health care, see health care
  undervaluation of, 45–6, 116
services
  domestic, see service
  financial, see financial services
  health, 79
  sexual, 39, 41, 75–7

sex work, 39, 41, 75–7
shops, 125–8
silk, 223–5
silkwomen, 138, 223–4
singlewomen
  as apprentices, 29
  as bakers, 185
  as money-lenders, 103–5
  as servants, 47–8
  pregnant, as boarders, 63–4
spices, 198
spinning, 212–16, 222
stalls, 128–30
Stow, John, 245–6, 247
Stretton, Tim, 21
Stubbes, Philip, 248
sumptuary laws, 247
surgery, 83

tallies, 88–9
Tamworth, Staffordshire, 17–18
  Chief Pledges of, 267–8
  concern over poverty in, 179–80
  concern over social misbehavior in,
      180–1
  disease in, 179
  drink trades in, 142–3, 152–5, 161–3,
      171–2, 176, 266, 267–8, 269
  food trades in, 183, 184, 187–8, 191,
      192, 194, 195, 201, 270, 271
  innkeeping in, 203
  occupational identity (in food/drink
      trades) in, 144, 145, 189, 271
  records of, 178, 256, 262
  servants in, 51
trade, foreign, 124–5

venereal disease, 26, 76–7, 83
victualers, 201–2

weaving, 217–19, 220, 222–3
wet nursing, 64
Whitney, Isabella, 245
widows
  independence of, 31
  as innkeepers, 206–7
  as money-lenders, 106–7
  maintaining late husband's business, 29,
      139, 165–6, 183, 191, 210, 226–7,
      234–5, 238
  as servants, 48–9
wine, 167–70
wiremaking, 236–7
wool, 210–11

Zell, Michael, 36

CPSIA information can be obtained at www.ICGtesting.com
Printed in the USA
LVOW10s1355130115

422563LV00006B/63/P